W9-AFD-695

FACTS ABOUT HUNGARY
THE FIGHT FOR FREEDOM

The crest on the cover, known as the Kossuth coat of arms, was first used during the 1848–49 freedom fight, then adopted by the post-war Hungarian Republic as its insignia. However, it was replaced by a Soviet-type emblem until the 1956 Revolution, when the Kossuth coat of arms appeared again as the symbol of national independence.

DB
957
.M3
1966

**FACTS
about
HUNGARY**

THE FIGHT FOR FREEDOM

Edited by Imre Kovács

THE HUNGARIAN COMMITTEE

NEW YORK, 1966

MAY 0 6 1998

493680

FACTS ABOUT HUNGARY
A COMPILATION
Revised Edition

COPYRIGHT 1966 BY THE HUNGARIAN COMMITTEE
NEW YORK, NEW YORK, USA
FIRST PRINTING SEPTEMBER 1958
SECOND PRINTING OCTOBER 1958
THIRD PRINTING JUNE 1958
FOURTH PRINTING OCTOBER 1966

Library of Congress Catalog Card No. 66-29871.

PRINTED IN THE UNITED STATES OF AMERICA
BY
WALDON PRESS, INC.
150 LAFAYETTE ST., NEW YORK, N.Y.10013
341

*TO THE HUNGARIANS WHO GAVE THEIR
LIVES FOR FREEDOM*

The Hungarian Committee is an exile poliical organization embracing the post-war democratic Hungarian political personalities and the representatives of the 1956 revolutionaries and freedom fighters. The purpose of the Committee is to work for the independence of Hungary and for the restoration of the freedom of the Hungarian people.

THE HUNGARIAN COMMITTEE
125 East 72nd Street
New York, N.Y. 10021
Telephone (212) RHilander 4–8210

CONTENTS

LIST OF CONTRIBUTORS

ISTVÁN BARANKOVICS, editor and writer; Member, Christian Democratic World Committee, Rome, Italy. Member Hungarian Parliament (1947-19); Leader Democratic People's Party of Hungary (1945-49).

ISTVÁN BORSODY, Ph.D., Professor of History, Chatham College, Pittsburgh, Pennsylvania, formerly Counsellor and Press Attaché, Hungarian Legation, Washington, D.C.; author, *The Triumph of Tyranny*, 1960.

GORDON GASKILL, free-lance American writer and journalist, residing in Europe.

WILLIAM P. JUHÁSZ, writer and cultural historian, Lecturer, Columbia University, New York, New York; Associate Professor of Comparative Cultural History, University of Szeged, Hungary (1945-48); author, *Megváltás Felé Egyháztörténet* (Toward Redemption, a General History of Religion), 1941, and *A Világ Népei* (The Peoples of the World), 4 vols., 1934-36.

PAUL KECSKEMÉTI, Ph.D., Senior Research Associate, Rand Corporation, Washington, D.C.

STEPHEN D. KERTÉSZ, LL.D., Professor of Political Science and chairman of the Committee on International Relations, University of Notre Dame, Indiana; Secretary General, Hungarian Peace Delegation, Paris (1946); Hungarian Minister to Italy (1947); author, *Diplomacy in a Whirlpool — Hungary between Nazi Germany and Soviet Russia*, 1953.

BÉLA K. KIRÁLY, Ph.D., Assistant Professor of History, Brooklyn College, Brooklyn, New York, formerly Commander-in-Chief, National Guard of Hungary and Chairman, Revolutionary Defense Committee (1956).

SÁNDOR KISS, Senior Editor, *East Europe,* New York, New York; Member, Hungarian Parliament (1945-46); Director, Hungarian Peasant Alliance (1945-46).

IMRE KOVÁCS, writer; Member, Hungarian Parliament (1945–47); Secretary General, National Peasant Party of Hungary (1939–46); author, *Néma Forradalom* (The Silent Revolution), 1939, and *The Ninety and Nine*, 1955.

ISTVÁN RÉVAY, Consultant, Free Europe, Inc., New York, New York; Director, Pál Teleki Research Institute, Budapest (1945–49).

EDMUND O. STILLMAN, Member, New York Bar Association, formerly associated with U.S. Department of State (1947–51); Senior Research Fellow, Russian Institute, Columbia University, New York, New York; author (with William Pfaff), *The New Politics*, 1961, *The Politics of Hysteria*, 1964, and *Power and Impotence — The Failure of American Foreign Policy*, 1966.

ZOLTÁN SZTÁRÁY, Director, Social Research Program, The Kossuth Foundation, New York, New York.

FERENC A. VÁLI, Ph.D., Professor of Government, University of Massachusetts, Amherst, Massachusetts, formerly Professor of International Law, University of Budapest; author, *Servitudes of International Law*, 1958; and *Rift and Revolt in Hungary — Nationalism versus Communism*, 1961.

LÁSZLO VARGA, LL.D., Member, New York Bar Association, Chairman, Federation of Free Hungarian Jurists, New York, New York; Member, Hungarian Parliament (1947–48).

PREFACE

On the tenth anniversary of the Hungarian Revolution of 1956 it seems appropriate to summarize once again what happened during those fateful days, how the Western Powers failed in their moral duty and political obligations, and what has occurred in Hungary since then.

This new, revised edition of *Facts about Hungary*—a compilation—contains as background a short history of the Hungarians, the story of their country's conquest by the communists, and analyses of the developments that led to revolution.

The twelve days that shook the Kremlin are recalled in detail. An evaluation of the revolutionary program reveals that Hungarians envisaged an independent country outside the power blocs, where a multi-party system, parliamentary democracy, the observance of individual human rights, and an economy based on the concept of social justice would prevail. Under the proposed economic plan, society as a whole rather than specific individuals would have controlled the main segments of the means of production.

That the United Nations could do no more than pass resolutions is evidenced by its own *Special Report on the Hungarian Uprising*. The dramatic timetable of failure made the reconquest of Hungary inevitable.

The post-revolutionary era, Hungary's present situation, and the problem of Hungarian minorities under Communist rule are dealt with by experts in their respective fields.

Our intent was to provide an objective presentation of the Hungarian question, still unresolved as regards the un-honored United Nations resolutions—namely, the withdrawal of Soviet troops and restoration of Hungary's freedom and independence.

I must thank Monsignor Béla Varga, Chairman of the Hungarian Committee (and President of the post-war Hungarian Parliament), for his encouragement and moral support in the publication of this revised edition of *Facts about Hungary*. May I also express my appreciation to the institutions, publishers, and authors who have graciously allowed the reprinting of their published material, to those who have provided new articles, and to Mr. Alexander Harsányi for invaluable editorial assistance.

Orthography follows that of the originals—some using accents for names as required in Hungarian writing, others omitting them. Therefore the same names may appear with or without accents in different articles.

New York, October 23, 1966

IMRE KOVÁCS

EARLY HISTORY
OF THE HUNGARIANS

Summary by Imre Kovács

At the close of the ninth century a people from the Urals settled in Europe: the Magyars. No people before them had succeeded in establishing a permanent state in the Carpathian Basin, and among similar ethnic groups only the Magyars, Finns and Bulgarians were able to remain in the European community.

The metamorphosis of the Hungarians into a European nation is a dramatic story. The difference between the nomadic life of the vast Steppe, stretching from the Great Chinese Wall to the Carpathian Mountains, and a feudal Europe just reborn in Christianity, indeed the difference between East and West made their assimilation very difficult, against the grain. Although they gradually assumed a European character and accepted Western attitudes, traces of their former life and culture, and elements of the Eastern way of thinking have lingered on, often causing emotional, intellectual and political conflicts, particularly in critical times.

As if not wanting them to leave, Asia often reached out after the Magyars. Up to the thirteenth century sporadic violent raids of nomad tribes disrupted their gradual consolidation. In the sixteenth and seventeenth centuries the Ottoman Empire subjugated them, but the Hungarians stubbornly resisted its despotic policies and oppressive economic and social system. And a mere two decades ago, the Soviet Union extended its sphere of interest to the Danube. Among the troops which crushed the Hungarian Revolution were many "kinsmen"—Mon-

gols, Kirghizes, etc., of similar build and skull structure
—from the Russian Steppes the Magyars had left centuries before.

NOMADIC LIFE

Many thousand years ago, when the various races of
mankind—Aryans, Hamites, Semites and Chinese—had
already emerged, another ancient people existed called
Ural-Altaics after their home, the Ural-Altai mountains.
Anthropologic, ethnographic and comparative linguistics
research have established the Ural-Altaic origin of the
Hungarians, as have early historiographic records. Their
direct lineage leads back to the Ural stock from which
the Samoyeds separated some four thousand years ago,
leaving behind the Finno-Ugrians.

The Finno-Ugric people's original home was along
the middle Volga, approximately the region bordered
by the Vyatka, and the lower reaches of the Kamma and
Belaya rivers and the central Ural mountains. About
3,500 years ago the Aryans penetrated the peaceful,
gleaning, fishing and hunting people, forcing one
branch, the Finns, northwestward. This group finally settled on the territory of present-day Finland. Another group, now called the Ugrians, was pushed back
beyond the Urals and settled in the sparse forests, along
the Ob, Tobol, Ishim and Irtish rivers. They lived under a loosely-knit social system based on blood-relation-
ships, the smallest organized unit being the clan (or
"large family"), comprising two or three sets of grand-
parents and their intermarried descendants, some fifty
to one hundred individuals.

Among clan members there was full equality, and the
land on which they lived, hunted, fished and gleaned
was considered common property, as were the tents, huts
and large items of equipment such as boats, fishing nets
and special traps. They had almost no personal possessions, just the bows, small nets, harpoons, primitive
hatchets and hammers indispensable in their daily life,
and of course their clothing. The primitive methods of
hunting, fishing and gleaning required that all work be
done by groups. The clan's head was the eldest, who

guided common efforts, led forays, negotiated with other clans, directed barter, took command in case of war.
(The ancient Ugrian name for "clan" was *had*, the Hungarian word for "army.") In negotiations and decision
making he was guided by custom and tradition, being
responsible to the "council of men."

As the Ugrians increased in number they branched
out onto the Steppes and extended their original settlement all the way to the Altai Mountains, south to the
Syr-Darya River and Lake Aral, and west to the Caspian
Sea. At that time, about 1500 B.C., the area known today as the Kirghiz Steppe was in the path of the great
Migration of Peoples.

On the Steppes, Hungarians turned from gleaning, fishing and hunting to stock-breeding, which transformed
their political, economic and social structure. Pastureland was still common property, but control over livestock, tents and major equipment gradually shifted to
the head of the clan. Even clan structure changed: the
matriarchal system of indirect inheritance, under which
all possessions went to the mother's brothers or her sis-
ters' male children, was replaced by male-line or direct
inheritance. The Ugric clan democracy was replaced
by a patriarchal system in which the head of the family held the real power.

The Hun Empire in Central Asia was overthrown by
the Chinese at the end of the first century A.D., and
the Huns, rushing westward, swept the Ugric people
along with them. Sometime between the first and fifth
centuries the Ugrians intermingled with a Turkic people
of Altaic origin, creating the ethnic group which has
been known ever since as the Magyars. (The name "Magyar"—in its original form Magyeri—comes from Män'-
si-eri. *Mänsi'* means *men*.) In the Hungarian language
Finno-Ugric elements or words predominate in the area
of family life, fishing, hunting, trading, etc.; Turkic roots
relate to livestock, to military and political organization.

The Ugrian and Turkic peoples merged in western
Siberia. During the second half of the fifth century the
Magyars moved from there to the area bordered by the
Black Sea, the Sea of Azov and the lower Don River. In

the course of their long journey and temporary settlements, they often engaged in warfare. Tempers flared easily on the Steppes and a victory usually meant considerable loot in men and stock. Captured prisoners were sold or kept to do manual work.

Land cultivation was limited to the small area around the temporary settlements, where millet and buckwheat were planted. For Steppe-people a settlement did not mean immobility. If their animals used up the land, the people moved to new pastures. Winter quarters were more permanent and often grew into large communities with haphazardly pitched tents and improvised corrals. During the summer the settlements were either completely abandoned, or old people, women and children were left behind with some of the slaves, while the men moved with the cattle, searching for better pastures, or engaged in warfare.

ORIGIN OF THE EARLY MAGYAR PEOPLE

URAL Stock		ALTAIC Stock	
Finno-Ugrians		Turkic peoples	Mongols
Finno-Perm Branch	Män'si Branch	Western Turks	Eastern Turks
FINNS	Män'si-eri (pre-Magyars)	Ogurs	Huns, Avars, etc.

MAGYARS

The chief was responsible for the tribal alliance, but did not have to account for every decision, and was actually a despotic ruler. Moving westward, the Magyars had to cross some half dozen large rivers and innumerable small ones. Women, children and small animals were floated across on leather drums while the men pushed into the stream on horseback, driving the cattle ahead of them. Each crossing was made along a good-sized stretch of river bank, and measures had to be taken to forestall surprise raids by enemy tribes. At such times the tribal chief was in absolute charge and his orders had to be obeyed without question.

Occasionally such a people on the move grew like an avalanche into a huge nomad empire by absorbing smaller groups they encountered. These empires were usually held together by a "Titan of the Steppes," but they seldom survived their founder, for there was nothing to keep them together. The conquered peoples continued to live by their own customs and codes, spoke their own tongue and generally maintained their culture. The only tie with their overlord was the submission of their own chieftain, who unconditionally carried out the orders of an Attila or a Genghis Khan. Each group of submerged people was given sufficient land and pasture and had its place in the army during a war or while on the move. The conquered peoples were usually sent ahead to man the more dangerous points, or brought up the rear. When the Khan or Mogul died and his empire disintegrated, the various tribes—their social systems and cultures untouched—went their own way.

The Magyars were variously identified by empires of Turkic peoples as Sabyrs, Turks, Onugurs, from the latter stemmed names like *Húngaro* (Spanish), *Hongrois* (French), *Ungarn* (German), and Hungarian.

According to legend, it was a miraculous stag that led the ancient Hungarians during their wanderings. Old King Nimrod, a giant, had two sons, Hunor and Magor. One day the two princes went hunting and saw a wondrous, regal stag in the distance. They kept pursuing it through more and more beautiful country and lush pastures until it vanished south of the Sea of Azov in the Meotis marshes.

The legend of the mythical stag reflects the ideas of the nomadic herdsmen. They were influenced by Central Asian religious philosophy, symbolized by the struggle between Fire and Darkness. The people of the Steppes conceived the fight between Evil and Good in terms of the Demon of Evil—a large beast of prey, often a mythical monster—attacking a tame animal, usually a doe, stag, sheep or goat, and inflicting a deadly wound. They drew pictures of such scenes, in which the monster cannot always be seen, but is intimated by the terror of the fleeing prey. These animals in flight, accurately carved in leather or cast in gold, were sometimes worn by nomad chiefs.

In the ninth century when the Magyars moved again, they first settled between the Don and Dnieper Rivers, then in the area bordered by the Dnieper and Dniester Rivers, and finally penetrated the Carpathian Basin. They were then a people of seven tribes (with 108 clans) numbering at least half a million, and governed by an intertribal council. The membership of this supreme political and judicial organ included the tribal leaders, those holding important offices, such as the shaman (high priest), medicine men and chief judge, plus specially invited tribal members. At its meetings, presided over by the chief of the tribal alliance, the membership discussed such things as the fair distribution of pastureland, smoothed over clan arguments or plotted some war action.

In 896 A.D., when the Hungarians crossed the Carpathian Mountains with their vast herds to settle in their present country, after the vicissitudes of three thousand years and wanderings covering thousands of miles, their social system was both democratic and despotic. A wealthy group of clans, risen above the others, was gaining increasing power and privileges. Other clans had been ruined in war or otherwise impoverished, formed a middle layer in transition toward the position of outcasts or captured slaves.

This society, clearly divided into social strata, was partially administered by councils of clans, tribes and tribal alliances, which served the interests of the community. However, the leaders could take arbitrary measures, in accordance with the practice prevalent on the Steppes. It was finally united by a military organization headed by an elected leader—at the time of the Conquest, Prince Árpád.

ENCOUNTER WITH FEUDALISM

The Hungarians, with their pagan, nomadic customs and numerous livestock, ended their wanderings in the Carpathian Basin, which reminded them of the Steppes. Here the Huns and Avars had established their states too. Attila's capital had been somewhere along the River Tisza. The "Scourge of God," as trembling peoples called him, was buried in the river-bed when he died in his sleep of a hemorrhage after a pagan orgy, and the Huns drifted back to Asia. The Avars, who built earthen forts and ruled the area of present-day Hungary in the seventh and eighth centuries, had been routed by Charlemagne.

Hungary was inhabited at the time of the Conquest by remnants of Zalan's Bolgar-Slav, Pribina's and Svatopluk's Slav states. The conquered Slavs, who had a fairly well-developed agriculture, became servants of the wealthier clan and tribal chiefs, and some of them even served the poorer freemen. The approximately one hundred thousand square kilometers of thin woodlands, meadows and pastures did not suffice for the Hungarian population—which, including the Slavs, now numbered about six hundred thousand—to lead a nomadic life, so they therefore gradually shifted to agriculture and livestock breeding.

The tribal chiefs were surrounded by freemen who had deserted their own poor or weak clans to enter the service of richer clans. In peacetime they tended livestock or supervised the work of slaves, and in war fought under the chief, or led auxiliary troops composed of slaves. They were often joined by adventurous youth from the smaller clans. Hungarians on predatory campaigns were led by the chieftains of tribes along the Western border, who had the best knowledge of routes leading west. For this reason, and because they had five to six thousand horsemen, their power grew. The raiders were strictly disciplined by their lieutenants, often with the whip.

At first Europe trembled. Eventually, though, other nations learned the Magyar tactics, and countered them with superior feudal war techniques. In 955 A.D. the army of the bravest Hungarian leader, *Bulcsu,* met with total defeat. In due time the Hungarian people learned their lesson, realizing that the only way to survive was to conform to the European order.

In 962, during the Byzantine revival, Otto the Great assumed the title of German Emperor and began to establish the Eastern provinces (*Markgravates*). At that time, being emperor meant defending the Christian world against barbarian harassments. A German alliance with Byzantium might well have driven the entire Hungarian nation back to the Steppes.

The weakened Hungarian tribes were fighting now each other, as their chiefs strove for power, some by seeking alliance with Byzantium. This intertribal rivalry ended with the victory of Prince Géza. His son, Vajk, became a Christian and the first king of Hungary, under the name István (Stephen). The crown Pope Sylvester II sent for his coronation in 1000 dramatically symbolized the conditions set by Christian Europe: join us, or perish.

Europe's political, economic and social order then was feudalism. At the peak of that pyramidal society stood the supreme ruler. Sloping gradually downward to a wide base were the noblemen and landowners, personally dependent on the ruler. The toiling masses comprised the foundation. A hierarchic chain of vassalage linked everyone to his immediate superior, from poorest through richer to wealthiest, right up to the ruler, according to rank and position.

King Stephen married a German royal princess. The cortège accompanying her to Hungary included priests and knights. The priests converted the Hungarians, the knights defeated the rebels, who lost all they had, even their freedom. Victorious King Stephen gave generous rewards. German and Italian soldiers of fortune obtained vast landed estates with many servants.

The feudal state replaced the system of clans and tribes. Its foundation was laid by Saint Stephen (canonized in 1083) and based on the Frankish pattern.

The basic unit of the Frank state was the county. Saint Stephen took over some counties surviving from the Slav states and established new ones. At first he only claimed the "unappropriated" lands located between the territories of tribes and clans as royal counties. But rivalries and murderous struggles resulted in the gradual incorporation of tribe and clan lands in the county system. Public administration became simply that of royal estates.

The king appointed bailiffs to administer the counties. These officials maintained law and order, led conscripts in wartime. The upper stratum of county society was composed of freemen in supervisory positions. Of equal rank were freemen who had lost contact with their clans and were managing their own small estates, usually with a few slaves. There was also a gradually increasing class of specialized freemen, described in the chronicles as ploughmen, vine-dressers, fishermen, hunters, swineherds, horseherds, coopers, smiths, cartwrights, carpenters, etc. These people lived either in the royal estate center or in villages. There were also freedmen, slaves gradually liberated as a result of Christian teachings, who were still servants (*servientes*) doing heavy field work. The more skillful among them were taken into the "courts"—the households of the king, landlords, bailiffs, or important freemen. They became cooks, footmen, coachmen, dog or falcon trainers, etc. If the king gave away one of his estates, which happened quite frequently, all the servants went with the estate and had to serve the new master.

The feudal aristocracy severed all links with the common Hungarians. Blood ties of the clans were long since disrupted, and people serving the upper classes were strangers or, if not, had to maintain a strictly subservient relationship. The great lords received high rank from the king in addition to their estates. Although numbering only a few hundred, their power became so great that the king was unable to act without their support. In time they incorporated their privileges into law and formed a Royal Council. In matters of national interest they spoke the decisive word.

At first the large estates (*latifundia*) were no more than the group of servants and freemen under the personal power of each landlord, that lived throughout the country in rural communities among other people. The landlord received a share of the produce grown by his serfs. This system was replaced in the thirteenth century by great estates formed by land accumulation, which remained the prevalent economic structure until the middle of the twentieth century.

THOUSAND-YEAR-OLD NATION

Original essay by William P. Juhász

The symbol of the nation's founding, Saint Stephen's coronation in 1000 A.D., involved no pledge of fealty. Emperor Otto III, whose dream was a Christian World Empire, looked on Hungary as an equal and independent partner in the great Western Christian community. Church life of that era was imbued with an ascetic spirit of reform fostered by the reshaped Benedictine order and the renewed Papacy. Saint Stephen associated himself closely with the work of religious reform. In the stern, virile personality of this monarch the Christian spirit joined with a magic inheritance of the Eastern khans and ancient high priests.

Magyar encampments gave way to villages, then cities. A network of bishopal sees and cloisters arose in addition to the royal administrative seats, propagating the ascetic spirit. An ever greater area than that of the original tribal holdings was occupied by the royal, and later, the clerical, estates. Stephen received foreigners—knights, craftsmen, tradesmen—with open arms, and they, in turn, helped the cities prosper. The king's typically Eastern tolerance towards strangers was voiced in an admonition to his son, the saintly Imre: "Weak is the land of one language."

The transcendental and spiritual content of the shamanist view of the world facilitated the nation's inner acceptance of Christianity, and inspired a live, original folk religiosity which—side by side, but never at odds with the church—permeates the peasantry to this day.

Even before Saint Stephen the Hungarians had become familiar with both Western and Eastern Christianity, and many became Christians.

The adoption of Western culture, the personalities of the ruling house and the presence of Western émigrés caused the land to look Westward, but, for all that, it was not unmindful of its Eastern heritage. Contact with the great nomad cultures of the Scythians, Huns and Avars survived with startling vividness through the poetic tales of Hungarian chroniclers of the eleventh through fourteenth centuries. Architecture, arts and crafts showed oriental impulses as well as the dominant Western influences in their part Eastern-pagan, part Byzantine works. The influence of Byzantium lasted until the end of the thirteenth century, although greatly subordinate to Western ideas.

Hungary was the easternmost area of Europe where the artistic and spiritual attainments of the Middle Ages rooted in congenial soil; and this is as true of early and late Gothic, Renaissance architecture and sculpture, as of the medieval legends and religious poetry. Hungarian spiritual life joined the great stream of medieval Western culture, while retaining its own individual color. Although strongly affected in its classical music by Gregorian and West European traditions, Hungary in folk music still clung to the age-old pentatonic scale, this area being the westernmost point of its spread.

The rising German Empire, which fought the Papacy throughout the Middle Ages, sought to extend its feudal rule over Hungary. This attempt, led by Emperor Conrad II, was foiled by Saint Stephen. His successors, kings of the House of Árpád, beat back each such try.

Again and again the Hungarian State faced incursions of pagan nomad horsemen—Petchenegs, Cumanians— which were parried by King Saint László (1077–1095) and others. Far graver, however, was the invasion of Hungary in 1241 by several hundred thousand mounted troops from Genghis Khan's Empire, which extended from southern Russia to the Persian Gulf, the Indian Ocean and the Yellow Sea. Within a year, they utterly sacked the land, slaying about half the population, dragging off many survivors as slaves—a blood-bath from which the country hardly recovered. A year later, the invaders left the ravaged land, as if sensing that they had come to a wholly alien world; but for centuries they held the Russian Steppe region, decisively influencing the life and culture of the emerging Russian Empire.

Saint László and Kálmán the Learned pushed Hungary's domain southwestward, and their successors pressed southward and to the north Balkan zone, whose political and spiritual orientation was uncertain for centuries (and still is) with respect to the West. The sole enduring result of Hungary's north Balkan expansion was to gain Croatia, the area between the Adriatic Sea and the Drava and Sava Rivers, a close geographical adjunct of Hungary. A running battle with the Venetian Republic for the possession of Dalmatia, on the narrow eastern coast of the Adriatic, drew on the nation's resources, especially during the fourteenth and fifteenth centuries, under the kings from foreign ruling houses.

HUNGARIAN RENAISSANCE

The latter, after a brief interregnum, were followed by Robert Károly (1308-1342) and his son Lajos the Great (1342-1382), two monarchs of the French-Italian House of Anjou—kin to the kings of Naples—who in the fourteenth century raised Hungary to heights outwardly even greater than that of the Árpád era. When their male line died out in the first half of the fifteenth century, Sigismund of Luxembourg (1387-1437), also Emperor of Germany, ascended the throne, to be followed by a Polish king and two kings from the House of Hapsburg, who, in the last decades of the fifteenth century, were succeeded by a national monarch risen from the lesser nobility, Mátyás Hunyadi (1458-1490). Under him the nation attained a new, sunset age of splendor. The varied series of rulers from the so-called mixed houses closed with two Jagiello scions.

Meanwhile the religio-magical spirit of the monarchy had faded. The nobles' vast estates, with their military might, constituted veritable princedoms. Against them a weak but ambitious young king, László IV, (1272-1290), vainly sought the aid of the still primarily nomadic, pagan Cumanians, who had settled the plains.

The kings of Hungary were chosen by a conclave of freeholders, high nobility, prelates and lesser nobles. These rulers—owing to their foreign origin and the mode of selection—could hardly be expected to evoke great respect for the throne. That respect was transferred to a symbol, the crown given the nation by the Pope, leader of Christendom. Until modern times (even under the centuries-long rule of the Hapsburgs) the crown enjoyed the devout regard of the freeholders and nobles, who avowed themselves supporters of this symbol of power.

In 1222, just six years after the promulgation of the English Magna Charta, King Endre II, under whom the power of the feudal lords had waxed great, issued the first Hungarian written constitution, at the demand of the militant freeholders, to safeguard their rights. The *Golden Bull* gave a firmer status, in public law, to the landed nobility. Yet at the same time some of those already free fell into a state of dependency, and the growing multitude of serfs progressively lost their political, social and economic independence. This led to the great peasant revolt of 1437, linked to the name of Antal Budai Nagy, and later to the rebellion under György Dózsa in 1514, involving the whole peasantry. This was precipitated by the high nobility's attempt to void the civil rights of peasants in the rural towns. The codification of the constitution after the revolt was crushed deprived the peasantry of the rights of free movement and property ownership, and placed it beyond the pale of the constitution, which applied only to the privileged classes.

The heresies so permeating the life of the Middle Ages formed a major counterpoint to the paramount spiritual power, the Catholic Church headed by the Pope. The Bogumil doctrines stemming from the Balkans—which sharply differentiated soul and body in terms of light and dark, relinquishing the world of the body to the devil—exerted no deep influence on Hun-

garian spiritualism, which perceived and respected the
supernatural through its appreciation of the sensual
world. This same leaning towards the sensuous also kept
the liturgical, introspective mysticism of the Byzantine
Church from making much headway. A far stronger influence on the Hungarian soul was the religious movement launched by Jan Hus early in the fifteenth century, with its social and political aspects. Its effect might
have been more enduring had not hostile hordes of Hussite forces broken into upper Hungary. Their assault,
while directed primarily against the nobles and prelates,
did not spare the people. Yet the movement left strong
traces on the religious life of the fifteenth and sixteenth
centuries, for example, in the first Hungarian Bible
translation, as well as in many Hungarian Hussite songs
and hymns.

The bases of contact with Western culture were primarily the cloisters, and the students who, during the
Árpád era and later, thronged to the West's great universities in Padua, Bologna and Paris; later, from the
fourteenth century on, to Cracow, Vienna and Prague;
and, in the sixteenth through eighteenth centuries, also
to the Protestant universities of Leyden, Utrecht, Wit-
tenberg and Oxford. Because of these students pouring
abroad, the Hungarian universities—that of King Lajos
at Pécs and that of King Mátyás at Pozsony—survived
only a short time. The pull of the Hungarian intellectual élite toward the West—ever tinged with disillusion
—was as alive then as now.

In the mid-fourteenth century Hungary was invaded
by another mounted nomad people, who, though their
central base was Asia, were able, partly with Western
help, to forge a firm empire at the edge of Europe. The
advance of the Osman Turks towards Hungary began
in the middle of the fourteenth century during the reign
of Lajos the Great of Anjou, and engaged Hungary's
full strength for three centuries. It had a fateful effect
on the nation's destiny; its historical, political and social
development.

During the fourteenth century, well before the capture of Constantinople, the Osman Turks conquered a

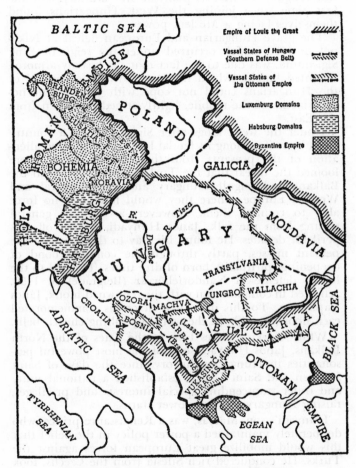

Legend:
- Empire of Louis the Great
- Vassal States of Hungary (Southern Defense Belt)
- Vassal States of the Ottoman Empire
- Luxemburg Domains
- Habsburg Domains
- Byzantine Empire

EAST CENTRAL EUROPE IN THE XIVTH CENTURY

great portion of the Balkans and met Hungarian forces in the north. The clash between Turks and Hungarians was religious as well as political and military. For the first time since joining the West, Hungarians found themselves facing a Moslem power.

The grave Hungarian and European defeat at Niko-pol in 1396, which occurred under the reign of King Sigismund, was due to the fact that the heavily armored mounted knights which the West rushed to the aid of the Hungarians could not cope with the ancient no-mad tactics of the mobile, lightly-armed horsemen from the East.

Under the weak kings after Sigismund, in a country riven by strife among its feudal lords, plus growing alien-ation of the peasants from the leading classes, there loomed the threat that the Turks might conquer all the Balkans and engulf Hungary and even Central and Western Europe, where they would have met no force able to counter them. However, a brilliant general sprung from the folk, János Hunyadi, fended off this peril for decades. He found his way to the hearts of the peasant masses, partly through the common bond of deepening spirituality born of dire times. This led to the heroic defense of Nándorfehérvár (Belgrade) in 1456, achieved in collaboration with the renowned monk, János Kapisztrán. To this day, that victory is commemorated each noon throughout the world by tolling church bells.

While Turkish forces beat at the gates of the North Balkans, János Hunyadi, one of the most powerful per-sonalities in Hungarian history since the days of Saint Stephen and Saint Lászlo, established a national unity and order transcending special interests and privileges, raising Hungary to great-power status.

Hunyadi's son, Mátyás, was a Renaissance prince, who deliberately maintained a power policy in the belief that this would mobilize great European forces against the Turks. He conquered rich Silesia from the Czechs, took Vienna and part of Austria. The realm of Mátyás and his prelates became the easternmost focus of humanism. Mátyás' court in Buda sheltered many eminent Italian and Austrian humanists, historians and natural scientists; he fostered the arts. A small fragment of his Buda library still extant, the Corvina, includes some of the finest examples of illuminated manuscripts. Despite all alien influences, Renaissance architecture, too, found its own distinctive expression in Hungary, as had Roman, Gothic and Renaissance painting and sculpture. The crenellated friezes of houses in the towns of upper Hungary give ample evidence of this.

Renaissance culture, in contrast to that of the Middle Ages, remained distant to most of the peasantry, and hardly reached the middle classes. But Mátyás' humanism was understood and preserved in many anecdotes about this king whom his people called "Mátyás the Just."

Two Milestones

After Mátyás' death, jockeying for power among the court cliques, the dwindling of royal sway, squabbles between high and lesser nobility, and their joint strife with the serfs, disrupted the nation at the very moment when Turkish power reached its zenith, vanquishing the northern Balkans, then taking two key Hungarian and European fortresses: Belgrade and Pétervárad (Petrovaradim). In the decisive battle at Mohács, in 1526 in southern Hungary, the great majority of the high clergy and the aristocracy perished, and the country lay open to the Turks.

At the time, the throne had two claimants: Ferdinand of Hapsburg, nephew of Charles V, and János Zápolya, the Hungarian noble who had crushed the Dózsa peasant rebellion in 1514. The rivalry for the throne was a sign not only of disintegration, but of tragic inner conflict. Some of the country's leaders believed that only a strong western power could save the land from Ottoman subjugation, and the annihilation of its Christian culture. Many clung to Hapsburg rule even in the status of an Austro-German colony. Another faction rallied round the idea of a national kingdom headed by Zápolya, deeming that the country could better preserve its independence through a certain degree of accommodation to Turkish suzerainty than by subjection

to Austria, which they felt did not particularly desire
Hungary's liberation. However, at this time, and during
the subsequent century and a half of Turkish rule, Hungarian leaders saw that the goal of survival under twofold pressure from Turks and Germans could be achieved only by accommodating outwardly to both, inward-
ly to neither. The more positive policy supported
Hapsburg rule in Hungary, despite actions inimical to
the nation, while the other group represented the passive force which has sustained long-suffering Eastern
peoples even under the direst tyrannies. More than once
this dual stand was taken by a single individual who,
so to speak, looked both West and East.

The first national leader to bear heroically this grave
conflict within himself was György "Fráter" Marti-
nuzzi Utyeszenics, the most influential man at the
courts of János Zápolya (1526–1540), Zápolya's widow
and his son, János Zsigmond, the first Prince of Transylvania (1559-1571). Fráter was first soldier on the frontier, then Paulist monk, finally Bishop of Várad and
Cardinal. He had to endure failure in both his stands:
the German Hapsburg power could not defend the country against the Turks or even restore its independence,
while the Turks would not permit even a quasi-national
kingship. Two impossibles neutralized each other, as it
were, to provide the sole path of action. To implement
his dual policy, Fráter supported the creation of an independent Transylvanian princedom, which split Hungary into three parts: the Hapsburg area in the west,
the central Turkish zone to the north—largest of the
three—and to the southeast the nominally free area of
little Transylvania, which, though it acknowledged
Turkish dominance, decisively contributed to the survival of Hungarian spiritual freedom.

The intellectual leaders of Hungary never allowed
the opposition viewpoint to perish. This was true of
pro-Hapsburg Catholics like Cardinal Péter Pázmány, the
royal viceroy Miklós Esterházy, and the great general
and poet of the fight against the Turks in the XVIth
Century, Miklós Zrinyi, Croatian by descent; as well as
of Protestants who co-operated with the Turks but at the

same time defended an independent Transylvania, men like István Bocskay, Gábor Bethlen and György Rákóczi I, of the early XVIIth century. The Transylvanians, who recognized Turkish dominance, would always negotiate with the Hapsburgs, even when warring with them, and pro-Hapsburg statesmen more than once saved Transylvania from destruction.

Austria looked on the Protestants as rebels, deeming that Protestantism heightened Hungarian independence efforts and anti-German feelings. Although most of the high nobility had become Catholic, it was perhaps in some measure due to these maneuvers of the Viennese Court that the lesser nobility and citizens of the towns generally remained so firmly Protestant. The lesser nobility organized the ancient counties into citadels of Protestantism and national resistance.

Bocskay and Bethlen, with their troops, forced the German power to sign a peace, one of whose cornerstones was recognition of Protestant religious freedom. Both men had seized large areas from the Germans. Both rejected the Hungarian crown offered to them, knowing that acceptance would lead to a clash between Turks and Hapsburgs and thus imperil Transylvania's independence.

One of Transylvania's great princes, István Báthory (1571–1581), was chosen by the Poles as their king in 1576, inaugurating a bright era in Polish history. His triumph over the forces of Czar Ivan the Terrible saved Poland and Central Europe from Russian invasion. Both Báthory and his contemporary, Cardinal Péter Pázmány, Archbishop of Esztergom and the greatest leader and writer of the Counter-Reformation, sought to establish a European league of nations against the Turks and Russians.

Battles between the royal and Turkish forces—always fought on Hungarian soil—caused the people, especially the peasantry, untold grief. Apart from the havoc wrought by regular troops, Turkish and Tartar auxiliaries slaughtered or drove off thousands, not sparing women and children. On the Great Plain the peasants left their villages for the fortified shelter of the rural towns, where at least they could escape the raids of irregulars. The peasants under Turkish rule were despoiled not just by the Turks but by feudal lords in Hapsburg territory who also demanded tribute.

This grave and insoluble German-Turkish conflict was aggravated by yet another: the religious rift. A trend towards worldliness and slack morals on the part of many prelates, the attempt of powerful nobles to seize the ecclesiastical estates, the unpopularity of the Catholic Hapsburg power, the Turks' relative tolerance of Protestants, and, even more, the strong practical sense of a good segment of the Hungarians, enabled Protestantism to win over the great majority of the people in the decades after the Mohács defeat. However, most of them became Catholics at the end of the sixteenth century. One reason being that the Catholic Church enjoyed Hapsburg support; then too, there was the moral and religious upsurge within the church and the proselyting of the new Jesuit Order; and also many preferred Catholicism's mystic aura to the barer Protestant ritual. However, the Catholic Church never again achieved a preponderance over the three main Protestant faiths— Reformed, Lutheran and Unitarian.

In almost all European states at this period, either the Catholics or the Protestants achieved decisive numerical and political superiority. Most of the Hungarian Catholic leaders naturally were more drawn to a Catholic great power, while the majority of Protestants leaned towards the Transylvanian princedom, which championed Protestant religious freedom. Essentially, however, the Catholics were no more "pro-German" than the Protestants were "pro-Turkish." No religious war of extermination ever occurred in Hungary, where Eastern tolerance created an acceptance of varying beliefs. That tolerance was uniquely manifested by the Transylvanian parliament at Torda in 1552, which guaranteed complete freedom of belief, stipulating that no one could be barred from public office for religious reasons.

In the seventeenth, and to a lesser extent in the eighteenth century the Viennese Court persecuted Protestants; in the second half of the seventeenth century it

actually sought to force a single religion on all its territories, citing the dictum *"cuius regio, eius religio."*

Towards the end of the sixteenth century, at the
peak of the Turks' advance, about two-thirds of the
country had fallen into their hands. During the seventeenth century the Ottoman Empire began its slow disintegration. At that time, after the victory at Szentgott-
hárd in 1664—the Hungarians came to believe that the
Viennese Court was not too anxious to free the land,
fearing that a united country might carve out its independence. However, it was the Thirty Years' War, and
then the French Wars, which kept the Hapsburgs from
pitting their full strength against the Turks. In 1683
the Turkish forces, already in steep decline, made a last
desperate attempt to destroy Hapsburg power. They
were routed, while besieging Vienna, by a coalition of
Austria, Poland, Venice and the Papacy, but primarily
by the direct intervention of King Jan Sobieski of Poland. As a result, Austria and several other European
countries resolved upon a war of liberation, during
which Hungarian forts taken by the Turks were recap-
tured. In 1686 they freed Hungary's ancient capital,
Buda, the center of the Turkish forces of occupation.

FREEDOM FIGHTS

The liberating armies swiftly retook most of the country; only the south remained in Turkish hands for a
few more decades. Eugene of Savoy, the great general
who advocated that the center of gravity of Hapsburg
lands be transferred to Hungary, and Louis of Baden
(*Türken Louis*) freed the south too, beating back the
Turks' last attempts at conquest and extending Hapsburg sway to the North Balkans, including the onetime
sphere of Hungarian influence. And finally a reunited
Hungary, plus Croatia, became part of the Hapsburg
Empire. (In 1691 Transylvania also lost its autonomy,
partly due to inner decline and a lack of able leaders,
partly to the end of the Turkish counterpoise.)

The excesses of the foreign soldiery, confiscatory taxes
and harsh economic exploitation plunged the country

into an impoverished colonial status. The bitterness of
the lesser nobility was augmented by the growing persecution of Protestants. In 1644 scions of the ancient
high nobility holding prominent posts in the land, headed by Viceroy Ferenc Wesselényi, joined with the lesser
nobility in an attempt to free Hungary from German
rule. Trusting in the promises of Louis XIV, they decided to revolt, but French aid failed to materialize.
The Viennese Court executed the leaders of this revolt,
which had existed only on paper, and launched an era
of absolutist terror in Hungary.

From the end of the sixteenth century on, the serfs,
fleeing persecution and ruin, joined with the lower
nobility and burghers to form Cossack-style troops, such
as the *Hajdus* led by Bocskay. These free forces, the so-
called *Kuruc* Army, fought foreign mercenaries and
others in the service of the King. Imre Thököly, a
descendant of the high nobility, became their able general. At the time of the last great Turkish drive before
the fruitless siege of Vienna, Thököly's *Kuruces* had
occupied a large part of upper Hungary, where some
of his less disciplined troops launched vengeful Catholic
persecutions. With the Turkish fiasco the star of Thököly and his forces declined and he himself died a captive
of the Turks.

At the start of the eighteenth century, a new national
revolt, the first universal fight for freedom against foreign oppressors, broke out, sparked by a mass rising of
peasants in northeast Hungary. The movement took on
a country-wide import when Hungary's wealthiest and
most distinguished aristocrat, Ferenc Rákóczi II—with
holdings vast as a small country—assumed its leadership
after an inner struggle. Three of his ancestors had ruled
Transylvania, his father participated in the Wesselényi
attempt; his mother, Ilona Zrinyi, descendant of great
soldiers and statesmen, had heroically defended the Fort
of Munkács against Caraffa, chief executor of absolutist
terror, on behalf of her second husband, Imre Thököly.
Rákóczi had been schooled first by Austrian Jesuits, then
at the Viennese Court. He himself was deeply Catholic
—his "Confessions" are a masterpiece of spiritual litera-

ture. Later, in France, he was drawn to the stern ascetic views of the Jansenists.

Louis XIV promised much, but did only enough to allow the patriots of a small nation to disquiet the menacing Hapsburg power. Rákóczi also received like promises from the Russian Czar, Peter the Great, which were honored only in their breach.

Actually the French and their allies, the Bavarians, were in no position to lend Rákóczi any potent aid, because the forces of the Hapsburg-English-Dutch coalition led by Eugene of Savoy and Marlborough roundly defeated them, preventing a breakthrough towards central Europe.

When the chance of French support ceased, the fight for freedom was doomed. In 1705, the parliament of the insurgents chose Ferenc Rákóczi as their monarch, dethroning the House of Hapsburg—mainly at the wish of the French. For a decade the impoverished country again became a battlefield. Drained of all its strength, further fighting would have been suicide, and the *Kuruc* forces surrendered in 1711. Rákóczi and his adherents fled to Poland. He met with Peter the Great in a vain attempt to gain Russian support, and then emigrated to France, where the court of Louis XIV received him as a distinguished but politically inconsequential guest. He died as an émigré in Turkey, where, after his death, his son also vainly tried to organize forces against the Hapsburg Empire.

Was Rákóczi's battle for liberty in vain? Were the Hungarian freedom fights of 1848 and October 1956 useless? For Hungarians, Rákóczi—as later, Kossuth too—is not associated with national defeat and collapse. The Rákóczi freedom fight awakened powerful forces among the people. Within a few years it brought about an amazing national renaissance, a reconciliation of the classes, rich forms of art, music and poetry which evoked the Hungarian outlook and spirit. The seeds of the Rákóczi revolt ripened later. His battle for liberty made it impossible for Austrian absolutism to maintain its terroristic oppression; the Rákóczi uprising ended enslavement. Even though oppression did not cease, the old methods could never recur. The Hungarian people had given proof of their vigor and will to live.

Maria Theresa's humanistic absolutism—she ruled from 1740 to 1780—took account of Hungarian strength and national aspirations. Hungarian troops played a major part in defending her realm from attacks on all sides. Hungarians played an outstanding role in her government. The noble youth of her Hungarian bodyguard brought the ideals of French enlightenment to Hungary. She reformed public education, which had been solely in the hands of the Catholic orders and Protestant denominations. New laws somewhat ameliorated the state of the peasantry, although their lot was not radically changed. Economic exploitation also was eased, yet did not cease. The Viennese Court still blocked the growth of Hungarian industry, for Austria looked on Hungary as a source of raw materials and food, and an outlet for her industrial goods.

Joseph II (1780–1790) was the standard-bearer of enlightened absolutism, modeling himself on his ideal, Frederick II of Prussia. His social measures sought to alleviate the plight of the peasants though they were opposed by the privileged orders, like those of his mother, Maria Theresa. Some of the peasants expected miracles of him, and the very backward Rumanian peasantry of Transylvania somehow got the idea that the king meant to destroy the Hungarian landowners with their help. For the first time in Hungarian history, oppression spread to the tragic area of minorities, when the revolt of the Rumanian peasantry led to horrible destruction. At the same time, however, Hungarian Transylvania was the site of early Rumanian cultural efforts. Here were printed the books that stirred the Rumanian national culture and consciousness.

Joseph II continued to promote tolerance towards Protestants. However, though he himself was a devout Catholic, his anti-church measures alienated some Hungarian Catholics, whose national pride was offended by the king's effort to streamline administration by making German the obligatory language. Some of the high nobility scarcely knew Hungarian, and all the privileged orders used Latin rather than Hungarian in official affairs, especially legal matters. Even so, however, Joseph II's action sparked a far-reaching spiritual revolt which underlay the great national resurgence of the 19th century. The country's youth and writers fought not only to preserve the national language but to make it sovereign. These two groups have initiated every freedom movement in Hungary through today.

1848

Joseph II finally had to withdraw his Germanizing decree. That victory, though, was only the first phase of the battle for the Hungarian language, literature and culture, and beyond that, for the recognition of Hungary as a social and political entity.

Hungarian literature was never *l'art pour l'art*. The ancient shaman texts, the heroic epics and even the old love songs are poetic works, but at the same time religio-magical texts in which each phrase, each image bears on the nation's destiny. The Hungarian author, whether writing in Latin or in his own tongue, never completely broke away from his ancient poetic-priestly and political role. He was not content to express his inner intent in artistic form; artistic creation was also a communal act for society, even when he was apparently in conflict with it. The great poets of the reform era, Mihály Vörösmarty, Ferenc Kölcsey, Dániel Berzsenyi, Mihály Csokonai Vitéz, later the great novelists of the age of revolt—Mór Jókai, Zsigmond Kemény, Joseph Eötvös—played leading roles in the formation of national life.

The writer's basic aim in the reform era, as in modern times, has been to portray the people to the upper classes and intelligentsia. The writer's subject was primarily the peasantry (comprising then about eighty per cent of the population); their outlook, interests, rich traditional experience, and needless suffering and poverty. Poetic creation was the bridge between the two worlds. This forms the deeper content of Hungarian folk literature as exemplified by that era's great apostles of poetry, Sándor Petőfi and János Arany.

The concepts for which the statesmen and youth of

the reform era fought in the National Assembly and at county meetings, as well as in books and in periodicals, can be listed under five headings.

> The serfs should be freed and given land.
>
> The rights of man must be assured.
>
> A system of popular representation should be established, with free elections and a government responsible to parliament.
>
> Special privileges and unequal taxation must be abolished.
>
> There must be social and economic reform, including a reform of public administration and the prisons; a modern credit system should be established and the guilds abolished.

These reforms were opposed not only by the Vienna Court, but by most of the Hungarian high nobility, prelates, and lesser nobility, who feared the consequences of abolishing serfdom, the basis of their economic and social existence. However, for the most part they too condemned Austria's oppression of Hungary.

The influence of the 1848 Paris revolt, which swept through Europe and temporarily overthrew the reactionary system associated with the name of Metternich, was decisive. This influence, absorbed and then projected by the young Hungarian intellectuals, launched the 1848 struggle for freedom.

Two positions, gradual reform versus radical change, crystallized around two great personalities. István Széchenyi, who had effected a long series of cultural, economic and technical advances, considered further reforms as the pre-condition of national and political transformation.

Heading the camp of swift revolutionary change, Louis Kossuth—who, as a young envoy, sat in the National Assembly—soon became the idolized leader of the country's youth. Defying censorship, he continued to issue reports on affairs in parliament and at county meetings, becoming a champion of freedom of the press. Like Széchenyi, he had a broad western education. Thrown into prison, he gained so fluent a command of

English there that later he was able to address English and American audiences in almost Shakespearean cadences. Kossuth's stand can be briefly summarized: freedom first—meaning the highest attainable degree of national independence and democracy—then all else. Kossuth brought ideals and endeavors of the reform age into a single focus: the achievement of liberty.

The youth of Pest, dissatisfied with the National Assembly, staged an enthusiastic mass demonstration in March, 1848, in collaboration with two great figures, the poet Petöfi and the novelist Mór Jókai. Defying the censor, they published Petöfi's rousing call to freedom, "Arise Hungarians!", as well as a twelve-point manifesto. This tradition was continued by Hungarian youth when in October 1956 they again listed their demands by points—many identical to those of 1848—in the face of new foreign oppression, this time Soviet Communist tyranny.

Petöfi, through his life and poetry, fulfilled the historic mission of Hungarian literature. His championing of the people's cause was reflected even by his death at the hands of Russian Cossacks who invaded Hungary to help end the fight for freedom.

Hungarian youth's March demands were: freedom of the press, a responsible cabinet, equality before the law, equal taxes, the abolition of serfdom, union with Transylvania (then governed separately so as to divide the Hungarians). The demonstrating throng freed the political prisoners, among them Mihály Táncsics, leader of the workers, who as yet had played hardly any political role.

The March events forced the Vienna Court to approve the April laws the National Assembly had passed, fired by the dynamism of Hungarian youth. The first responsible Hungarian cabinet was formed. Kossuth became the soul of the freedom movement, blending youthful verve with responsibility in running the country.

Széchenyi, shattered by the thought of the destructive storm the revolt would bring, felt sure that the cause of Hungarian independence must fail in a showdown

with Vienna and the aroused minorities. He retired to
an Austrian sanitarium, and in 1860 committed suicide.

Until now there had been no real minority question
in Hungary. The status of peasants of whatever nationality, was the same. The Turks had by and large destroyed the Hungarians on the Great Plain, and spared
the minorities who dwelt in the hills. Thus, when they
withdrew, the proportion of other nationalities had
risen sharply. Surging Hungarian national consciousness
spurred that of the minorities too, and the Vienna Court
fanned the flames so as to keep Hungary in check. From
the first decades of the nineteenth century this nationalistic trend also was aided by Russian pan-Slavism. As
a counterpoise to the Hungarian freedom movement, the
reactionary Austrian Court, curiously enough, supported
the liberal and even radical efforts of minority leaders,
whose nationalistic and democratic movements relied
largely on the aid of Austrian reactionary circles. The
Vienna Court even went so far as to encourage revolts
by minorities whose intelligentsia was primarily embittered by the use of Hungarian as a state language, a
parallel to the former rift between the Hungarians and
Austria.

Seizing a moment when the fight for freedom seemed
under control, Vienna stripped Hungary of her constitution. At this, the National Assembly dethroned the
House of Hapsburg on April 4, 1849, proclaiming Hungary's emancipation from Austria, and chose Louis Kossuth as governor of independent Hungary.

The revolutionary army had fine leaders, especially
Arthur Görgey, a former officer of the guards, and
Joseph Bem, hero of the Polish Revolt of 1831, who
also participated in the Viennese revolt. Among the officers were idealistic foreigners, too, defending the cause
of universal freedom on Hungarian soil, while the rank
and file was made up of the Hungarian peasantry.
Though short of money and arms, the army scored cru-
cial victories and at one point drove the Austrians quite
out of the country. But the fate of the revolt was sealed
when young Franz Joseph called in the Russian Czar,
Nicholas I, to suppress it. Without arms and outside

help, facing overwhelming force, further resistance
would have been suicidal, as in the days of Rákóczi's
battle for freedom; and Görgey, as plenipotentiary of
the fleeing Kossuth, surrendered at Világos on August
13, 1849.

The Austrian terror then loosed by General Haynau
took thousands of victims. Most of the military and political leaders of the revolt were executed, among them
thirteen generals. Others escaped by fleeing abroad. Kossuth emigrated to Turkey, where Bem joined the Turkish forces to fight for the third time against Russian
czarism. Kossuth sailed for Britain on an American
naval vessel and his electric presence contributed to the
fall of the English Conservative Party. Then he went
to the United States, to be feted as no one since Lafayette. Finally he settled in Torino, center of the Italian
freedom movements, where he evolved a significant plan
for a Danubian Confederation linking Hungarians,
South Slavs and Rumanians into a bloc strong enough
to ward off Austrian encroachment.

LIGHTS AND SHADOWS

Grave defeats, the loss of the Italian provinces and
her complete elimination from the German empire,
forced Austria into a settlement with Hungary. Most
Hungarians saw that a compromise was the only realistic
solution; so the advocate of the new approach, Ferenc
Deák engineered the Compromise of 1867 between Hungary and Austria, by whose terms the ruling house entered into a personal union with Hungary. Foreign and defense affairs, as well as tariffs and monetary matters were
to be handled jointly. Until the First World War the
Compromise was recognized as a basis of national policy
by all leading Hungarian statesmen, among them Julius
Andrássy, supporter of the monarchy's pro-German policy, and Kálmán and István Tisza, broadly cultured
representatives of the landowning lesser nobility, who
were backed by the semi-liberal majority party.

The movement for complete independence continued,
though now based more on dreams than reality. Indeed
the Independence party was accused—not without some

truth—of waging a campaign to distract public opinion
from urgent social and cultural reforms. Yet it is also
true that the conservative framework of the Monarchy
precluded radical reform—essential for that was national
independence.

In the shelter of a European power, in the calm of
the Franz Joseph era (1848–1916), the country thrived,
developing industry and trade. Travel and communications improved, a network of banks appeared, and
urbanization—especially in Budapest—made great strides.

At the end of the century came the first labor movements and strikes, and the first meaningful agrarian and
socialist movements. Demands for social improvement
led inevitably to political demands—above all, the right
to a universal secret ballot. Here the workers of Budapest played an energetic role.

The transition period, lasting well into the first decade of the twentieth century, was intellectually a time
of retrospection, drawing inspiration from the preceding
great decades, but neglecting grave and timely problems,
the hidden social and human conflict which it should
have explored.

Music, creative arts, architecture, and the humanities
were inspired by the Reform Age and Freedom Fight to
an even greater extent than literature. The work of
Franz Liszt, one of the top composers of the period and
a precursor of modern music, was shaped to a great
extent by the revolutionary experiences of the Hungarian nation. The same inspiration moved other key
composers of the epoch (Ferenc Erkel, Mihály Mosonyi);
its painters (Mihály Munkácsy, László Paál); sculptors
(Miklos Izso, János Fadrusz); architects (Miklos Ybl,
Frigyes Feszl), and those engaged in the flourishing historical sciences.

In the years before World War I, Hungarian writing
resumed its old communal mission. The new literature
had two faces. The first found Hungarian spiritual life
stagnant through loss of contact with Western life, literature, art and science. These writers declared that only
contacts with the West could rouse Hungarian society
from its vegetative stupor. Their revolt was expressed by

the magazine *Nyugat* (The West), founded in 1908. This literary spirit facing Westward was represented by the poets Endre Ady, Mihály Babits, Dezsö Kosztolányi, Árpád Tóth and later by the novelist Sándor Márai. Ady was also a brilliant publicist, Babits and Kosztolányi were outstanding novelists and short story writers.

No less important was the new literature's other face, which did not gaze afar, but was concerned with the Hungarian land and the country's subterranean forces. This group gave impetus to a salient phenomenon of modern Hungarian spiritual life: Populism. For writers, artists, musicians, teachers, historians and agrarians, life in Hungary—especially the life of Hungarian peasants—became an artistic and human experience with basic social and political overtones, bringing an awareness that Hungarian society and culture could not be reborn without ending the impoverishment of the villages. Endre Ady also represented this side of the new literature, together with the prophetically passionate "unmasker" of the postwar era, Zsigmond Móricz. They were joined by the novelist Dezsö Szabó, and the poet, Gyula Juhász. Móricz and Szabó were social and political publicists in the deeper sense of the word.

In the first generation of new creativity was the musical genius, Béla Bartok, a great initiator even from a global standpoint. In him this duality of the new Hungarian spirit, melding Western and folk elements, was harmoniously at one. No composer has ever given a more vital voice to Nature, in the world's universal, religious sense—meaning not pantheism but the symbol-language of being. His revolutionary achievement (shared by his eminent partner, the composer Zoltán Kodály) was to create forms which gave the world of individual feeling and passion a mythic perspective. By their rediscovery of Hungarian folk music, these two men made the nation aware of a spiritual treasure, a means of expressing the most sharply differentiated individual intents. The personal influence of these two composers, their brave resistance to all tyranny, swayed youth as much as their art.

This populist trend has found expression in the style,

composition, and color of the last fifty years of Hun-
garian painting, from the pioneers (Pál Szinyei Merse,
László Mednyánszky, Simon Holóssy, Károly Ferenczy,
József Rippl-Ronai) through the seekers of new forms
(Gyula Rudnay, József Koszta, István Csók, Tivadar
Csontváry) to the present generation (József Egry, István
Szönyi, Aurél Bernáth). Present-day Hungarian sculptors
express this approach in their search for new forms to
represent the human figure (Ferenc Medgyessy, Miklós
Borsos, Tibor Wilt, Dezsö Bokros-Birman, Géza Csorba).
Architecture, like music, has developed a modern airy
sunny style drawn from the ornamental forms of the
people's art (Ödön Lechner, Béla Lajta, etc.).

The Western face of the new revolutionary spirit more
than once seemed master of the field, but never could
obliterate the folk spirit entirely. Where this Western
outlook prevailed, it produced a wholly urbane literature and art which, though often seemingly at odds with
folk art and literature, actually formed a rich equation,
trend balancing trend.

As a result of the defeat of the Monarchy in 1918
Hungary suffered an unprecedented loss of land and
population, though surely not chargeable with any imperialistic aims. Hungary was allowed to keep 28.6 per
cent of her former territory, 31.5 per cent being annexed
to Rumania, 19.6 per cent to Yugoslavia, 18.9 per cent
to Czechoslovakia, 1.2 per cent to Austria, and small
fragments to Poland and Italy. The country lost 71.4
per cent of its total territory and 61 per cent of its total
population. Over three million Magyars, more than a
fourth of the total population, were assigned to these
"successor states."

The lost war tore open old wounds. The October 1918
revolt, which can hardly be called that, since it had practically no opponents and so occurred quite bloodlessly,
firmly achieved the inevitable break with Austria and
the ruling house; and enabled the country, which had
at last regained its freedom, to undertake a democratic
and social transformation. That road, however, was
blocked not only by a latent and ever more strongly
organized inner subversion, but primarily by the hostil-

ity to Hungary of the Western Powers, notably France, then dominant in continental affairs. These forces swept the country towards communism which—then, too—was forced on the people by a tiny minority, consisting mainly of former war prisoners trained in Russia. They sweetened the bitter pill with a promise that the Soviet Union, then advancing towards Poland, would help restore a great portion of Hungary's territorial integrity. Since such Soviet aid did not materialize, the dictatorship of the proletariat in Hungary soon crumbled in the face of Czech, Rumanian and Hungarian troops backed by the French. Actually, however, it was not outside force that caused its collapse after four months, but the peasantry, which, despite all social oppression, abhorred terror.

NEO-BAROQUE SOCIETY

After the fall of the first Hungarian "Commune," the country was reorganized by conservative forces, whose spirit a noted modern Hungarian historian named the neo-Baroque, alluding to its overemphasis of old forms to cover lack of content. With the aid of military force, the Parliament elected as Regent the leader of the troops entering Budapest, Admiral Nicholas Horthy, last commander of the Austro-Hungarian fleet. The law it enacted dethroned the Hapsburg ruling house, but in principle retained the Hungarian kingship, despite the fact that the returning Charles IV had been turned back twice by force of arms. The troubled country was consolidated by Count Stephen Bethlen, Prime Minister from 1921 to 1931.

The neo-Baroque order socially and spiritually ostracized the nation's two great basic strata, the vast majority of the population: the peasants and the workers, the latter by now organized along social-democratic lines by the trade unions. It scoffed at land reform, an inescapable condition for a unified society, and refused to countenance attempts to bring the economic status of workers and peasants into balance. This led to the emergence of a sort of half proletariat, intellectual and non-intellectual, which strongly affected public opinion and proved fertile soil for fascist ideas.

After the triumph of Italian Fascism and then of German National Socialism, the influence of the anti-democratic forces grew apace, abetted by fear of increasing Soviet power beyond the border, as well as by a tacit awareness that the great social problems remained unsolved. This political orientation, combined with the ruling neo-baroque society's views, led to growing isolation from the era's progressive current of ideas.

The writers again undertook to lead the nation out of its political, social and spiritual impasse, voicing solutions for the fateful problems which the official world would not face. Hungary was still a predominantly agrarian state and each social, economic and spiritual crisis was linked in some way to the widening gulf between leading classes and peasantry.

Folk literature continued to reveal the Hungarian world, depicting its human, spiritual and moral values, but also the inhuman conditions many millions of Hungarians had to suffer. Above all, it never ceased to stress that the key to any Hungarian renaissance was improvement of the peasant's lot by radical land reform.

Poets, novelists and dramatists, essayists, publicists, agronomists and teachers comprised the community of populist writers which, with that generation, became a true movement. Gyula Illyés, József Erdélyi, Imre Kovács, László Németh, János Kodolányi, Péter Veres, Zoltán Szabó, Ferenc Erdei, József Darvas, Pál Szabó, György Sarközi, Géza Féja, Sándor Karácsony are its best representatives. Many eminent spirits of the age were akin to them without being openly engaged in their activities. Thus the magic style of Áron Tamási, the Transylvanian novelist, short story writer and dramatist, which lent mythical perspective to the life of the peasant, and the exquisite music of Lörinc Szabó's verses, also blazed the way for a young literary élite. They kept in close touch with the chief figure of the new generation of poets, the spokesman of social justice, of the city proletariat, Attila József.

But all in vain. Hungary fell under the sway of the

Nazi and Fascist movements, and pent-up resentments of the lower middle class found an outlet in strong anti-Semitism. Broad strata of the population were influenced by Hitler's and Mussolini's clever move, the so-called Vienna Awards, 1938–40, which restored to Hungary significant Hungarian-populated areas of Czechoslovakia and Rumania.

In 1941 the Germans forced participation in the campaign against Yugoslavia, using as bait the return of its Hungarian-populated northern areas. Premier Paul Teleki, realizing the fateful significance of restitution via terroristic regimes, committed suicide.

The new Prime Minister, László Bárdossy, was an ardent supporter of German policy. Hungary declared war on the Soviet Union, then on the Western Allies, and joined the German campaign against Russia. In March 1942 Miklós Kállay took over the premiership and, as events turned against Germany (the Allied landing in Africa and especially in Italy, the Battle of Stalingrad), he established contacts with the West. In August 1943, the Kállay government declared its readiness to accept the Casablanca formula of unconditional surrender, should the Allied forces reach the frontiers of Hungary. The Germans, getting wind of this, occupied Hungary in a surprise move on March 19, 1944, and appointed a Quisling government.

One immediate result of the German occupation was that several hundred thousand Jews were hauled to death camps abroad. In October, 1944, when Soviet advances already threatened Hungarian soil, Regent Horthy and his circle once more tried to break off hostilities. The Germans arrested him, along with many thousands of Hungarians; other thousands only escaped by going underground. The Germans entrusted the government to the extreme rightist Arrow-Cross faction led by Ferenc Szálasi; all hopes faded.

COMMUNIST CONQUEST
OF HUNGARY

Excerpts from the study of Stephen D. Kertész:
"The Methods of Communist Conquest: Hungary
1944–47," WORLD POLITICS, Volume III. No. 1. 1950
(Center of International Studies, Princeton University, Princeton, New Jersey.)

In the general picture of Eastern European developments the Hungarian scene has some peculiar features.
Hungary did not succeed in changing sides effectively
during the war and at the close of hostilities was probably in the worst political position among the former
Axis satellites. She did not enjoy much sympathy in the
West, and was positively disliked by the Russians. In
point of time Hungary was the last of the Axis satellites
to conclude an armistice treaty with the three major
Allies (January 20, 1945).

The invading Russian army found in the devastated
country an almost complete vacuum of political power.
The old administration was nonexistent, or not recognized by the occupying army, which with the help of
experienced Communist advisers created an entirely new
political organization. Despite or perhaps because of
these circumstances, Hungary is the only former Axis
satellite state where free and unfettered elections took
place according to the Yalta Agreement.

Hungary was politically isolated in the months following the close of hostilities. She had neither diplomatic
representatives abroad nor friends among the victorious
states. She was occupied by Russian troops, and, until

September 1947, under the strict rule of the Russian-dominated Allied Control Commission. In the armistice period she could not renew diplomatic relations without the permission of the A.C.C. This permission was in some cases delayed, in others, refused. The Hungarian people still retained vivid recollections of the 1919 Communist regime of Béla Kun. They also remembered that the Hungarian revolution of 1848–49 had been crushed with the help of the Russian Imperial Army.

While Budapest and western Hungary were still in German hands, the Moscovite Communists, moving around the liberated areas in Russian army cars, picked up a few members of the former opposition parties and escorted them to Debrecen, the chief town in north-eastern Hungary. This group of hand-picked politicians approved a Communist proposal to convoke at Debrecen a Provisional National Assembly. In the larger villages and towns the National Committees organized meetings which elected representatives by acclamation.[1]

The Provisional National Assembly consisted of 230 deputies, of whom 72 were Communists, 57 Smallholders, 35 Social Democrats, 19 representatives of trade-unions, and 12 members of the National Peasant Party. The rest of the deputies were without apparent party affiliation or belonged to insignificant parties. Seven Moscovite Communists became members of the Assembly.

At the first session of the Assembly (December 21, 1944) one of the leading Moscovites, E. Gerő, emphasized that "the policy of the Hungarian Communist Party is a Hungarian, democratic, and national policy." The next day the Assembly elected the Provisional National Government and authorized the new government to conclude an armistice with the Allied Powers.

The exterior appearance of the Provisional National Government seemed excellent. Even conservative people were agreeably surprised. The Communists, Smallhold-

[1] Altogether thirty-eight towns and villages, representing 1,381,-000 people in the Russian liberated areas, took part in these "elections," though some three and a half million people dwelt there. Regular elections, of course, could not have taken place in those apocalyptic days.

ers, and Social Democrats each had two portfolios, the
Peasant Party one. Besides these seven party men, five
non-party men sat in the cabinet. The prime minister,
Béla Miklós, and two ministers were generals of the
Horthy regime. There was even a Count in the cabinet,
Géza Teleki, son of the popular late prime minister,
Count Paul Teleki, who killed himself when Hungary
joined Germany in the attack on Yugoslavia.[2] A fifth
non-party appointee, Erich Molnár, turned out later to
be an old member of the underground Communist
Party.

The whole political setup created at Debrecen, and
particularly the composition of the new government, exposed clearly one of the main principles of Communist
politics: a constant pattern of giving formal authority
to non-Communists while retaining effective control in
the hands of Communists or fellow travelers. Communists in the new government had all the key positions
in terms of real power. Fellow travelers, moreover, were
tolerated only while they proved to be useful as a front,
i.e., as non-party advocates of Communist policy. Communist and Russian consent was necessary for the appointment of all important officials, particularly cabinet
ministers.

POLITICAL CONDITIONS

The Debrecen government endeavored to function
under miserably difficult conditions. All its offices were
jammed into one building, and the effectiveness of all
governmental measures depended entirely on the good-
will of the Russians. The central government truly was
little more than a show window. There was no regular
railroad, telegraph, or postal communication. The *Official Bulletin* published in Debrecen could not be forwarded beyond the outskirts of the town. The real

2 Count Géza Teleki and General Gábor Faragó were sent by
Regent Horthy to Moscow in September 1944 to negotiate an armistice agreement, General Miklós commanded the first Hungarian
Army fighting against the Russians and General János Vörös was
chief of the General Staff. Both Miklós and Vörös went over to
the Russians after the armistice proclamation of Regent Horthy.
Faragó and Vörös became members of the Miklós cabinet.

power lay in the hands of the occupying Russian forces. In addition, communist-dominated local National Committees and communist-organized police actually administered the country. The Debrecen government's feeling of deprivation and absolute dependency on the Russians also had an important psychological impact even subsequently when the situation improved somewhat.

The Russians had a wide choice of means for exerting pressure, for they had practically unlimited power. The daily bread of the population, personal liberty, and other primary necessities of life depended entirely upon them. The devastated country had to feed an occupying force of several hundred thousand men. Factory equipment was removed at will as war booty. Food supplies were seized. Civilians by the thousands, and from eastern Hungary even women, were taken to Russia as war prisoners. Public safety did not exist; there was no authority capable of giving protection against the Russians. Even when the period of large-scale kidnapping came to an end, people were arrested and judged by Russian military tribunals on fantastic charges, sometimes for having carried out instructions of the Hungarian Government. In such cases, of course, there was no question of legal assistance or due process. The accused simply disappeared.

When the government moved in April 1945 to the devastated capital, Budapest, the Russians, the Communist Party, and the various communist-sponsored organizations already were occupying the choice spots. Since many government buildings were destroyed during the siege, the government agencies obtained only battered tenements. It was characteristic of conditions that the foreign ministry had to move into a shabby old apartment house, while the communist-organized "Democratic Youth Movement" occupied a magnificent palace.

Using the stipulations of the Socialist-Communist agreement of October 1944 which provided for the immediate unification of the workers through the unions, the Communist Party seized control of the trade unions. (In Hungary the trade union movement had been intimately connected with the Social Democratic Party.) Under the German Occupation, they of course were dissolved and their leaders arrested.

In 1944, the thirty-one trade unions in Hungary had a membership of about 100,000. After the liberation twenty new trade unions were formed and membership rose to 850,596 in December 1945 and to 1,288,905 by January 1947. Unions appeared in all branches of state administration, private enterprise, and the free professions. Practically all working men had to belong to a union; and the unions, as mass organizations, became important tools in the hands of Communist policy-makers. Top posts in the National Federation of Trade Unions and in the Trade Union Council went to Communists. A delegate of the trade unions sat in every denazification committee, in every People's Court, and in every National Committee, on equal footing with representatives of the four political parties. This in each case resulted in double Communist representation. In the factories various committees were organized through which the Communist Party further strengthened its hold on the workers.

The fate of the Social Democratic Party was similar to that of the trade unions. After Charles Peyer, the old leader of the party, was deported by the Germans, Árpád Szakasits, former editor of the Social Democratic Party newspaper *Népszavat,* took over. Szakasits, a fellow traveler, was eager to accept Communist suggestions when he reorganized the party after the Russian liberation. Left-wing Socialists got key positions. The moderate and independent elements of the party were branded rightist deviationists, traitors to worker unity. When in May 1945 Peyer returned from the Mauthausen concentration camp, he was offered a diplomatic post by way of honorable exile. He did not accept, but courageously carried on a losing battle. Disappointed, Peyer eventually resigned from his party and finally fled the country with other Socialists. *In absentia* he was tried and sentenced as a spy and traitor.

Thus Communists soon gained by force an absolute majority in all agencies established by the coalition parties. The trade unions and the leftist Socialist dele-

COMMUNIST CONQUEST OF HUNGARY

gates invariably supported the Communists. Since the attitude of the National Peasant Party was uncertain, the Smallholder representative usually remained isolated.

The history of the National Peasant Party is characteristic of the political evolution in Hungary. The party was founded in June 1939 by a populist writer, Imre Kovács, as a more radical party than the Smallholders. During the war years it worked underground in scattered groups throughout the country without parliamentary representation. Radical populist writers—the so-called village explorers—and a group of progressive intellectuals formed the core of the party. Some members were secretly Communists. After the war, these crypto-Communists with the help of radical slogans and the intervention of the Communist Party gradually seized control. Progressive intellectuals lost all power positions.[3]

The Russians and Communists controlled mass media such as radio, movies, and newspapers. First the Russians, later the Communists, allocated all newsprint. Publication of newspapers was authorized through a licensing system. At the outset only the Communist and Socialist Parties, and later only political parties of the coalition, could publish newspapers. There was also other pressure. For instance, printers would refuse articles the Communist Party objected to.

But despite these and other difficulties, a strange optimism prevailed in the coalition parties. An important fact one cannot overlook is that the non-Communist parties were almost as progressive on social, economic, and cultural questions as the Communists themselves professed to be.[4] All the coalition parties were in opposition during the Horthy regime and co-operated underground with the Communists during the German occu-

[3] The founder of the party, Imre Kovács, resigned as Secretary General when the party joined the leftist bloc in 1946, and resigned from the party when the Secretary General of the Smallholders Party, Béla Kovács, was arrested by the Russians on February 25, 1947.

[4] Cf. Oscár Jászi, "The Choices in Hungary," *Foreign Affairs*, XXIV (1946), 462. Jászi points out that "the Small Landholders' Party is not reactionary, not even conservative; it is a progressive party in favor of social and cultural reforms."

pation. As throughout Nazi-oppressed Europe, so in Hungary the common fight against the Nazi foe developed a sort of camaraderie between the Communist and non-Communist politicians. It was like a miracle that Hungary had been able to avoid complete annihilation at war's end, and the leading politicians of the new order seemed determined to make the most of a desperate situation. This task needed courage and an optimistic outlook, especially as regarded the chances of cooperation with the Russians and Communists. And above all a great common task faced the parties: the rebuilding and rehabilitation of a devastated country. And there the Communists displayed zeal and energy. Non-Communist leaders "thought it natural that the Communist Party should be more radical than other parties, but expected it would work shoulder to shoulder with the others in reviving the country."[5]

All political parties recognized the impact of Russia's overwhelming power in the Danubian area, but a spirit of wishful thinking nevertheless prevailed. Soviet Russia appeared a newcomer in the society of great powers. Her harsh manners seemed due to a different tradition and not to ill will. After the armistice period she would withdraw into the vastness of Russia and refrain from interfering in the internal affairs of Hungary. Even a few non-Moscovite Communists, who pictured the future along lines that today would be considered Titoism, shared these views. Then this view was no crime. Communist leaders and the Russians, moreover, professed and openly encouraged it.

It took some time to realize that Communists hated left-wing politicians or Socialists of independent views more than they did the former Nazis. In a number of cases former Nazis were welcome in the Communist Party and became obedient tools. Gradually it became clear that in decisive questions the Communists did nothing but carry out the orders of Moscow and that actually the Communist Party was a disguised third branch of the Soviet administration represented in Hun-

[5] Ferenc Nagy, *The Struggle Behind the Iron Curtain*, New York, Macmillan, 1948, p. 72.

gary outwardly by the Red Army and Soviet diplomacy. Lacking popular support, it could rely only on the Russians. Under these conditions genuine co-operation between Communist and non-Communist parties never took place. Political expediency at all times guided the Communist attitude. They sought control. That was the aim of all Communist actions. Economic and social reforms played only a secondary, tactical role. In pursuing this aim the Communists sometimes veered quite suddenly, without any apparent motive or reason. Always, however, they invoked the "will of the people," which, of course, they cleverly manipulated through their press and organized mass demonstrations.

FREE ELECTIONS

The fall elections in 1945 marked a turning point in postwar Hungarian politics. The Communists arranged to have the Budapest municipal elections on October 7, a month before the general elections, certain that the working-class districts of the capital would assure a sweeping victory for the joint Communist-Socialist ticket. But the outcome was the first major disappointment for the Communist brain trust, for the Smallholders got an absolute majority—even in the capital.[6]

Feverish Communist efforts followed this defeat. They proposed a single electoral ticket for the forthcoming general elections. A.C.C. chairman Marshall Voroshilov himself intervened and eventually offered 47.5 per cent of the single list to the Smallholders, who refused. The embittered Socialists also insisted on separate electoral lists since they attributed their defeat in Budapest to the people's anti-Communist sentiments. Instead of setting a single block ticket, the four parties agreed to continue

[6] The results of the Budapest municipal elections:

	Votes	Seats
Smallholders Party	285,197	121
United Socialist-Communist ticket	249,711	103
Civic Democratic Party	22,392	9
National Peasant Party	11,741	5
Hungarian Radical Party	5,013	2

the coalition government, whatever the results of the election. The Communists still were optimistic. They enjoyed tremendous advantages. Besides the support of the occupying forces, they had plenty of newsprint and transportation facilities, in contrast with the non-Communist parties.

It was a shock to the Communists and the Russians when at the general elections on November 4, 1945, the Communists polled only 17 per cent. The Smallholders got almost 60 per cent of the seats in Parliament.[7] This defeat proved that the Communists had not won over the former agrarian proletariat, which had been their greatest hope. A considerable number of the new land-owners, no matter how small their allotment, had grown class-conscious, and staunch supporters of private owner-ship. Communism did not appeal to them.

After the elections Voroshilov was quick to point out to Smallholder leaders that "the Soviet Union wished to base its friendship with Hungary on its relations with the Smallholders Party."[8] The Smallholders, glowing with victory, were most pleased by this statement. They visualized a new era of constructive Hungarian-Soviet co-operation. The apparently passive Soviet attitude at the elections encouraged everyone.

The Communists, though flabbergasted, were not greatly disturbed. They had to change tactics and Mátyás Rákosi, their leader, had to explain to Moscow. On the whole, however, the political situation remained favor-able to them. The aristocracy and landowners had al-ready been liquidated. Land reform had also deprived

[7] THE RESULTS OF THE 1945 GENERAL ELECTIONS:

| | Seats in Parliament | |
	Total number	Percentage
Smallholders Party	245	59.9
Communist Party	70	17.11
Social Democratic Party	69	16.9
National Peasant Party	23	5.6
Civic Democratic arty	2	0.49
Total:	409	100.00

[8] Ferenc Nagy, *op. cit.*, p. 154.

the Church of its main economic base. The middle class lived in complete insecurity, gradually selling off their belongings in order to exist. Inflation on an unprecedented scale, moreover, increased the general hardship and confusion. The Communists held all key posts, and controlled the country by means of the National Committees and the police. Trade unions and factory committees were firmly in Communist hands. Fifth columns were carefully planted in all parties. The continuance of coalition government was assured by the pre-election arrangement. Thus the Communists hoped to rule the country conveniently behind the screen of a coalition, as in other satellite countries.

After the elections it was agreed that the Interior Minister should be a member of the Smallholders Party. Five days later the Communists said they must have that post, since Voroshilov—astonished to hear that in Hungary the situation would be different in that respect from other countries friendly to the Soviet Union—had vetoed the proposition. The Smallholders yielded. Otherwise they obtained an imposing number of cabinet seats but, of course, not the real power positions. The prime minister, one minister of state, seven other members of the cabinet, president of the Assembly, and later the President of the Republic[9]—all were Smallholders. The Communist and the Socialist Parties each obtained three portfolios, the Peasant Party one. In addition, the Communist and Socialist Parties each had a deputy premiership.

The coalition honeymoon did not last long. Mass meetings and other Communist-organized demonstrations of the workers, synchronized with Russian political and economic pressures, moved the government leftward. The most skillful tactical step in undermining the Smallholders was the formation of a left-wing bloc by Communists, Socialists, the Peasant Party, and the Trade Union Council. Thus the Communists isolated the Smallholders within the coalition, took the offense, and began to address *ultimata* to them "in the name of the Hun-

[9] Hungary was declared a republic by a law promulgated on January 31, 1946.

garian people." Politicians opposing the demands of the leftist bloc were denounced as "Fascists" and "enemies of the people." A tense revolutionary atmosphere was created, making impossible a normal function of parliament.

Gradually the Smallholders Party was maneuvered into a self-liquidating process which began in March 1946 with the expulsion from the party of twenty-one deputies, attacked by the Communists as "reactionaries." This was followed in ensuing months by other unwarranted expulsions and by various Russian- and Communist-dictated political and economic measures.

Early in 1947 the discovery of a large-scale conspiracy against the Hungarian Republic was announced. Communist newspapers soon connected the conspiracy with the Smallholders Party. One of the Smallholders cabinet ministers and several members of the party were arrested. Their "confessions" implicated Béla Kovács, Secretary General of the Smallholders. Parliament refused to suspend his immunity but he offered to testify before the political police. After this hearing, Soviet authorities arrested him on February 25, 1947, on charges of espionage against the Soviet Army.

In this political crisis the cabinet was reorganized. Three Smallholder ministers resigned to be replaced by left-wing Smallholders. In April the People's Court sentenced three alleged conspirators to death, the others to long penal servitude. On May 18 the exhausted Prime Minister, Ferenc Nagy, went to Switzerland for a rest. On May 28 the Russians very belatedly forwarded Béla Kovács' "confession" of March 9 to the Hungarian Government whose head conveniently happened to be, in the absence of Nagy, Deputy Prime Minister Mátyás Rákosi.[10] The confession implicated some of the leading Smallholders, among them the Prime Minister himself. Nagy, notified of these events, decided to return at once, but was advised from Budapest not to do so. He resigned

[10] This text was published in *White Book Documents on the Conspiracy Against the Hungarian Republic and Democracy* (in Hungarian), by the Ministry for Propaganda, Budapest, 1947, pp. 110–13.

on May 29, and has since remained in exile.[11] Another Smallholder leader, Msgr. Béla Varga, President of Parliament, fled Hungary on June 2 to avoid arrest.

With Smallholder leadership liquidated, the stage was set for the next act: the elections of August 31, 1947. Under the new Prime Minister, Lajos Dinnyés, whose appointment was engineered by General Sviridov, deputy of Marshal Voroshilov, Smallholder co-operation became total submission to the Communists. A modification of the electoral law was voted and the Communist Party felt it necessary to adopt different tactics than in 1945.

In 1945 opposition parties were not allowed. Only two insignificant non-coalition parties took part in the elections. These were mere fronts. One obtained two seats, the other none.

In 1947, reverse tactics seemed opportune for the final disintegration of the Smallholders Party. Besides the four coalition parties, the Allied Control Commission authorized six opposition parties. This gave a democratic aspect to the elections and confused the Smallholders, disgusted anyway by the subservient party leadership. In addition, the new electoral law assured important advantages to the coalition parties, especially by granting them the so-called premium seats, and made possible quasi-unlimited exclusion from the vote under various pretexts.

Further, its provisions served to eliminate from the public life the most important opposition leader, Dezső Sulyok. He was designated Prime Minister in January 1946, but this was vetoed by the Communists. Sulyok was excluded from the Smallholders Party in March 1946, and after much haggling the A.C.C. authorized in October the formation of the Freedom Party under his leadership.[12] Publication of the party newspaper *Holnap* (Tomorrow), however, was blocked and party meetings

11 Ferenc Nagy gives an account of the "conspiracy," the abduction of Béla Kovács by the Russians, and his forced resignation. *Op. cit.*, pp. 311–425.

12 Concerning the history of the Freedom Party, see Desiderius Sulyok, *Zwei Nächte ohne Tag, Ungarn unter dem Sovietstern*, Zürich, 1948, pp. 358–379.

were constantly broken up by Communist-organized mobs. Police protection was nil. The activities of the Freedom Party thus becoming practically impossible, it disbanded in July 1947.

This was when one of the expelled leading members of the Smallholders Party, Zoltán Pfeiffer, founded the Independence Party. Most of the terror and violence of the regime was concentrated against him and his party during the election campaign. The Independence Party was considered, in a way, as successor of the Freedom Party. The Communists supposed that the other opposition parties, authorized at the last minute, lacking organization, skilled leadership, money, and courage in the face of terror, could not obtain a substantial number of votes.

Election results proved, however, that the Communist policy-makers had miscalculated again. The four coalition parties barely obtained a majority. They received about the same proportion of votes as the Smallholders alone in 1945. The Communist Party polled 22 per cent instead of 17, but the five per cent gain stemmed from the use of "flying squadrons" and other frauds.[13] Among the losers was the Social Democratic Party, which polled only 14.9 per cent. They protested sharply, citing the many electoral frauds organized by Communist Minister of the Interior, László Rajk.

The great surprise of the elections was that the Democratic People's Party polled the most votes, after the Communists.[14] The other striking phenomenon was the complete disintegration of the emasculated Smallholders Party, which got just 15 per cent of the votes. The oppo-

[13] The new law permitted persons absent from their residence to vote with so-called blue tickets. These tickets were issued to Communist brigades who were transported from one place to another and voted ten to twenty times. A great many persons were excluded from the polls on ridiculous charges.

[14] The Democratic People's Party, better known as the Barankovics Party, was belatedly accepted by the Supreme National Committee as eligible to take part in the 1945 elections. However, by then it was too late for proper preparations; being denied all means of conducting a successful campaign, the party decided against running. Through the rights established, it participated in the 1947 elections as an opposition to the coalition parties.—Ed.

sition had divided into two major and four smaller parties. But by and large the proportion of anti-Communist votes did not change basically despite electoral abuses.

RESULTS OF GENERAL ELECTIONS, 1947

	Seats from the constituencies No.	%	Premium seats	Seats on the national list	All seats in Parliament
Coalition Parties:					
Communist	79	22.27	18	3	100
Smallholders	54	15.4	12	2	68
Social Democratic	53	14.9	12	2	67
National Peasant	29	8.31	6	1	36
Opposition Parties:					
Democratic People's	58	16.41	—	2	60
Hungarian Independence	47	13.42	—	2	49
Ind. Democratic	18	5.21	—	—	18
Radical	6	1.68	—	—	6
Christian Women's League	4	1.39	—	—	4
Civic Democratic	3	1.01	—	—	3
Total	351	100.00	48	12	411

Understandably the Communists were disgusted by the parliamentary elections, and hence resolved to liquidate even the appearance of parliamentarianism. The Russian Minister to Hungary, Georgi M. Pushkin, remarked sourly that the Hungarian people did not appreciate the numerous Russian gestures, not even Moscow's ratification of the Hungarian peace treaty, which was purposely announced two days before the Hungarian elections.

After the second electoral failure, the Communists started their new policy with the elimination of the opposition parties. The forty-nine members of the Hungarian Independence Party were attacked shortly after the elections as "Fascists" and deprived of their seats in the National Assembly. Their leader, Zoltán Pfeiffer, fled Hungary. The Democratic People's Party followed a cautious policy and continued to exist for another year. In connection with the ensuing Mindszenty trial, however, the Communists wanted to use this Catholic party for their own ends. To avoid this, its leader, István Baran-kovics, dissolved the party and fled from Hungary in February 1949. The two major opposition parties van-ished from the scene.

Naturally the new alignment of political forces affect-ed the composition of the cabinet. The Smallholders and Socialists now had four portfolios each, five ministers were Communists, and two were National Peasants. But the shift in distribution of portfolios did not reflect more important changes within the parties.

The Smallholders majority was not only smashed and split, but the remnant was thoroughly intimidated. Doc-ile fellow travelers took over its leadership, ruthlessly eradicating all inclinations toward an independent policy. The show window, however, did not change for a while. Both the President of the Republic and the Prime Min-ister remained Smallholders. But on July 30, 1948, the President of the Republic, Zoltán Tildy, was forced to resign,[15] being replaced by Árpád Szakasits, pro-Commu-nist Socialist leader.

Before the complete liquidation of the parliamentary system, the last important item on the Communist time-table appeared to be the absorption of the Social Demo-cratic Party, as provided in the Kallai-Szakasits agree-ment of 1944. This was carefully planned, step by step. Leading Social Democrats, unwilling to become Commu-nist stooges or fellow travelers, were gradually elimina-ted. The new Socialist leader Árpád Szakasits, was usual-ly just the mouthpiece of Communist leader Mátyás Rákosi, but under the pressure of the majority of tough Socialist workers even he tried to resist the Communists from time to time. On such rare occasions he would be attacked by the Communist press as "a rightist devia-tionist." Finally, after a series of Communist-organized

---

[15] The reason for Tildy's resignation was the arrest of his son-in-law, Victor Chornoky. He was recalled for "consultation" from his post as Minister to Egypt, then arrested, charged with treason, sen-tenced, and hanged on December 6, 1948.

purges,[16] fellow traveler Socialist leaders moved on June 12, 1948 to merge with the Communist Party (by now the Hungarian Workers Party) against the will of the membership.

All independent political parties having ceased to exist, the Republic of Hungary became a "People's Republic."

Nothing could better reveal the transformation of Hungarian political life and the background of the Communist "elections" than the following official explanation published for Western consumption:

> Since the elections of 1947 the political and economic structure of Hungary has undergone a thorough change. The opposition parties, which at the elections of 1947 received a proportion of the votes, have since disappeared from the political scene. . . . It became evident that beyond their anti-Communist and anti-labor slogans, the agents of capitalists and large-estate owners, the saboteurs of production and nationalization, were seeking cover. The leaders of these parties fled from the country, deserting their followers, and the parties themselves were dissolved. . . .
>
> The old Parliament did not represent any longer the will of the people. Therefore, it became necessary to set a date for new elections. . . . Two opposition parties [Father Balogh's Independent Hungarian Democratic Party, and the Hungarian Radical Party] have become convinced in the interval since 1947 that they can do good work for the sake of the people only if they go along with the other three parties [Hungarian Working People's Party, Smallholders Party, and National Peasant Party] which at the beginning of February 1949 formed the Hungarian People's Independence Front to replace the Hungarian National Independence Front, and joined the Peoples Front.[17]

Of the votes at the May 15, 1949 elections, 5,478,515 were cast for the list of the People's Front (ie., 95.6 per cent) and 165,283 against. The number of ballots invalidated was 86,721.

[16] Secretary General Antal Bán, Minister of Industry and Labor, Imre Szélig and others had to flee the country, and many leading Social Democrats, among them Anna Kéthly, Vice-President of the Parliament, were imprisoned.—Ed.

[17] *Hungarian Bulletin*, May 21, 1949, pp. 1, 7-8. This Bulletin is distributed in the United States by the Hungarian Legation.

Monolithic Dictatorship of the Proletariat

"A People's democracy is, according to its function, a dictatorship of the proletariat without the Soviet form," said the Communist dictator of Hungary, Mátyás Rákosi.[18] To establish this kind of totalitarian dictatorship the Soviet satellites were isolated from the West. The Communists pursued throughout Eastern Europe a ruthless policy of eliminating all actual or potential opposition. In Hungary, simultaneously with the liquidation of the non-Communist parties, they terrorized the Catholic and Protestant Churches,[19] put through extreme nationalization,[20] seized foreign investments, and launched a large-scale purge in the Communist Party.[21] In the course of this, the former Minister of the Interior and Foreign Minister, László Rajk, and a group of Communist leaders were arrested on charges of Titoist conspir-

[18] *New York Times*, January 23, 1949.

[19] The order of persecution of Catholics and Protestants is only a question of timing. The Catholic Church is enemy number one, for Catholics are more numerous in Eastern Europe and the centrally organized Catholic Church is a world-wide obstacle to communist expansion. In Hungary, however, Lutheran Bishop Ordass was imprisoned before the Mindszenty trial. His successor was a Lutheran priest, a member of the Communist Party. The first great onslaught against the Catholic Church occurred in July 1946, when the government was quick to dissolve all Catholic youth organizations on unsubstantiated Russian accusations. Their buildings were given to Communist organizations. The Church schools were nationalized in June 1948. The Calvinists accepted a compromise solution negotiated with the Government and thus kept some of their schools. Since Joseph Cardinal Mindszenty followed an uncompromising policy, he was arrested and sentenced to life imprisonment in February 1949.

[20] During 1946 the coal mines and the electric power stations of a capacity above 20,000 kilowatts were nationalized and the five largest heavy industrial enterprises of the country placed under state control. In November 1947 the large banks were nationalized. In March 1948 all industrial plants employing one hundred or more workers were nationalized. The nationalization decree of December 28, 1949, seized all enterprises in which the total number of employees reached ten, and in some cases even five.

[21] Rákosi noted in an address to Czech workers at Prague that 200,000 persons had been expelled from the Hungarian Communist Party (*New York Times*, June 24, 1949). This action reversed the first stage of Communist policy, which was a drive for mass membership.

acy. The subsequent trial and executions were designed to provide ammunition for anti-Titoist propaganda. They also served as deterrents to deviation from the party line and eliminated potential leaders of a national Communist movement.

In all phases of Hungarian politics, energetic Russian intervention helped the Hungarian Communist Party. If the Hungarian Government was not responsive enough to suggestions, there quickly followed threats, ultimata, and the use of naked force. The methods by which the transformation of Hungary's political structure has been manipulated were repeatedly admitted and even described by leading Communists. Joseph Révai, one of the chief Communist theorists in Hungary, declared:

> We were a minority in Parliament and in the Government, but at the same time we represented the leading force. We had decisive control over the police. Our force, the force of our party and the working class, was multiplied by the fact that the Soviet Union and the Soviet army were always there to support us. . . .[22]

Moreover, the preamble of the new Constitution of the Hungarian People's Republic, which entered into force on August 20, 1949, did not try to conceal but rather stressed the fact that Soviet Russia has been the deciding factor in the postwar transformation of Hungary's political structure.[23]

[22] Joseph Révai, "On the Character of Our People's Democracy." The original article appeared in *Társadalmi Szemle*, Budapest, March-April, 1949. An English translation of the article was published in *Foreign Affairs*, Vol. 28 (1949) pp. 143–52.

[23] *"The armed forces of the great Soviet Union* liberated our country from the yoke of the German fascists, crushed the power of the great landowners and capitalists who were ever hostile to our people, and opened the road to democratic progress to our working people . . . the Hungarian working class, in alliance with the working peasantry and *with the generous assistance of the Soviet Union*, rebuilt our war-ravaged country. Led by the experiences of the Socialist revolution of 1919 and *supported by the Soviet Union,* our people began to lay down the foundations of socialism and now our country is advancing towards Socialism along the road of a people's democracy." [Italics added]—*Constitution of the Hungarian People's Republic, Budapest,* 1949.

FOUR HORSEMEN OF THE APOCALYPSE

.. The four horsemen of the Apocalypse rode behind the Red Army as its hordes poured like a dark flood over the Hungarian plain. Thirteenth-century chronicles describing the Tartar invasion pale beside the horrors the Hungarian people had to suffer while the Red barbarians turned their garden-like state into a vale of terror. They raped and dishonored our women in ways so fiendish that they surpass belief.

... When the Red Army invaded the country in 1944, 160 well-trained Communists of Hungarian extraction arrived straight from Moscow, with detailed blueprints for the liquidation of our social, political and economic structure, and for the complete communization of the country. ... So confident were the Communists, that of all their conquests in Eastern Europe they singled out Hungary as the first country to hold general elections. Here they expected their greatest victory.

The elections were to occur in two stages: first in the capital and then country-wide. The future of the whole resistance was to be decided at the polls in Budapest. Great was our surprise when the final count resulted in my party's winning an absolute majority, polling 50.5 percent of the votes. No one expected any party to win a majority in the Budapest City Council, but the mystery of this miraculous success cleared up when the count in the newly formed suburban precincts disclosed larger majorities of the Smallholders than in the old city. Great was our rejoicing, because this victory of October 7, 1945, heralded an even greater triumph in the national elections a month later. Here the Communists suffered a smashing defeat, being reduced to a minor party. They polled only 17 percent of the total vote, in spite of Red Army support; in spite of all pressure, terror, and intimidation. The Smallholders captured more than 57 percent of the total vote. ...

Statement by Msgr. Béla Varga, Chairman of the Hungarian Committee, before the Subcommittee on Hungary, House of Representatives, Washington, D.C., August 20, 1954.

ROAD TO THE REVOLUTION

Excerpts from the study of Paul Kecskeméti:
"Limits and Problems of Decompression: The Case
of Hungary," THE ANNALS, May 1958, American
Academy of Political and Social Science, Philadel-
phia, Pennsylvania.

When Stalin died, Matyas Rakosi was the undisputed
boss of Hungary. Not content with the position of Secretary General of the Hungarian communist party (officially designated as Hungarian Workers' party), he also
assumed the office of Prime Minister in August 1952—
up to that time, he had been Vice Premier in a number
of successive cabinets of varying composition. Such a
cumulation of offices, however, could not endure long
after Stalin's death. The new Soviet leadership proceeded to dilute authority at the top: control of the
party apparatus was separated from leadership in the
administration. Hungary, of course, had to follow suit,
but Rakosi was not allowed to redistribute authority as
he saw fit. It would have been easy for him, if left alone,
to divest himself of some of his offices and fill them with
his own dummies; and this was precisely what he set
out to do when Moscow instructed him to replace "one-
man rule" by "collective leadership." But the center was
in dead earnest about diluting authority. In May 1953
Rakosi was summoned to appear in Moscow *ad audien-
dum verbum,* and to take along not only his faithful
henchmen, Erno Gero and Mihaly Farkas, but also two
mavericks, Imre Nagy and Istvan Dobi.

This was a straw in the wind. It indicated that Mos-

cow not only wanted to replace one-man rule by colle-
giate government in Hungary, but also was interested
in giving authority within the new government body to
people who did not see eye to eye with Rakosi on certain important matters. The choice of the outsiders
whom Rakosi was instructed to take along much against
his will was significant. Dobi was not even a member
of the communist inner circle but a former Smallholder
Party man turned communist; Nagy, an old party wheel-
horse and former émigré in Moscow, had only recently
been reinstated as a member of the Hungarian Politburo
after being under a cloud for Titoist deviations. Both
were known to be extremely critical of Rakosi's policy
of forced collectivization of peasant holdings. By giving
them the nod, the Moscow center intimated its desire
for concessions to the peasantry.

Appearing early in June before the Moscow Presidium
with his ill-matched companions, Rakosi was forced to
listen to a scathing denunciation of his stewardship
during the past years. Beria, Malenkov, Molotov,
Khrushchev, and Kaganovich took him severely to task.
He was told that his attempt to build up a gigantic
heavy industry in Hungary under his Five-Year Plan
of 1950, expanded further in 1951, was unsound, ex-
travagant adventurism. His farm policy, determined in
the needs of industrialization, had also been disastrous.
It drove hundreds of thousands of peasants from the
countryside, swelling the ranks of industrial workers
who could produce only at a loss while leaving the land
without people to work it. The country lacked food and
the mood of the people was bitter. If the situation was
not remedied, the government would eventually be
"booted out."[1]

---

[1] A deliberately vague summary of the Soviet leaders' denunciation of Rakosi's policy is found in *Imre Nagy on Communism*
(New York: Frederick A. Praeger, 1957), p. 66. The last remark
about the Hungarian government facing the risk of being "booted
out" is attributed there to Khrushchev. Nagy also states that at
the June meeting, Molotov and not Beria (*sic*) told the Hungarians that there was no objection to permitting the dissolution of
kolkhozes (*ibid.*, p. 153). The covert meaning of this pointed reference to Beria will become clearer as we proceed with our narrative.

"Thaw" in Hungary

The Hungarian delegation returned to Budapest with precise instructions. The Central Committee was to meet and condemn Rakosi's policy of overindustrialization and forced collectivization. Rakosi was to abandon the premiership and hand it to Imre Nagy, whose mission was to placate the peasantry by stopping the collectivization drive and to emphasize production of consumer goods at the expense of heavy industry. There were also to be other reforms, notably the relaxation of police terror. At the same time, Rakosi was to remain head of the party apparatus; the party under Rakosi and the administration under Nagy were to work hand in hand to correct the mistakes of the past and create more tolerable conditions.

The Hungarian communist party did as told: meeting on June 27–28, the Central Committee duly condemned Rakosi without deposing him as party leader and adopted new policy directives in accordance with Moscow's wishes. On July 4, Nagy was appointed Premier. Presenting himself before the National Assembly on the same day, he announced a bundle of reforms. Peasants, he said, will no longer be forced to join kolkhozes or even to remain in them against their will; the people will be given more consumer goods; police terror will be abolished.

This was the beginning of "decompression" in Hungary. While Rakosi's regime had been, in some respects, the most Stalinist of all, the "thaw" under Nagy was the most sudden and most radical. To be sure, the Hungarian innovations were not unique; but it was only in Hungary that the announcement of the new course created the impression of a substantial change in the nature of the system itself.

The Moscow center neither anticipated nor desired this, and Nagy himself was too orthodox a communist to conceive his role in such terms. He neither wanted to change the nature of the system nor aspired to set up a "national communist" régime independent of Soviet tutelage. In fact, in all he was doing, he felt he was merely carrying out Moscow's instructions, as imple-

mented by the Hungarian party's Central Committee.
Hence, from Nagy's point of view, there was no reason
why Rakosi should not go along with him. The differences between them concerned only tactics, and the
highest party authorities had pronounced his, Nagy's,
tactical approach to be the correct one. As a disciplined
communist, Rakosi had had no choice but to co-operate
in putting Nagy's reforms into practice.

Rallying the party apparatus which he still controlled,
Rakosi gave out the watchword that Nagy's drive was
full of danger and must be stopped. In fact, within a
few days after Nagy's speech, the whole countryside was
in uproar; the peasants decided to disband the kolkhozes
before the harvest rather than wait for the directives
which the government promised to issue after it was
completed. This led to many clashes, a situation which
Rakosi exploited to discredit Nagy. At a meeting of
the Budapest party organization on July 11, he sounded
the alarm about kulaks moving to destroy the socialist
order. All those present understood that Rakosi's real
target was the Nagy government. Thus, the beginning
of the "thaw" in Hungary also marked the beginning
of the split in the communist leadership.

At first, the split was not a matter of clashing doctrines. Rakosi did not say that Nagy's reform program
was wrong in principle. What Rakosi told his followers
was to keep their powder dry; he, Rakosi, would soon
be back in Moscow's favor, and the apparatus would
then be restored to supreme authority. There were, indeed, capital developments in Moscow which nourished
Rakosi's optimism: Beria, who had carried the ball at
the Moscow conference which condemned him, was
liquidated soon afterwards.

Rakosi, however, expected in vain that Beria's "un-
masking" would lead to his rehabilitation, even though
he kept urging the point in Moscow. The center, apparently, was quite happy about things as they were,
with the state machinery and the party apparatus locked
in stalemate. Moscow also was far from being dissatisfied with Nagy's reform policy as such, in spite of such
initial mishaps as the peasant revolts of the summer of

1953 which Rakosi took such pains to exploit against his rival. In 1953 and 1954, when Malenkov's authority was at its height, there was not much chance of undermining a policy based upon making concessions to the people and relaxing terrorism.

In May 1954, the Hungarian leaders went on another pilgrimage to Moscow, asking the center to arbitrate their differences. Rakosi trotted out his Beria argument; but was told that Beria, scoundrel though he was, had for once been quite correct in so far as he, Rakosi, was concerned. This is what Khrushchev, according to Nagy, said on that occasion:

> In June 1953, we correctly passed judgment on the Hungarian party's leadership, and that judgment is still entirely correct today. They can't hide behind Beria as Rakosi is trying to do. We were there, too, when these errors were ascertained, every one of us! We were right, and what we decided then is also right today. This should have been acted on already![2]

The last cryptic sentence in Khrushchev's speech is particularly revealing. Nagy does not explain it; this is understandable, since his book is a brief he composed after his exclusion from the party in the fall of 1955, arguing the case for his reinstatement. To the party audience for which Nagy's text was written, the allusion was perfectly clear. What Khrushchev had in mind was that the Hungarian party's Third Congress, scheduled to meet on April 18 to elect a new Politburo from which some of Rakosi's followers were to be dropped, had been postponed at Rakosi's urging to give him a chance to plead his case once more in Moscow. The delay, Khrushchev implied, was totally unnecessary: the prearranged script was not to be changed. Thus, the pilgrims having returned from Moscow, the Congress convened on May 24; on the 30th, it elected the new Politburo minus the three Rakosites whose elimination Moscow had prescribed.

[2] *Ibid.*, p. 143.

FREEING OF POLITICAL PRISONERS

The Moscow meeting of May 1954 also decided in Nagy's favor a policy dispute of long standing between him and the apparatus, a decision which was to have extremely far-reaching consequences in the sequel. The dispute concerned the release of many thousands of political prisoners detained in concentration camps and penitentiaries. In his inaugural speech of July 1953, Nagy had promised to put an end to the system of arbitrary police arrests, to dissolve the concentration camps, and to review the cases of all those who had been incarcerated on political charges during the Rakosi era. Rakosi fought this policy tooth and nail and with considerable success. To be sure, there were no more political arrests after Nagy assumed the government, and many totally innocuous and obscure internees were freed. Rakosi had no objection to this; but he was vitally interested in blocking the review of the cases of hundreds of people, mostly communists and social democrats, who had been arrested, tortured, and sentenced on fictitious charges in the vast purges he had instituted in 1949–52. For about a year, Rakosi had his way, but Nagy continued to press the matter. When the question came up at the May conference, the Soviet leaders expressed displeasure with the dilatory way in which the issue was being handled and ordered the release and rehabilitation of the victims of Rakosi's purges. For Moscow, this was a matter of course. There had been a political amnesty in Soviet Russia the year before; no satellite government could be allowed to follow a different path.

The Hungarian case, however, was not comparable to the Russian. No mass purges had occurred in Russia since before World War II, and the amnesty of 1953 was not calculated to raise grave moral problems among communists brought face to face with the enormity of synthetic trials and extorted confessions. By contrast, when hundreds of Hungarian communists and social democrats returned from prisons and concentration camps and told their friends what had happened to them, the moral effect was devastating.

These tales, of course, were not published at that time. The public comments made by Nagy and the spokesmen of his régime after the rehabilitation campaign was nearly completed in the fall of 1954 were stern enough, but still remained on a general plane. Nagy, for example, wrote in an article in *Szabad Nép* on October 10, 1954:

> The party's June resolutions[3] have been put into effect by the rehabilitations, by the liberation of unjustly sentenced comrades. . . . In this sphere, too, we must and will liquidate the grave mistakes of the past. This demonstrates the party's sense of justice and its strength, as well as the wisdom of collective leadership.

There was nothing in this to disturb the peace of mind of the general reader. There had been faults, but the party in its wisdom had seen to it that they should be corrected. At the nerve center of the party, however, the rehabilitations had entirely different repercussions.

Many of the former political prisoners were left-wing intellectuals, writers, and journalists who had always moved in the Budapest literary set and now made it a point to tell all to their erstwhile cronies. Nights were spent going through what had happened—a story of unspeakable, gruesome tortures, revealing the communist state apparatus as a monster of depravity. The recipients of these confidences wished they were dead, for as communist writers they had provided a richly orchestrated literary accompaniment to the purges. They had exhausted the remarkable resources of the Hungarian language to vilify the victims and render thanks to their torturers for saving humanity and socialism from harm. Now they felt they had no excuse whatever and began to hate themselves and communism, the cause of their utter moral degradation. This was one of the decisive impulses behind the revolt of the communist writers

[3] The reference is to the Central Committee's resolutions of the previous year (June 1953) which censured Rakosi's policy and spelled out the "New Course." Nagy and the publicists of his régime were constantly invoking the "June resolutions" which, however, were withheld from the general public: Rakosi had succeeded in obtaining a party decision blocking their publication.

which set the stage for revolution two years later. It
must be stated here that the greatest figure among the
communist writers, Tibor Dery, did not need this kind
of shock to see the light: he never lent his name to Rakosi's manhunts and was in opposition throughout the
latter's reign.

Another momentous consequence of the rehabilitation was that many party functionaries who had gone
through the inferno of Rakosi's jails and camps were
restored to high or middle party offices. The best known
of these is Janos Kadar, one of the architects of the October Revolution who was to betray it; he was made First
Secretary of the communist party organization of the
Thirteenth District of Budapest, a working-class quarter which early in 1956 became one of the focal points
of the intra-party revolt against Rakosi.

NAGY'S FALL

In October 1954, Nagy's position seemed impregnable
and Rakosi appeared to be on his way out. He was absent from the Central Committee meeting of late October which again condemned the forced industrialization policy of the Rakosi era and gave the green light
to Nagy for a reorganization of the economy with emphasis upon consumer goods. A few months later, however, Nagy was ousted; and Rakosi was back. The wind
suddenly changed in Moscow: Malenkov was forced to
resign in February 1955; and on March 9 the Central
Committee of the Hungarian communist party, following instructions from Moscow, condemned Nagy's reform policy as a "rightist deviation." From then on,
Nagy's political decline was rapid. On April 14, the
Central Committee not only deposed him as premier
but also dropped him from the Politburo; in November
he was expelled from the party.

Nagy, as we see, was treated far more rigorously than
Rakosi had been when he fell out of favor. The Soviet
center, in fact, no matter how displeased with Rakosi's
conduct of Hungarian affairs, always viewed him as an
insider, an important figure in international communism, whereas Nagy was expendable. To be sure, after

Nagy's fall Rakosi was not permitted to combine his party office with the premiership; the latter post went to Andras Hegedus. But this separation of offices had no real significance: Hegedus, a nonentity, was completely dominated by Rakosi. Hungary seemed to have returned to one-man rule in substance if not in form.

The main reason for Nagy's fall was that his key policy, the reconversion of industry, was anathema to the anti-Malenkov group which got the upper hand in Moscow. The chief stumbling block was that new capital would have been needed to put reconversion into effect, but Hungary had no money and Moscow firmly refused to foot the bill. It was now Nagy's turn to be criticized for extravagance. He pleaded for an expansion of trade exchanges with the Soviet Union, but Moscow told him that Soviet supplies to Hungary would be cut in half in 1955. He then proposed to increase trade with the "people's democracies," but learned that these were moving toward autarchy. In desperation, Nagy decided to try to finance his experiment by trade with the Western countries.[4] This definitely was the last straw; the idea of financing his domestic schemes by sources outside the "camp of peace and democracy" put Nagy's communist loyalty in doubt. Rakosi's past crimes were venial by comparison. Nagy had to be dealt with harshly; he had no roots in the apparatus, and he dabbled in heresy.

Nagy's policy appeared costly and dangerous in other ways too. The economic report submitted to the October meeting of the Central Committee admitted that labor productivity in 1954 had dropped 3.3 per cent; this was due to the relaxation of the Rakosi régime's slave-driving methods. That tendency, too, had to be stopped. Whatever the merits of Rakosi's industrial policies had been, Moscow now decided that Hungary had better get along with the industrial plant that was there, forgetting about reconversion and higher standards of living. Rakosi's reinstatement was the logical consequence of this decision.

It would be a mistake to interpret Rakosi's comeback

4 *Ibid.*, pp. 184 ff.

as a return to Stalinism. The *status quo ante* was restored in some respects, notably as regarded labor policy; conservatism was the order of the day, and all ambitious reform plans were shelved in the chilly new climate of retrenchment. But wholesale terror was not resumed, no new collectivization drive got under way, and, most important, the policy of rehabilitation was not rescinded. Rakosi had to endure the presence in the apparatus of returnees from the camps who thirsted to get even with him. Khrushchev's pet foreign political scheme, the reconciliation with Tito, was also potentially dangerous for him, since Tito was not likely to forget the exceptional viciousness of Rakosi's conduct toward him—and, incidentally, toward Yugoslav minorities and residents in Hungary—during the conflict. Rakosi's enemies in the party could count upon the warm support of Tito whose star was rising in Moscow.

Rakosi, in fact, regained only the shadow rather than the substance of his erstwhile power. The old party bureaucracy continued to back him almost to a man, but the newly integrated functionaries back from prison hated him; and the communist intellectuals, too, now were his fierce enemies. These opponents adopted Nagy as their hero, the man who had attempted to humanize the regime but was brought low by Rakosi's intrigues. It was after his fall that Nagy became the center of a cult among disgruntled communists.

OPEN REBELLION

The first symptoms of overt rebellion in the party appeared in the fall of 1955 with a bristling note to the Politburo denouncing the régime's cultural policies and signed by all prominent communist writers of the country. The Politburo reacted with a sharp resolution verbally castigating the writers, but nobody was arrested; there were only a few disciplinary punishments which the writers shrugged off. In the winter, critical articles began to appear in the official organ of the Writers' Association, the *Literary Gazette* (Irodalmi Ujság).

These were only isolated incidents. After the Twentieth Congress of the Soviet Communist Party in February 1956, however, all hell broke loose. Khrushchev's secret speech became known overnight. Khrushchev spoke only about Stalin, but his revelations seemed to suit Rakosi to a T; and the latter's foes in the Hungarian party immediately concluded that the new party line, as formulated by Khrushchev, authorized them to denounce the boss openly and in public.

The subsequent press compaign against Rakosi and his system, conducted mainly in the columns of the *Literary Gazette*, has since been described in Western publications, and so has the series of explosive meetings in the Petofi Circle, a discussion club operating under the auspices of the Communist Youth League.[5] It is less well known that rebellious voices of extreme bluntness were frequently heard in the spring of 1956 at party meetings in various working-class districts of Budapest. The party rebels at first did not know the magnitude of the risks they were taking; they reckoned with the possibility of being arrested. But it soon became clear that there would be no arrests: the police were not permitted to touch Rakosi's critics.

After the Twentieth Congress, the Old Guard retreated step by step. On March 2, Rakosi publicly admitted that the most prominent victims of his purges, Rajk and the other alleged Titoist conspirators executed with him, had been innocent. This admission gave new impetus to the outcry against the boss. He was now commonly referred to as the "bald-headed murderer"; his authority in the party and in the country sank to zero. Moscow at first sought to keep him in power: the only real alternative, in fact, was Nagy, but the center still regarded him as impossible. In the end, a weak intermediate solution was adopted.

Realizing that Rakosi had outlived his usefulness, Moscow let him go. The axe fell on July 18, but this time there was no pilgrimage to Moscow: instead, Miko-

5 See United Nations, *Report of the Special Committee on the Problem of Hungary*, New York, 1957, paras. 379–385. The fullest documentation on the intellectuals' report is found in a special issue of *Les Temps Modernes*, Paris, Vol. 12, Nos. 129, 130, 131 (January 1957).

yan came to Budapest. He told the Hungarian party to
remove Rakosi as First Secretary and replace him with
Erno Gero.

This did not appease the critics; Gero, in fact, had
always been closely identified with Rakosi; and he had
been one of the driving forces behind Rakosi's Five-Year
Plan, the source of Hungary's misfortunes. He was in
a difficult position. He could not change basic economic
policy since Moscow's objections to reforms in this field
remained in force. But the people now demanded tan-
gible improvements, and the Poznan Riots of June 1956
had shown that violent outbreaks were no longer unthinkable. In his quandary, Gero tried to create a better atmosphere by wooing the party opposition. He
promised freedom of criticism and sought to improve
his position by diverting popular wrath against the political police. The solemn re-burial on October 6 of
Rajk and some of his co-victims was an astonishing spec-
tacle; it was essentially a demonstration under government auspices against the political police. A few days
later, Mihaly Farkas, the chief torturer of Rajk and his
associates, was arrested. But this move could as little
save Gero as Strafford's execution could save Charles I.
Nor was Nagy's readmission to the party on October 13
sufficient to stem the rising tide of revolt.

HEROIC DAYS

OCTOBER 23.

Student demonstration in Budapest takes place in front of the statue of General Bem and the Polish Embassy. Students demand reforms, democratization, the return of Imre Nagy. Police try to disperse crowd when students attempt to be heard over Budapest radio. Tear gas is used; then students are arrested. Crowd attempts to free the students and police open fire. The demonstration turns into a riot and street fighting breaks out.

Martial law is declared, a call for Russian troops issued; during the night, Soviet tanks and jets are reported used against demonstrators.

OCTOBER 24.

Additional Soviet military units enter Budapest at the request of the Communist regime. Fighting breaks out between Soviet troops and the Hungarian people. Changes in the party Central Committee and in the government are announced. Imre Nagy replaces András Hegedüs as Premier, but Ernö Gerö remains First Secretary of the Party. Nagy appeals to the people to stop fighting. Surrender deadlines are announced as fighting continues. The deadlines are moved forward several times, and finally abandoned. Rebels capture factories in Budapest. Fighting reported in Debrecen, Szolnok, and Szeged.

OCTOBER 25.

The Nagy government claims its forces have restored order in Budapest, but admits fighting continues. Ernö Gerö is relieved as First Secretary of the Party and replaced by János Kádár. Nagy and Kádár announce that,

*following restoration of order, negotiations for with-
drawal of Soviet troops will be initiated. Nagy promises
to reconvene parliament and to consider a reform program and reorganization of the government.*

OCTOBER 26.

*Fighting continues throughout the country. Insurgents
take the entire area between Magyaróvár and the Hungarian frontier station of Hegyeshalom. The Party Central Committee pledges: (1) election of a new government
based on the Patriotic People's Front; (2) correction of
past mistakes; (3) negotiations with the Soviet Union
for withdrawal of Soviet troops; (4) establishment of
relations between the two countries on the basis of complete equality; (5) acceptance of workers' councils and
raising of wage rates; (6) a complete amnesty to all participants in the fighting.*

OCTOBER 27.

*Formation of a new government is announced. The
cabinet is headed by Imre Nagy. Non-Communists in
the government include Zoltán Tildy, former President
of the Republic, and Béla Kovács, former Secretary General of the Smallholders Party.*

OCTOBER 28.

*Local negotiations with Soviet troop commanders re-
ported; in some cases Soviet forces join the insurgents.
The government announces a cease-fire. Nagy states
that Soviet troops will withdraw from Budapest immediately, and that the security police will be dissolved.*

*An emergency committee, composed of János Kádár,
Antal Apró, Károly Kiss, Ferenc Münnich, Imre Nagy
and Zoltán Szántó, assumes temporary leadership of the
Party.*

*Spontaneous rise to power of revolutionary workers'
councils and local national committees. A series of political and economic demands are made. The major ones include: withdrawal of Soviet troops, political and economic equality of relations between the
Soviet   Union and Hungary, revision of the economy,*

*democratization, changes in government organization
and personnel, dissolution of the security police, protection of those taking part in the revolution, withdrawal from the Warsaw Pact, Hungarian neutrality, a call
for free elections, free speech, press, assembly and worship.*

*The Patriotic People's Front announces that a coun-
try-wide Committee has been created to co-ordinate the
activities of these various committees. Budapest Chief of
Police announces formation of Hungarian National
Guard Units.*

OCTOBER 29.

Central Party organ SZABAD NÉP *(Free People) answers
the Soviet Pravda attack on the revolution and defends
the Hungarian uprising.*

*Radio Free Miskolc calls for immediate withdrawal of
Soviet troops from Hungarian soil, not merely their return to bases outside Budapest. The Minister of Defense
announces withdrawal of Soviet units from Budapest,
Hungarian Army units replacing them.*

*Heavy fighting continues in Budapest, particularly at
Kilián (Maria Theresia) Barracks.*

OCTOBER 30.

*Nagy announces abolition of one-party system, a
return to the political conditions prevailing after 1945,
and negotiations for immediate withdrawal of all Soviet
forces from Hungary. A new coalition government is
formed with Imre Nagy as Premier: Béla Kovács, Zoltán
Tildy and Ferenc Erdei are included.*

*The recall of the Hungarian "representative" to the
U.N., Soviet citizen Péter Kos, is announced.*

*Tildy calls for reconstituting the Smallholders Party;
Ferenc Erdei makes a similar appeal for the Peasant
Party, and Kádár implies to Communist Party members
that he agrees with both.*

Cardinal Mindszenty is freed.

*Revolutionary Home Defense Committee forms. Co-
chairmen: Gen. Béla Király and Gen. Pál Maléter.*

Hungarian Air Force threatens to bomb Soviet tanks

unless they leave Budapest. Insurgents storm security police headquarters in Pest, burn down Party headquarters in Buda. Security police appeal to Writers' Union to intervene for its 10,000 members: they will surrender if guaranteed amnesty.

OCTOBER 31.

Radio Free Kossuth broadcasts Soviet declaration concerning changes in relations between Soviet Union and Satellite States. Ministry of Agriculture announces suspension of compulsory deliveries of farm produce.

Cardinal Mindszenty arrives in Budapest.

Independent Smallholders Party announces formation of a new executive committee and resumes control of its former newspaper, KIS UJSÁG (Little Journal). Hungarian Social Democratic Party is reorganized in Budapest, with Anna Kéthly as president, and NÉPSZAVA (People's Voice) as its official publication.

Pal Maléter replaces Lajos Tóth as First Deputy Defense Minister and Istvan Kovács takes Tóth's former job as Army Chief of Staff. Nagy announces that the Hungarian government is prepared to leave the Warsaw Pact and has asked for negotiations on withdrawal of Soviet forces from Hungary.

The Council of Ministers appoints Maj. Gen. Béla Király as military commander of Budapest.

A Trans-Danubian National Council is organized from various county councils. It requests immediate evacuation of Soviet troops, repudiation of the Warsaw Pact, free elections, a declaration of Hungary's neutrality, and freedom of speech, press, assembly and worship.

NOVEMBER 1.

Imre Nagy announces Hungary's withdrawal from the Warsaw Pact, proclaims Hungarian neutrality, and asks the United Nations to put the Hungarian question on its agenda. NÉPAKARAT, (People's Will), newspaper of the Free Hungarian Trade Unions, is published for the first time. The National Peasant Party, now called Petöfi Party, is reorganized, its daily SZABAD SZÓ (Free Voice) is again published. Kádár attacks past leaders and policies *of the Hungarian Communist Party and announces the reorganization of the Party under the name of the Hungarian Socialist Workers' Party.*

Co-ordinating and controlling all the Revolutionary forces, National Guard formed. Commander-in-chief: Běla Király. Deputy: Police Colonel Sándor Kopácsy.

Soviet units surround Hungarian airfields, allegedly to protect evacuation of Soviet dependents. Budapest ringed by Soviet tanks. Social Democrat leader Anna Kéthly goes to Vienna to attend the meeting of the Socialist International.

NOVEMBER 2.

Hungarian government protests to the Soviet Embassy the re-entry of Soviet troops on Hungarian soil. The United Nations is notified of Soviet activities in the second official note within two days, and is requested to appeal to the great powers to recognize Hungarian neutrality.

Soviet troops take rail line from Zahony to Nyiregyháza; hold Budapest International Airport, and Kalocsa Airfield. United Hungarian Youth Federation is organized in Budapest.

The Budapest National Committee elects József Kővágó its president, Mayor of Budapest.

NOVEMBER 3.

Considerable Soviet reinforcements and troop movements to the Austro-Hungarian border are reported. Russian tanks surround uranium mines at Pécs.

The Hungarian government is reorganized after resignation of most of its ministers. The new ministers, many of them non-Communists, take over the administration. New cabinet includes: Imre Nagy, Premier and Minister of Foreign Affairs. Zoltán Tildy, Istvan Bibó, Anna Kéthly, Ferenc Farkas, Géza Losonczy, and János Kádár as Minister of State, and Pál Maléter, Minister of Defense.

Negotiations for withdrawal of Soviet troops continue; further Soviet troop movements are reported.

Cardinal Mindszenty addresses the people.

József Kővágó elected Secretary General of the Small-holders Party.

The National Council of Dunapentele appeals to all free radio stations to broadcast to Soviet troops in Russian to counteract Soviet propaganda.

NOVEMBER 4.

Imre Nagy announces Soviet attack on Budapest. Russian forces take over most of the country: airfields, highway junctions, bridges, railway yards. Heavy fighting reported in Csepel and Köbanya. Soviet paratroops in action near Győr. Fighting at Pécs as Hungarian troops resist Soviet efforts to take uranium mines and airfields. Heavy fighting in Budapest. Győr and Sopron fall to the Russians. Fighting continues in all parts of the country. The situation remains confused.

New communist government formed in Szolnok: János Kádár, Premier; Ferenc Münich, Deputy Premier and Minister of Security; Imre Horváth, Minister of Foreign Affairs; István Kossa, Minister of Finance; Antal Apró, Minister of Industry.

State Minister Bibó: "I appeal to the great powers of the world for a wise and courageous decision in the interest of my enslaved nation and of the liberty of all Eastern European nations. God preserve Hungary ..."

Repeated free radio broadcasts call for Western help.

The Hungarian Writers' Union appeals for Western aid: "To every writer in the world, to all scientists, to all writers' federations, to all science academies and associations, to the intelligentsia of the world! . . . HELP HUNGARY!"

WE WANT TO BE FREE!

*We Hungarians feel that mankind looks to the United
Nations for an answer to the burning question: must the
governments, whether of small or large nations, act on moral
principles, or may jungle law be permitted to reign un-
curbed. The answer to this hinges on the case of the numer-
ically small, but spiritually great nation, to which I belong ...*

*Truth outdoes fiction in this epic struggle written in blood;
a struggle where the participants rose high above the measure of mortals, where 14-year-old children rose to the heights
achieved by ancient heroes and 70-year-old grandmothers
acted like Roman matrons. And yet my task is to relate this
in a manner conveying a sense of reality.*

*There are memories of glorious days followed by gloom.
First the joy of rapturous crowds in the smoke-filled streets;
later the sombre calm of men to die in the rubble of the
wounded city.*

*The Hungarian Revolution proves that the fate of nations
is molded by the emotions of the people. Even the creation
of this great institution, the United Nations, is due to the
ardent desire of millions to be able to rely on an international forum to mediate between the nations and to seek just
solutions on the basis of moral principles ...*

*I wish to emphasize that the Hungarian Revolution was
not premeditated, not organized by anyone. Hungarian youth
as one man strained against the Communist shackles, break-
ing them with volcanic force. In the heat of this sacred fire
Communist indoctrination melted within minutes. The truth
was suddenly revealed, and the rpulsive farce of Communist
lies and doctrines became apparent. These young people rose
as one, rejecting Leninist-Stalinist teachings in a single re-
sounding outcry.*

*The very same evening hundreds of thousands of Hungar-
rians voiced one wish with all their hearts:*

"We want to be free!"

Mayor József Kővágó, before the United Nations Special
Committee on the Problem of Hungary, Jan. 29, 1957

IDEOLOGY OF THE REVOLUTION

Excerpts from the booklet of Edmund O. Stillman under the same title, published by the Free Europe Press, New York, New York, 1957.

From October 23, the first day of the rebellion, the Hungarian nation issued demands in astonishing volume, and in the form of resolutions, manifestos, handbills, and brief tracts. Later, as radio stations were seized by the revolutionaries, political demands were broadcast daily, and almost by the hour. It was as if a nation, long silenced, were indulging itself in the sheer functional pleasure of speech.

The radio broadcasts provide the best single source on the ideology of the revolution, for all of them were monitored abroad and each station broadcast the demands of the significant groups within its locale. This is not to say that *every* ideological current in Hungary between October 23 and November 9 may be studied in this record, for undoubtedly there were isolated groups on the periphery of the revolution, who rejected the general tenor of the demands; but they do not seem to have qualified as major forces, since the radio stations were unquestionably in the hands of those with broad popular backing.

It is not this burgeoning of demands everywhere that is so surprising, for demands as such are a standard feature of revolutions. As G. S. Pettee, a student of revolutions, observes: "The attacks on the dominant classes . . .

[are] one of the characteristic symptoms of a coming revolution, and naturally . . . [they] continue in ever increasing volume during the course of the revolution until the position of the obnoxious . . . institutions is completely undermined."

What is impressive in the Hungarian demands is their virtual unanimity. There were traces of ideological differences between, say, Radio Free Miskolc which seemed to represent the Hungarian "left" and Radio Free Győr which took its stand with what might be termed the "center"; but even Győr was explicit on October 28, when it stated flatly:

> This is not a counter-revolution, but the national movement of the Hungarian people. *The workers and peasants in Győr-Sopron counties do not want the restoration of the power of manufacturers and landlords*; the national revolution is not aimed at the restoration of the old regime. (Italics added.)

From the date of the first revolutionary outbreak through November 4, when the Soviet armies returned to the attack, a totalitarian society was in dissolution. But just as surely contact between classes, or between regions, was never wholly lost. As the revolt progressed a consensus slowly emerged. "In the course of our several days of fighting for freedom the joint demands of the entire country are beginning to take shape. Therefore, we workers, students, and armed forces under the leadership of the workers' council and student parliament of Miskolc submit the following proposals. . . ."

This growth of cohesion among the revolutionary forces is one of the most striking features of the revolt. Despite the disorganization that followed the collapse of the Gerő regime on October 23–24, anarchy was short-lived. Within a matter of days "revolutionary councils," "workers' councils," "*kolkhoz* [collective farm] councils," and "student parliaments" spring up everywhere as a kind of counter-government. Very slowly they began to establish links—by courier and radio. It was as if social discipline were an ingrained feature of the revolutionaries; and as the authority of the central government dis-

integrated in town after town, or in government department after department, the need for a new source of
authority was increasingly felt.* Gradually these councils
took on functions of local administration, and even some
of the attributes of central power. Thus existing institutions—press, civil defense, sanitation, production, and
even foreign affairs—fell into the revolutionary orbit.
The Hungarian News Agency, itself revolutionized by
that date, reported on October 30:

> The Revolutionary Committee of the Ministry of Foreign
> Affairs has resolved: (1) No time should be lost in elabo-
> rating the basic principles of an independent Hungarian
> foreign policy. . . . (2) We condemn the declaration made
> by Peter Kos, the Hungarian UN representative. . . .
> (4) The workers of the Foreign Ministry will take part
> with all their energy in assuring order. . . . (5) We call
> on [ministerial] workers . . . to report at their offices on
> Wednesday morning.

It is this gradually emerging order among the revolutionaries which accounts, in part, for the multitude of
demands. After a decade of enforced silence, the people,
organized or represented in councils, were declaring
themselves. The demands are then as much a statement

---

* Soviet writers on the Revolution of 1917 are fond of dwelling
on a similar phenomenon, which they call *dvoevlastie*, or "dual
power." As the revolutionaries seceded from the moribund Czarist
regime, they set up in Petersburg, Moscow, and other regions, a
revolutionary counterpart in the form of workers' and peasants'
soviets. These soviets at first represented all shades of revolutionary
opinion and were only later captured by the Bolsheviks under
Lenin's direction.
    Crane Brinton discusses the issue of *dvoevlastie* in his *Anatomy
of Revolution:* "In *all* our revolutions [1642, 1775, 1789, and 1917]
. . . the legal government finds opposed to it, once the first steps in
actual revolution have been taken, not merely hostile individuals
and parties . . . but a rival government, better organized, better
staffed, better obeyed. . . . At a given revolutionary crisis they [the
leaders of the new representative bodies] step naturally and easily
into the place of the defeated government."
    It is a wry comment on history that the nearest analogue to this
proliferation of democratic, or revolutionary, councils in Hungary
in 1956 should be the soviets of 1917. But within a generation a
derivative of those soviets, the Hungarian Worker's Party (Communist) had come to stand for the *ancien régime*.

of the fundamental of a new Hungarian social order—
an attempt to establish the broad consensus—as a series
of peremptory ultimata to a disintegrating regime.

DEMANDS IN DETAIL

Between October 23 and November 9 a total of 225
major demands were broadcast by the revolutionary stations and monitored abroad. By category these demands
were:

	NO. OF INSTANCES	PER CENT OF TOTAL
National Independence	78	35
Political Reform	69	31
Economic Reform	63	28
End of Censorship	8	3
Religious Freedom	7	3
Total	225	

(*All percentages rounded*)

The largest single category thus dealt with the
issue of national sovereignty and the Gerő regime's
subservience to the Soviet Union, and confirms the
initial impression that this was a nationwide rebellion against a foreign power as well as a foreign
political *system*. Again, of these demands, 162 dealt with
issues which may be termed political or social, in contrast to economic—and even in this last category the
number of demands dealing with purely economic matters such as wages, as against quasi-political issues like
worker-management of industry, is comparatively small.
The great weight of demands addressed to the need for
political and social reform further suggests that poverty,
while real, was only a secondary complaint, subordinate
to freedom as such. (The impression is reinforced by con-
versations with representative Hungarian refugees. Thus
of 18 Hungarian students and intellectuals interviewed
in detail shortly after the revolution, given a hypotheti-
cal alternative fully 15 chose political freedom as pref-
erable to economic security under totalitarian conditions. Only one refugee chose economic security at the
price of "freedom," while two were in doubt.)

Despite this emphasis on the political and social, the overwhelming majority of the demands are specific and practical. There were very few generalities. The typical formulation of demands in Hungary was—"We demand that our uranium mines be placed under immediate Hungarian control," or "We demand that free elections be held at once, without the supervision of any foreign state," or "Far-reaching financial assistance must be granted to independent [i.e., non-collective] peasants." Occasionally demands for reform are put in terms of principle—"Complete rejection of Stalinist peasant policy," or "true Socialist democracy"—but these are exceptions to the general rule. The impression is overwhelming that these demands are addressed to the immediate issues of the day: there is *no* single instance of a "philosophical law" put forward in justification of the revolution. This is in marked contrast to such revolutionary documents as the *Declaration of the Rights of Man* in 1789, which states: "Men are born and remain free and equal. . . . Law may rightfully prohibit only those actions which are injurious to society. . . ." In the Hungarian revolution all matters of theory were deferred until such time as Soviet troops might withdraw and conditions of political security prevail. In this respect the Hungarian demands show a clear ancestry in the pre-revolutionary "literature of protest" which similarly avoided any approach to abstraction.

On the other hand, if the Hungarian revolutionaries rejected theory, there is ample evidence for the general shape of the society they wished to see. Few of the demands could be classified as "rightist" except by a doctrinaire of the discredited "Stalinist left." There was, for example, no case of demands for the return of pre-war governments—Hapsburg or Horthyite—or for the restoration of capitalism as such. Disclaimers on this point were frequent and explicit. The nationalization of large- and medium-scale industry was to be left intact; and so far as de-nationalization was an issue at all, it centered on agriculture and small trade.

Thus the Communist policy of *forced* collectivization, or peasant oppression, was frequently the target of the demands; but the collective farms, as such, were seldom attacked. Indeed, of 22 demands dealing with the question of agriculture, eight specify that collectivization must be voluntary, or rid of the element of compulsion. The three separate demands for financial aid to private farming would suggest that the peasants foresaw a "Socialist" sector of agriculture as continuing if local farmers wished it so.

The nine demands of the "Hungarian agricultural population," as broadcast by Radio Budapest on November 1, are a good summary of the peasant position midway through the revolt:

—Complete rejection . . . of Stalinist policy. A decree must be issued ordering the dissolution of weak [agricultural] collectives and collectives established by means of violence. Peasants must be granted the right to leave collectives. . . . The land, property, and animals which they brought to the collectives must be given State support. The present system of State assistance to collectives must be discontinued. State support must be administered by a collective center . . . elected by collective members.

—An agricultural delegation composed of peasant representatives, members of new parties, agricultural experts and journalists must be sent to study the system of large-scale farming in Western Europe—Denmark, Holland, England, the northern countries [Scandinavia]—and the United States, and their experiences must be used to benefit Hungarian agriculture.

—The present setup of the machine tractor stations [MTS] must be discontinued.

—Far-reaching financial assistance must be granted to independent peasants.

—We approve the discontinuation of the compulsory delivery system . . . but this is only a first step. The extremely high peasant taxes must be reduced immediately and the present system of taxation must be revised. . . .

—The old system of selling and purchasing land must be restored.

—State farms whose output and profits are inadequate must be liquidated.

—The Ministry of Produce Collection must be abolished,

the Ministries of Agriculture and State Farms merged, and the bureaucratic apparatus reduced.

—Peasant Revolutionary Committees must be established in all villages. Members of the Committees should be recruited from the democratic parties and should take power until elections are held.

The moderate position is significant since, on November 1, the general impression was that the Hungarian revolution had "won." Consequently, there was little tactical advantage to be gained at that point by hiding fundamental beliefs.

So far as demands dealing with industry go, the majority had a distinct left-wing flavor, and were in every sense normal demands of a militant Central European working class. Thus there were four separate demands for worker management of industry, a quasi-"Titoist" or, perhaps, syndicalist feature; six demands for the right to strike; six for the establishment of free trade unions; and five for the abolition of the "speed-up" and norm system in the factories. All were compatible with the modern socialist state.

Radio Free Miskolc probably spoke the consensus of the Hungarian industrial workers on October 25, when it declared:

. . . Let them withdraw Soviet troops from Hungary. Strike! We have had enough of this. Enough of the autocracy of certain leaders. We too want Socialism but according to our own special Hungarian conditions, reflecting the interests of the Hungarian working class, the Hungarian nation, and our most sacred national sentiments.

Proceeding to the specific, Miskolc demanded:

. . . the elimination, without any other considerations, of all persons who compromised themselves by the cult of personality.

We demand that those Communists and non-Communists who, in obeying the principles of proletarian internationalism, honor above all our Hungarian national tradition and thousand-year history be given the most important positions in the party and government.

We demand the revision of the institutions of the State security authorities and the immediate elimination of all leaders and functionaries who are the slightest degree compromised. . . .

With regard to the grave errors committed in the field of planned economy, we demand the immediate dismissal of the responsible leaders of the planning organs.

We demand an increase of real wages.

We believe our demands will be realized if our parliament ceases to be an election machine, and the members of parliament cease to be yes-men.

We demand that March 15 be proclaimed a national holiday. . . .

Thus there was very little of the doctrinaire in the demands of the Hungarian working class. Surprisingly, this was as true of the Communists who joined the ranks of the revolutionaries (in large numbers) as of the non-Communist left. A mobile transmitter which called itself Free Radio Rajk (after the "National" Communist Minister of Foreign Affairs executed in 1949) expressed solidarity with national demands in a broadcast on November 1:

Comrades, if the Communist Party wishes to continue in the leading and guiding role . . . it must proclaim and demand . . . all that the Hungarian people rightly ask. It is up to us, the Communist Party . . . to ask . . . withdrawal of the Russian Army. . . .

As the revolution progressed even the government of Mr. Nagy, once again Premier from October 24 forward, shared this view. An interview with Gyorgy Lukacs, a Communist and Minister of People's Culture in the government of October 27, expresses a sense of resignation. According to the correspondent of the Polish weekly *Nowa Kultura,* Mr. Lukacs felt:

[The second wing of the Communist Party] is revolutionary, wishing to break completely with Stalinist traditions . . . to create a new Marxist party. . . . The new Party will not be able to expect rapid success—Communism in Hungary has been wholly disgraced. . . .

Evidently between October 23 and November 9 there were few significant political differences which divided the Hungarian people, and these are difficult to evaluate. There were 14 "free" stations in operation at one time or another in the course of the revolt, and of these only six used the demand form as such—the remainder confined themselves to general political commentary, reportage, military movements, and so forth.* Nor was "demand activity" evenly distributed among the six:

	NO. OF INSTANCES	PER CENT OF TOTAL
Budapest (Free Kossuth)	108	48
Free Miskolc	73	32
Free Gyor	27	12
Szombathely	9	4
Free Rajk	2	1
Unidentified	6	3
Total	225	

Yet, it would probably be inaccurate to conclude that demands as such were foreign to the majority of the nation, or that the concept was limited to a few locales.** Radio Budapest, for example, broadcast the demands of widely dispersed organizations and, as the voice of the capital, saw itself as speaking for the country at large.

Again there are some interesting divergencies in the *share* of each class of demands in the total demand activity of the stations—in other words, in the emphasis:

* The 14 "free" stations were Budapest (Radio Free Kossuth, after October 30), Debrecen, Dunapentele Eger, Gyor, Kaposvar, Miskolc, Nyiregyhaza, Pecs, Szombathely, whose locations are all known; and Csokonay, Rakoczi, Roka, and Rajk, whose locations were not discovered.

** Thus of a total of 78 demands for national sovereignty, 30 were voiced by Radio Budapest in the capital, 25 by Miskolc in northeastern Hungary, 15 by Gyor in the northwest, five by Szombathely on the Austrian frontier, two by Radio Rajk, the mobile transmitter, and one by an unidentified source.

	PERCENTAGE OF ALL DEMANDS BROADCAST BY SOURCE		
CATEGORY	I. Budapest	II. Miskolc	III. Gyor
National Independence	28	34	55
Political Reform	30	33	30
Economic Reform	34	27	15
End of Censorship	5	3	—
Free Religion	3	3	—

The two outlying stations (Miskolc and Gyor) show a strong emphasis on the issue of national sovereignty; indeed Gyor seems preoccupied with the fundamental issues of the revolution, independence and political freedom, to the exclusion of much else. Conceivably Gyor, which was isolated in the northwest and farther from the threat of Soviet power, felt freer to voice this demand; but the demand, as such, appeared in the capital, in Miskolc, in Gyor, in Szombathely, and over one unidentified station as well as the mobile transmitter Radio Free Rajk. Apart from drawing the conclusion that national sovereignty was the *basic* demand (a conclusion supported by the fact that of eight demands broadcast over Szombathely, five were for independence, and that both of the two demands broadcast by Radio Free Rajk were for independence as well) no generalizations are possible.

DEMANDS VARYING

Four distinct phases of the revolution can be distinguished. In the first, from October 23 through October 24, the revolt had the character of a disorganized outbreak. Fighting was sporadic and the government, though now headed by Mr. Nagy, treated it as a temporary disturbance. In this period, apart from the Petoefi Club and the Writers' Union, few demands were put forward. These dealt with limited reform of the existing system.

In the second phase, which extended from October 25 through October 29, the revolution gained strength, the armed forces went over to the people, and the government of Mr. Nagy was forced into a series of concessions. The revolutionaries seized the radio stations in Gyor, Pecs, Szombathely, and elsewhere and voiced the majority of the demands of the nation. It was in this period that the people burst the bounds of the existing system and, in the words of a Polish Communist who observed these events, pressed for "a curious synthesis: a basic realization of people's democracy (land in the hands of the peasant, socialization of factories and banks) and of a pluralism of parties, freedom of the press, and all the other liberties inherent in a liberal democracy." Similarly, as clashes between Hungarian revolutionaries and Soviet troops grew more bitter, a parallel theme developed—the immediate withdrawal of all foreign troops from Hungary, the abolition of the Warsaw Pact, and, as a logical corollary, the declaration of Hungary's "neutrality" between East and West.

In the third phase, October 31 through November 4 —the period of Hungary's brief freedom—the nature of the demands changed: the Social Democrats, the Smallholders, the "Petoefi Peasants" resumed political activity as free parties and the *form* of demands, as such, fell more or less in disuse. As the government was gradually broadened, and Mr. Nagy in effect joined the revolution, the following type of political address became usual. On October 31 Bela Kovacs, former General Secretary of the Smallholders' Party and a Minister of State in the new government, declared:

> The [Smallholders'] party has full liberty to reassemble, but the question is whether, in its constitution, the party will proclaim its old ideas again. No one should dream of going back to the world of aristocrats, bankers and capitalists. That world is definitely gone! A true member of the Smallholders' Party cannot think along the lines of 1939 or 1945. The last ten years were bitter, but they also provided a useful lesson.
>
> . . . We must make use of the lesson . . . draw up a new party program. . . . I cannot and do not wish to define the new program. . . . I must first discuss it with the Party leaders in Budapest. . . . But one thing is certain: It must be based on the creation of a new Hungary. . . .

When the Hungarian freedom fighters battled against the Russian tanks, they fought for the country's independence. This does not mean that we regard the Russian people as our enemies, but one cannot follow a unilateral policy. . . . It is necessary to establish relations, based on equal rights, with all nations, and one cannot tie the country's fate to one or another military bloc. The Hungarian people want a neutral Hungary.

Mr. Kovacs' views were a typical expression of the political thought of those days, and, on the face of it, moderate enough. In the brief period of political activity allowed the nation, the demands for neutralization of Hungary came to the fore. Mr. Nagy formally proclaimed neutrality on November 1, in an address broadcast over Radio Budapest:

The Hungarian people, on the basis of independence and equality and in accordance with the spirit of the UN Charter, wish to live in true friendship with their neighbors, the Soviet Union, and all the peoples of the world . . . without joining any power blocs. . . . We appeal to our neighbors, and to countries far and near, to respect the unalterable decision of our people . . . [for a] free, independent, democratic, and neutral Hungary.

However moderate the official position might be, the Soviet Union saw in such a program a threat to its interests. On November 4 it returned to the attack, and the final phase of the revolution began. The free radios resumed their activity, but, as they fell to the Soviet armies, were silenced. In this period the broadcasts dealt chiefly with appeals to the UN, proclamations of strikes and resistance, and military movements.

The last rebel broadcast in Hungary was heard on November 11, over Free Radio Rajk, the mobile transmitter of the Communist revolutionaries. It was no longer a demand on the Hungarian government, but an appeal to international law: "We request . . . the free nations of the world to assert what moral influence they can. . . . If UN observers were sent to Hungary it would be disagreeable not [only] to Janos Kadar, but to his Soviet masters."

The end of radio broadcasts did not spell the end of resistance. For more than a month Hungary was paralyzed by a general strike. In this period the position of the revolutionaries grew steadily weaker, and their demands, so far as they are known, more modest. Until the end, however, the demand for free elections and the withdrawal of Soviet troops remained fixed.

1. We wish to emphasize that the revolutionary working class considers the factories and the land the property of the working people.

2. The Workers' Parliament recognizes the Kadar government as a negotiating party, provided that the government, to assure its own legality, will reorganize itself to conform with the will of the people.

3. The people have put their faith in the workers' councils to make certain that the will of the people continues to be carried out. We demand that the authority of the workers' councils be expanded and reaffirmed by the government in the economic, cultural and social fields.

4. In the interest of preserving order and re-establishing peace, we demand that a date be set for free elections in which only those parties may participate that recognize and have always recognized the Socialist order, based on the principle that means of production belong to society.

5. We demand the immediate freeing of the members of the Imre Nagy government which was elected by the revolution, as well as the release of the freedom fighters.

6. We demand that a cease-fire be ordered immediately as well as the prompt withdrawal of Soviet troops from Budapest, since Hungarian authorities can assure order through the labor force. And we demand that as soon as workers have resumed work, the Hungarian government open negotiations for the gradual and orderly withdrawal of Soviet troops from the territory of the country, and keep the public informed on the progress of these negotiations.

7. The police force must be organized from the honest workers of the plants and from the Army units loyal to the people.

8. It is requested that the above points be made public by the government on the radio and through the press.

Conclusion: We shall immediately begin with reconstruction, work toward supplying the people with food,
and re-establish transport facilities, but other tasks will be
undertaken only after recognition of our demands and after they are carried out.

—Workers' Councils of the 11th District
Budapest, November 12, 1956.

These demands were circulated in the form of crudely
printed handbills by such organizations as the Workers'
Councils of Csepel or Sztalinvaros. But with the final
suppression of the revolution, and the reorganization of
the secret police in December, the cycle of political activity which had begun with the Petoefi debates in the
spring of 1956 came to its end.

NEHRU ON THE HUNGARIAN REVOLT

" . . . what happened in Hungary (Oct. 23–Nov. 4,
1956) demonstrated that the desire for national freedom
is stronger even than any ideology and cannot ultimate-
ly be suppressed. What happened in Hungary was not
essentially a conflict between communism and anti-com-
munism. It represented nationalism striving for freedom
from foreign control."

Prime Minister Jawaharlal Nehru:
The Tragic Paradox of Our Age,
The New York Times Magazine, Sept. 7, 1958

OUR LOVE OF LIBERTY . . .

There is no country which in the course of its thousand years of history has suffered more than we. Hungarians have had to wage incessant struggles for independence, mostly in defense of the Western countries. These struggles interrupted the continuity of our development and we always had to rise again by our own efforts. In the course of history this is the first occasion that Hungary has enjoyed the sympathy of all other civilized countries. We are deeply moved by this, and every member of our small land rejoices that, because of our love of liberty, the nations have taken up its case. . . .

Yet we, even in our dire situation, hope we have no enemies, for we are the enemies of no one. We want to live in friendship with all people and all countries. . . . We Hungarians want to live and progress as standard-bearers of the family of peaceful European nations. We want to live in a spirit of friendship with all the peoples of Europe and not on the basis of an artificially created friendship. And turning our eyes toward more distant parts, we, a small nation, want to live in friendship, in undisturbed, peaceful and mutual esteem with the great United States, as well as the powerful Russian Empire, and in good-neighborly relations with Prague, Bucharest, Warsaw and Belgrade.

. . . Now we need general elections, free from abuses, in which all parties can nominate candidates. The elections should be held under international supervision.

. . . I must stress that we have a classless society and a State where laws prevail. We support private ownership which is rightly and justly limited by social interests. This is the wish of the Hungarian people.

As head of the Hungarian Roman Catholic Church I declare . . . that we do not oppose the justified development of our country. We only desire that this development be sound. . . .

Radio Statement of József Cardinal Mindszenty, November 3, 1956.

UNITED NATIONS SPECIAL COMMITTEE ON THE HUNGARIAN UPRISING

Reprinted from the UNITED NATIONS REVIEW, August 1957, Volume 4, Number 2. A Summary of the Report of the General Assembly's Special Committee: THE PROBLEM OF HUNGARY.

When the General Assembly established a five-nation fact-finding committee in January 1957 to gather information on the Hungarian revolt and its suppression, it was generally recognized that the assignment was an extremely difficult one. Some opinion tended toward the view that it was a virtually impossible task, considering the position taken by the Soviet Union and the Hungarian authorities. The mandate to the Committee was explicit, but the problem of where and how to begin the study was a large one. The new Hungarian Government headed by János Kádár flatly refused to permit the Committee or its staff to enter Hungary, on the grounds that the political and military developments following the uprising were an "internal" affair, and that establishment of the Committee was an "illegal" act in violation of the United Nations Charter. The evidence, therefore, had to be gathered outside the country from reliable and knowledgeable sources.

Five months after it came into being, the Special Committee on the Problem of Hungary reported its findings. The evidence showed that the revolt which began in October 1956 was a spontaneous national uprising, and that it had no outside assistance; that the Soviet Union intervened twice, first to crush the uprising, and a second time to overthrow the legal and popularly supported Hungarian Government; and that the Kádár regime installed by the Soviet Union did not have the confidence or approval of the Hungarian people.

These conclusions are the core of the historic Committee report released on June 20, 1957. It is a clear and concise document of 148 printed pages, summarizing testimony from 111 eyewitnesses, information from governments which had diplomatic establishments in Hungary during the course of the revolt, memoranda provided by non-governmental organizations, official Hungarian and Soviet statements, and broadcasts of official and unofficial Hungarian radio stations. The verbatim record of hearings runs to some 2,000 pages.

Members of the five-nation Committee were K. C. O. Shann of Australia (Rapporteur), R. S. S. Gunewardene of Ceylon, Alsing Andersen of Denmark (Chairman), Mongi Slim of Tunisia, and Enrique Rodríguez Fabregat of Uruguay. There was no minority report and no dissent from the general conclusions. Questioned at a press conference on this unanimity, the Committee Rapporteur declared: "I do not suppose there was any particular unanimity amongst the members of the Committee for some time. It took us some time to get into the work. It took us quite a long time to make up our minds what had happened. But after a certain period, general unanimity in the Committee as to the broad outlines of what took place in Hungary existed, and continued to exist right through to the end."

SPONTANEOUS UPRISING

The Committee found that what took place in Hungary in October and November 1956 was a spontaneous national uprising which developed from "long-standing grievances which had caused resentment among the people." One of these grievances was the inferior status of Hungary in its relations with the Soviet Union. The system under which the Hungarian people were governed was reinforced by "the weapon of terror" wielded by the secret police and "a complex network of agents and informers permeating the whole of Hungarian society." Soviet pressure was resented in other respects also. "From the stifling of free speech to the adoption of a Soviet-style uniform for the Hungarian army, an alien influence existed in all walks of life." Hungarians felt no personal animosity towards the individual Soviet soldiers, the report notes, "but these armed forces were symbols of something which annoyed a proud people and fed the desire to be free."

The claim made in support of Soviet intervention that the uprising was fomented by "reactionary" circles in Hungary and that it drew its strength from outside "imperialists" failed to survive the Committee's examination. "From start to finish," the report declares, "the uprising was led by students, workers, soldiers and intellectuals, many of whom were communists or former communists." Most of the political demands put forward during the revolt included, in fact, stipulations that "democratic socialism" should be the basis of the Hungarian political structure, and that such social achievements as the land reform were to be safeguarded. At no time was any proposal made for return to power of any person associated with prewar days. "Fascists" and "saboteurs" from the outside could not possibly have entered the country under conditions prevailing at the frontiers or have landed at the airports which were under Soviet supervision.

It was the universal testimony of witnesses that the uprising was not planned, and that developing events took the participants by surprise. "No single explanation can determine exactly why the outbreak occurred just when it did," the report says. But communist spokesmen, including János Kádár, had recognized both the grievances of the Hungarian people prior to October 23, and the "broad, popular movement" which was caused by bitterness and indignation. The Committee concluded that two factors seem to have brought popular resentment to a head. The first was the news of a successful Polish move for greater independence from the Soviet Union. This news was largely instrumental in bringing Hungarian students together in the meetings of October 22. The second factor was the acute disappointment felt by the people when the First Secretary of the Central Committee of the Hungarian Workers' (Communist) Party in a speech on October 23 failed to meet any of the popular demands and adopted what was considered a truculent tone toward his hearers.

Although the uprising was not planned in advance, and though its whole development "bears the hallmark of continuous improvisation," Soviet authorities had taken steps as early as October 20 to make armed intervention possible. Troop movements and projected troop movements were noted from that date on. The Committee found that Soviet troops from outside Hungary were employed even in the first intervention, and that no clause of the Warsaw Treaty provides for intervention by armed forces of the Soviet Union to dictate political developments within any signatory's frontiers.

When the demonstrations began on October 23 they were "entirely peaceful," the investigation found. None of the demonstrators appears to have carried arms, and there was no evidence of any kind that resort to force was intended. For the transition of the peaceful demonstrations into an armed uprising, the actions of the AVH (security police) in firing on the people outside the Radio Building were largely responsible. Within a few hours Soviet tanks were in action against the Hungarians. The appearance of Soviet soldiers in their midst, not as friendly allies but as enemies in combat, "had the effect of still further uniting the people."

Regarding the request alleged to have been sent out by the Hungarian Government to Soviet authorities for assistance in quelling the uprising by force, the Committee report observes that Prime Minister Imre Nagy "has denied, with every appearance of truth, that he issued this invitation or was even aware of it." Since Soviet tanks appeared in the streets of Budapest at approximately 2 a.m. on October 24, the Committee declared, "it would have been impossible for him to have addressed any official message to the Soviet authorities, since he held no government post at the time when the tanks must have received their orders." Nor was any evidence uncovered which might substantiate the claim of János Kádár that he had invited the second Soviet intervention. There was "abundant evidence," however, that Soviet preparations for further intervention, including the movement of Soviet troops and armor, had been under way for some time. The report observes that "Mr. Kádár and his Ministers were absent from Budapest during the first few days after he formed his government, and administrative instructions to the people of Hungary were issued by the commanders of the Soviet troops."

PEOPLE'S INITIATIVE

When Imre Nagy became Prime Minister, the Committee said, he was not in the beginning able to exercise the full powers of that office because of the influence of the AVH (security police). Only when the grip of the AVH was loosened by the victory of the insurgents was he able to take an independent stand. "By this time, the real power in Hungary lay with the Revolutionary and Workers' Councils, which had sprung up spontaneously in various parts of the country to replace the collapsing communist party structure." Though a communist of long standing, Mr. Nagy invited non-communists into his new government and listened to the demands of the Revolutionary and Workers' Councils. The Prime Minister himself, like the country at large, was surprised by the pace of developments. "However, seeing that his countrymen were united in their desire for other forms of government and the departure of Soviet troops, he threw in his lot with the insurgents." Although Mr. Nagy had not instigated the uprising and was never its actual leader, he became a symbolic figure.

The few days of freedom enjoyed by the Hungarian people "provided ample evidence" of the popular nature of the uprising. A free press and a free radio came to life throughout the country, and there was general rejoicing over the disbanding of the security police. Steps were taken by the Workers' Councils to give the workers real control of nationalized industrial undertakings and to abolish unpopular institutions such as production norms, which were widely resented as being unfair to workers and interpreted as an indication of secret trade agreements for the benefit of the Soviet Union. During these days of freedom, while negotiations went on for the withdrawal of Soviet troops, attempts were made to clear the streets of battle debris, and life was beginning to return to normal. There were a number of beatings and lynchings by crowds during this period, in almost all cases confined to attacks on members of the AVH or those who were believed to have cooperated with them.

Regarding the violations of basic human rights prior to the uprising, particularly up to the autumn of 1955, the Committee said that on the evidence it was convinced that numerous accounts of inhuman treatment and torture by the AVH were true. Also on the evidence, it had to be acknowledged that numbers of Hungarians, including women and children, were deported to the Soviet Union. These deportations were designed to break the back of the revolution. The momentary success of the uprising succeeded in ridding the country for a few days of the apparatus of police terror, but this democratic achievement succumbed to the counter-revolution, with Soviet armed forces setting up János Kádár and his colleagues "in opposition to a Government which enjoyed the overwhelming support of the people of Hungary."

Following the second Soviet intervention on November 4, the Committee found, there was no indication of any popular support for the Kádár Government. Violations of basic human rights were reinstituted. Mr. Kádár successively abandoned most of the points contained in the revolutionary program which he at first promised to the Hungarian people. In the beginning he accepted the popular demand that Soviet troops should be withdrawn, but soon refused to discuss the matter further. "Against the workers, he has proceeded step by step to destroy their power and that of the Workers' Councils," with capital punishment now applicable to strike activities, the report states. The Social Democratic Party was again forcibly liquidated. General elections were postponed for two years. Writers and intellectuals were subjected to repressive measures. Of the 190,000 Hungarians who fled the country, mostly young people, "only a small fraction" returned.

Soviet action in Hungary, the Committee concluded, was "a massive armed intervention by one power on the territory of another," with the avowed intention of interfering in its internal affairs.

BACKGROUND OF REVOLT

Political developments in Hungary leading up to the events of October-November 1956 were these:

A general election was fought in 1945 by six political parties authorized by the Allied Control Commission, five of whom won seats in Parliament. The Smallholders Party won 245 seats, the Social Democrats 69, the Communists 70, the National Peasants 23 and the Democratic Party 2. The four major parties formed a coalition, but communist influence steadily asserted itself. By 1948, the Committee report recalls, leaders of non-communist parties "had been silenced, had fled abroad, or had been arrested." In 1949 Hungary officially became a "People's Democracy," with real power in the hands of Mátyás Rákosi, a communist trained in Moscow. Under his regime "free speech and individual liberty ceased to exist," with arbitrary imprisonment becoming commonplace. Purges took place both within and outside the communist party. In June 1949 Foreign Minister László Rajk was arrested, charged with attempting to overthrow the regime, and hanged. Numerous others were victims of similar actions. These purges were facilitated by the apparatus of the security police.

The Twentieth Congress of the Communist Party of the USSR early in 1956 encouraged a movement within the Hungarian Workers' (Communist) Party which aimed at a measure of democratization and national independence and a relaxation of police rule. In March of that year, Rákosi announced that the Supreme Court had found that László Rajk and others had been condemned on "fabricated charges." This official admission of crimes by the regime had profound repercussions. Rákosi was dismissed in July, and in the presence of large crowds Rajk and other victims of the 1949 trials were reburied with ceremony. Rákosi was succeeded as First Secretary of the Central Committee of the party by Ernö Gerö, and Hungarians looked for a softening of the regime.

As early as 1955 protests against the dictatorial regime had been voiced by Hungarian writers. These protests mainly concerned the doctrine of party allegiance in literature. Although a number of writers were arrested, the scope of the protests gradually widened to take in other grievances of the Hungarian people. On October 19, 1956, the Minister of Education announced certain changes as a result of requests put forward by Hungarian students, one of which concerned abolition of compulsory teaching of the Russian language in schools. This announcement, the Committee report observes, was followed by student demands of more far-reaching character in Szeged and other towns. News of developments in Poland was received with enthusiasm.

The Committee found evidence that as early as October 20, steps were being taken by Soviet authorities for use of armed force in Hungary, though the mass demonstrations did not occur until three days later. On October 20 and 21 floating bridges were assembled at Záhony on the Hungarian-Soviet frontier. On October 21 and 22, in neighboring areas of Romania, Soviet officers on leave, as well as reserve officers speaking Hungarian, were recalled to duty. Soviet forces in western Hungary were observed moving toward Budapest on October 22.

On that same date a number of student meetings were held in Budapest. At the most important of these meetings, students of Building Industry Technological University adopted a list of sixteen demands which expressed their views on national policy. They included the immediate withdrawal of all Soviet troops, the reconstituting of the Government under Imre Nagy (who had served as Prime Minister from 1953 to 1955), free elections, freedom of expression, re-establishment of political parties, and sweeping changes in the conditions of workers and peasants. It was learned during the meeting that the Hungarian Writers' Union proposed to express its solidarity with Poland on the following day by laying a wreath at the statue of General Bem, a hero of Hungary's 1848–49 War of Independence, who was of Polish origin. The students decided to organize a silent demonstration of sympathy on the same occasion.

Early next morning, the Committee report recounts, the students' demands became known throughout Budapest. Radio Budapest referred to the planned demonstration, and later announced a communiqué from the Minister of the Interior prohibiting it. However, the ban was lifted in the early afternoon, when the demonstration was already under way. Thousands of young people took part, including students, factory workers, soldiers in uniform and others. A similar demonstration took place at the statue of Sándor Petöfi (a nationally honored Hungarian poet, 1823–49). At the statue of General Bem, the President of the Writers' Union, Péter Veres, read a manifesto to the crowd, which also heard a proclamation of the students' "sixteen demands." Most of the crowd later crossed the Danube to join demonstrators outside the Parliament Building. By 6 p.m. between 200,000 and 300,000 persons were gathered at this site. Repeated calls for Imre Nagy eventually brought the former Premier, and he addressed the crowd briefly from a balcony of the Parliament Building.

Up to this point there had been nothing to suggest that the crowds would not disperse in due course and return home. But at 8 p.m. the First Secretary of the Central Committee, Ernö Gerö, who that morning had returned from a visit to Marshal Tito of Yugoslavia, broadcast a speech. "The general hope," says the report, "was that he would take account of the popular demands voiced by the students and would make some conciliatory announcement in connection with them. The speech, however, made none of the hoped-for concessions, and its whole tone angered the people." At about this time, another crowd had undertaken to carry out one of the students' demands—the removal of the statue of Stalin. By 9.30 p.m. they had overturned it from its pedestal.

On the evening of October 22 some of the students had tried to have their demands broadcast by Budapest Radio. The censor, however, had been unwilling to broadcast demands for free elections and withdrawal of Soviet troops, and the students would not agree to have their demands expurgated.

The following day a number of students went again to the Radio Building with the intention of making another effort to have their demands broadcast. What followed, in the words of the report, was this:

"A large crowd gathered at the Radio Building, which was guarded by the AVH or state security police. The students sent a delegation into the building to negotiate with the director. The crowd waited in vain for the return of this delegation, and eventually a rumor spread that one delegate had been shot. Shortly after 9 p.m., tear gas bombs were thrown from the upper windows and, one or two minutes later, AVH men opened fire on the crowd, killing a number of people and wounding others. Insofar as any one moment can be selected as the turning point which changed a peaceable demonstration into a violent uprising, it would be this moment when the AVH, already intensely unpopular and universally feared by their compatriots, attacked defenseless people. The anger of the crowd was intensified when white ambulances, with Red Cross license plates, drove up. Instead of first-aid teams, AVH police emerged, wearing doctors' white coats. A part of the infuriated crowd attacked them, and in this way the demonstrators acquired their first weapons. Hungarian forces were rushed to the scene to reinforce the AVH but, after hesitating a moment, they sided with the crowd."

Meanwhile, workers from Csepel, Ujpest and other working-class districts heard of the situation by telephone. They seized trucks and drove into Budapest, obtaining arms on the way from friendly soldiers or police, or from military barracks and arms factories known to them. Starting at about 11 p.m., the Radio Building came under attack with light arms. At midnight the radio announced that clashes had taken place at various points in the city. Early on October 24 the demonstrators seized the Radio Building, but were driven out again. Elsewhere in the city the AVH guards opened fire on unarmed demonstrators. While fighting was in progress at the Radio Building, the first Soviet tanks made their appearance in Budapest—about 2 a.m.—and soon went into action, though no official announcement of the Soviet intervention was made until seven hours later. Radio announcements gave the impression that Imre Nagy, appointed Chairman of the Council of Ministers during the night, had invited the Soviet intervention, even though it was clear he held no responsible office at the time the invitation would have to have been made.

Armed Uprising

First shots at the Radio Building marked the beginning of a bitter five-day battle in which the people of Budapest found themselves in combat with Soviet armor and with the AVH. The ordinary police sympathized with the insurgents and gave them weapons or fought at their side. The Hungarian army as a whole began to disintegrate with the start of the uprising. Wherever they could do so, Hungarian soldiers gave weapons and ammunition to their compatriots, and in many instances deserted to join them, sometimes in complete units. "There was no single instance recorded," the Committee determined, "of Hungarian troops fighting on the Soviet side against their fellow countrymen." The Hungarian resistance was composed primarily of workers and students. They usually fought in small groups. Against Soviet tanks the "Molotov cocktail"—a simple bomb made of gasoline—was used with effectiveness. The tanks had difficulty in maneuvering in the narrow streets, and the mechanized forces had insufficient supplies and infantry support. There was evidence that some of the Russian soldiers disliked the task assigned to them; many of them had established friendly relations with the Hungarian population. Most of the then available Soviet forces had been sent to Budapest, and there was comparatively little fighting in the provinces.

In the capital, the first few days of the uprising were marked by the transfer of power from the communist bureaucracy to the new Revolutionary and Workers' Councils. In most instances these Councils took over without opposition the various responsibilities of local government. There were also Revolutionary Councils or Committees in the army, in government departments, and in professional groups and centres of activity such as the radio and telegraph operations. The most influential of these bodies probably was the Transdanubian National Council, representing the people of Western Hungary. Using the Free Radio Station at Györ, this Council demanded that Hungary should denounce the Warsaw Treaty and proclaim her neutrality. Workers' Councils sprang up in industrial plants of various kinds, in factories and mines. Their principal purpose was to secure for the workers a real share in the management of enterprise and to set up machinery to protect their interests. The emergence of the Councils throughout the country "represented the first practical step to restore order and to reorganize the Hungarian economy on a socialist basis, but without rigid party control or the apparatus of terror."

Imre Nagy's period of office in the premiership from 1953 to 1955 had been marked by a loosening of controls imposed earlier by Rákosi. He had been attacked as a deviationist, and while he escaped trial, he was expelled from the communist party and divested of all his offices. In the minds of numerous Hungarian communists his name came to stand for more liberal policies, and many wished for his return to public life. Prior to the uprising, Nagy was readmitted to the party. During the formative hours of the demonstration, his reputation was high with the Hungarian people, though it became somewhat clouded by Budapest Radio's attempt to tie him to the Soviet intervention.

A serious episode occurred on October 25 which embittered the population and further turned popular sympathy away from Nagy. Soviet tanks guarding the Parliament Building opened fire on unarmed demonstrators in support of the AVH. Many people lost their lives, and the incident shocked the nation, which was not aware that Nagy was at that time detained at communist party headquarters. On the same day Ernö Gerö was replaced by János Kádár as First Secretary of the Central Committee of the party. Subsequently, Gerö fled to Soviet territory. The former Premier, András Hegedüs, also fled from communist headquarters.

Mr. Nagy was now free to move to the Parliament Building, and on October 27 he formed a Government into which he invited both communist and non-communist members. The non-communists were serving in a personal non-party capacity, and several "Stalinists" were retained. The Central Committee of the party now announced that the Government would start negotiations for immediate withdrawal of Soviet forces.

Fighting stopped on October 28, largely on terms offered by the insurgents. The Prime Minister announced he would abolish the AVH after the restoration of order. Popular resentment against the AVH was so deep, however, that Mr. Nagy carried out his promise without further conditions on October 29, and as a result he was for the first time free of control by the state security police. The following day Mr. Nagy announced that the Cabinet had abolished the one-party system. Speaking in the name of the communist party, János Kádár, still First Secretary of the Central Committee, agreed with this step, to avoid "further bloodshed." Plans were launched for free elections.

"Once the AVH had been disbanded," the Committee found, "Mr. Nagy felt free to explain his actions on and immediately after October 24." These clarifications, and the various steps he had taken, served to dispel popular doubts about his attitude toward the uprising, and his popularity quickly returned. Soviet armed forces began to withdraw from Budapest on October 30.

As for the communist party, it realized that a drastic overhaul of methods would be required to regain the confidence of the Hungarian people. Mr. Kádár announced that a reformed party was in the making. The new party would defend the cause of socialism and democracy "not by slavishly imitating foreign examples, but by taking a road suitable to the economic and historic characteristics of our country." He urged the newly formed parties to "overcome the danger" of intervention from abroad by consolidating the Government. "We do not want to be dependent any longer," he declared; "we do not want our country to become a battlefield."

On November 3 the Government was again reconstituted. Three ministries each were allotted to the communists, the Social Democrats and the Independent Smallholders, and two to the Petőfi Party. The parties of the new caretaker Government were the same which in 1945 had received the blessings of the Allied Control Commission, of which the USSR was a member. It was announced that they were agreed that the Government would retain such socialist achievements as could be used in a free, democratic and socialist country, in accordance with the will of the people.

Neutrality, Second Intervention

The Prime Minister told the Soviet Ambassador on November 1 that authoritative information had arrived confirming the entry of new Soviet military units in Hungary. He declared that this was a violation of the Warsaw Treaty, which the Hungarian Government would denounce if the reinforcements were not withdrawn. The Soviet Ambassador stated later that day that the new troops had entered only to relieve the Russian forces who had been fighting, and to protect the Russian civilian population in the country. He said the Soviet Government was ready to negotiate a partial withdrawal, and suggested that two delegations be appointed, one to discuss political, the other technical, questions. At 2 p.m. that day Mr. Nagy informed the Soviet Ambassador that more Russian troops had crossed the border. For this reason and effective immediately, he declared, Hungary was withdrawing from the Warsaw Treaty. At 4 p.m. the Council of Ministers, including János Kádár, approved the action without dissent and adopted a declaration of neutrality for the country. This information was conveyed to heads of diplomatic missions in Budapest. They were informed also that the

Prime Minister had communicated with the United Nations, asking for the aid of the four Great Powers in defence of Hungary's neutrality. The declaration itself was broadcast by Mr. Nagy that evening.

Negotiations continued, meanwhile, for the withdrawal of Soviet troops. By the afternoon of November 3 agreement seemed close, with only some technical details remaining to be settled. A Hungarian delegation, consisting of the Minister of Defence, the Minister of State, the Chief of Staff and another military representative, was invited to settle the remaining details at the Soviet Military Command at Tököl, near Budapest, at 10 p.m. The Hungarian negotiators attended a dinner given for them by Soviet military representatives at Tököl. At approximately midnight, General Serov, Chief of the Soviet Security Police, entered the dining room accompanied by NKVD officers and ordered the arrest of the Hungarian delegation.

Soviet armored forces continued to advance toward Budapest in battle formation. It was estimated that 2,500 Soviet tanks and 1,000 supporting vehicles were in Hungary by this time. Mr. Nagy, who was not yet aware of what had happened at Tököl, was still awaiting word from his negotiators, and he gave specific instructions that the invading Soviet forces were not to be fired upon. These instructions were not changed until news was received that János Kádár had set up a rival Hungarian Government. The Prime Minister then announced over the radio that Soviet troops had attacked the capital "with the obvious intention of overthrowing the legal Hungarian Democratic Government." He declared that the Government was at its post and that Hungarian troops were in combat. The Hungarian Army, the National Guard and groups of freedom fighters, equipped mostly with light arms, fought side by side against the advancing tanks. By 8 a.m. of November 4, Soviet tanks had broken through the defences of Budapest. Bitter fighting continued in various parts of the capital until the evening of November 6, with some resistance continuing both inside and outside the city several more days.

Mr. Nagy took refuge in the Yugoslav Embassy on the evening of November 4, and Soviet commanders assumed control of the Government. They issued orders to the Hungarian people regarding the surrender of arms, movements in the streets, supply of food, and other matters normally within the province of civil administration.

"Having taken over Hungary by armed intervention," the report of the General Assembly's Special Committee states, "the Soviet authorities were compelled by reason of the administrative vacuum to administer a country whose popularly supported Government they had overthrown. The Soviet-installed Government of Mr. Kádár commanded no following in the country, with the exception of individual members of the former AVH, a few senior officers of the Hungarian Army, and a small segment of former communist party officials, who had been dismissed during the uprising. Having broken the armed resistance of the Hungarian people in a massive attack, the Soviet authorities found themselves facing the passive resistance of the Hungarian population."

Confronted by this nationwide resistance, the Soviet military command resorted to mass arrests. Many apprehended persons had not been directly involved in the fighting. In numerous cases, captives were not turned over to Hungarian authorities, but loaded onto trains or trucks and deported, under Russian escort, to the Soviet Union.

When János Kádár announced the formation of his "Hungarian Revolutionary Worker-Peasant Government" he had with him three former members of the Nagy cabinet. They declared they had left the Government because of its inability to fight "the counter-revolutionary danger." The purpose of the new Government, they said, was to defeat "fascism and reaction." Mr. Kádár declared that reactionary elements were seeking to overthrow socialism in Hungary and restore capitalists and landowners to power, and that he had requested the help of Soviet troops to defeat these "reactionary forces." He gave no explanation of his reversal of position since his broadcast supporting Mr. Nagy on November 1. "There is no evidence," the report states, "that he had taken any steps to disassociate himself from Mr. Nagy's policies or to resign from his Government." It is known that Mr. Kádár visited the Soviet Embassy after his broadcast on November 1, and that he and his Ministers were briefly in Moscow some time prior to their taking the oath of office on November 7.

The Committee found no evidence to suggest that any Hungarian group opposed the actions of Imre Nagy, which in most cases merely reflected what the Revolutionary and Workers' Councils had insisted upon from the beginning of the uprising. All the evidence shows that the Soviet troops fought alone against the Hungarians, except for some former members of the AVH and a small group of former party officials. Among the new Soviet troops who came in with the second intervention were a considerable number from distant regions of Central Asia, many of whom believed at first that they were in Egypt, with the mission of fighting the Anglo-French "imperialists." It would seem, says the report, "that the Soviet authorities had more confidence in troops who had no opportunity to be affected by European associations and who might be counted upon to behave with indifference to the attitude of the Hungarian people."

NAGY'S ABDUCTION AND THE DEPORTATIONS

Shortly after Imre Nagy took refuge in the Yugoslav Embassy, he was joined there by other leading Hungarians, along with fifteen women and seventeen children. During negotiations which ensued between the Yugoslav Government and Mr. Kádár, the Yugoslav Government proposed that Kádár should provide a written guarantee that Mr. Nagy and his party would be allowed to return freely to their homes or, if this were not possible, to go to Yugoslavia. A suggestion by Mr. Kádár that they should seek asylum in Romania was rejected by Mr. Nagy. Other demands which Mr. Nagy rejected were that he should resign from his position in the Government, offer a self-criticism of his ac-

tivities, and should declare himself in sympathy with
the Kádár regime.

Eventually the Yugoslav Government declared that it
would agree to the departure of Mr. Nagy and his friends
only if Mr. Kádár, as President of the Hungarian Government, guaranteed in writing that the party would be
granted safe conduct to proceed freely to their respective homes. In reply, Kádár confirmed in writing that
the Hungarian Government did not desire to apply sanctions against Nagy and the members of his group for
their past activities. What followed, in the words of the
Committee report, was this:

"The next day, November 22 at 6:30 p.m., a bus arrived at the Yugoslav Embassy to take the party to their
homes. Soviet military personnel arrived and insisted on
entering the bus, whereupon the Yugoslav Ambassador
asked that two Embassy officials should accompany the
bus, to make certain that Mr. Nagy and his party
reached their homes as agreed. The bus was driven to
the headquarters of the Soviet Military Command, where
a Russian lieutenant-colonel ordered the two Yugoslav
officials to leave. The bus then drove away to an unknown destination escorted by Soviet armored cars."

The Yugoslav Government, in a *note verbale*, condemned the Hungarian action as "a flagrant breach" of
agreement. The note recalled that Mr. Nagy and his
party had refused to go to Romania, and it condemned
the Hungarian move as completely contrary to the generally accepted practices of international law. Nevertheless, Mr. Kádár's Government announced publicly that
Mr. Nagy and some of his colleagues who had sought
asylum in the Yugoslav Embassy had gone to Romania
in accordance with their own request.

As a result of its study of eye-witness testimony and
other confirming evidence, the Committee reached the
conclusion that "beyond doubt, deportations to the Soviet Union had indeed taken place . . . in considerable
numbers," and that official statements denying the deportations were not in accordance with the facts. Among
the witnesses were seven men and boys and one young
girl, a first-aid nurse, who had been among the depor-

tees. In addition, the Committee heard from a number of others who had been placed in deportation trains, but who had been liberated by Hungarian workers or freedom fighters. Some of the evidence was given by persons who had helped to stop trains or trucks to liberate prisoners.

The deportations began after the second Soviet intervention. Witnesses declared that on some days several trainloads of prisoners left Budapest. Deportation trains were reported to have arrived in the Soviet Union as late as mid-December, and some Hungarians are believed to have been deported in January of this year.

Most of the arrests in Budapest were made in a haphazard manner. People were rounded up in the streets in groups that ran into hundreds, and sometimes included elderly people and children. "According to witnesses," the report states, "the general practice was to close off a part of a street by stationing a tank at each end. Anyone found within the area was taken away." One case was reported in which fifty people were liberated from a truck; following this, Russian soldiers arrested fifty other people to take their place. Some of the deportees were seized in resistance centres, others in house-to-house searches after the fighting had ended. In some cases the entire Revolutionary Council in a town or the whole Workers' Council in a factory was taken.

The prisoners were carried in trucks or armored cars to political prisons or other assembly places such as underground halls at the railroad stations, military barracks and churches. Most of the deportation trains passed through Záhony, the frontier station between Hungary and the Soviet Union, but some trains were also reported to have crossed into Romania. The trains to the Soviet Union usually consisted of from twenty to thirty sealed freight cars or cattle trucks, with thirty to seventy persons in each car. Soviet troops guarded every car, and the engine drivers sometimes were Russian.

Many of the prisoners threw notes out of the cars appealing for help, giving their names and addresses so that their families could be notified. A considerable

number of messages were picked up by Hungarian railroad workers and forwarded to families of the deportees. When freedom fighters stopped a deportation train
by removing the rails or setting signals, heavy fighting
usually took place before the captives were liberated,
but in one instance the Russian guards fled without
resistance.

The eight witnesses who had been taken to the Soviet Union were imprisoned at Uzgorod. Other captives
were taken, reportedly, to prisons in Mukacevo and
Kolomea in the same district, and to Stryj. Guards informed them that Uzgorod was a place of assembly for
prisoners who were to be taken eastward from that
point. The Uzgorod prison was believed to hold 2,000
Hungarian prisoners at a time.

In general, the Committee heard, the treatment given
to deportees in the Soviet prisons was better than in
Hungarian prisons. Food and general conditions improved after their arrival, and they were not obliged to
perform forced labor. They were taken from the crowded
cells only for interrogation or for exercise in the yards.
Witnesses testified that Russian guards showed sympathy
and friendliness.

Interrogations were conducted by Russian officers and
members of the NKVD. "In the opinion of the witnesses,"
the report says, "the principal purpose of the interrogations was to obtain information about the cause and
organization of the uprising, about foreign assistance
the Hungarians were thought to have received and about
conditions in Hungary before the uprising. It was the
impression of the witnesses that the interrogations were
not aimed at determining the guilt or innocence of the
individual prisoners, but rather at finding out why the
Hungarian people rose in arms and how they had succeeded in doing so."

Of the eight deportees questioned by the Committee,
one had succeeded in escaping from the Soviet Union
with five friends. The other seven had been returned by
January 5. After arriving in Hungary they were kept in
prisons for periods of from a few days to several weeks.

Their decision to escape from Hungary arose from their fear of further arrest.

The Committee estimated that the number of persons deported ran into the thousands, and it was unable to find evidence that many of them have been returned to Hungary.

DEVELOPMENTS UNDER KÁDÁR

In an effort to win popular support, Mr. Kádár declared that the policy of his Government would include implementation of various demands made during the uprising, including raising the standard of living, factory management by Workers' Councils, and the abolition of compulsory agricultural deliveries by the peasants. These promises failed to satisfy the Hungarian people, who continued to press for withdrawal of Soviet troops, for free elections, and for the return of Nagy. Industrial production had been completely disrupted and continued to deteriorate, since the workers refused to return to the factories unless the Government gave evidence it would comply with their demands. Workers' Councils still remained the principal channels through which demands were conveyed to the Kádár regime. On November 14 the factory Councils established the Greater Budapest Workers' Council in order to present a united front. "It became clear from the Government's attitude," the report says, "that it was in no position to satisfy the workers' demands."

Meanwhile new security forces were organized, including among their numbers many former members of the AVH. Arrests of members of the Workers' Councils began, and party personnel were infiltrated into key posts of the Councils. When the Greater Budapest Council called for a forty-eight-hour strike to take place on December 11 and 12, the Government decreed the abolition of all Councils above the factory level. Decrees were also issued instituting the death penalty for a large category of offences, including participation in strikes.

Factories had been almost entirely idle for about two months. Because of a slow-down strike of the coal miners, electric power plants were able to produce only a minimum of electricity. But by mid-December, dire necessity forced a resumption of work. The Hungarian workers now found themselves in factories and mines policed by Russian soldiers.

A State Information Office to control the press was inaugurated, the Revolutionary Council of Intellectuals was dissolved, and the Petöfi Club ceased to function. The Writers' Union, which had branded the Soviet intervention a "historic mistake," was disbanded. By the beginning of 1957 non-communist organizations had in effect been barred from any role in public life. The mandate of the present Hungarian Assembly was due to expire last May 17, but an amendment of the Constitution postponed its termination for two more years.

The Committee observed in its report that it was twice refused permission by the Kádár Government to enter Hungary in pursuance of its fact-finding mission. This not only compelled the Committee to gather its testimony from persons outside the country, but deprived it of an opportunity of hearing representatives of the Kádár Government express their views directly. Nevertheless, it declared, in its effort to present an objective picture of developments it felt obliged to include in the report a representation of the opinions expressed by the Government of the USSR and that of Mr. Kádár.

No evidence was found that either of them had published anything in the nature of an objective statement of the facts behind the uprising, the Committee declared. But there are various indications that the Soviet authorities "were baffled by the spontaneous uprising of the Hungarian people" and that they did try to obtain information on it from various sources. The phenomenon of a working class movement "directed against cherished communist methods and ideals and against emblems of the Soviet Union as symbols of those methods" seems to have caused misgivings. Some Hungarians received the impression that their interrogators were not unsympathetic.

The memorandum circulated by the Hungarian delegation to the United Nations on February 4 alleged that the aim of the Hungarian "counter-revolution" was to "reinstate the system of capitalists and estate owners, who have never given up hope since their defeat in 1945." A *Pravda* article suggested that no one regarding himself as a Marxist could fail to understand that radical change in Hungary's political system would inevitably mean the restoration of capitalism. Spokesmen for the USSR and Mr. Kádár have acknowledged a number of legitimate grievances about which the Hungarian people had complained before and after the date of the revolt. "These concerned manifest errors and shortcomings of the Government headed by Rákosi, who failed, as did his successors, to meet even the most justified demands."

But the Kádár-Soviet view maintains that reactionary elements within Hungary and "imperialist circles" abroad took advantage of such legitimate grievances and the unrest they generated "to mislead the people and to strive by violence to overthrow the People's Democratic Republic."

In the Hungarian White Book on the uprising, *The Counter-Revolutionary Forces in the October Events in Hungary,* Rákosi policy is described as "criminal." It is said to have aroused "deep indignation and a broad popular movement." However, the White Book asserts, "the dark forces of the counter-revolution tried from the very beginning to take advantage of the movement . . . in order *to overthrow the people's power*" [italics in original]. The Soviet Union's Minister of Foreign Affairs, D. T. Shepilov, told the United Nations General Assembly on November 22: "For the first time since the defeat of fascism in the Second World War, the world was witness to an open attempt by the underground fascist forces to defy the forces of democracy and to stage a comeback by means of an armed struggle." The Hungarian White Book charges that the instigators of the armed uprising were "foreign agents, Horthyite émigrés and leaders of the underground organizations in the country, who took an organized part in the mass demonstrations and increasingly assumed a leading role in them. . . . The only possibility of saving popular power and eliminating the threat of a new, devastating war in the Danube Valley was to suppress counter-revolution." The White Book declared that the real objectives of the uprising were quite different from its publicly announced aims. Only the assistance of Soviet troops, it is claimed, enabled the true leaders of Hungary to throw back the armed forces of reaction.

Despite the Soviet Union's and the Kádár Government's self-justification, however, the Committee found the interventions to be against popular will.

"It is incontrovertible that the Nagy Government, whose legality under the Hungarian Constitution, until it was deposed, cannot be contested, protested against the entry and the use of Soviet forces on Hungarian territory, and not only asked that these forces should not intervene in Hungarian affairs, but negotiated and pressed for their ultimate withdrawal. The actions of the Nagy Government give proof of the firm desire of the Hungarians, as long as they could publicly express their aspirations, to achieve a genuinely independent international status for their country.

"It is no less incontrovertible," the report says, "that the Nagy Government was overthrown by force. Its successor assumed power as a result of military aid by a foreign state. The Nagy Government neither resigned nor transferred its powers to the Kádár Government. Noteworthy is the acceptance by the Kádár Government, after initial declarations to the contrary, of the continued presence of Soviet forces in Hungary.

"There is no doubt as to the aspirations of the immense majority of the Hungarian people. The presence of the Soviet army on Hungarian territory is for Hungarians the visible attestation of Hungarian subordination to an outside power, and of the impossibility for their country to pursue its own ideals. The aspiration for the withdrawal of the Soviet armed forces is based on the deep patriotic feelings of the Hungarians, having their source in their historic past. Their will for regaining full international independence is powerful, and has only been strengthened by the role played by the Soviet military command in the postwar years by the establishment of a political regime patterned after that of the

Soviet union, and more recently by the Soviet military intervention to guarantee that regime's continuance."

The Committee did not find that Hungarian feelings and aspirations were antagonistic to the USSR as a state, or to the Soviet people as individuals. Furthermore, Hungarian feelings did not exclude sympathy in many quarters for a number of features of the Soviet economic and social system.

How the Committee Worked

The Special Committee on the Problem of Hungary was established on January 10. It held its first meeting one week later at United Nations Headquarters and elected Alsing Andersen as Chairman and K. C. O. Shann as Rapporteur. It had been charged by the General Assembly with the duty of assembling "the fullest and best available information regarding the situation created by the intervention of the Union of Soviet Socialist Republics, through its use of armed force and other means, in the internal affairs of Hungary, as well as regarding developments relating to the recommendations of the Assembly on this subject."

Following a preliminary examination of available documentation, the Committee gave hearings to thirty-five witnesses at United Nations Headquarters, after which it went to Europe. From March 11 to April 16 it held meetings in Geneva, and thereafter in Rome, Vienna, London and again in Geneva. The Committee's last meeting was on June 7 in New York. One hundred and eleven witnesses were heard, including twenty-one in Geneva, sixteen in Rome, thirty in Vienna and nine in London. The first three witnesses were heard in open meetings. They were Miss Anna Kéthly, Minister of State in the Hungarian Government of Imre Nagy; Major-General Béla Király, Military Commander of the City of Budapest and Commander-in-Chief of the National Guard during the uprising; and József Kővágó, Mayor of Budapest during the years 1945–47, and from October 31 to November 4, 1956. These three witnesses and other prominent Hungarians requested the Committee to hear certain other witnesses. Suggestions were also made in this regard by the Governments of Belgium, Canada, Denmark, France, Italy, the United Kingdom and the United States. During the hearings various witnesses also proposed the names of persons whose testimony might be taken to confirm or supplement evidence already given. More than 200 Hungarians wrote letters on their own initiative, asking to be heard.

The witnesses were selected "under the authority of the Chairman and the Rapporteur." The primary consideration on which selections were made was the witnesses' capacity to bring before the Committee evidence based on direct and personal knowledge of the events in Hungary. Attention was paid to ensuring that the witnesses were drawn from all segments of Hungarian life, and from all parts of the country.

Among them, the largest number were skilled and unskilled workers. Many had participated in the revolt as ordinary "freedom fighters," but several had been leaders in various spheres during the uprising. They included members of the Revolutionary Councils in Budapest and the provinces, leading members of the Workers' Councils, engineers, technicians, managers in state enterprises (including the uranium mines in Pécs), and communist and non-communist intellectuals. There were writers and journalists, an actress, an artist, an architect, professors of law, medicine, philosophy, history, science, technology, economy and agriculture, and several lawyers, including an assistant public prosecutor. Hearings were given to high school and university students of both sexes, including members of students' councils, to officers and soldiers of the Hungarian Army and Air Force, members of the National Guard and ordinary police. Leaders of the revolutionary forces who testified included the Commander and Deputy Commander of the National Guard at Csepel; the Commander of the Corvin Block; the Commander of the revolutionary forces of southern Budapest; and the leader of the "freedom fighters" and guerrilla forces in southwestern Hungary. Doctors and nurses who had cared for the wounded and carried out Red Cross duties also testified. Other witnesses were these:

railroad and communications workers, who gave evidence regarding troop movements; government officials, a number of whom had high rank or who were closely associated with Hungarian politicians or cabinet ministers of various parties; and former members of Parliament or leaders of political parties. One man had been a stenographer for the security police.

None of the witnesses had left Hungary before the October revolution. Some had escaped only a few weeks before being heard by the Committee.

At the beginning of his testimony, each witness would usually give his personal data and background, and would then make an introductory statement regarding events of which he had special knowledge. The witnesses were instructed to give evidence based on first-hand experience. Following the introductory statement, the witnesses were subjected to cross-examination by the Committee members. Some witnesses submitted documents, and some prepared memoranda to support or elaborate their testimony.

"Throughout its work," the report states, "the Committee has sought scrupulously to assess the value of the testimony and of the documentation placed before it. Care has been taken to subject witnesses to detailed interrogation in order to test the reliability of their evidence. The Committee has on many points been in a position to check the testimony of one witness with the testimony of others and with the documentation available. . . . As the hearings progressed, it became possible to put to witnesses questions of a more and more precise nature."

The Committee requested at an early stage, through the Secretary General, that the Hungarian Government extend assistance or facilities for its work, but permission to enter the country was denied. Later, while in Europe the Committee renewed its request, with a similar refusal from the Hungarian Government. The Committee requested that it be permitted to interview Imre Nagy, in Rumania, an appeal which the Rumanian Government rejected.

In concluding comments of the first chapter of the report, the Committee declared:

"The Committee has sought throughout its work to apply to the evidence the tests of authenticity and coherence which provide the essential criteria of the objectivity of any such investigation. While therefore bearing in mind the resolutions of the General Assembly, the Committee has approached its task of investigation without prejudgment, deeming it essential to present a factual report based exclusively on the careful examination of reliable evidence. It has consistently sought to avoid any emotional evaluation of the facts. It has endeavored to depict in restrained language the situation as revealed by the evidence received."

HAMMARSKJÖLD AND THE HUNGARIAN REVOLT

The Hungarian refugees, 200,000 of them who in the days of the uprising had fled into adjacent countries, as well as their sympathizers, blamed Hammarskjöld for their plight. They said that during the Nagy regime there were twenty-four hours when he might have gone to Budapest, and history would have taken another turn. Three years later, before the Students' Association in Copenhagen, Hammarskjöld explained, "In the Hungarian crisis, the United Nations confined itself to an 'expression of principle' . . . with the exception of one or two of the smaller countries, no one in the United Nations urged measures going further than those which were taken."

Emery Kelen: HAMMARSKJÖLD, G. P. Putnam's Sons, New York, New York, 1966.

TIMETABLE OF A FAILURE

Excerpts from the article of Gordon Gaskill published under the same title in THE VIRGINIA QUARTERLY REVIEW, Volume 84, Spring 1958, Charlottesville, Virginia.

NOVEMBER 1

At 10:26 a.m. on Thursday, November 1, 1956, a teleprinter on the twentieth floor of the United Nations building in New York City suddenly began clocking out a call that has no parallel in UN history.

An unidentified station asked: UNITED NATIONS NEW YORK . . . ARE YOU THERE?

The UN operator replied: YES WE ARE STILL HERE.

The unknown station identified itself: DIPLOMAG BUDAPEST CALLING.

The UN operator, not recognizing the codeword Diplomag, consulted a codebook and found that it meant the Hungarian Foreign Ministry. Such a call has never reached the United Nations before or since. Normally a member nation sends its messages to its own UN delegation, which relays them to the Secretary General. At this hour, however, the Nagy government of Hungary had no delegation it could trust. Thus, on this day and on this day only, the UN building was directly connected to Budapest, by a Telex circuit that went from Budapest to Vienna by landline, and then to New York by wireless. Whatever the nameless operator typed on teleprinter No. BP 679 in Budapest was instantaneously reproduced on teleprinter No. MNY 0544 at the UN.

The call from Budapest was so unusual that UN operators gathered around the machine, watching curious-

ly to see what it would print. Nine different times Budapest asked the UN to identify itself, and nine times the
UN patiently complied. Budapest, reassured, spoke of
a message it would send soon. New York waited; the
machine whirred; the contact with Budapest remained
unbroken, but no message came. Only scraps of technical talk were transmitted.

At 10:42 Budapest typed: FOR SECRETARIAT UN: IF YOU
ARE BUSY I CALL A FEW MINUTES LATER. OUR MESSAGE WILL
BE READY. OKAY? PLEASE ANSWER.

The UN, which had said nothing at all about being
busy, replied: WE ARE NOT BUSY. CAN WAIT IF YOU WANT.
In retrospect, the first four words have prophetic overtones.

Budapest broke the connection at 11:14 a.m. No real
message had been sent out. UN operators gossiped about
the odd exchange, but no one thought to notify the
Secretary General's office that the Hungarian Foreign
Office was on the point of sending a message which, in
the circumstances, must be of considerable importance.
The connection lasted 48 minutes.

In Budapest, during these 48 minutes, Premier Imre
Nagy was holding the most grave and momentous cabinet meeting of his career. Unquestionably, he had ordered that the teleprinter link to the United Nations be
established and kept open during it, ready for any emergency. During the last 10 minutes of the 48 minutes, he
had cast the die, irrevocably. This cabinet meeting was
the climax of a morning of furious activity, both anxious
and ominous.

At about 6 a.m. (noon in Budapest) Nagy had protested to Andropov, the Soviet ambassador, against new
Russian troops coming into Hungary. Andropov was
conciliatory; he said they had come only to relieve and
replace departing Russian soldiers exhausted by fighting,
and to protect Russian civilians in Hungary. Nagy replied bluntly that this explanation did not satisfy him.
He said that if the Soviet troop influx was not halted
instantly, he would appeal to the United Nations. Andropov promised that no more troops would enter.

At 8 a.m. (2 p.m. in Budapest) Nagy telephoned Andropov again and said, indignantly, that the troop influx had not stopped, and that, on the contrary, new Russian soldiers had been pouring in steadily for the last three hours. Because of this, he said, Hungary was going to withdraw immediately from the Warsaw Pact. Andropov continued to be conciliatory, but warned Nagy against doing anything rash.

At 10 a.m. (4 p.m. in Budapest) Nagy summoned his special and historic cabinet meeting. He informed his ministers of his decision to leave the Warsaw Pact. They backed him with a unanimous vote, and then drew up a proclamation of Hungarian neutrality, and approved the text of his appeal to the United Nations. They then suggested that the Soviet ambassador himself be summoned to their presence, and hear with his own ears what they had decided.

At 11 a.m.—while the teleprinter connection to New York was established but idle—Andropov arrived to face the Hungarian cabinet. Nagy read out, solemnly, with a full sense of their great meaning, the decisions he and the cabinet had taken. Andropov remained impassive but still conciliatory. He assured Nagy several times that the Russian troops would be quickly evacuated to Russia, all of them, and begged Nagy to withdraw his proposed appeal to the United Nations. Nagy said that he would send it anyway to New York (the line was open and ready) but that he would withdraw it when—and only when—the Soviet troops actually left Hungary. In all this, no minister seemed more enthusiastic or determined than Janos Kadar, a close and trusted collaborator of Nagy. Deeply moved, with tears in his eyes, Kadar faced the Soviet ambassador and said: "I know my political future may be obscure now, but as a Hungarian, I would come down into the streets, if necessary, and use my bare hands to fight against your tanks." Thus far, the great decisions had been made, but they were still not public. Nagy had informed all chiefs of diplomatic missions in Budapest about his forthcoming steps, but this was still secret, in official channels. At 12:15 p.m. he took the final, irreversible step. Radio Budapest went on the air and told the whole world what had been decided. Now Nagy's bridges to Russia were burned; he had set out into the unknown. And he gave the word to proceed with sending the Hungarian appeal to the United Nations.

At almost the very second this broadcast ended, the UN teleprinter sprang to life again—at 12:21 p.m. BUDA-PEST CALLING. ARE YOU READY PLEASE?

Twice again the UN identified itself. Then the formal Nagy appeal for UN help came through briskly, in excellent English, without a halt, and almost without a typographical error. It was addressed to Dag Hammerskjold, Secretary of the United Nations, and said:

> Reliable reports have reached the Government of the Hungarian People's Republic that further Soviet units are entering into Hungary. [The Prime Minister] summoned M. Andropov, the Soviet Ambassador, and expressed his strongest protest against the entry of further Soviet troops into Hungary. He demanded the instant and immediate withdrawal of these Soviet forces.
>
> He informed the Soviet Ambassador that the Hungarian Government immediately repudiates the Warsaw Treaty, and, at the same time, declares Hungary's neutrality, turns to the United Nations, and requests the help of the great powers in defending the country's neutrality. . . .
>
> Therefore I request Your Excellency promptly to put on the agenda of the forthcoming General Assembly of the United Nations the question of Hungary's neutrality and the defence of this neutrality by the four great powers. . . .

It was signed: "Imre Nagy, President of the Council of Ministers of the Hungarian People's Republic, designated Minister of Foreign Affairs."

At the end, Budapest asked: DO YOU RECEIVED [SIC] PLEASE?

New York replied: RECEIVED WELL THANKS VERY MUCH, and then typed out the formal acknowledgement and the exact hour: 12:27 (p.m.) EASTERN STANDARD TIME UNITED NATIONS NEW YORK.

12:27 p.m. on Thursday, November 1, 1956.

At that moment Hungary's appeal for help came legally and officially into the hands of the United Nations.

And at that moment a time-clock began to tick, unheard by almost everyone. It would tick for 58 more hours, and then it would strike—with the violent Russian counterattacks that swept away the Nagy government and drowned the revolution in blood.

No one in the United Nations that Thursday afternoon could know (nor could Nagy himself in Budapest know) that there would be only 58 hours. This is purest hindsight. Yet the hours did exist, and to some UN delegates, looking back now with uneasy hearts, they seem an all-too-brief period of grace during which, had the UN acted with furious energy and resolution, something might yet have been done to save Hungary. Probably this is over-optimism; but it is worth exhuming the 58 hours to learn, by autopsy, how they slipped through the fingers of the UN, unused. This is the timetable of a failure, but it is also a lesson for future crises.

The 12:27 message from Nagy utterly changed the United Nations' legal position toward Hungary.

Only five days earlier, Hungary had taken a completely opposite stand in the UN. It is not yet clear whether on this day—October 28—Nagy was still controlled, against his will, by Communist police guards, or whether in his own mind he had not yet come to desire UN intervention. On October 28, he was still surrounded by guards of the hated AVH security police; on October 29 he appeared for the first time without them, unquestionably a free agent at last.

At any rate, on October 28, Dr. Peter Kos, actually a Soviet citizen named Leo-Konductorov, acting as Hungary's permanent delegate to the UN, and speaking in the name of the Nagy government, formally told the Security Council that events in Hungary were purely internal affairs, and no legal concern of the UN. This stand (which Nagy might have rescinded the following day, but did not) was later to be reaffirmed by the puppet Kadar government, and thus used to stop any UN action, even the entry of UN observers. But in the five days since October 28 events in Hungary had changed fantastically, and Nagy had changed with them. Now he completely reversed his stand. Now the legal government

of Hungary was not only permitting UN intervention;
it was literally begging for it. During those 58 hours it
would have welcomed any number of UN observers,
probably even UN troops, had any been available. During most of the 58 hours—but never before and never
since—Hungary lay wide open to the West, its borders
with Austria free and inviting.

Only about four hours after the Nagy appeal arrived,
the General Assembly was to meet in momentous and
extraordinary session about Suez. The third World War
seemed possible, even probable, and in the corridors of
the UN there were foreboding and almost unbearable
tension.

The UN teleprinter office recognized the Nagy message as something out of the ordinary and sent it by
special messenger to the Secretary General's office. It arrived about 12:35 p.m. and created little or no excitement. Mr. Hammerskjold's office too had all its ener-
gies aimed at Suez. Further, it was the lunch hour. Not
only did the Secretary General's office make no announcement of the message; it was soon to deny that it
had ever come in at all.

News agencies, having monitored the Nagy broadcast
in Europe, noted that he said he was appealing to the
United Nations; now they checked to see if, in fact, any
such appeal had arrived in New York. It had, but
through confusion or oversight, the Secretary General's
office said it had not. The reports from Europe were so
authentic, however, that the UN press chief finally went
in person to the Secretary General's office and, with some
digging, found the message. He summoned a flash conference of UN correspondents and read out the text—at
2 p.m.

At this moment in Hungary, Radio Budapest began play-
ing Mozart's "Requiem" for the martyrs of the revolution.
It was night, the eve of All Souls' Day, and throughout
the darkened city hundreds of thousands of candles burned
in the windows, mourning the Hungarian dead. The city
was uneasy. Already the elation aroused by Nagy's broadcast was being blunted by ominous rumors. They were
justified. In the darkness, Russian tanks moved up to sur-

round the city's three airdromes. In eastern Hungary, Russian armor suddenly began moving westward, from Debrecen toward Szolnok.

At 2:30 p.m. in New York the Nagy appeal was circulated in mimeographed form to all UN delegates, but it bore no marks of urgency and was mingled in their boxes with innumerable other mimeographed notices. Most delegates did not actually see it until late that afternoon, and many not until late that night.

Not everyone in the UN building that day was hypnotized by Suez to the exclusion of Hungary. As the afternoon drew on, there arose an odd and entirely informal group, which one of its members has called the *Cassandra Club*. It included a few members of the UN Secretariat who, for one reason or another, had a special interest in Eastern Europe. It included some Hungarian-Americans and some leading Hungarian exiles. It included also a minority of UN delegates, especially those from Catholic countries.

Particularly active was Dr. Emilio Nuñez-Portuondo of Cuba, who for five years had been tireless in talking about Soviet oppression in Eastern Europe. As soon as he learned of the Nagy appeal, he immediately began a championship of Hungary which was to bring him more than 11,000 congratulatory letters and telegrams. He began buttonholing large numbers of other delegates, trying passionately to convince them that the call from Hungary was urgent and desperate, and that the UN should act at once, this very night.

He did not succeed. Time after time he and other members of the Cassandra Club were told, in effect: "There are only troop movements in Hungary, but there is actual shooting in Egypt. Let us settle Suez first; then we will take up Hungary." This was especially true of the powerful Afro-Asian-Arab bloc, which has the balance of power in Assembly voting. The AAA was in full cry after the British and French, and suspected anything else as being a diversion.

At 4 p.m., while Nuñez-Portuondo pleaded in New York, Janos Kadar was speaking over Radio Budapest in praise of "our glorious uprising." But immediately after the broad-cast he went, by a circuitous route, to the Russian embas-sy, and there had long talks. It was unquestionably at this time that he decided to desert Nagy—"seized by fear," as Nagy was to say later. But Kadar kept his decision se-cret; Nagy suspected nothing of it, and kept Kadar as a trusted ally until the very last.

In the darkness, 160 Russian tanks had moved up to sur-round all three of Budapest's airdromes in a ring of steel. More Soviet armor moved steadily east, south, and west of the city, cutting off one road after another.

In New York, Nuñez-Portuondo and his supporters were getting nowhere, and the General Assembly was to meet—on Suez—in less than an hour's time. They were bogging deeper and deeper into long legalistic argu-ments about parliamentary procedure. Some delegates argued that since this afternoon's Assembly had been called to discuss Suez, it could not legally discuss any-thing else. Nuñez-Portuondo denied this. He pointed out that this would be the first extraordinary session ever held under the "Uniting for Peace" procedure adopted in the days of Korea, and that no precedents of any kind existed. "We are going to make our own precedents to-day," he said. "Let us make good ones." He insisted that once the Assembly was in session, it was master of its own agenda and could, by two-thirds vote, take up any matter it liked.

Others argued that since the Security Council was still "seized" of" the matter of Hungary, the Assembly could not yet legally discuss it. Nuñez-Portuondo (whose Cuba happens to be one of the eleven Council members) pointed out that the Council could meet quickly—to-night—introduce a resolution, receive the expected So-viet veto, then vote the matter over to the Assembly.

A third objection carried great weight with many del-egates, and with the Secretariat itself—ironically, an ob-jection which need never have arisen had it not been for a blunder of the Secretariat. This was the argument about whether Nagy meant, when he said "forthcoming Assembly," the regular session which would not sit un-til November 12 or this afternoon's special session. The objectors speculated that since today's special session had not been called until last night, Nagy, far away in Hungary, probably did not even know it was being held.

In this they were wrong, but Nuñez-Portuondo and his adherents could not prove it. All they could do was to argue that, with new Russian troops pouring into Hungary, Nagy certainly did not mean a delay of eleven more days. They also argued (correctly) that every radio set in Hungary that could get foreign broadcasts would be tuned in to see what the West, especially the UN, was doing, and that Nagy probably knew of the special session as soon as the general American public did.

The argument could have been settled by the Secretariat's asking Nagy which he meant, but this was not done. Communications with Hungary were free and open all this afternoon and much of the evening. The Secretary General, however, did not get around to acknowledging the Nagy message until 1:05 a.m. the next morning—twelve hours later—and by this time the lines were cut, and his acknowledgement had to be sent to Geneva, for possible relay on to Budapest somehow.

But the debate about Nagy's intent could have been settled instantly if the Secretariat had not overlooked the meaning of a document which had been in its offices for several hours. At 12:45 p.m. this same afternoon, only 18 minutes after the formal Nagy appeal had come in, the same teleprinter had come alive with the third and last direct contact with Budapest. It brought a one-sentence message, again addressed to Mr. Hammerskjold, again signed by Nagy himself:

"I have the honour to inform you that Mr. Janos Szabo, First Secretary of the Permanent Mission, will represent the Hungarian People's Republic at the special session of the General Assembly of the United Nations to be convened November 1, 1956, at New York."

This was crystal clear, and would have decided the matter forever. But the significance of this message was entirely overlooked by the Secretariat; it was considered purely an administrative matter and was not circulated to the delegates. More than 24 hours later the Under Secretary General still did not know of it and assured the Security Council that no such message had been received. He was quickly corrected.

At 5 p.m. the General Assembly began its extraordinary session to discuss the crimes of Suez.

At the same hour in Budapest, the Russian embassy admitted that Soviet tanks were surrounding the three airdromes, but explained that it was merely to protect the evacuation of Russian personnel. The embassy made no mention that the surrounding roads were cut. By now only one major road was still open, to Vienna.

In the General Assembly the debate on Suez was long and bitter. The very word "Hungary" was mentioned only once at this session, in a casual remark by a British delegate: "I cannot help contrasting [our actions at Suez] with the armed actions of the Soviet Union aimed at perpetuating its domination of Hungary."

John Foster Dulles spoke about 7 p.m. and said: "I doubt that any representative ever spoke from this rostrum with as heavy a heart as I have brought here tonight." This, however, had nothing to do with Hungary, which he did not mention. It was because, he said, America felt compelled to vote, on Suez, against its friends Britain, France, and Israel. When Dulles finished —at 7:40 p.m.—the Assembly adjourned this session. A second session would meet later.

While Dulles was speaking in New York, a large Soviet armored force rolled westward into Kisvarda. Another strong force of tanks appeared in the Gyoengyoes area, 50 miles northeast of Budapest, and began entrenching itself.

To a man like Vitetti of Italy, it seemed unthinkable that this night should pass without at least a gesture of help. He soon discovered, as Nuñez-Portuondo had discovered, that any real move to act tonight would lead to endless parliamentary arguments on the floor. Therefore, about 10 p.m., he settled for the only tactics that seemed possible. He would wait until after the vote on Suez and then would rise, on a point of order, to mention the urgency of Hungary. This device, mild at best, had American approval. It very specifically did not have

American backing in the sense that America would press for action tonight. It was, and was in advance known to be, an empty gesture, a device to get the name of Hungary on the record, a proof that it had not been overlooked.

NOVEMBER 2

At 9:50 p.m. the Assembly opened its second session of the evening, and the great debate on Suez swept on. Cassandra Club members haunted the news agency tele-printers on the third and fourth floors, collected every scrap of news about Hungary. One Cassandra concentrated on the Reuters tickets, believing that they somehow had faster, more detailed reports. As midnight neared, he asked anxiously if the circuits would be kept open, and was assured they would be. At 1:25 a.m. came a dispatch he had expected and feared, a long account, in alarming detail, of Russian troop movements in Hungary. It quoted a dismayed Hungarian as asking: "Are we going to be another Korea?"

He got copies of this dispatch, sent one to the Secretary General's office and others to various delegations—especially the American one. John Foster Dulles himself read it, while the debate on Suez droned on. It was not until about 2:30 a.m. that the name of Hungary was spoken on the floor. Lall, of India, made a passing reference to "some difficulties in Hungary."

There were indeed some difficulties in Hungary. At almost the moment Lall was speaking, two armored trains rolled slowly out of Russia and into Hungary, at the border point of Zahony. Hungarians could see, across the frontier, great masses of Russian troops, waiting. The armored trains occupied the Zahony station and moved steadily on, deeper into Hungary, taking over the main line to Nyiregyhaza. Farther along the line lay Budapest.

In New York Vitetti of Italy fretted with impatience. He could not speak until the Suez vote came; it was growing very late; he knew in his heart that it was already too late now to act this night on Hungary, even if the Assembly wished. The Suez vote did not come until about 3:30 a.m. The American resolution against Britain, France, and Israel passed triumphantly, 64 to 5, with 6 abstentions.

Vitetti rose to his feet. "I have asked to speak on a point of order." He referred to the Nagy appeal, which, he said, "has just been circulated to us." He underlined the urgency of events in Hungary and said: "I hope that the United Nations—and if necessary this special emergency session—will take immediately whatever action is possible, with regard to the request of the Hungarian people." Then he sat down. It was no motion, merely a point of order. Belaunde of Peru said that he agreed with it, then he too sat down. That was all. The speeches went on—about Suez.

At about 4 a.m. John Foster Dulles rose to speak again, on Suez, but in closing he mentioned Hungary. He looked drawn and haggard. It was very late and, although not even he suspected it, he would be under a surgeon's knife on the morrow.

"I want to express my endorsement," he said, "of the intervention made by the representative of Italy with reference to the Hungarian situation. . . . I hope that this matter, which is on the agenda of the Security Council, will be kept urgently before it, and we shall not be preoccupied with the Middle East to the exclusion of assisting the State of Hungary to regain its independence." A few minutes later—at 4:20 a.m.—the Assembly adjourned.

Exhausted by sleeplessness and the tensions of Suez, delegates went home to sleep. During the new day about to dawn neither the Assembly nor the Council planned any meetings. It was to be a day of rest.

There was little rest in Hungary. Government loudspeaker trucks roved Budapest proclaiming: "Do not be alarmed! The Russian troop movements are only to protect evacuating Russian personnel!" They reassured no one. The Russian intent seemed too clear and ominous now.

The alarm, and the Russian intent, seemed at last crystal clear in New York, too, as the sun reached Manhattan. The *New York Times* had banner streamers:

SOVIET TANKS AGAIN RING BUDAPEST: NAGY
DEFIANT, APPEALS TO UN. Western delegates, still
sleepy, were telephoning each other, long-faced, discuss-
ing the blackening news from Hungary. By late morning, America, Britain and France agreed that there must
be a special Council session today after all. They drafted
a two-sentence letter which, in effect, summoned the
Council to meet, and called a special messenger to deliver it, by hand, to the new Council President, Entezam
of Iran.

> While the special messenger hurried across Manhattan,
> Radio Budapest carried an appeal for Western help from
> the Jewish community of the city. It was followed by one
> from the chief Lutheran bishop: "I ask you in the name
> of Jesus Christ to help us."
> And, about this same hour, an American diplomatic con-
> voy was only a few miles from the Austrian frontier and
> safety. Then Russian tommy-gunners astride the road
> stopped them. To American protests, the Russian com-
> manding officer said curtly: "There is no use arguing. You
> must return to Budapest." Reluctantly, the convoy turned
> back.

In New York, the special messenger was not able to
deliver the American-British-French letter to the Security Council President until 1 p.m.
Twenty-four of the fifty-eight hours were gone now.
Entezam of Iran read the letter. "In view of the critical situation in Hungary, we have the honour on behalf
of our governments to request you to call an urgent
meeting of the Security Council this afternoon." President Entezam decided that it would be impossible to
collect eleven delegates before 5 p.m., and sent out a
call for that hour.

Word that the Security Council would sit in extraordinary session spread quickly through New York, and
to the world. It caused mounting excitement and hope,
not least of all in Hungary. Now at last, it seemed, the
UN would rise like an avenging angel and do something.

At 1:20 p.m. Radio Budapest came on the air with disturbing news. Most ominous of all was a second Nagy pro-

test to the Russians about the increasing stream of Soviet
troops entering Hungary. Nagy pressed, with mounting urgency, for their immediate evacuation. He sent a second
appeal to the United Nations.

This second Nagy appeal came more slowly. The direct telex circuit to Budapest no longer existed and,
anyway, Nagy now had a UN delegation that he could
trust—or so he believed. But the message was not urgently handled, and again it did not reach most delegates until late that night.

This second appeal, again direct from Nagy to Hammerskjold, recalled that in yesterday's appeal he had reported new Soviet troops entering Hungary. "[Today]
further and exact information . . . reached the government . . . that large Soviet military units crossed the
border, marching towards Budapest." He described some
of the troop movements and said: "On the basis of the
above-mentioned facts, the Hungarian government
deemed it necessary to inform the USSR and all the
other diplomatic missions in Budapest about these steps
directed against our People's Republic." Nagy said he
had made concrete proposals to the Russians about withdrawing their troops, had suggested a place for negotiations on the subject, and named the Hungarian negotiators. "I request Your Excellency to call upon the
Great Powers to recognize the neutrality of Hungary,
and ask the Security Council to instruct the Soviet and
Hungarian Governments to start the negotiations immediately."

Tension increased in the UN building as the afternoon drew towards 5 p.m., when the Council would
meet. No one, of course, expected the Council to take
any real action, because of the sure Soviet veto. But it
could clear the track for real action, by voting on a
resolution, having it vetoed, then voting the "end-run"
strategy to transfer the matter into the Assembly. Delegates and informed correspondents were certain that it
was what Henry Cabot Lodge of America would do: he
would be carrying the ball since Britain and France
were still in Coventry over Suez.

Lodge's way was clear. He needed only seven Council votes for the end-run play, and he was absolutely sure of at least eight: the United States, Britain, France, Australia, Belgium, China, Cuba, and Peru.

Promptly at 5 p.m. in New York the Council met in extraordinary session, and immediately fell into an hour-long legalistic argument about the rights of Janos Szabo of Hungary, who had been invited to attend as a guest. This argument, begun by China and the United States, grew quite involved. Did Szabo really represent Hungary? If so, should he be allowed to speak? And, if so, should he speak before or after the regular Council members spoke?

Mr. Hammerskjold was not himself present, being busy with Suez, but was represented by his Under Secretary General, Protitch.

The Council asked Protitch whether the Secretariat thought that Szabo was entitled to represent Hungary. He replied that it had only Szabo's word for it, and added: "We have not yet officially received in the Secretariat any particular information on any credentials from the Hungarian government itself." One of his aides leaned over to whisper to Protitch, and the Under Secretary seemed taken aback. He rose to make a correction: "I have just been informed by the Legal Office that a cable has been received from the Hungarian Government appointing Dr. Janos Szabo at the emergency session of the General Assembly yesterday." It was obviously the first time that the Under Secretary General had heard of this cable, which had arrived nearly 30 hours before.

As the debate on Szabo continued, even Henry Cabot Lodge, who had helped to start it, grew bored. He asked dryly: "Is it in order now to begin talking about the situation in Hungary?" "No," said President Entezam, "it is too early."

In Hungary it seemed very late. At almost the moment Entezam spoke, Soviet bombers, flying from Russia, touched down on the Hungarian airfields of Kecskemet and Szeged. In the darkness, ever more Russian troops came in, and not only from Russia itself. They came also from Ruma-

nia, and Hungarian watchers could see Rumanian roads
jammed for several kilometers with troops waiting their
turn. Russian railways were so choked that some troops
were routed via Czechoslovakia, and began pouring into
Hungary over the Danube bridge at Komarom. In nearly
the whole of eastern Hungary, all railway lines were now
commandeered by the Russian Army.

About this hour, too, the American diplomatic convoy,
turned back by the Russians, reached Budapest again. By
this time, also, the new American Minister, Wailes, had
finally reached his post and was trying furiously to find
out what the situation was.

In New York the arguments about Szabo at last sub-
sided (he could speak only after any Council member
who wished had spoken) and Henry Cabot Lodge rose
to his feet. He began a long and spirited speech which,
on the surface, seemed exactly what the Hungarians
were waiting for. He made a graceful reference to Louis
Kossuth, the great Hungarian freedom fighter of 1849,
who had been defeated by Russian and Austrian arms,
and had come to America in 1851, seeking help for his
country. (Kossuth had been received in America with
universal, almost hysterical adoration and was com-
mended to Congress in a special message by President
Fillmore. But he left America seven months later, having received not an ounce of real help for Hungary.) As
Lodge continued, the Cassandra Club, the press galleries,
and many delegates looked puzzled. It was an excellent
speech, but where was the resolution he was supposed
to introduce, to bring matters to a head, and pass them
to the Assembly?

It neared adjournment time, and the question arose
about when the Council should meet again—always a
good test of the degree of urgency with which various
delegates view the situation. President Entezam seemed
in no hurry at all; he suggested that next Monday, November 5—three days away—would be soon enough. Immediately delegates from many countries protested that
affairs in Hungary were too urgent to lie over so long.
Cuba suggested that it was dangerous to delay later than
3 p.m. tomorrow, November 3. Nobody objected, and

Nuñez-Portuondo's suggestion was adopted. The session adjourned at 8:50 p.m.

NOVEMBER 3

In Hungary, the students of Sopron University looked up, stricken, from the commandeered radios that formed their impromptu listening post. "Nothing!" one student whispered, as if unable to believe his ears. "Nothing! Not even a resolution!"

All over Hungary the Soviet Army was on the move this night, their noises partly cushioned by thick snow. A great mass of tanks and machine-gun units moved through Szolnok, steadily westward. Two hundred more tanks had been motionless for several days between Szolnok and Abony; now they too were in motion, westward. Russian infantry moved into Nagyrede almost silently, under cover of darkness. A steel ring of tanks moved up to surround the uranium center of Pecs.

The miners made plans to flood the precious uranium mines, so that the Russians could not use them. Within a few hours, they executed their plans to perfection.

About 4 a.m. (10 a.m. in Hungary) a report swept Budapest like wildfire, that a plane with 16 United Nations observers had just landed outside the city. It brought a surge of hope and caused even blacker disappointment when it proved to be utterly false.

About 6 a.m. (noon in Hungary) Nagy announced a new "streamlined" government, saying that 20 of his former ministers had "been relieved of their posts at their own request." In fact, some of them had been such old-line Communists that the insurgents no longer accepted them and, in a few cases, even prevented the so-called ministers from entering their own offices. Others among them, fearful of the gathering storm, were glad to leave the Nagy government while there was still time. The new 12-person government included only three Communists, and one of them was still Janos Kadar.

Also at 6 a.m. Hungarian and Soviet generals held their first meeting to work out plans for the total evacuation of all Russian troops from Hungary. Nagy himself attended part of this meeting. It seemed to be making smooth progress; the atmosphere was correct, almost cordial; the Soviet generals were accommodating. The complete Russian evacuation was taken for granted by both sides, and the only difference was the date on which it was to be completed. The Hungarians asked for December 30, the Russians held out for January 15 "for technical reasons." The Hungarians agreed that departing Russian soldiers would be treated with full ceremonial, including military music by Hungarian bands for the last units to leave. The Hungarians also agreed to rebuild and maintain Soviet war memorials damaged in the revolution—although the destroyed Stalin statue in Budapest was tacitly omitted.

When this session ended, the negotiators agreed to hold a second meeting that night at 4 p.m. (10 p.m. Budapest time) to iron out further details. The Russians, headed by General Malinin, suggested that since the first meeting had been at the Hungarian Parliament building, the second should be at Soviet military headquarters, at Tokol, on the outskirts of Budapest. He pointed out that from there he had a direct telephone line to Moscow, a useful matter for the negotiations. The hopeful Hungarian negotiators, led by Major General Pal Maleter, a hero of the revolution and now Minister of Defense, agreed.

By 7 a.m. strong Russian forces occupied the road junction at Gyor, and now even the road to Sopron was cut. The Russians told Hungarians in Gyor that they had been traveling steadily for 600 kilometers. Now all the borders with the West were held by Russian troops, except the small bulge of Sopron, and the neck of this bulge was in Russian hands, which sealed it off from the rest of Hungary.

In Washington at 7 a.m., John Foster Dulles awoke with very sharp abdominal pains. He was taken at once to Walter Reed Hospital, and would be operated on at 1:35 p.m. for a cancerous condition. Thus, at this critical hour, the Department of State lost its chief, and the direction of affairs fell to Under Secretary Herbert Hoover, Jr. Supreme control remained, of course, in the hands of President Eisenhower, who in less than 75 hours would go before the voters, seeking re-election.

Nothing of moment happened in New York this last

morning of Hungarian freedom. In the United Nations attention was centered on what was expected to be the climactic Assembly session on Suez, to begin this evening. It was expected to vote into existence a special force of UN troops to be rushed to Egypt.

At 3 p.m., thanks to the insistence of Cuba yesterday, the Security Council met again about Hungary. At last the United States introduced its long-awaited resolution. *Fifty of the fifty-eight hours were gone now.*

Hardly had the Council come to order when Brilej of Yugoslavia moved for adjournment! He argued that since Hungary and Russia seemed to be negotiating now, the Council should not interfere, but should wait to see how the negotiations worked out.... "We believe," Lodge said hopefully, "that adjournment for a day or two would give a real opportunity to the Hungarian government to carry out its announced desire to arrange for an orderly and immediate evacuation of all Soviet troops." No other Western delegate shared Lodge's optimism about Russian good faith. Said Walker of Australia: "Unfortunately, the world has had some experience of the course that 'negotiations' sometimes take in a country where the Soviet Union has been able to establish military supremacy."

Sir Pierson Dixon of Britain said: "It would be quite wrong, misleading, and unfair to the Hungarian people to take the comfortable view, as the representative of Yugoslavia seems to do, that we can now safely leave the Hungarian question to settle itself." He urged the immediate passage of the United States resolution and concluded: "I do not frankly see how the Council can do less."

De Guiringaud of France joined in, with all-too-accurate prophecy: "We have not only the right but the duty to find out whether [these Russian troop movements] are not rather a re-grouping of Soviet forces so that they will be able to intervene with such suddenness as to make possible the establishment of a régime to the liking of the Soviet Union."

As de Guiringaud spoke, events in Hungary were confirming his fears. For the last hour, Hungarian outposts on all

the major roads near Budapest had been telephoning in
alarm to the Ministry of Defense. They reported that hundreds of Soviet tanks were moving slowly and steadily toward Budapest, and asked permission to fire on them.
"No," answered the Ministry, to dozens of such requests.
"Do not fire." Nagy had given the strictest orders that no
Hungarian would fire the first shot. He still had a for-
lorn and fading hope—there seemed no other—that the
Tokol negotiations might produce a miracle. Thus the
tanks moved on, nearing the outskirts of the capital,
watched by anguished and helpless Hungarians.

In New York . . . Janos Szabo of Hungary sat impassive, having said almost nothing. But at last, about 4
p.m., several delegates asked Szabo to tell the Council
officially whether or not there were really serious negotiations going on in Hungary. Yes, Szabo replied, there
were. "I should like to inform the Council with satisfaction about the following promising information received from Hungary today: The leaders of the Hungarian and Soviet armies met at noon today (Budapest
time) and both parties expressed their views on the technical questions of withdrawing the Soviet troops. They
agreed that they would study the proposals of each other,
and they would meet again at 10 o'clock tonight, Budapest time."

It was now that hour—10 p.m. in Budapest. General Maleter and his Hungarian negotiators arrived promptly at the
Russian HQ in Tokol. Apparently some negotiations were
carried on, and the Hungarians had a direct telephone line
back to Nagy's office in Budapest proper. Soon the Russian leader, General Malinin, suggested that they should
all have something to eat and drink, and he led the way
to the banquet. Shortly after this, the telephone link to
Budapest was abruptly cut. This alarmed Nagy and the
military commander at Budapest, General Bela Kiraly. The
latter ordered patrols to move out towards Tokol to see
what was wrong. The patrols never returned.

In the UN, having heard Szabo's report about the
negotiations, delegates were eager to hear a more authoritative source: Arkady Sobolev of Russia. Usually Sobo-

lev is voluble in obstruction, but during this session he said hardly a word. Delegates asked, prodded, even taunted him to say something about these famous negotiations. "I think we really must hear him," said Dixon of Britain. Walker of Australia observed: "It seems that the absence of any comment from him would be rather ominous." At last, about 6 p.m., Sobolev was goaded into making his only statement of the evening, and one of the shortest he has ever made. In English translation it takes only 51 words, and its crux was: "I can confirm that such negotiations are in progress."

At almost the same moment Sobolev spoke in New York a short man in uniform without rank markings suddenly entered the room at Soviet headquarters, interrupting the banquet for the Hungarian negotiators. The host, General Malinin, seemed indignant at the interruption. The visitor whispered something in his ear. Malinin shrugged his shoulders, then ordered his own negotiators to leave the room. The mysterious visitor had identified himself as General Ivan Serov, the notorious chief of Soviet security. He and his men immediately seized all the Hungarians.

In New York there was still no vote on the American resolution, and de Guiringaud of France wondered "why, in this case, the draft resolution is not being put to a vote?" Other nations asked the same question. President Entezam announced that this session must end quite soon, because the Assembly was to meet at 8 p.m. about Suez. This raised immediate protest from the delegations of China, Australia, France, and Britain—but America did not join them. The other nations argued that the Council could go on meeting on Hungary, even while the Assembly discussed Suez. They offered to split their delegations, and thus hold simultaneous meetings. They got no support from the United States, and the proposals were dropped.

Again came the question: when to meet again. President Entezam still said that next Monday, November 5, at 10:30 a.m. would be soon enough. Again there were many protests that this was too late—and again no protest from the United States. Australia suggested that things in Hungary were desperate, and wanted to meet not later than tomorrow, Sunday, November 4, at 5 p.m. Sighing, Entezam put this to a vote. Only he and Lodge voted against it—and thus for further delay. But Peru, Russia, and Yugoslavia had abstained; thus the Australian proposal did not get the necessary seven votes, and failed. Entezam's idea of next Monday was then adopted, Australia abstaining till the last. And Walker of Australia, joined by de Guiringaud of France, rose immediately to say that if anything came up before Monday, they reserved the right to have the Council meet sooner. Certainly, agreed Entezam. All too soon, they were to remember this.

The Council adjourned at 6:55 p.m. Again it had achieved nothing. Again the long-expected "end-run" into the Assembly had not materialized. As the delegates left the hall, they had had their last chance to act.

Less than four hours were left now.

The Council delegates ate a hasty dinner and then hurried to the session of the General Assembly, which began at 8 p.m.—on Suez.

> At this hour, great masses of Soviet armor were already inside Budapest. One strong column advanced from the south, along the Danube, and had already invested the important Soroksari Avenue. This cut off Csepel Island, the heart of Hungarian industry, packed with intrepid workmen who had done so much of the freedom fighting, from the inner capital. Another great column moved into the city from the north, along Vaci Avenue. Still, not a shot had been fired yet.

NOVEMBER 4

In New York, the Assembly rang with some of the bitterest speeches ever heard on the East River. Speaker after speaker denounced "this bloody, brutal, premeditated armed attack" . . . "the furious frenzy of a monster unchained" . . . "this hideous crime of aggression. . . ." All this invective, however, had nothing to do with Hungary. It was aimed solely at Britain, France, and Israel, for their actions in Suez. And it was while this great debate swept on that

The clock struck in Hungary.

At 10:24 p.m. (4:24 a.m. in Budapest, November 4) the first Russian shot was fired in the great counterattack. Soviet guns opened up against Hungarian barracks on Budaorsi Avenue. Immediately, cannon fire broke out all over the city, and the Hungarians began to fight back, fiercely.

New York learned nothing of this for another hour and 25 minutes. Meanwhile, the storm about Suez raged. Arkady Sobolev of Russia seemed especially indignant about Anglo-French actions in Egypt. Gone was his reticence of a few hours before, in the Security Council. In a long speech, he accused the British and French of "barbarity" and of "sowing death among the peaceful inhabitants, among women and children," and of "wilfully ignoring the United Nations."

At 11:05 p.m. (5:05 in Hungary) a strange voice came from a strange radio transmitter in Hungary. It was the voice of Ferenc Munnich, an old-line communist recently dismissed from the Nagy cabinet. It announced the formation of the puppet Kadar government, known as the "Hungarian Revolutionary Worker-Peasant Government." Munnich asserted that Kadar, he, and two others had parted ways with the Nagy government on November 1. The new régime asked for Russian armed help in fighting "fascism and reaction and its murderous bands."

Even this telling announcement attracted little attention in the West, for it was not widely heard. It was broadcast from Szolnok, a Hungarian city about 65 miles southeast of Budapest, already in Russian hands. It came on a wave length of 1187 kilocycles, a wave length normally used by the Balaton-Szabadi transmitter far away in the west of Hungary. It was a second Hungarian broadcast, five minutes later, that really broke the news to the world.

At 11:20 p.m. (5:20 a.m. in Hungary, November 4) Radio Budapest came on the air in great excitement. "Attention! Attention! Premier Imre Nagy will address the Hungarian people!" A moment later came the Prime Minister's shaken voice. "This is Premier Imre Nagy speaking. Today at daybreak, Soviet troops attacked our capital with the obvious intent of overthrowing the legal democratic Hungarian government. Our troops are in combat; the government is at its post. I notify the people of our country and the entire world of this fact." This was repeated every five minutes, in German, French, and English, interspersed with the Hungarian national anthem.

The horrifying news came quickly to New York. At 11:49 p.m. the Reuters teleprinters in the UN building tapped out a bulletin from its Vienna office. The news spread swiftly; delegates went about with thoughtful, stricken faces. In the Assembly the debate droned on, about Suez. About 12:30 a.m. (it was now November 4 in New York, too) an agonized group of Hungarians in exile, headed by Monsignor Bela Varga, insisted on seeing Lodge. They were told that he was busy; they persisted and, in their desperation, a minor scuffle followed with a junior American official. UN guards came up to remove the Hungarians.

In the Western camp there were consternation, heartache, and guilt. The worst fears of the Cassandra Club had been justified, but it was no time for I-told-you-so's. Walker of Australia went to Lodge and said: "What are we going to do about this?" He suggested a Council meeting the following afternoon—about 15 hours later. But Walker had had enough delay. He said, in effect: "We have already waited too long. We are probably too late now, but we cannot wait any longer." He proposed, and Lodge finally agreed, that the Council should have a special session this same night—or, technically, morning.

About 1 a.m. Walker interrupted the Assembly debate on Suez and, on a point of order, brought the first official news of the Russian attack. He read aloud the Reuters bulletin, in grim tones, and then said: " . . . In view of this news, I am now asking the President of the Security Council to invite the members of the Council to meet with him within half an hour in his office for a consultation regarding the next steps—and the immediate steps, I trust—to be taken by the Security Council."

About 20 minutes later, Lodge also rose on a point of order, to repeat substantially what Walker had already said, except that he quoted an American news agency, the Associated Press, and added the news that the American Legation in Budapest was under fire, its staff sheltering in the basement.

Lodge was shaking with indignation, perhaps the special indignation of optimism betrayed. "And I sat here," he said, white-faced, "and heard the representative of the Soviet Union talking about stopping bloodshed in Egypt. Heaven knows I want to stop bloodshed in Egypt, but I think there is a cynicism about the Soviet Union representative talking about it at the very moment when they were shedding blood in Budapest. This will horrify everybody who knows about it.

"When I saw the first press dispatches, I immediately asked for a meeting of the Security Council, and I was very glad to learn that it will be called soon. I simply wish to say in this great General Assembly of the United Nations how much our hearts go out to the people of Hungary, and with how much warmth and feeling we think of them, and wish for them a happy issue out of their trials, and a future of independence."

To continue the chronology further is hardly worth while. The Assembly adjourned at 3 a.m. and the special Council session opened five minutes later. It was short, bitter, and now completely useless. With indignation spurring him now to true urgency, Lodge rammed through in only two hours the "end-run" tactics he had been expected to use two days before. Only Russia opposed it, and it was voted over to the Assembly, 10–1. The Assembly met Sunday afternoon at last—its first session on Hungary—and within four hours rushed through an American resolution condemning Russia, asking her to withdraw her troops at once. It passed by 50 votes to 8, with 15 nations abstaining.

But it was far too late now. The fifty-eight hours had run out; the clock had struck; the deed was done.

DOUBLE STANDARD OF MORALS

I arrived at the Headquarters of the United Nations more than two months ago as the only legal representative of the Imre Nagy Government. I requested on several occasions a hearing by the pertinent organs of the United Nations so that I might justify the appeal made by Mr. [Imre] Nagy to the United Nations and ask for action on this appeal. We have waited with great patience for this occasion and during this time of waiting the oppression of our small country continues. By armed force a group has been put into power which has no legal right to consider itself Hungary's Government....

This period of waiting has meant, for the Hungarian people, a great deal of suffering, the deportation of the country's youth, the flight en masse of thousands to escape deportation, the terrible sentences — often the death sentence — passed against those who remained back home. . . .

All this damage, all this suffering would have been avoided, in our opinion, if the United Nations had heeded in time the appeal of the Imre Nagy Government and had taken appropriate action. Such action was all the more necessary because the Hungarian question does not concern Hungary alone. It raises in the United Nations the question of whether a Great Power which is a Member of the United Nations and has accepted the obligations of the Charter has the right to use arms to force a small country, also a Member of the United Nations, to accept a political and economic order it does not want.

. . . The United Nations was formed as a bulwark against dictatorships. If it cannot be maintained as such — if the United Nations cannot ensure that small countries will have the same rights as the big countries—the United Nations has no raison d'être, and the consequences cannot be other than the bellum omnium contra omnes (nations all warring with each other). This, in the epoch of atomic and hydrogen bombs, would mean the extermination of the world. If the task assigned to it cannot be carried out by the United Nations, it will be succeeded by the horrors of the Apocalypse. . . .

Madame Anna Kéthly, before the United Nations Special Committee on the Problem of Hungary, January 28, 1957.

THE UNITED NATIONS ON THE IMRE NAGY CASE

Acting Rapporteur: Dr. E. Ronald Walker of
Australia. New York, New York, July 14, 1958.

I

1. As defined by resolution 1132 (XI) of the General
Assembly of the United Nations on 10 January 1957, the
functions of the Special Committee on the Problem of
Hungary were to collect "the fullest and best available
information regarding the situation created by the intervention of the Union of Soviet Socialist Republics,
through its use of armed force and other means, in the
internal affairs of Hungary, as well as regarding developments relating to the recommendations of the General
Assembly on this subject." The Special Committee was
instructed to report its findings to the General Assembly
"at its eleventh session, and thereafter from time to time
to prepare additional reports for the information of
Member States and the General Assembly if it is in
session."

2. In pursuance of its functions, the Committee submitted a first Interim Report on 20 February 1957.[1] A
fuller report was submitted on 12 June 1957[2] and endorsed by the General Assembly by resolution 1133 (XI)
adopted at the resumed meetings of its eleventh session,
on 14 September 1957.

[1] A/3546.
[2] *General Assembly Official Records, Eleventh Session, Supplement* No. 18 (A/3592).

3. In its main Report, the Committee dealt with all aspects of the intervention of the Union of Soviet Socialist Republics in Hungary, by armed force and by other means, and the effects of that intervention on political developments and on the observance of human rights and fundamental freedoms in Hungary. Among the actions by Soviet forces on Hungarian territory which the Report related was the arrest of General Pal Maleter and the abduction of Premier Imre Nagy and his companions. Reference was also made to official Hungarian announcements of many arrests and trials of persons having participated in the uprising and to unofficial reports of secret trials and executions.

4. In view in particular of continued reports from Hungary of completed or contemplated trials of participants in the uprising, the Committee had thought it necessary to keep under review such reliable information as can be obtained concerning developments falling within its terms of reference.

5. On the night of 16 June 1958, the world learnt that Imre Nagy, Pal Maleter, and two of their associates had been executed by the Hungarian Government.[3] The Committee met as a matter of urgency and issued on 21 June a communiqué deploring these tragic events.[4] After further consideration of the available information, the Committee decided to prepare a special report to bring to the attention of the United Nations the circumstances of these executions, which have evoked expressions of profound indignation from leading figures and many organized groups, as well as numerous individuals, in many countries. The Committee also considered several proposals submitted by its members,

[3] An English translation of the relevant communiqué was issued by the Permanent Mission of the Hungarian People's Republic to the United Nations on 18 June 1958. The announcement of the trial and execution was made by the Hungarian Ministry of Justice, broadcast originally by Budapest Radio, Home Service, 16 June, 2300 hrs. GMT, and was carried by the Moscow Radio, Home Service, 17 June, 0830 hrs. GMT. The communiqué was published in the 17 June issue of *Nepszabadsag*, and was carried on the same day in the Soviet newspapers *Pravda* and *Izvestia*.

[4] Annex I.

which have been recorded in the Committee's records.

6. The Committee informed Prince Wan Waithaya-kon, the Special Representative of the General Assembly on the Hungarian Problem, of its action and received the following reply:

> "I warmly appreciate excellent communiqué issued by Special Committee which has received wholehearted approval throughout the world. After careful reflection I am of opinion that Special Committee is doing the right thing in collecting more information for report to General Assembly which alone can determine further action."

II

7. The Special Committee recalls that from the beginning of its activities it has spared no pains to obtain the fullest and most authentic information on the questions which the General Assembly charged it to investigate. For this purpose, it has made repeated approaches to the Hungarian authorities, who were obviously in the position to provide facts germane to its inquiry. It has also applied to the Governments of the Union of Soviet Socialist Republics and of Rumania, but none of these Governments has co-operated with it in any respect.

8. The Governments referred to have throughout maintained that the Committee is illegal and its activities contrary to the provisions of the Charter, particularly to paragraph 7 of Article 2. This view was, however, decisively rejected by the General Assembly when, on 10 January 1957, it created the Committee by a vote of 59 to 8, with 10 abstentions, and again rejected on 14 September 1957, when the General Assembly endorsed the Committee's report by 60 votes to 10, with 10 abstentions. On the former occasion, the General Assembly called upon the USSR and Hungary, as well as all other Member States, to assist the Committee in its task; on the latter occasion, the General Assembly expressed its regret that "the Union of Soviet Socialist Republics and the present authorities in Hungary have failed to co-operate in any way with the Committee."[5]

[5] Resolution 1133 (XI) of 14 September 1957.

9. It should be recalled that, with a view to obtaining such co-operation from these Governments, the following steps have been taken:

(a) On 25 January 1957, in communicating the text of resolution 1132(XI) to the Governments of the USSR and Hungary, the Secretary General drew their attention to the paragraph in which the General Assembly called on those Governments to permit the Committee and its staff to enter Hungary and to extend all appropriate co-operation to them. This request was rejected.[6]

(b) On 14 March 1957, the Committee requested the Government of the Rumanian People's Republic to enable it to meet Imre Nagy, as the evidence of Mr. Nagy who, as Prime Minister of Hungary, had appealed to the Security Council, would be of outstanding importance. Its request was rejected.[7]

(c) On 19 March 1957, the Secretary General transmitted to the Permanent Mission of Hungary a copy of a letter from the Chairman of the Special Committee, saying that it was the Committee's expectation that the authorities concerned would reconsider their previous position and enable it to conduct the necessary investigation in Hungary. The Hungarian Government maintained its previous position.[8]

(d) On 20 December 1957, the Chairman of the Special Committee wrote to the Minister of Foreign Affairs of Hungary asking for information about the reports of trials alleged to be proceeding in Hungary against participants in the 1956 uprising, including General Maleter and Colonel Kopacsi. The Permanent Representative of Hungary refused to transmit this letter to his Government.[9]

10. Following an appeal by the Committee to interested Governments on 21 June 1958 to make available to it any information at their disposal regarding the arrest, trial and execution of Imre Nagy, Pal Maleter

---

[6] Report of the Special Committee on the Problem of Hungary (A/3592), para. 32.

[7] Report of the Special Committee on the Problem of Hungary (A/3592), para. 34.

[8] Ibid., para. 33.

[9] Annex II.

and their companions, the Committee addressed letters
to the Foreign Ministers of Hungary, Rumania and the
Union of Soviet Socialist Republics, asking for specific
information regarding these matters. These Governments have refused to accept the Committee's letters.[10]
In the face of the Hungarian Government's refusal to
make fuller information available, the Committee has
concentrated in this present report on Hungarian Government official texts and communiqués, and on reports
in officially licensed Hungarian newspapers and broadcasts of statements by Hungarian Ministers, high officials
and Party leaders.

III

11. The communiqué issued by the Hungarian Ministry of Justice and published in Budapest and Moscow
on the night of 16–17 June 1958[11] announcing that death
sentences had been pronounced and carried out against
Imre Nagy, Pal Maleter, Miklos Gimes, and Jozsef Szilagyi also stated that Sandor Kopacsi had been sentenced
to life imprisonment, Ferenc Donath to twelve years'
imprisonment, Ferenc Janosi to eight years, Zoltan Tildy
to six years, and Miklos Vasarhelyi to five years. Imre
Nagy, Pal Maleter, Ferenc Donath, Miklos Gimes, Zoltan Tildy, Sandor Kopacsi, Jozsef Szilagyi, Ferenc Janosi and Miklos Vasarhelyi had been charged with the
"crime of having formed an organization aimed at
overthrowing the Hungarian People's Democratic State
order." In addition, Imre Nagy had been accused of
"treason," and Sandor Kopacsi and Pal Maleter of
"mutiny."[12]

[10] Copies of the letters and of the replies from the Permanent
Representatives of these three Governments are in Annex III.

[11] See footnote 3.

[12] Zoltan Tildy, an ordained Minister in the Reformed Evangelical Church, was Prime Minister of Hungary in 1945 and became the first President of the Republic in 1946. Sandor Kopacsi
was head of the Budapest Police between 1952 and 1956. Ferenc
Donath, Miklos Gimes and Miklos Vasarhelyi were journalists, and
Jozsef Szilagyi, a writer; all four were close political associates of
Imre Nagy. Ferenc Janosi, the son-in-law of Mr. Nagy, was an
ordained Minister of the Reformed Evangelical Church, and also
held several government posts.

12. The Special Committee, as noted earlier, found that General Maleter was arrested on 3 November 1956 in the Soviet Headquarters at Tököl on Csepel Island, where, as Minister of Defence in the Nagy Government, he was leading the Hungarian military delegation,[13] which was negotiating with the Soviet Command, in which capacity he was entitled to special protection accorded under the recognized principles of international law. It should be noted that at the meeting of the Security Council on 3 November 1956, the representatives of Hungary declared, and the representative of the USSR confirmed, that these negotiations were taking place.[14]

13. The Committee also examined the circumstances in which Imre Nagy and his party were abducted by Soviet military personnel on 22 November 1956, after they left the Yugoslav Embassy in Budapest, where they had been granted asylum.[15] They did so under a promise of safe conduct and immunity given by Mr. Kadar, in his capacity as Chairman of the Council of Ministers, in a letter addressed to the Government of the Federal People's Republic of Yugoslavia on 21 November 1956. Mr. Kadar stated:

> "In the interest of terminating the matter, the Hungarian Government, agreeing to the proposals contained on page 3, section 8 of the letter of 18 November 1956 addressed to me by the Yugoslav Government, hereby confirms in writing its verbal declaration that it does not desire to apply sanctions against Imre Nagy and the members of his group for their past activities. We take note that the asylum extended to the group will hereby come to an end and that they themselves will leave the Yugoslav Embassy and proceed freely to their homes."[16]

14. On 23 November 1956, the day following Mr. Nagy's abduction, a Hungarian Government communiqué announced that he and some of his party had

---

[13] *Report of the Special Committee on the Problem of Hungary* (A/3592), para. 290.

[14] S/PV. 753, paras. 62 and 132.

[15] *Report of the Special Committee on the Problem of Hungary* (A/3592), paras. 80-82 and 630-639.

[16] TANJUG, 28 November 1956.

gone to Rumania, in accordance with a request they had submitted previously.[17]

15. The Yugoslav Government on 24 November 1956 lodged a protest with the Hungarian Government against the violation of the written agreement guaranteeing the safety of Mr. Nagy and his companions. The note also stated that Mr. Nagy had rejected an offer to go to Rumania, which had been made to him while he was still on the Embassy premises.[18]

16. A statement made by the Foreign Minister of Rumania at the General Assembly on 3 December 1956 may be recalled in connection with the assurances given to the Yugoslav Government by Mr. Kadar. On that occasion, Mr. Preoteasa stated that, on being approached by the Government of Hungary with reference to Mr. Nagy, the Rumanian Government "gave the assurance that the stay of the group in Rumania would be marked by all the rules of hospitality and that all necessary steps would be taken to guarantee the personal safety of Mr. Nagy and his friends. Similarly, the Rumanian Government gave the assurance that it would observe the international rules relating to political asylum."[19]

17. The Committee recalls the efforts it made in March 1957 to obtain the assistance of the Rumanian Government to enable it to meet Imre Nagy.[20] The Committee notes that the circumstances in which Mr. Nagy subsequently departed from Rumania have never been revealed. Indeed, the first official indication of his having been brought back to Hungary was given after the announcement of his execution.

18. It is significant that a number of references to Imre Nagy were made by Mr. Kadar while Mr. Nagy was still in the Yugoslav Embassy and during the first days of his detention in Rumania, in which Mr. Kadar gave assurances to the effect that his Government was not intending to prosecute Mr. Nagy for his part in the

[17] *Report of the Special Committee on the Problem of Hungary* (A/3592), para. 638.
[18] TANJUG, 24 November 1956.
[19] A/PV. 605, para. 202.
[20] See para. 9 (b) above.

uprising. On 11 November 1956, Mr. Kadar declared:

> "I, who have myself been a member of Nagy's Government, hereby state that according to the best of my knowledge, neither Imre Nagy nor his political group has willingly supported the counter-revolution."[21]

On 14 November 1956, Mr. Kadar told a delegation of Hungarian workers that he did not believe that Imre Nagy had deliberately and willingly helped the "counter-revolution." Rather, he had been carried away by events. "Imre Nagy is not under arrest," he added. "He left the Parliament Building of his own free will and neither the Government nor the Soviet troops wish to restrict his freedom of movement. It depends entirely on him whether or not he participates in politics."[22] On 27 November 1956, Mr. Kadar declared:

> "We have promised not to start any punitive proceedings against Imre Nagy, and we shall keep our word."[23]

19. In March 1957, however, speaking in the Kremlin, Mr. Kadar accused Mr. Nagy of not only undermining the Party from within, but of preparing its destruction from without, in alliance with the dark forces of reaction.[24] Attacks on Nagy reached a new intensity in December 1957, when volume IV of the *Hungarian White Book* stated that he "violated his oath of office, and instead of defending constitutional order, he exploited his post of Prime Minister to uphold the attempt at the violent overthrow of constitutional order."[25] Other denunciations of Imre Nagy that month were made before the Academy of Sciences, by Dezso Nemes, editor of *Nepszabadsag*,[26] and before the National Assembly, by the Chief Public Prosecutor, Geza Szenasi.[27]

---

[21] Budapest Radio, 11 November 1956, 1000 hrs. GMT.
[22] *Nepszabadsag*, 14 November 1956.
[23] *Nepszabadsag*, 27 November 1956.
[24] *Nepszabadsag*, 28, March 1957.
[25] *The Counter-Revolutionary Forces in the October Events in Hungary*, Volume IV. Published by the Information Bureau of the Council of Ministers of the Hungarian People's Republic [Budapest, 1957], page 90.
[26] *Tarsadalmi Szemle*, January 1958, pages 44-59.
[27] *Nepszabadsag*, 22 December 1957.

20. On 12 June 1958, in a front-page article, Mr. Kadar spoke contemptuously of "characters like Imre Nagy, who fell into the quagmire of treason."[28] Four days later came the announcement in Budapest and Moscow that Imre Nagy had been sentenced to death and executed.

21. Following this announcement, the Yugoslav Ambassador in Budapest, on 24 June 1958, handed a note of protest to the Hungarian Foreign Ministry.[29] "The Yugoslav Government, and our people," declared the note, "have received the sudden news about the secret trial and the execution of Imre Nagy with profound indignation." The Yugoslav note of protest recalled the exchange of letters between the Yugoslav and Hungarian Governments on 18 and 21 November 1956. In them, agreement was reached on the question of the asylum of Imre Nagy and other persons given asylum in the Yugoslav Embassy in Budapest, by which the Hungarian Government guaranteed their personal security and free departure to their homes immediately after leaving the Yugoslav Embassy building and undertook that "it would not apply any sanctions against them for their activities." The note of 24 June also revealed that the Yugoslav Government had protested on 24 November 1956 to the Hungarian Government that this agreement had not been implemented, and that the Hungarian Government, by its reply of 1 December 1956, had rejected the Yugoslav protest. The Hungarian Government asserted in its reply that the fact that the persons concerned had not returned to their homes was "a secondary question of technical importance," and that it was otherwise keeping to the obligations of the agreement. It reaffirmed that it was prepared to guarantee their personal security and declared that "it did not intend to punish them for their past activities." The Yugoslav note of 24 June 1958 added that:

> "It is obvious that the Government of the Hungarian People's Republic has on two occasions harshly offended the obligation it gave to the Government of the Federal

28 *Nepszabadsag*, 12 June 1958.
29 TANJUG, 24 June 1958.

People's Republic of Yugoslavia: by not making possible the free return of Imre Nagy and other persons to their homes, but instead sending them to the Rumanian People's Republic for a compulsory stay; and by the fact that, contrary to the given guarantees regarding personal security and impunity because of their past action, it brought some of these persons to a secret trial, and sentenced Nagy and some of his companions to death, which punishment was executed. . . ."

IV

22. The execution of Imre Nagy and his companions has special significance because Mr. Nagy, as the Prime Minister of the Government of Hungary (of which Mr. Kadar was also a member) had appealed directly to the United Nations on 1 and 2 November 1956.[30] The fate of Imre Nagy, however, should not be allowed to distract attention from the fact that since the intervention by Soviet armed forces on 4 November 1956, many other sentences have been officially announced concerning persons accused of being connected with the 1956 uprising. It cannot, however, be taken for granted that all sentences have been published. Most of the victims have no famous name to bring their sufferings to the notice of the world. A list of sentences announced by the Hungarian Government-licensed press and radio and all apparently referring to persons associated with the 1956 uprising, is submitted in an annex to this report.[31] From this list, it appears that at least thirty persons were sentenced to death between 20 June 1957, the date of publication of the Committee's main Report, and 21 June 1958.[32]

23. In addition to these officially announced sentences, many reports have been received from unofficial sources of trials now under way or contemplated. Among the many names mentioned in such unofficial reports are

[30] *Report of the Special Committee on the Problem of Hungary* (A/3592), para. 326.

[31] Annex IV.

[32] This figure is additional to the thirty-one death sentences mentioned in the *Report of the Special Committee on the Problem of Hungary* (A/3592), para. 760.

those of Mrs. Laszlo Rajk, widow of the former Minister of Foreign Affairs executed in 1949 and later rehabilitated before the uprising of October 1956; Gabor Tanczos, former Secretary of the Petöfi Club, Peter Erdös, György Fazekas and Sandor Haraszti, prominent journalists; and Szilard Ujhelyi, a close associate of Mr. Nagy and former Director of the Hungarian Radio. Except for Mrs. Rajk, Peter Erdös and Szilard Ujhelyi, these persons were mentioned in the communiqué issued by the Hungarian Ministry of Justice as being associated with Imre Nagy and other condemned persons, on 16 June 1958. Although no confirmation by the Hungarian authorities is available, the Committee cannot ignore these reports, in view of the earlier circulation of similar unofficial reports regarding pending or current trials of Imre Nagy and Pal Maleter.

24. In its main Report, the Committee referred to the regime of "summary jurisdiction" prevailing in Hungary since November 1956.[33] No real alleviations have been introduced by the Decree-Laws of 15 June and 3 November 1957,[34] as to the sentences to be imposed or the summary procedures to be followed. Minimum sentences of five or ten years' imprisonment are still provided for; the majority of the members of the "People's Court" still consists of revokable appointees of political organs, whose names are not made public; the accused may still be obliged to select counsel from a list compiled by the Minister of Justice. The Committee's main Report also includes evidence regarding the methods by which so-called confessions have often been obtained from political prisoners accused of disloyalty to the regime.[35] The continued presence of foreign armed forces in Hungary is likely to prevent the expression of the feelings of the people against such procedures by the Hungarian Government. The presence of the Hungarian security police, whose activities were referred to

[33] *Report of the Special Committee on the Problem of Hungary* (A/3592), paras. 753-757.

[34] *Magyar Kozlony*, No. 66, 15 June 1957; No. 117, 3 November 1957.

[35] *Report of the Special Committee on the Problem of Hungary*, (A/3592), paras. 771-775.

in the main Report of the Committee, there being no evidence that this has changed, is an essential factor restricting the free expression of the people's feelings.

25. The Committee recalls that the Hungarian authorities failed to respond to the efforts made in 1957 by the Special Representative of the General Assembly, Prince Wan Waithayakon, to achieve the objectives of the United Nations, as set out in the relevant General Assembly resolutions.[36] The recent sentences are all the more disturbing because they came after a number of public assurances by Hungarian leaders that a period of stabilization had begun and that proceedings against persons accused of participating in the uprising were virtually over. Thus, on 1 April 1958, the Minister of Justice, Ferenc Nezval, speaking before the Legal and Judicial Committee of the National Assembly, declared that the "trials of provincial counter-revolutionary criminal cases are already concluded. The final liquidation of counter-revolution cases and a conclusion of trials may be expected soon."[37] Despite such assurances, unofficial reports of further trials and executions continue to be received.

V

26. In its examination of the circumstances surrounding the arrest of General Maleter and the abduction of Mr. Nagy, the Committee has emphasized that, in both cases, the action was taken by Soviet security personnel and not by members of the Hungarian armed forces or security police. The Warsaw Treaty of 14 May 1955 (which the Hungarian Government, under Imre Nagy, decided on 1 November 1956 to repudiate, as announced by their cablegram to the United Nations[38]) and the Hungarian-Soviet Agreement of 27 May 1957,[39] are invoked to justify the presence of Soviet forces in Hungary. Despite this, in September 1957, the General As-

[36] A/3774.

[37] *Esti Hirlap,* 2 April 1958.

[38] A/3251.

[39] *Report of the Special Committee on the Problem of Hungary* (A/3592), Annex A to Chap. VIII.

sembly, in resolution 1133 (XI), found that "The Union of Soviet Socialist Republics, in violation of the Charter of the United Nations, has deprived Hungary of its liberty and political independence," and reiterated its earlier resolutions calling for the withdrawal of Soviet armed forces. On 24 May 1958, Mr. Kadar announced the withdrawal of 17,000 Soviet troops from Hungary,[40] but gave no information as to the nature of the troops withdrawn or the troops that remained. Neither this announcement nor any other available evidence has enabled the Committee to conclude that there has been a complete withdrawal of Soviet armed forces, as urged by the General Assembly, and it is not contested that Soviet armed forces are still in Hungary.

27. While the arrest of General Maleter and the abduction of Mr. Nagy and his companions were undertaken by Soviet personnel, nevertheless, the Hungarian Government, in announcing the subsequent trials and executions, has accepted full responsibility. These secret trials and executions evidence continued disregard for the resolutions of the General Assembly and for human rights, as defined in the Universal Declaration of Human Rights and the Charter of the United Nations. Moreover, although Mr. Kadar is reported as recently as 1 July 1958 as having denied that the Hungarian Government had broken its word, the record clearly shows that the action of the Hungarian Government in bringing Imre Nagy to trial was contrary to solemn assurances, which Mr. Kadar, on behalf of the Hungarian Government had previously given, including those confirmed by letter to the Yugoslav Government.

28. The executions of Pal Maleter and Imre Nagy and their companions are striking, but unhappily not isolated, examples of the continued policy of repression carried out at the present time in Hungary in conditions described in this Report and the previous Report of the Committee.

29. In view of the continued prevalence of unofficial reports for further secret trials and executions, the Com-

[40] *Nepszabadsag,* 28 May 1958.

mittee expresses the hope that the Government of the Hungarian People's Republic, hearing the voice of public opinion in many countries, will cease carrying out new death sentences and, bringing to an end the present harsh repression, will effectively re-establish the inalienable principles of human rights. In view of these conclusions, and since the Committee cannot submit this Report to the General Assembly directly, in view of resolution 1132 (XI), it is transmitting it to the Governments of Member States for such purposes as they may deem appropriate in relation to measures that may be taken by the General Assembly or initiatives that may be undertaken by Governments in this matter.

VOROSHILOV ABOUT IMRE NAGY

During his visit at the Brussels (Belgium) World's Fair in 1958, stopping in front of the panoramic view of Budapest in the Hungarian pavillion, the then Soviet chief of state, Marshal Kliment Y. Voroshilov stated:

> What a beautiful city, what a beautiful country. But such foolish things have happened there. Some people have called it counter-revolution, some called it revolution. I think it was just foolishness... Here in the West they raised a big fuss because Imre Nagy was given too harsh a sentence. Perhaps it would have been possible not to give Imre Navy such a harsh sentence because he was just a fool. Nagy never helped us, never raised his finger to help us. He was not a real Communist...

New York Times, Aug. 14, 1958

SUMMARY OF
UNITED NATIONS ACTIONS

Compiled by László Varga

The action taken by the United Nations on the *"Situation in Hungary"* can be divided into six distinct phases:

1. PRELIMINARY ACTION by the Security Council (exclusive of the General Assembly), October 28-November 4, 1956. The Security Council, unable to act because of a Soviet veto, decided to summon the General Assembly into emergency session (invoking the "Uniting for Peace" resolution as provided in Chapter VII of the United Nations Charter).

2. EMERGENCY SESSION: November 4 and November 8-9, 1956.

3. REGULAR (ELEVENTH) SESSION: November 19-21, December 3-4, and December 10-12, 1956.

4. SPECIAL COMMITTEE ON HUNGARY: After several unsuccessful attempts to directly observe the situation on Hungarian soil, the Secretary General proposed, on January 5, 1957, the establishment of a Special Committee for continued observation of the Hungarian situation. The General Assembly selected and authorized a five member committee for this purpose on January 10, 1957.

5. DEBATE ON THE NAGY CASE: Following the official Hungarian announcement of the execution of Imre Nagy and his associates on June 17, 1958, the Special Committee immediately began a new investigation and issued its special report on July 14. The General Assembly put the Nagy case on the thirteenth session's agenda on September 22nd and discussed it on December 11-12.

6. SPECIAL REPRESENTATIVE: Accepting the special

report on the Nagy case, the General Assembly abolished the Special Committee on Hungary and nominated Sir Leslie Munro of New Zealand to report on "significant developments" in Hungary. Abolition of his office—the Secretary General takes over.

In all, the General Assembly passed twenty-five resolutions on Hungary between November 4, 1956 and February 8, 1963. Of these, thirteen were political, three humanitarian, one procedural, and eight dealt with the credentials of the Hungarian representatives.

PRELIMINARY ACTION

The first official word that the situation in Hungary was being brought to the attention of the United Nations came on the afternoon of Saturday, October 27, 1956.

Three permanent members of the Security Council—France, the United Kingdom and the United States—asked for an urgent meeting under Article 34 of the United Nations Charter, which empowers the Council to "investigate any dispute or any situation which might lead to international friction or give rise to a dispute" to determine whether its continuance is likely to endanger the maintenance of international peace and security.

Shortly before the Council was due to meet on the afternoon of Sunday, October 28th, word was received that the Government of the Hungarian People's Republic had "categorically" protested the Council's consideration of "any question concerning the domestic affairs of Hungary."

However, by a vote of nine to one (the USSR voted no and Yugoslavia abstained) the Council decided to place an item entitled "The Situation in Hungary" on its agenda.

Three days later on November 1st, Premier Imre Nagy cabled the Secretary General of the United Nations requesting help "in defending the country's neutrality" and asked Mr. Hammarskjold to include this request on the agenda "of the forthcoming General Assembly meeting."

The Security Council met again on the afternoon of November 2nd, and a new communication from the Hungarian Premier was circulated, asking the Council "to instruct the Soviet and Hungarian Governments to start negotiations immediately."

The following day the United States introduced a draft resolution urging the Soviet Union to cease intervention in Hungary. The Council, however, did not vote on the U.S. proposal.

New developments were announced early on the morning of November 4th in the General Assembly, which was then giving its attention to the Middle East crisis. Soon after midnight, Ambassador Henry Cabot Lodge, Jr., asked for a point of order to tell the Assembly that Budapest was under heavy bombardment and that the Security Council would soon meet on the matter.

Within three hours, at 3 a.m. on November 4th, the Council was called to order. However, a modified U.S. draft resolution was rejected because of the negative vote (veto) of one permanent member (USSR).

The Security Council then decided, by a vote of 10-1 (USSR) to invoke the "Uniting for Peace" resolution and call an emergency session of the General Assembly to "make appropriate recommendations concerning the situation in Hungary."

EMERGENCY SESSION

The General Assembly of the United Nations met on the afternoon of November 4th, and promptly put the "Situation in Hungary" on its agenda. The vote was 53 to 8, with 7 abstentions.

Ambassador Lodge then introduced a resolution calling on the USSR to stop all forms of intervention in Hungary's internal affairs. In spite of strong opposition by the Soviet Union's representative, Arkady A. Sobolev, the Assembly passed the resolution by a vote of 50 to 8. There were 15 abstentions. Hungary was not represented.

The resolution called upon the Government of the USSR to desist forthwith all armed attack on the people of Hungary and to withdraw all its forces without delay from Hungarian territory. It also called upon the Governments of the USSR and Hungary to permit observers designated by the Secretary General to enter the territory of Hungary, to travel freely therein, and to report their findings to the Secretary General.

The next morning Secretary General Hammarskjold received a cable dated November 4, 1956 from the new Hungarian Premier, János Kádár. The cable claimed that previous requests by the Nagy Government to have the Hungarian question discussed in the United Nations "have no legal force" and categorically objected to any such discussion. This question, added the cable, was "within the exclusive jurisdiction of the Hungarian People's Republic."

Three days later, on November 8th, the General Assembly reopened the debate on the "Situation in Hungary."

The credentials of the Hungarian representative were discussed at some length and were referred to the Assembly's Credentials Committee, which permitted Kádár's man, Mr. Szabó, to be seated "provisionally."

Shortly after the debate began, it became evident that the USSR, Communist Hungary and the other Soviet-dominated countries would base their case on the contention that the events in Hungary fell within the exclusive jurisdiction of the Hungarian People's Republic.

On November 9th, the Assembly voted on three resolutions before it:

1. The Five-Power (so-called Cuban) resolution which recalled the resolution of November 4th, and suggested that free elections be held in Hungary under United Nations auspices. It was adopted 48 to 11 (India was among those voting against it) with 16 abstentions.

2. The United States resolution in which the Assembly called upon the USSR to cease immediately actions against the Hungarian population and to facilitate the receipt and distribution of food and medical supplies. It was adopted 53 to 9 with 13 abstentions.

3. The Austrian resolution, of strictly humanitarian character, which called upon all Member States to undertake large scale immediate aid by furnishing medical supplies, foodstuffs and clothes, was passed without opposition. Sixty-seven delegations voted in favor and eight abstained.

The next afternoon, November 10th, the special emergency session of the Assembly decided to transfer discussion of the Hungarian situation to the Agenda of the Assembly's eleventh regular session, as "a matter of priority." The decision was approved by a vote of 53 to 9, with 8 abstentions.

Regualr [Eleventh] Session

The debate began with a formal accusation by Cuban representative Nuñez-Portuondo that Hungarians were being deported to the Soviet Union.

That charge was made on November 15th, with the circulation of a proposal that the General Assembly urgently call upon the Soviet Government and Hungarian authorities to halt these deportations.

Three days later, the "Revolutionary Workers' and Peasants' Government" of Hungary issued a communique, later distributed to Assembly members, stating that "false" and "provocative panic rumors" were being spread by hostile "counter-revolutionary" elements to the effect that arrests were taking place in Hungary and that young people and others were being deported to the Soviet Union.

Debate on the deportation issue opened on the morning on November 19th, when a revised version of the Cuban proposal was presented. The Assembly also had before it two other resolutions: the Three-Power Resolution (Ceylon, India and Indonesia) calling for U.N. observers to travel freely in Hungary, without prejudice to Hungarian sovereignty; and the Four-Power Resolution (Argentina, Belgium, Denmark and the United States), urging continued aid to refugees.

After a three-day debate, the General Assembly adopted all three resolutions late on the afternoon of November 21st.

The Cuban resolution was passed by a vote of 55 to 10 with 14 abstentions. Burma and Ceylon split the unity of the Colombo Powers by voting in favor of the proposal, while India and Indonesia abstained.

The Resolution on observers was adopted 57 to 8. Fourteen delegations abstained, among them Poland and Yugoslavia.

The Assembly then overwhelmingly approved continued aid to refugees by passing the Five-Power Resolution by a vote of 69 to 2 (Hungary and Romania). There were 8 abstentions.

On November 30th, Secretary General Dag Hammarskjold notified Assembly members, in a written report, that he had no information available at that time about steps taken to comply with Assembly decisions on the withdrawal of troops or political matters. He also stated that no permission had

so far been given by the Hungarian Government for observers named by him to enter Hungary for on-the-spot examination of the situation.

Three days later, on December 3rd, Hungary's Acting Foreign Minister, István Sebes, cabled Mr. Hammarskjold re-
affirming the Hungarian Government's view that "permission
for United Nations observers to enter the territory of Hungary would violate the sovereignty of Hungary and would
be contrary to the principles of the United Nations Charter"
and that the recent events in Hungary were exclusively an
internal affair and thus outside the competence of any international organization.

The same day, debate was resumed in the General Assembly at the request of the United States, which joined thirteen
other members in presenting a proposal repeating earlier
Assembly demands for the entry of United Nations observers
into Hungary, and asking the Soviet Government and Hungarian authorities to notify the Secretary General of their
consent not later than December 7, 1956. In the meantime,
the draft recommended that Mr. Hammarskjold arrange for
the immediate dispatch of observers named by him to Hungary and to "other countries as appropriate."

On December 5th, Radio Budapest announced that Secretary General Hammarskjold's proposed visit of December
16th would be unsuitable at that time.

Following this broadcast on December 6th, Ambassador
Lodge issued a statement to the press declaring that if the
statement was authentic it raised a question as to the good
faith of the Hungarian spokesman, Imre Horváth, who extended the invitation.

The next day, however, the Hungarian delegation declared
that Mr. Lodge's comment on Mr. Horváth was "absolutely
unfounded." It further declared that the Hungarian delegation was continuing its discussion with the Secretary General,
since the date of his proposed visit to Budapest was "quite
obviously subject to mutual agreement . . ."

The scene of action shifted back to the Assembly on the
morning of December 10th. Seventeen nations proposed that
the Assembly condemn the USSR's violation of the United
Nations Charter in depriving Hungary of its liberty and independence and the Hungarian people of the exercise of

their fundamental rights. It further proposed that the Assembly call on the USSR to make immediate arrangements for the withdrawal, under United Nations observation, of its armed forces from Hungary and to permit the re-establishment of Hungary's political independence. Colombia, the Dominican Republic, Turkey and Spain later joined the sponsors of this proposal, bringing the number to twenty.

On the morning of December 11, 1956, during the course of the debate the Hungarian delegation walked out of the Assembly. Mr. Horváth announced that the Hungarian delegation "will not participate in the proceedings of the eleventh session of the General Assembly as long as the discussion of the Hungarian questions does not proceed in the spirit of the United Nations Charter."

On December 11th, the Assembly asked Secretary General Hammarskjold to take any initiative he deemed helpful in regard to the Hungarian problem in conformity with the principles of the Charter and the Assembly's resolutions.

On the afternoon of December 12th the Assembly finally decided in favor of the so-called Twenty-Power resolution. The vote was 55 to 8, with 13 nations abstaining, among them Yugoslavia, Haiti, Hungary and South Africa were absent. Burma, Ceylon, Nepal, Lebanon and Libya voted in favor of the proposal.

SPECIAL COMMITTEE ON HUNGARY

Several attempts by the General Assembly to obtain permission for either the Secretary General or an observers' team to visit Hungary and report to the General Assembly on the resolution and its suppression were thwarted by the Soviet and Hungarian governments. Therefore, on January 10, 1957, the General Assembly accepted by a majority vote a resolution introduced by 24 member states which read *inter alia*:

". . . desiring to ensure that the General Assembly and all Member States shall be in possession of the fullest and best available information regarding the situation created by the intervention of the Union of Soviet Socialist Republics, through its use of armed forces and other means, in the internal affairs of Hungary as well as regarding developments relating to the recommendations of the General Assembly on this subject,

1. It establishes, for the above mentioned purposes, a Special Committee, composed of representatives of Australia, Ceylon, Denmark, Tunisia and Uruguay, to investigate and to establish and maintain direct observation in Hungary and elsewhere, taking testimony, collecting evidence and receiving information as appropriate, in order to report its findings to the General Assembly at its eleventh session, and thereafter from time to time to prepare additional reports for the information of Member States and of the General Assembly if it is in session ... "

The resolution further calls on the Governments of Hungary and the Soviet Union to grant permission to the Special Committee and staff to enter the territory of Hungary and travel without restrictions.

The resolution also requests the members of the General Assembly to put all information in their possession at the disposal of the Committee, and requests the Secretary General to provide all means necessary to the effective functioning of the Committee.

Finally, the resolution calls upon the members of the General Assembly to make every possible effort to carry out the previous resolutions as well as the present one, and repeatedly requests the Secretary General to take the necessary steps, in accordance with the Charter and previous resolutions, to promote the solution of the Hungarian question.

Fifty-nine votes were cast in favor of the resolution and eight against it. Ten members abstained. (The usual ten negative votes of the Soviet bloc were reduced to eight, because the Hungarian delegation had withdrawn from the session and Yugoslavia abstained, with Afghanistan, Cuba, Egypt, Finland, India, Jordan, Saudi Arabia, the Sudan and Syria.)

On January 23, 1957, the General Assembly accepted a report by the United Nations High Commission on Refugees and then requested the High Commissioner "in consultation with the Secretary General and with the governments concerned, to develop a comprehensive assessment of the needs, both material and financial, of the Hungarian refugees to be submitted to the United Nations Refugee Fund Executive Committee for its approval at the earliest possible date." Forty-nine members voted for the resolution, and not one negative vote was cast; nineteen members abstained.

On February 21, 1957 the General Assembly accepted a suggestion from the Credentials Committee to "take no decision regarding the credentials submitted on behalf of the representatives of Hungary." The Hungarian Communist delegation thus became the first and only member of the United Nations whose credentials were not accepted by the General Assembly. According to Clause 85 of the rules of procedure the *de facto* recognition of a delegation and the toleration of its presence permits it to participate fully in the activities of the General Assembly until such time as a final decision is made regarding its credentials.

Through the Secretary General, the Special Committee requested the Hungarian Government to admit it into Hungarian territory. On February 5, 1957 the Hungarian regime answered "that in the opinion of the (Hungarian) Government, the Committee violates, in its function, the Charter of the United Nations . . . consequently, the Hungarian Government is not in a position to permit the members of the Special Committee and its staff to enter into the territory of Hungary."

During its stay in Europe, the Committee repeated its request, and it was again refused by the Hungarian Government on March 25, 1957. Also rejected was a Committee request to the Government of Romania for permission to visit Imre Nagy, then being held in that country.

After a long and heated debate, the General Assembly accepted the Special Committee's unanimous report in a September 14, 1957 resolution, 60 (ten more than on November 4, 1956) to 10, with 10 abstentions.

In favor: Israel, Italy, Japan, Jordan, Laos, Lebanon, Liberia, Libya, Luxemburg, Mexico, Morocco, Netherlands, New Zealand, Nicaragua, Norway, Pakistan, Panama, Paraguay, Peru, Philippines, Portugal, Spain, Sudan, Sweden, Thailand, Tunisia, Turkey, United Kingdom, USA, Uruguay, Venezuela, Argentina, Australia, Austria, Belgium, Bolivia, Brazil, Burma, Cambodia, Canada, Chile, China, Colombia, Costa Rica, Cuba, Denmark, Dominican Republic, Ecuador, El Salvador, Ethiopia, France, Ghana, Greece, Guatemala, Haiti, Honduras, Iceland, Iran, Iraq, Ireland.

Against: Poland, Romania, Ukraine, USSR, Yugoslavia, Albania, Bulgaria, Bylorussia, Czechoslovakia, Hungary.

Abstaining: Nepal, Saudi Arabia, Syria, Yemen, Afghanistan, Ceylon, Egypt, Finland, India, Indonesia.

The resolution *"Notes* the conclusion of the Committee that the events which took place in Hungary in October and November 1956 constituted a spontaneous national uprising;

Finds that the conclusion reached by the Committee on the basis of its examination of all available evidence confirms that:

(a) The Union of Soviet Socialist Republics, in violation of the Charter of United Nations, has deprived Hungary of its liberty and political independence and the Hungarian people of the exercise of their fundamental human rights;

(b) The present Hungarian regime has been imposed on the Hungarian people by the armed intervention of the Union of Soviet Socialist Republics;

(c) The Union of Soviet Socialist Republics has carried out mass deportations of Hungarian citizens to the Union of Soviet Socialist Republics;

(d) The Union of Soviet Socialist Republics has violated its obligations under the Geneva Convention of 1949;

(e) The present authorities in Hungary have violated the human rights and freedoms granted by the Treaty of Peace with Hungary;

Condemns these acts and the continued defiance of the resolution of the General Assembly;

Reiterates its concern with the continued plight of the Hungarian people;

Considers that further efforts must be made to achieve the objectives of the United Nations in regard to Hungary in accordance with the Purposes and Principles of the Charter and the pertinent resolutions of the General Assembly;

Calls upon the Union of Soviet Socialist Republics and the present authorities in Hungary, in view of evidence in the report, to desist from repressive measures against the Hungarian people, to respect the liberty and political independence of Hungary and the Hungarian people's enjoyment of fundamental human rights and freedoms, and to ensure the return to Hungary of those Hungarian citizens who have been deported to the Union of Soviet Socialist Republics."

The resolution further calls on Prince Wan Waithayakon, President of the General Assembly's eleventh session, to take all steps he considers necessary on the Hungarian question, in accordance with the resolutions passed hitherto.

The twelfth session of the Credentials Committee again took up the question of the Hungarian delegation's credentials and suggested that the General Assembly, as at its previous session, abstain from final decision. The Committee recommended this procedure in view of the fact that no new information was received to contradict the Assembly's statement that "the present Hungarian regime exercises its power not by the will of the people but as a result of the armed interference of the Soviet Union." The General Assembly accepted the Credentials Committee's report on December 10, 1957.

THE NAGY CASE

On the evening the June 16, 1958, the Hungarian radio announced the execution of Imre Nagy, Pál Maléter and two of their associates. The Special Committee met immediately after the announcement to debate this Soviet and Hungarian brutality and prepared a report which was sent to all members of the General Assembly on July 14, 1958.

On September 22, 1958, the General Assembly placed the Hungarian question on its agenda 61 to 10, with 10 abstentions. The debate took place on December 12, 1958.

The resulting resolution condemns the execution of Imre Nagy, Pál Maléter and the other Hungarian patriots, expresses regret that in Hungary, under the threat of Soviet arms, basic human rights have been continuously violated, and condemns the Soviet and Hungarian regimes for refusing to implement the General Assembly's resolutions.

It further calls on the Hungarian and Soviet regimes not only to refrain from violating the human rights of the Hungarian people but to respect those rights.

The resolution sanctions the July 14th report of the Special Committee, expresses thanks to the Committee and to Prince Wan Waithayakon for their work and appoints Sir Leslie Munro of New Zealand "for the purpose of reporting to Member States of the General Assembly on significant developments relating to the implementation of the resolutions of the General Assembly on Hungary."

The resolution also declares that "the United Nations will

continue to be seized of the situation in Hungary in view of the fact that the Government of the USSR and the present authorities in Hungary are disregarding the above mentioned resolutions of the General Assembly on Hungary."

The resolution was presented by thirty-seven Member States. Fifty-four votes were cast in its favor. The Soviet bloc, i.e., ten members, voted against it, fifteen delegations abstained (Saudi Arabia, Sudan, United Arab Republic, Afghanistan, Ceylon, Ethiopia, Finland, Ghana, Greece, India, Indonesia, Iraq, Lebanon, Libya and Morocco). Two members (Yemen and Israel) were absent.

The Credentials Committee again took up the question of the Hungarian delegation's credentials during its thirteenth session. Henry Cabot Lodge, the United States Delegate, declared that "The United States and humanity in general will never give up its insistence that the day will come when the people of Hungary will be truly represented in the United Nations. But as long as everything in Hungary—including the recent so-called elections—is conducted under Soviet domination, the representatives of the present Hungarian regime cannot have the approval of those who prize the dignity of man."

On December 12, 1958, the Credentials Committee recommended that the General Assembly "take no decision regarding the credentials submitted on behalf of the representatives of Hungary," since "the present Hungarian regime has been imposed on the Hungarian people by the armed intervention of the Union of Soviet Socialist Republics."

The report of the Credentials Committee was accepted by the General Assembly on December 13, 1958.

SPECIAL REPRESENTATIVE

In the resolution of December 12, 1958, the General Assembly requested the Union of Soviet Socialist Republics and the "present authorities in Hungary" to co-operate with the United Nations Representative that he might perform his duties.

On December 10, 1959, the General Assembly accepted the recommendations of the Credentials Committee which once again refused to accredit the "representatives" of the Kádár regime. The vote was 72 to 1 with one abstention (Romania).

The rejection was repeated three times in 1961; on April 21, August 24 and December 19.

The General Assembly considered the report of the Special Representative, Sir Leslie Munro, on December 21, 1961, and deplored the continued disregard of the General Assembly resolutions concerning the Hungarian situation by the Union of Soviet Socialist Republics and the Communist Hungarian regime. The vote was 49 to 17, 32 abstaining.

The "last legal battle" in the Hungarian case was on December 20, 1962, when the General Assembly reaffirmed the basic resolutions 1004 (ES-II), 1005 (ES-II), 1127 (XI), 1131 (XI), 1132 (XI), and 1133 (XI), in which the General Assembly, by a great majority, requested—among other things—the withdrawal of Soviet armed forces from Hungary and an assurance to the Hungarian people of their fundamental rights, freedom and independence.

The General Assembly resolved that the "position of the United Nations representative on Hungary need no longer to be continued," and requested the Secretary General to "take any initiative that he deems helpful in relation to the Hungarian question." The vote was 53 to 13, 43 abstaining; three were absent.

The credentials of the representatives of the Communist regime in Hungary were accepted by the Credentials Committee, and its report was approved by the General Assembly on January 8, 1963.

The Secretary General visited Budapest in 1963 but so far has not submitted any report to the Assembly or taken any initiative in the Hungarian question.

ALBERT CAMUS:

The subjugated and enslaved Hungary did more for the cause of freedom and justice than any other people in the world during the last 20 years.

September 1, 1957

RECONQUEST OF HUNGARY

Original contribution by Béla K. Király

In the small hours of November 4, 1956, Soviet Army combat divisions and Air Force units launched a massive attack on Budapest: the reconquest of Hungary—the third phase of the revolution and freedom fight—had begun.*

Two other phases of the revolution had preceded the reconquest. The first had taken place between October 23 and 28. At 12:20 P.M. on October 28 Prime Minister Imre Nagy announced a ceasefire which put an end to the first Soviet attack, a ruthless police action against the Hungarian people. During that first phase the Soviet Army was opposed only by the uncoordinated resistance of small groups of freedom fighters. The moral—and indeed the actual—victory of this phase of the struggle had gone unquestionably to the freedom fighters. Despite announcement of the armistice of October 28, coordination and organization of the small freedom-fighter groups into a revolutionary force, the National Guard, still continued apace.

During this second phase of the revolution the organizers of the national defense faced three major problems: to insure the loyalty of the Army; to maintain public order; and finally, to seek ways and means of defending the nation in case of renewed Soviet aggression.

One of the mysteries of the Hungarian revolution that

* There are indications that prior to the Hungarian and Polish unrest a major Soviet force of "volunteers" had already concentrated in the Ukrainian S.R. for contingent use in the Middle East in connection with the Suez crisis. These forces were thus available to be moved into Hungary in October.

is not yet fully explained is what were the real causes of the Soviet armed attacks. Some observers assume that the Soviet leaders' main goal was to prevent a chain reaction of Hungarian-type revolutions in other captive countries. Others emphasize the naked military objective —"Military Base Hungary" was indispensable to the Soviet system, Hungary had to be reconquered.

Marshal V. D. Sokolovsky's book, *Military Strategy* (Frederick A. Praeger Publisher, New York, 1963), presents a fair interpretation of Soviet strategic thinking. According to this source, until the meeting of the Supreme Soviet in January, 1960, the old post-World War II strategic concepts prevailed in the U.S.S.R. Under this way of thinking, Soviet military planning was still based on the possibility of a third world war fought primarily by conventional forces, most probably in the "European Theater." Nuclear weapons and missilery were still considered only secondary means of warfare. To the Soviet strategists of 1956, "Miliary Base Hungary" may still have been an indispensable site from which a major blow could be launched against the West.

Since early 1960, however, the "radical military thinkers," supported by Nikita S. Khrushchev, gradually gained sway. Consequently, the conventional "theater" concept was replaced by intercontinental strategy. By this theory, the major strategic blows against the West, previously planned to be carried out by Army Groups, were now to be delivered by massive missile and nuclear attacks. "Military Base Hungary," or Rumania or wherever else, today play a much less important role in the Soviet military system than they did in 1956. One is inclined to wonder whether this is the reason why the Hungarian revolution was suppressed while the Rumanian diplomatic discord is tolerated ten years later.

It is not yet known whether the Soviet decision on Hungary had been taken at the beginning of the revolt or whether the U.S.S.R. was sincere in the diplomatic negotiations preceding and following the October 28 armistice.* But the negotiations kept alive the hope that

---

* According to Colonel Oleg Penkovskiy, there was confusion and hesitation in the Kremlin regarding the Hungarian events

Hungary might be able to assume a Finnish or Austrian type of neutrality as the Hungarians earnestly wanted. The policy of the Hungarian government was based on this popular aspiration. Neither the government nor the populace had any intention of joining in an alliance with the foes of the U.S.S.R.

This was a just goal and in no way overstepped the Hungarian people's right to self-determination. Yet both people and government always had to keep in mind the possibility of further Soviet aggression. And the revolutionary leadership had the utmost difficulty in attempting to prepare for such an attack.

The foremost difficulty was the notorious sensitivity of the U.S.S.R. Any major strategic movement in Hungary—even of a defensive nature—would have been viewed by the Soviet authorities as a hostile move against the U.S.S.R. Nor was there any feasible line of defense in Hungary along which deployment of even all the armed forces could have halted a massive Soviet assault for just a few days. But the government was in no position to make such strategic moves even if it had wanted to, for many key positions in the Army were still in the hands of Stalinist generals who might have been able to obstruct such action. These Stalinist senior officers also could not be removed hastily, again because of Soviet sensitivity.

If conventional strategic defense against massive Soviet aggression were not feasible, why did not the revolutionary government prepare an all-out guerrilla war for such an eventuality? First of all, Imre Nagy and his government refused to be party to any kind of war against the U.S.S.R. But also, for purely physical reasons, such a guerrilla war was out of the question in Hungary. Hungary is essentially a flat plain devoid of sizable mountains or forests or rugged terrain. Without such geographical formations no standing guerrilla base

and the Suez crisis: "We in Moscow felt as if we were sitting on a powderkeg. Everyone in the General Staff was against the 'Khrushchev adventure.' It was better to lose Hungary, as they said, than to lose everything." (*The Penkovskiy Papers*, Doubleday & Company, Inc., Garden City, New York, 1965, p. 411.)

could be built up and consequently no lasting guerrilla war could be waged. Guerrilla war, just as a conventional war, was outside the realm of reality for the Hungarian government in 1956.

In view of all these factors, the Hungarian government did not prepare an all-out defensive war against the U.S.S.R. but rather made every possible effort to forestall Soviet aggression.

Despite the peaceful intentions and actions of the revolutionary government, and indeed of the whole people, the leadership of the Hungarian Armed Forces still had to take certain defensive measures, not, of course, in the hope of a final victory in the case of Soviet attack, but to secure a few days' or perhaps hours' respite for the Imre Nagy government to make its dispositions. A plan was evolved that, in case of a Soviet attack, the capital city of Budapest should be defended, and to this end a defensive ring was to be built around the city. On November 1, Colonel András Márton, the Commandant of the Zrinyi Academy [General Staff College] and a member of the highest revolutionary organ of the Armed Forces, the Revolutionary Council of National Defense, was named commander of the outer defense ring around Budapest. The Stalinist officers in the General Staff sabotaged preparations for even this minimal defensive system.

Because the buildup of defense around Budapest was proceeding slowly, this writer, as Military Commandant of Budapest, set up a cordon of infantry, field artillery, anti-aircraft artillery and freedom-fighter units round Budaörs airfield, five miles south-west of Budapest. Two small aircraft waited there at the government's disposal. Until the second Soviet attack overran the defenders at Budaörs, the airfield remained in the hands of revolutionary troops.

Meanwhile, as Soviet emissaries were negotiating with Hungarian officials, simultaneously the gradual invasion of Hungary began, though there was no firing on Hungarians. As early as October 29 the first reports of the entrance of new Soviet troops into Hungary reached Military Headquarters in Budapest. By October 31 most of the roads into Hungary from the U.S.S.R. and Rumania were thronged with Soviet vehicles.

The Hungarian government's first official statement about these military movements was issued on November 1. The Government protested and informed the U.N. about "the re-entry of Soviet troops into Hungary." By November 2, Soviet troops entering from Rumania had penetrated as far as the Great Hungarian Plain, reaching Szeged, Szolnok and Kiskunhalas. At the same time Soviet military authorities seized the Northeastern Hungarian railway system, including the railway junctions of Zahony, Kisvarda and Nyiregyhaza. During the night of November 1–2, all Hungarian airfields were occupied by a coup. The Soviet Embassy announced to the Hungarian authorities that the "seizure was necessary to ensure the peaceful transfer of Russian families by air from Hungary as well as to prevent possible attack by the Hungarian Air Force on Soviet units that were being evacuated [sic] from Hungary." On November 2 and 3 two main Soviet army concentrations were formed, one along the main highway from Miskolc to Budapest, the other along the highways between Szeged and Budapest. As a matter of fact, by November 3 Budapest was strategically encircled by massive Soviet Army units.

Nevertheless, Prime Minister Imre Nagy still made efforts to arrive at a pacific solution with the U.S.S.R. An agreement was reached during the afternoon of November 3 between the Soviet and Hungarian plenipotentiaries on the withdrawal of the Soviet troops from Hungary to be completed by January 15, 1957. Minister of State Ferenc Erdei and Generals Pál Maléter and István Kovács, who had been authorized to represent the government of Imre Nagy, went to the Soviet Military Headquarters in the evening merely to settle a few very slight amendments before signing the agreement reached during the day. They arrived at the Soviet Headquarters at Tököl, on Csepel Island five miles south of metropolitan Budapest, at 10 P.M. on November 3. Their arrival coincided with the start of the second Soviet offensive and they were promptly arrested by the Soviet secret police.

It was around midnight of November 3–4 that the Headquarters of the National Guard of Hungary received the first reports from the town of Kecskemét, then shortly afterwards from the town of Kiskunhalas, that Soviet armed forces had begun a ferocious attack against barracks and military installations and against the civilian population. About 2 A.M. the outer perimeter of the defenses of Budapest also reported Soviet attacks on various sectors. By this time, however, the sounds of battle could already be heard at National Guard Headquarters.

In the meantime two major Soviet artillery strongpoints were set up, one at Kelenföld, a southwestern suburb of Budapest, and the other at Nagyrákos military parade ground, in Köbánya, a suburb northeast of Budapest. In the small hours of November 4 these concentrations of several hundred pieces of Soviet artillery opened up with a heavy barrage against the capital. The barrage seemed intended to terrorize rather than to achieve purely military goals. This was evident from the haphazard aiming of the fire, which struck civilian housing, street corners and squares of no military significance. But the heaviest shelling fell on the Kilián Militady Barracks. This area sustained extensive damage. Four thousand buildings containing about 40,000 apartments were destroyed in Budapest. The Hungarian capital had never suffered such devastation apart from the Soviet destruction of the city during World War II.

The battle of Budapest raged for ten days. In other large cities, like Pécs and Miskolc, the subjugation of the Hungarian freedom fighters also became an extended military operation. With Czechoslovak permission a Soviet division crossed into Hungary at Komárom [Komorno] and gradually sealed off the Austrian frontier.

This writer was in charge of the joint staffs of the Commander in Chief of the National Guard of Hungary and the Revolutionary Council of National Defense, both housed in the Police Headquarters in the center of Budapest. The other staff which served the Headquarters of the Commandant of Budapest was stationed in the building of the Ministry of National De-

fense nearby. The operational head of this latter Head-
quarters was the Chief of Staff, Major General István
Kovács, directly under the writer's orders. At the time
of the second Soviet attack I happened to be at the
Headquarters of the National Guard on Deák Square.
To issue orders to the defense perimeter, I telephoned
Major General Kovács. Instead of taking orders, the
General passed the receiver to Lieutenant General
Károly Janza, the dismissed Stalinist Minister of Defense, who was not even authorized to be present at the
Headquarters. General Janza asked me to join them at
the Ministry of Defense and help them to prevent "the
activities of fascist bands." In other words, their behavior showed that even as the second Soviet attack was
being launched, the Stalinist officers had managed to
take over the most important military staffs as well as
the Ministry of Defense.

It was impossible, therefore, to send orders to the
troops through the proper command channels. Recognizing this agonizing fact, this writer repeatedly requested
the Prime Minister to go on the air (the radio was still
in our hands) and issue general orders of resistance so
that the army and freedom-fighter units should know the
intentions of the political leadership. Since Imre Nagy
refused to do so, I requested permission to do so myself.
This the Prime Minister forbade outright. Such an appeal, he claimed, would be legal recognition of a state
of war with the U.S.S.R., or might even be interpreted
as a declaration of war, which the Government would
never allow.

The Hungarian troops were very uncoordinated because of the sabotage of the Stalinist Hungarian officers
and because the Soviet forces were advancing rapidly in
overwhelming numbers. It was thus time to secure the
revolutionary military leadership by moving it to a command post where it would be less exposed than in the
building in the center of Budapest where it was then
located. Such a command post had been prearranged in
the *Manresa,* the former Jesuit monastery on Szabadsághegy [Freedom Hill] overlooking Budapest. There we
could be sure of safety for hours, perhaps for days, for

the revolutionary military leadership and even for the Government if it chose to join the Military Headquarters. This was suggested to the Prime Minister. He rejected the proposal and went to the radio studio in the Parliament building to broadcast the following announcement:

"This is Imre Nagy speaking, Chairman of the Council of Ministers of the Hungarian People's Republic. Today at dawn Soviet troops launched an attack against our capital with the obvious purpose of overthrowing the lawful and democratic government. Our troops are fighting; the government it at its post."

After the broadcast, it was no longer possible to reach the Prime Minister. Later on he sought refuge in the Yugoslavian Embassy to save what he could through negotiation before everything was lost in a fight imposed upon the Hungarian people by Soviet aggression.

Without political leadership the revolutionary military leadership faced a grave decision. Should it call on the nation to resist the Soviet aggression in a guerrilla war, or start armistice negotiations, or just lay down arms? No other alternative existed. These three possibilities were discussed at the Central Military Headquarters on Szabadsághegy under the leadership of this writer. There we received information about a spontaneous meeting of revolutionary leaders, local freedom-fighter leaders, and workers' representatives, who gathered at the Bólyai Military Academy [Training School for Political Officers] in the Hüvösvölgy, a western suburb of Budapest. When the meeting was called to order, a resolution was passed inviting the writer to preside over the meeting and to extend it as broadly as possible to represent all possible strata of the revolution. This enlarged meeting was then to consider a draft resolution for an immediate armistice offer to the Soviet High Command. About half of the freedom fighters who were serving at the Headquarters on Szabadsághegy elected to participate in the meeting. The rest felt that, even if further fighting seemed in the final outcome hopeless, they would not lay down arms before the Soviet invaders. They were unwilling to put their arms or themselves at the mercy of the Soviet troops. They were also in principle reluctant formally to renounce the goals of the revolution in that manner. This writer joined the latter group.

The Soviet Army was absolutely superior in numbers and equipment. During our next few days at the Headquarters on Szabadsághegy, it was clear from the regrouping of Soviet troops that an all-out attack against the hill was being planned. So the Headquarters was moved to Nagykovácsi, a small town some 20 miles west of Budapest. From there the Headquarters tried to contact and coordinate those freedom-fighter groups still resisting in the immediate vicinity and in the mining areas of Piliscsaba, Dorog and Tata. Superior Soviet forces discovered the location of the Headquarters and on November 11 launched an attack against it with tanks, jet fighters, artillery and infantry. A bloody encounter ensued, known today in Hungary as the "Battle of Nagykovácsi." After heavy losses, the Headquarters was withdrawn during the night toward the west.

We bivouacked then on various ridges of the Pilis, Vértes and Bakony Mountains, while Soviet helicopters hovered overhead, tracking our line of retreat. Anxiously we listened to foreign radio broadcasts, waiting and hoping for an eventual change that somehow at some point would force the Soviet Union to negotiate with Imre Nagy after all. We hoped that then we could offer him again the services of the only surviving central organ, the Headquarters of the National Guard and the Revolutionary Council of National Defense, to help him to rebuild from the ruins. But as the days passed, that hope faded away. At last we realized that the tide could never be turned by battle, could not be turned by political means either. If there was no place for Imre Nagy and for his political solution, nor could there be any place for us.

On November 14, the last pocket of resistance in Budapest collapsed when the workers on Csepel laid down their arms. In mid-November, threatened by Soviet encirclement again, this writer gave orders that the Hungarian Military and freedom-fighter High Command and the units immediately supporting it withdraw from the country in small units. This operation was completed during the second half of November. We laid down our arms on Austrian soil, not before the Soviet Army.

John F. Kennedy:

October 23, 1956, is a day that will forever live in the annals of free men and free nations. It was a day of courage, conscience, and triumph. No other day since history began has shown more clearly the eternal unquenchability of man's desire to be free, whatever the odds against success, whatever the sacrifice required.

Americans will never—at any summit meeting, in any treaty declaration, in words or even in our minds—recognize Soviet domination of Hungary. Hungary's claim to independence and liberty is not based on sentiment or politics. It is deeply rooted in history, in culture and in law. No matter what sort of puppet government they may maintain, we do not mean to see that claim abandoned.

Americans intend to hasten by every honorable and reasonable means the arrival of the day when the men and women of Hungary will stand again in freedom and justice. On this anniversary we must, with Abraham Lincoln "Here highly resolve that these dead shall not have died in vain. . . . It is for us the living . . . to be dedicated to the unfinished work which they so nobly advanced."

(Message to the Commemorative Concert on October 23, 1960 in the Hunter College, New York, New York)

SOVIET ARMED FORCES
IN HUNGARY

I

Reprinted article of Ferenc A. Váli, "Soviet Troops in Hungary: Legal Aspects," THE FLETCHER REVIEW (Summer 1959, Vol. 2, No. 1), Medford, Massachusetts.

Under the terms of the Armistice Agreement with Hungary[1] her territory remained occupied by Allied (Soviet) troops.

Article 22 of the Treaty of Peace with Hungary[2] provided:

> Upon the coming into force of the present Treaty all Allied forces shall, within a period of 90 days, be withdrawn from Hungary, subject to the right of the Soviet Union to keep on Hungarian territory such armed forces as it may need for the maintenance of the lines of communication of the Soviet Army with the Soviet zone of occupation in Austria.

Accordingly, after the coming into force of the Peace Treaty, Soviet troops were to remain in Hungary for the purpose of maintaining communication with the Soviet troops of occupation in Austria, as long as Austria was to be subject to such an occupation. The Treaty of Peace came into force on September 15, 1947.

Under the Four Power Agreement and the *Staatsvertrag* with Austria of May 15, 1955,[3] Soviet armed forces

---

[1] Armistice Agreement with Hungary signed at Moscow on January 20, 1945. See Manley O. Hudson, International Legislation, Vol. IV, 1950, pp. 276-282. Harvard University Press.

[2] American Journal of International Law Supplement, 1948, pp. 225-251.

[3] *Ibid.*, 1955, pp. 162-194.

evacuated Austria. Thus the above clause under which Soviet armed forces remained in Hungary after the coming into force of the Peace Treaty with Hungary ceased to be operative. It is still an open question why signatories to the Treaty of Peace with Hungary did not invoke this clause and invite the Soviet Union to evacuate Hungary. That the Hungarian government did not protest against stationing of Soviet troops on Hungarian territory, needs no explanation.

After the first, and also after the second intervention by Soviet forces in October and November, 1956, the world was told that these Soviet units were stationed in Hungary, and had intervened under the Warsaw Treaty.

The Treaty of Friendship, Cooperation and Mutual Assistance signed at Warsaw on May 14, 1955,[4] between Albania, Bulgaria, Czechoslovakia, the German Democratic Republic, Hungary, Poland, Rumania and the U.S.S.R. declares in its preamble that it wishes to promote:

> ... respect for the independence and sovereignty of States and non-interference in their internal affairs.

Article 1 of the Treaty reads as follows:

> The Contracting Parties undertake in accordance with the Charter of the United Nations Organization to refrain in their international relations from threat or use of force, and to solve their international disputes peacefully and in such manner as will not jeopardize international peace and society.

Article 4 provides:

> In the event of armed attack in Europe on one or more of the Parties to the Treaty by any state or group of states, each of the Parties to the Treaty . . . shall immediately, either individually or in agreement with other Parties to the Treaty, come to the assistance of the state or states attacked with all such means as it deems necessary, including armed forces. . . .

There is no direct clause in the Treaty which would justify one of the signatories stationing troops on the

4 *Ibid.*, 1955, pp. 194-199.

territory of the other, although there is a provision for a Joint Command of their armed forces which runs as follows:

> Article 5.—The Contracting Parties have agreed to estab-
> lish a Joint Command of the armed forces that by agree-
> ment among the Parties shall be assigned to the Command
> which shall function on the basis of jointly established
> principles. They shall likewise adopt other agreed measures
> necessary to strengthen their defensive power, in order to
> protect the peaceful labor of their peoples, guarantee the
> inviolability of their frontiers and territories, and provide
> defence against possible aggression.

It has been maintained that the right to station troops on Hungarian soil may be deduced from the above Article.[5] Such an opinion, however, is by no means convincing.

Simultaneously with the signing of the Warsaw Treaty a declaration was issued concerning the establishment of a Joint Command. Marshal of the Soviet Union I. S. Konev had been appointed Commander-in-Chief of the Joint Armed Forces to be assigned by the signatory states. A Staff of the Joint Armed Forces to be set up under the Commander-in-Chief, would include per-manent representatives of the general staffs of the sig-natory states. The Staff would have its headquarters in Moscow. The last paragraph of this declaration provides:

> The disposition of the Joint Armed Forces in the territories
> of the signatory states will be effected, by agreement among
> the states, in accordance with the requirements of their
> mutual defence.

Article 5 of the Warsaw Treaty as well as the above declaration refer to an "agreement" which, however, was never published. Thus the real source, if any, of the stationing of Soviet troops in the territory of Hungary remains obscure.

It seems characteristic for the prevailing circumstances that the Soviet Union, after the suppression of the Hun-garian uprising, found it necessary to have a special

---

[5] See: Quincy Wright, "Intervention, 1956," American Journal of International Law, 1957, p. 275.

treaty signed with the Kádár government on May 27, 1957, relative to "the legal status of Soviet forces temporarily stationed on the territory of the Hungarian People's Republic."[6]

But this latter Treaty does not contain provisions as to a consent by Hungary to the "temporary stationing" of Soviet forces; it presumes their existence within the borders of Hungary, and only provides regulations concerning their status, their placing, jurisdiction over their members and compensation for damages, etc.

The preamble of this Treaty recalls "the present international situation . . . when West Germany is being remilitarized . . . when the United States and other participants in the North Atlantic Alliance are maintaining numerous forces and military bases in close proximity to socialist States . . .," and thus continues:

> . . . taking note of the fact that in these conditions the temporary stationing of Soviet forces on the territory of the Hungarian People's Republic is expedient for the purpose of safeguarding joint defence against the possibility of aggression and that it accords with international agreements. . . .

Article I of this Treaty reads as follows:

> The temporary presence of Soviet forces on the territory of the Hungarian People's Republic in no way affects the sovereignty of the Hungarian State; the Soviet forces do not interfere in the internal affairs of the Hungarian People's Republic.

Similarly ludicrous statements are to be found in Article II of the Treaty:

> 1. The numerical strength of the Soviet forces temporarily on the territory of the Hungarian People's Republic, and the places of their stationing, are determined on the basis of special agreements between the Government of the Hungarian People's Republic and the Government of the USSR.
>
> 2. Movements of Soviet forces on the territory of the

[6] See: U.N., Report of the Special Committee on the Problem of Hungary, Eleventh Session, Supplement 18, pp. 60-62.

Hungarian People's Republic outside the places of their stationing require in each case the agreement of the Government of the Hungarian People's Republic or of the Hungarian organs authorized by the Hungarian Government to act for it.

3. The training and maneuvers of the Soviet troops on the territory of the Hungarian People's Republic outside their stationing areas are carried out either on the basis of the plans agreed on with the proper Hungarian Government bodies, or with the approval in each case of the Government of the Hungarian People's Republic or of the proper Hungarian authorities.

The relationship between the Soviet Union and its European satellites, including such treaties and agreements as the Warsaw Treaty of 1955, or the "status of Soviet forces agreement" with Hungary, cannot be considered as a relationship between independent states under international law or international politics. Accordingly, all such conventional provisions as referred to above can only be envisaged in the knowledge that they serve to camouflage the real state of affairs: the complete subordination of satellite (in our case, Hungarian) governments and authorities to the will of Moscow. Therefore, the stationing of Soviet forces in Hungary ought never be and can never be considered in the same light as, for instance, the legal status of the United States or British armed forces in foreign lands.[7]

The presence of Soviet forces in Hungary, though open to legal examination and scrutiny—the result of which can hardly be considered satisfactory—does not rely on the consent of the Hungarian people. It is at present the outcome of Soviet intervention in the affairs of Hungary, the consequence of an elimination by force of the recognized government of Hungary, and of the establishment by same armed intervention of a slavishly subservient puppet-government.

[7] See: F. A. Vali, "Servitudes of International Law, A Study of Rights in Foreign Territory," London, 1958, p. 217.

II

Reprinted from Ferenc A. Váli, RIFT AND REVOLT
IN HUNGARY—*Nationalism Versus Communism*
(Cambridge, Massachussets, 1961, pp. 431–434) with
the permission of Harvard University Press.

The Soviet forces that suppressed the Revolution amounted to three army corps, which included eight tank and armored divisions, two infantry divisions, and additional artillery, air force, and other ancillary units. These forces were successively reduced during the following three years. In March 1958 (before Khrushchev's visit), 17,000 men were ostentatiously withdrawn from Hungary as part of the Soviet attempt at partial disarmament. In 1959 the number of Soviet soldiers on Hungarian soil was estimated at some 45,000 to 50,000 men.[8] Their distribution in the country revealed, according to military experts, the real purpose of their presence. While officially it is claimed that the Soviet Army, under an agreement with the Hungarian government concluded in accordance with the terms of the Warsaw Treaty, is stationed in Hungary for protecting that country and the Communist bloc against potential aggressions of the imperialist West, its geographical allocation confirms its function as a force of occupation in hostile territory. The troops were concentrated around Budapest and some other industrial cities, or else stationed in encampments within easy approach to the capital, whereas the western and southern borders (with Austria and Yugoslavia) were not guarded by Soviet forces. The pressure exercised by the Soviet Army against internal uprisings in Hungary was enhanced by the presence of considerable Soviet troop concentrations in the Carpatho-Ukraine and on the Rumanian side of the Hungaro-Rumanian frontier, at places from which

8 See *Hungary under Soviet Rule III: A Survey of Developments from the Revolution to August 1959*, ed. A. A. Berle, Jr., *et al.*, and published by the American Friends of the Captive Nations (New York, 1959), p. 7. *The Times* (London), on April 29, 1960, estimated the total of Soviet forces at some 37,000.

Soviet troops poured into Hungary during the Revolution.[9]

Since the end of 1957 the Soviet forces have tried not to be noticeable, except near their garrisons. Officers, when in towns or when attached to Hungarian military or police headquarters, wear mufti. Both officers and men are again strictly isolated from the Hungarian public. The Soviet Military Command with its hundreds of officers is located in Budapest; but these quarters, together with the Soviet embassy, form a Soviet enclave in the city where officers, officials, and their families are accommodated and have their special shops and other facilities.

The stationing of Soviet troops in Hungary had been the principal complaint voiced throughout the nation during and after the Revolution. The crushing of the revolt by those troops and the resolutions of the United Nations General Assembly demanding their withdrawal focused world attention on their presence in Hungary. Prime Minister Kádár, in his radio address of November 8, 1956, and in his negotiations with workers' councils and other representative bodies, promised the withdrawal of foreign troops "as soon as peace and order are restored." On the other hand, General Grebennik, the Soviet commander of Budapest, had replied to a similar demand made to him by representatives of the workers' councils: "Soviet troops will leave Hungary only when crayfish whistle and fishes sing." On November 19, 1956, the Soviet Foreign Minister, Shepilov, said in the United Nations General Assembly that "by agreement with the Hungarian government Soviet troops will be promptly withdrawn from Budapest, once normal conditions are restored in the Hungarian capital. At the same time, the Soviet government will begin negotiations with the government of the Hungarian People's Republic, as a party to the Warsaw Treaty, on the question of maintaining Soviet troops on Hungarian territory." Willingness to negotiate for the withdrawal had been declared by "both sides"—the Soviet government and the Hun-

[9] *Hungary under Soviet Rule III*, pp 8-11; *Hungarian Freedom Fighter*, September 1959.

garian government which it had installed by force. Soviet pronouncements and those of the Kádár regime referred to the Soviet declaration of October 30, 1956,
which laid down the principle that Soviet forces could
only be withdrawn from Hungary after an agreement
to this effect among all the members of the Warsaw
Treaty.[10]

The question of withdrawal from Hungary has not
ceased to occupy foreign and Hungarian public opinion. It is coupled with another: would Soviet forces,
once withdrawn from Hungarian territory, again intervene in case of another revolt against the regime? This is
a question that also concerns satellite countries in which
no Soviet forces are stationed, and also affects any international settlement which might induce the Soviet
Union to withdraw its forces from East-Central Europe.
Khrushchev during his visit to Hungary in April 1958
made contradictory statements on this issue. On April
5 he declared in Sztalinváros: "You must not again depend on the Russians coming to your assistance in the
event of another counter-revolution. Therefore, you
must become stronger and stronger."[11] On April 8 he
said he had been misquoted by Western journalists, and
he really meant to say that Hungarian Communists
"should manage their efforts so that there should be no
new counter-revolution and we Russians should not be
obliged to come to your assistance."[12] Subsequent to
these pronouncements, the principle of assistance by the
Soviet Union and other Socialist countries in case of a
"counterrevolution" in any Socialist country seems to
have been adopted.

Another trial balloon was launched by Kádár himself
when he declared on August 20, 1959, that "the time
will come when Soviet troops will be withdrawn from
Hungary."[13] A whispering campaign presaged an official

10 For Grebennik's statement (an adaptation of Russian prov-
erb), and Soviet pronouncements in remainder of paragraph, see
U.N. Report, pp. 57-58.

11 New York Times, April 6, 1958. The Hungarian press did
not report that passage of the speech.

12 Népszabadság, April 9, 1959.

13 Népszabadság, Aug. 21, 1959.

announcement of this withdrawal at the Hungarian
Party Congress scheduled for December of that year. It
was not Khrushchev, present at the Congress, but Kádár
who disappointed wishful thinkers by declaring that
"Soviet troops will only be withdrawn when their presence is no more warranted by the international situation."[14] Two weeks before the Kennedy-Khrushchev
meeting in Vienna of June 1961, Kádár told a meeting
of factory workers that Hungary's friends cannot be expected "to defend our frontiers and national independence to the end of time." These words he said with reference to antiaircraft missiles recently supplied to the
Hungarian forces by the Soviet Union.

Hungarian public opinion, convinced that the Soviet
Army could always return if not obliged by international convention to abstain from renewed interventions,
desires their withdrawal for reasons of national prestige
and in order that the demands of the Revolution may
be fulfilled. The people, moreover, hope that the absence of foreign troops would have a restraining effect
on the government and oblige it to give greater heed
to the public interest. They hope that with the departure of Soviet troops, external influence would diminish, opening the way for an evolution more in conformity with national sentiment.

[14] *Népszabadság*, Dec. 2, 1959.

To the West

You still want to come?
Too late, to late.
We are cut and fallen
like weat in the reaper ...
Süddeutsche Zeitung, Munich, 15 December, 1956

WHY THE UNITED STATES
FAILED TO ACT

I.

The reason why the US Government did not offer concrete help to the Hungarian freedom fighters is given by Robert Murphy, then Undersecretary of State, in his memoirs, DIPLOMAT AMONG WARRIORS, *pp. 428–432. (Doubleday & Company, Inc., Garden City, New York, 1964.) Reprinted by permission of the Publisher.*

I must admit that I did not expect that an anti-Soviet revolution would spread through Hungary like a forest fire, but I never doubted that if a revolt did break out, the U.S.S.R. would use every means no matter how brutal to suppress it. The United States Government had no advance information about this uprising, no plan of action. And neither did Tito in Belgrade nor the authorities in Budapest nor the rulers in Moscow. The State Department had welcomed the stimulation which Tito seemed to be giving to a liberalizing trend, but nobody anticipated anything like this Hungarian insurrection. The American Legation in Budapest was even without a Minister at the climax of the disorders. Christian M. Ravndal had done a superb job of reporting the political maneuvers which preceded the revolt, but he had been appointed in July as Ambassador to Ecuador. His successor, E. T. (Tom) Wailes, who had been Ambassador to the Union of South Africa, could not reach Budapest until November 2 and he never did present his credentials there. Although Wailes' experience and wisdom were invaluable during the last weeks of the crisis, many members of Congress were critical of the State Department and of American intelligence services for having been caught so completely by surprise. The movement into Hungary by large numbers of additional Russian troops was the most acute international situation since the invasion of Korea six years before, and far more dangerous because there was possibility of direct American contact in Europe with the Red Army itself.

While I was receiving in my office a stream of anxious visitors who where distressed because the State Department did not know what was going on behind the scenes in Hungary, other critics were accusing the State Department of having actively fomented the Hungarian uprising. It seemed to be a case of damned if we didn't, and damned if we did. Charges of our complicity in the rebellion were based chiefly on broadcasts from Radio Free Europe, a station maintained in Munich by an American organization. Radio Free Europe employs a number of Europeans to broadcast news and speeches in European languages, and it was only natural for the Hungarian announcers to give encouraging accounts of the rebellion in their native land. It is not unlikely that Hungarian challenges from the American broadcasting station did help to incite some patriotic insurgents, thus giving credence to the rumor that the United States was a party to the uprising, but actually we had nothing to do with it.

The impression that our government was sponsoring the Hungarian revolt was unfortunately enhanced by an appeal to Marshal Bulganin from President Eisenhower, who urged the Russian Premier to withdraw Soviet forces from Hungary and permit the people to exercise their rights in freedom. Eisenhower issued a statement declaring: "The United States considers the developments in Hungary as a renewed expression of the intense desire for freedom long held by the Hungarians." While I agreed with this sentiment, I regretted that the President expressed himself as he did just at that time, because the Russians were trying to blame the Americans for the human slaughter which was occurring in Hungary. When the grim fighting finally ended on November 14, Eisenhower thought it advisable to issue another public statement explaining that he never had advocated open rebellion by an undefended population against forces over which they could not possibly prevail.

While the rebellion was blazing, everyone in the United States wanted to help the brave Hungarians, and the State Department was inundated with proposals ranging from outright military action to plans for welcoming thousands of refugees. Members of Congress and ambassadors from several embassies in Washington came to my office to urge "action," and some of our critics were bitter. I would analyze for each complainant the possibilities of "action" adequate to liberate Hungary, and would point out that palliatives could not possibly settle the issue but would only provoke the powerful Soviet armies to further massacre.

One suggestion frequently made was that the United States Air Force should at least fly in supplies to the patriots. But the geographic position of Hungary made this unfeasible. Our planes could not fly over Communist-controlled East Germany, Czechoslovakia or Yugoslavia, so we could approach Hungary only through Austria, and Austria declared in no uncertain terms that it would resist any form of overflights. Discussions with my visitors would conclude by my asking the complainant whether he would support a policy which would inevitably lead to a direct military attack by American forces against Russian forces. The sympathizer always would reply that he meant "action short of war." American policy of promoting liberation of captive nations always stopped short of war, and this was well known.

The Yugoslav Ambassador in Washington, Leo Mates, called on me several times. The Ambassador's forehead was wet with perspiration as he described the tense attitude of his government regarding the Soviet armies which were moving along the Yugoslav frontier. He was greatly alarmed by the clamor in the United States for counteraction against the Russians, and he begged that provocation be avoided. He believed that his country was trembling on the thin edge of war against the Soviet Union, and he urged that everything be done to confine the conflict to Hungary.

From the Yugoslav sources I learned confidentially

that before the Soviet Government decided on the grave step of military intervention, there were three days of violent discussion in the Kremlin. I was informed that strong influence was exerted by Peiping to induce Moscow to intervene in Hungary. Perhaps Peiping did support this brutal move, but even if the Chinese had opposed it, Moscow would have intervened anyway because its entire Eastern European security system was at stake. Once the decision was taken—and I was told that it was taken with the greatest reluctance—Marshal Zhukov was authorized to use every force needed for total suppression of the revolt. From the Russian point of view this was an absolute political and military necessity, and once the offensive was launched, they followed through. Putting ethics and the humanities aside, their judgment was sound. They understood the requirement to win.

The ruthless suppression of the Hungarian rebellion was somewhat dimmed by the Suez crisis, which could not have been timed more advantageously for the Russians. On October 24, units of the Red Army already stationed in Hungary went into action, and additional units invaded the country during the following days. On October 29, Anglo-French-Israeli forces invaded Egypt. The Russians were determined in any case to crush the Hungarian insurrection, but the attack against Egypt provided them with an admirable distraction. For instance, when the President of Syria was urged at the United Nations to indicate some indignation about Russian conduct in Budapest, that estimable gentleman declared he did not care if there were fifty Budapests— what concerned him was what might happen to Syria as a result of the attack on Egypt. The concomitant of the military operations in Hungary and Egypt burdened the State Department with its most intense responsibilities since World War II, causing me and some of the other officers to work around the clock, while Secretary Dulles went to New York to take personal charge, with Ambassador Lodge, of the simultaneous proceedings in the United Nations.

Dulles succeeded—with cynical support from the Soviet Union!—in sponsoring measures in the UN which resulted in a cease-fire in Egypt. But measures adopted by the UN against Russia had no effect whatever on the situation in Hungary. The first step taken by Dulles was to have a resolution presented to the Security Council affirming the right of the Hungarian people to choose their own government, and calling upon the Soviet Union to desist forthwith from any form of intervention. Yugoslavia abstained from voting on this resolution and the Soviet representative—to the surprise of no one —vetoed it. The United States Government, under the direction of Dulles, then took the initiative in the General Assembly which passed a sturdy resolution by 53 to 9, with 13 abstentions, calling for immediate cessation of Soviet intervention in Hungary and providing for UN representatives to observe conditions in that country and to submit a report. But the Soviet Union would not permit Sir Leslie Munro of New Zealand to visit Budapest as an observer. We pushed as hard as we could in the UN forum, but we failed in our essential objective—release of the Hungarian people from bondage.

In the end, our government was reduced to the minimal policy of providing assistance to Hungarian refugees, and to impact on world opinion—whatever that may mean. On the assumption that the American people did not desire to go to war against the Soviet Union, and in Washington it was believed that they did not, there seemed no other policy to pursue. The American Legation in Budapest gave sanctuary to Cardinal Mindszenty; 21,500 refugees were offered asylum in the United States; and our government engaged in sundry welfare work for the Hungarian people. This was not a glorious position for the United States, and the words "roll back the aggressors" no longer appeared in speeches. General Ivan A. Serov, Soviet State Security Chief, arrived in Hungary and apparently was in charge of deportations which assumed massive proportions. Many patriotic men and women were executed.

Morally, the Soviet Union undoubtedly suffered in Western opinion. For one thing, the Soviet action doomed the "Spirit of Geneva" which had been exercising a divisive influence in the West and which was beginning to pay off for the Russians. But the U.S.S.R., as a practical matter, incurred little or no visible damage to its own world position. In fact the element of fear plays an important role in international affairs, and the effe.. of Hungary on some countries was evident in their subsequent willingness to yield to Soviet influence in the United Nations. In retrospect, world acceptance of the Russian aggression in Hungary is still incredible. For sheer perfidy and relentless suppression of a courageous people longing for their liberty, Hungary will always remain a classic symbol. Perhaps history will demonstrate that the free world could have intervened to give the Hungarians the liberty they sought, but none of us in the State Department had the skill or the imagination to devise a way.

II.

EXCHANGE OF LETTERS
BETWEEN THE EDITOR OF THE HUNGARIAN QUARTERLY AND
AMBASSADOR HENRY CABOT LODGE
IN CONNECTION WITH THE HUNGARIAN
QUESTION DEBATED AT THE UNITED NATIONS ON
NOVEMBER 3, 1956, A FATEFUL DAY.

January 2, 1961
New York, New York

Dear Ambassador Lodge:

I am sending you herewith the January, 1961 issue of *The Hungarian Quarterly*. It contains an article by Sen. Thomas J. Dodd with critical remarks on the U.S. attitude toward Hungary during the 1956 revolution.

Sen. Dodd questions in particular your support of a proposal to adjourn discussion of the Hungarian situation in the U.N. on Nov. 3, 1956, (when messages from Budapest requested such a discussion in view of Soviet troop movements) and discusses several alternative courses of action.

We would be most interested in exploring those questions regarding the 1956 Hungarian events which have not yet been fully clarified. We would, therefore, be very glad if you would summarize for the next issue of *The Hun-*

garian Quarterly what took place in the U.N. between Oct. 23 and Nov. 4, 1956, and particularly, what motivated the stand of the United States delegation in the Hungarian issue.

Hungarian exiles are well aware of your sympathy for the Hungarian cause. They would be grateful to hear the whole story from you, a person whom they trust and respect. Moreover, I am sure that this particular aspect of the Hungarian problem would be of general interest to all readers.

The next issue of *The Hungarian Quarterly* goes to press on Feb. 15. Should you find it impossible to write a more comprehensive article, we would be glad to publish your comments on Sen. Dodd's article, as a brief note, or letter to the editor.

Sincerely yours,

IMRE KOVACS, Editor

Beverly, Massachusetts
January 16, 1961

Dear Mr. Kovacs:

This acknowledges your letter of January 2, enclosing an article in *The Hungarian Quarterly* for January, 1961 by Senator Thomas J. Dodd.

Unfortunately, I have not time to write an article for your next issue on everything that took place concerning Hungary in the United Nations between October 23 and November 4, 1956, as you request.

But I accept your invitation to comment on Senator Dodd's statements concerning me.

1. I refer particularly to Senator Dodd's statement on page 17 that when the Security Council met on Saturday, November 3, "it met, to our eternal shame, not at the request of the United States, but at the urgent insistence of Dr. Emilio Portuondo of Cuba."

There was nothing shameful about this. The people of Hungary had many friends in the United Nations. There was no reason why the then Representative of Cuba should not request the meeting rather than the

United States. We, of the United States Delegation, supported his request. If he had not asked for the meeting, we, or someone else, undoubtedly would have. It is really looking for trouble to see anything shameful in that.

2. Senator Dodd then quotes me as saying at the 753rd meeting of the Security Council on November 3, 1956:

"We believe that adjournment for a day or two would give a real opportunity to the Hungarian Government to carry out its announced desire to arrange for an orderly and immediate evacuation of all the Soviet troops."

This quotation is taken out of context. When read in context it gives a different picture of the United States position. Here is my complete statement:

"On the question of adjournment the United States view is as follows:—Secretary of State Dulles at the General Assembly meeting on 1 November said: 'I think we must not allow our preoccupation with what is going on in the Middle East to keep us from also observing with equal intensity what goes on in that part of the world'—that is in Eastern Europe.

"We are still disturbed by the wide differences between Soviet Union words about troop withdrawals and Soviet Union actions as evidenced in news reports. We believe accordingly that adjournment for a day or two would give a real opportunity to the Hungarian Government to carry out its announced desire to arrange for an orderly and immediate evacuation of all Soviet troops. But clearly the Security Council must keep this matter under urgent consideration. It may well be necessary for the Council to meet tomorrow as the Representative of Cuba suggests if events do not bear out the reports which we have heard today. In this spirit I should be willing, as I said, to adjourn until tomorrow or the next day, but I should wish to hear the Soviet Union Representative, if it is agreeable to him, before we adjourn today—and, of course, any other Representative who may wish to speak."

3. Senator Dodd says he does not understand my statement that the United States supported this adjournment

proposal on the announced desire of the Hungarian Government to arrange for an orderly and immediate evacuation of all the Soviet troops.

Would Senator Dodd have had the United States ignore the announced desire of the Hungarian Government to arrange for an orderly and immediate evacuation of the Soviet troops?

The United States was doing what it could to help the anti-Communist Government of Hungary—not to hinder it. The fact that a short time later it became clear to the Hungarian Government that the Soviet Union was lying does not alter the fact that on November 3 the Hungarian Government had some hope that the Soviets were telling the truth. This was a decision which it was the Hungarian Government's to make.

4. Senator Dodd writes of the motivation of my statement. Its motivation was instructions from Washington. At that particular time, Washington could not be sure of all of the facts of the situation and a moment's reflection will show why this was so. Washington was confronting these things: the Suez crisis; a fog of uncertainty about events in Hungary; and the very real possibility of a clash with the Soviet Union—with the world-shattering consequences which this could entail. A false move could not only have been very dangerous for the United States, but also devastating for Hungary. For Washington to have acted precipitately would have been extremely imprudent.

The United States Government did everything that could be done, short of taking steps which would have led to war. In the evolution of the United States foreign policy I carried out only one part, but that part speaks for itself. As you yourself are kind enough to say—and many Hungarians have generously echoed—I was (and am) filled with sympathy for the Hungarian cause and I left no stone unturned to do what I could to help.

Very sincerely yours,

HENRY CABOT LODGE

III.

In a special program entitled EISENHOWER ON THE PRESIDENCY, PART II, *on November 23, 1961, the Columbia Broadcasting System (CBS) presented, among other topics, the former President's views on the Hungarian Revolution. The following dialogue took place between General Eisenhower and CBS reporter Walter Cronkite:*

CRONKITE: There's one other point when we talk about natural aspirations for freedom of men, and this is Hungary. What were the limitations that kept us from moving into Hungary?

EISENHOWER: Well, the only way that the United States could have ever moved would have been one as of coalition, because you couldn't have jumped over Germany, Austria or France, or any other direction and gone in there, because it would not have been allowed. You were dealing with sovereign countries. There was no European country, and indeed, I don't believe ours, ready to say that we should have gone into this thing at once and tried to liberate Hungary from the Communist influence. I don't believe, at this time, that we had the support of the United Nations to go in and make this a full-out war. The thing started in such a way, you know, that everybody was a little bit fooled, I think, and when suddenly the Soviets came in in strength with their tank divisions, and it was a fait accompli, it was a great tragedy and disaster. But I don't believe that as of this day, even second sight, which is usually 20–20, I don't believe that the United States or any other country was ready to go to major war on that basis at that time.

CRONKITE: You had no doubts, in your own mind, that commitment in Hungary would lead to a major conflict with Russia?

EISENHOWER: Oh, it would have bound to have, in my opinion. Yes.

CRONKITE: Well, Mr. President, there was criticism, as I know you're aware, because in the nineteen hundred and fifty-two campaign, and thereafter, there were pledges that we were going to help liberate the peoples behind the Iron Curtain.

EISENHOWER: I was always very careful in the 1952 campaign; I always said, "By every peaceful means." I said, we will never accept the theory that these nations are to be forever enslaved. But we are not going to war to liberate them. We are going to use every peaceable means open to us, and I think we should always do that.

CRONKITE: Well, in the case of Lebanon, you did move . . .

EISENHOWER: Yes.

CRONKITE: Quickly and adroitly to put American troops ashore, although the Russians were threatening to intervene with volunteers?

EISENHOWER: They were threatening a lot of things, but what we did—we took a number of our combat teams from Europe and put them right ashore, and there we operated on the basis that a friendly government, with whom we had friendly relations, had asked for protection against this outside infiltration and almost invasion. We did it and were ready and prepared to take the consequences of it because we believed it was right, and quickly as they saw we meant business, why everything went very well, and it wasn't long before we could get out.

CRONKITE: You don't think that their reaction would have been the same in Hungary? I mean, when they see we mean business?

EISENHOWER: Not at that time, no—not at that time, because first of all, we had no agreement by Hungary. We had no government that was asking us to come in and it wasn't until there was a sort of a, I think, a very brief revolutionary government was set up, that we had any communication with them. So I don't know. It wasn't the same case at all.

HUNGARY TODAY:
THE ESTABLISHMENT

Reprinted (and supplemented) article of Imre
Kovács: "The Establishment in Hungary," EAST
EUROPE, May, 1956, Volume 14, Number 5. New
York, New York.

Developments in Hungary since World War II have
been marked by pendulum-like swings. The 1945 free
elections gave the non-communist parties an 83 per cent
majority. Yet in two years the Communist Party—aided
by Soviet Russia—staged a coup that forced the cruelest
type of communism on a nation long noted for its independent free spirit, its love of liberty.

Stalin's death in 1953 brought down Mátyás Rákosi
too, the Kremlin's viceroy, along with his Moscow-
trained cadre; and Imre Nagy, succeeding him as Prime
Minister, set a "new course" for Hungary in a desperate
effort to revise the ugly trends of communism. Fake
trials and arbitrary methods were abjured, political
prisoners freed, rehabilitated, even compensated; deportations ceased. The new communist regime pledged "socialist legality," improved working conditions, encouraged peasants to dissolve or leave the collectives and
abolished compulsory deliveries. Intellectuals regained
a degree of creative freedom. But haunted by the inevit-
ability of a built-in democratic escalation of liberal communism, hard-core stalwarts led by the re-emerging Rákosi, quashed the "new course" and put Hungary back
on the old track. They did not fully succeed in restor-
ing communist stupidity and rigidity, yet the people
grew alarmed, and when re-Stalinization touched the
most sensitive fields of national interest, revolt erupted
with volcanic force.

Massive Soviet military intervention on November 4, 1956, dashed the dreams of a free, independent Hungary; still life beats the strongest tyranny, and gradually changes were achieved—the pendulum swung again ...

The man the Russians chose to re-establish communism, János Kádár, was really a compromise—neither an Imre Nagy, caught up in the October Revolution, nor a Rákosi provoking it. Kádár is certainly a devoted communist, even an aspiring ideologist, as indicated by the title of his collected speeches and writings, FORWARD ON THE ROAD OF MARXISM-LENINISM. He has stated repeatedly his aim of a "positive relation" to the Soviet Union, and is quick to attack any hint that his regime might in any way oppose Soviet interests. While he has pushed various internal reforms, these are not to be considered "liberalization," he insists, but "humanization"—that is, they are not a movement away from communism but simply an effort to make it more livable.

VICTORY IN DEFEAT?

In an effort to achieve some degree of reconciliation between party and nation, Kádár has been applying a policy of measured concessions. However, these are quite limited and cannot be construed as meaning that the 1956 revolution is being carried out by those who suppressed it. Some Western circles rashly concluded that many of the revolutionary demands—ranging from 15 to 80 percent—have been implemented by Kádár, French publicist, Claude Bourdet, even described the situation as "victory in defeat." (*Les Temps Modernes,* March 1964.)

What is the truth? Between October 23 and November 9, 1956, Hungarian radio stations under revolutionary control broadcast 225 major demands. Of these, 35 percent called for national independence; 31 percent for political reform; and 28 percent for economic reform. The revolutionary program might be summed up in three points: national independence, withdrawal of Soviet troops, and free elections. Have these key demands been met? The country is perhaps more autonomous, but certainly not independent. The government remains a monopoly of the communists; and there are still 80 thousand Soviet soldiers in Hungary. Thus no matter how Kádár's changes are appraised, the things left undone are precisely those which would bring Hungary independence and freedom.

The party, with a membership of 550,000 (about five percent of the population, or a little over half its peak size in the Rákosi era), is the same power structure as in the other East European countries where communism was imposed by the Soviet Army. But some of its functions have been transferred to various front organizations, including the trade unions and social, professional and cultural groups. Unlike Poland and East Germany, where several tame political parties are allowed to function alongside the communists, Hungary has only the People's Patriotic Front—a firmly controlled, standard communist device intended to give mass appeal to the party's election campaigns. Even so, at its last congress in March 1964 there was talk of the possibility of replacing the single ticket with separate election districts or constituencies in which two or more candidates would vie for office.

Parliamentarianism and the multi-party system, however, are "needless," as party ideologist Dezső Nemes avers in the November 1964 issue of *Társadalmi Szemle* (Social Review)—though conceding that the dissolution in 1949 of the non-communist parties was too hurried— since the "socialist system and forms of organization ensure the development of the people's civic activities." And blandly he lists the organizations of "indirect" democracy, as: the Communist Party, the Communist Youth Federation, the trade unions, the Patriotic People's Front committees, the production and factory councils, the agricultural and craft co-operatives, the associations of scientists and scholars, the Hungarian Red Cross, the volunteer firefighting groups, the National Sports Federation, the stamp collectors' and hunters' associations, the fishermen's federation. Indeed three quarters of society is organized: "Socialist democracy assures the people the right of assembly better than the workers ever managed to achieve it."

Dezső Nemes further boasts: in the preceding year (1963), at the parliamentary and council elections, 70.5 percent of the population was entitled to vote and the "privilege" was exercised by 97.2 percent of those eligible. "The elections of course were secret." Yet another bizarre statement: "In our country the multi-party system is desired only by isolated reactionary elements who thereby hope to break out of their isolation and conduct effective machinations to disrupt the new political unity and its creative forces."

Nevertheless, Hungarian politics today is haunted by the ghost of parliamentary democracy. Official spokesmen labor to convince the public that nothing essential is lacking and that—to quote Premier Gyula Kállai—"the Hungarian parliament is more democratic than that of any capitalist country." (*Népszabadsag* [People's Freedom], December 25, 1964.) But under these pronouncements runs a current of doubt. Kállai himself admitted at the last congress of the PPF that not everyone was happy with single-list elections; on the other hand, in his December article he merely proposed to increase the number of candidates for the single ticket. "Since our society is led by the party of the revolutionary working class . . . we ourselves must simultaneously be the opposition party." Apparently the idea is to allow more approved non-communist candidates on the ticket, thus widening the regime's electoral base. This might conceivably open the way to broader policies reflecting the desires of the people, provided of course that the political status quo and existing "social achievements" are not threatened.

Freer and more democratic electoral procedures are in fact being adopted in various political bodies, reluctantly but steadily, from the parliament and party down to local councils. The parliament is no longer just an assembly of yes-men; it has acquired a more business-like atmosphere in which the deputies talk frankly and critically (though not, of course, challenging the regime's basic policies). The question period has been brought back, when ministers must answer to the deputies, and the Budapest radio has a regular program ("Between Sessions") where ministers and deputies are asked whether promised action was taken. The revamped parliamentary committees discuss special issues such as budget, education, foreign affairs, the planned economy, etc., in closed-door sessions, and groups of deputies hold regional meetings at their respective county seats.

THE ORGANIZATION MEN

While the backbone of the Kádár regime is still the party, the government's main support comes from an élite of bureaucrats and technocrats who know how to run a modern state. One of the most intriguing phenomena of present-day Hungary is the quiet takeover of the state economy and important segments of the civil service by old-timers and various experts. "Proletarian origin" or "movement merits" no longer count, and party hacks without enough education to meet the new standards are being pushed aside. In higher education, talent and ability now have priority; the graduate schools are open only to those who can pass the entrance examinations.

The appearance of the "organization" man in Hungary raises serious questions for the party. How much authority can be turned over to experts and technocrats without undermining the system, in terms both of power and ideology? "The currents of present-day bourgeois ideology which are the strongest in Hungary do not attack Marxism frontally," warned *Társadalmi Szemle* (Social Review) in November, 1964, "but try to reconcile Marxism and bourgeois ideology."

One of these currents is the bourgeois approach to economic, sociological, political and other problems of socialist development, *e.g.*, the concept of a "united industrial society," which, with regard to technical and scientific development, ignores the differences between the social systems of capitalism and communism. Another characteristic of bourgeois ideology is the existentialist concept of the individual. This expresses itself in the abstract and unhistorical treatment of ethical questions, in doctrinaire sermonizing, in confusion on the conflict between power and

morals, and, finally, in the confrontation of an isolated personality with an alien society. And a claim of "neutrality"
is frequently heard with regard to the ideological approach
to science and neo-positivism.

The ideological confrontation has also led to friction
between party members and non-party experts, the former complaining that they are being unjustly shunted
aside and that the new intelligentsia gets undeserved advantages. Party spokesmen reply that the policy is one
of "national unity" aiming to win over the intelligentsia; adding that if party loyalty is not enough to build
socialism under modern conditions, neither is just technical expertise.

Such sophistry would have foundered in the old days,
but the party is no longer what is was, and shrugs off
the concern of the onetime main cadre. The revolutionary stance would seem to have been a pretence, a "passing fever" which they admit was "inescapably" displaced
by a sobering-up. In the March 1964 issue of *Les Temps
Modernes,* Claude Bourdet observes that "the law of
progress make the (Hungarian) Communist Party re-
semble an English club or a university alumni organization, where professionals and experts with similar interests gather, rather than the earlier revolutionaries."
Népszabadság shudders at the thought, and protests ve-
hemently at the idea that the future might belong to
the technocrats, "the much touted professional barbarians" . . .

Nevertheless, Hungary has now been taken over by a
new class, or more accurately a new bourgeoisie. The
makeup of this Communist establishment, comprising
about one percent of the population, is rather heterogeneous. It includes the upper strata of the party, civil
service, state-run economy, planning office and trade
unions; senior officers of the army and security police;
privileged scientists; highly qualified experts; and the
usual upper crust of artists and writers. While they have
no common language, since communists and non-communists think and talk quite differently, they do have a
common past: most all of them suffered under Rákosi in

the days of Stalin, and some were his followers as well.
And they share a common interest: to keep things running and retain power.

The new Hungarian ruling class claims much the same
perquisites—homes, villas, pleasures, cars, travel—as its
pre-war counterpart, and is no less selfish, detached, ar-
rogant and corrupt. Below the top élite is another stratum of managers who run the state and local administration, the government enterprises, collective farms,
banks, educational and propaganda network, etc. They
are tough, unmannered, poorly educated. While they
follow orders from above, they do not always show a
sense of responsibility. Far, far below this feudal hierarchy lies the rest of the nation—the peasants and workers. Although national income is better distributed than
in pre-war Hungary, this class lives just above the poverty line.

ECONOMIC PROBLEMS

While lip service is still paid to traditional Marxist-
Leninist economic theories, a pragmatic approach to central planning and the new perspectives in East-West relations brought important changes in the Hungarian
economy. Under the pressure for more, better and var-
iegated consumer goods, and as a result of COMECON
measures for "international distribution of labor"
spurred by the high economic standards of the European
Common Market, production profiles and goals are being constantly revised.

A slow growth rate, low production and productivity
levels, and low quality are the most acute problems of
Hungarian industry. A steel plant in West Germany,
whose capacity equals that of the whole Hungarian nationalized steel industry, produces twice as much with
half as many workers. An American miner's output is
ten times that of a Hungarian. In Hungarian goods produced for export there is more work per unit than in
imported goods which, along with the grave deficit, is
a measure of inferior management. Economist István
Földes notes the vanity of boasting of advances when
the "standard is not our own past, but world technol-

ogy, whose progress has quickened by leaps and bounds" (*Népszabadság,* August 9, 1964). Hungarian industry produces slowly and expensively on outmoded machines, "shackled by equipment ten or more years old." Some lathe models are seven or eight years old, others date back fifteen or twenty years. Half the high-voltage products of the machine tool industry are pre-war models. Plant design is unsuitable; furnaces, foundries and power plants are undersized. The proud Hungarian flour mill industry cannot compete with even the bloc countries: it grinds at forty to fifty percent higher cost.

Quality falls below specifications. So "over the years there has been a great pile-up of goods," notes Deputy Premier Jenö Fock, chief of economic planning. State enterprises won't accept shoddy half-finished and finished goods from each other, but the public also shies from inferior products. Generally a quarter of the vacuum cleaners, washing machines, shoes, textile goods are unsalable rejects which can only be dumped at year-end sales. The growth of Hungarian exports is hindered by undependable shipments; orders are canceled for lateness, wares sent back if not as specified. Modernization is blocked by servile imitation of Soviet plant design and production clichés, by the unwieldiness of central control and an almost ritual bureaucratism. In vain have special skills been offered greater scope, the expert still faces party stubbornness and caprice at every turn.

The high cost of production is passed on to the public. That is why living standards sag. At the same time they foster the illusion of full employment through tricks of capital outlay so as to save face. About a third of plant workers just do make-work unrelated to production, at most carting raw material or finished goods back and forth. Jenö Fock also complains that the state enterprises "in the last few years have been employing an unjustifiable number of white and blue collar workers . . . the roll of administrative employees has grown faster than that of technical workers." Some sectors show a lack of skilled labor; at the same time "the number of helpers and assistants has needlessly ballooned." The improper use of time and men calls for stern measures involving the complete overhaul of labor utilization in the state enterprises, the political impact of which, however, so scares the communist regime that it rather struggles along with things as they are. Such urgent, and eventually inescapable overall rationalization might suddenly reveal the concealed unemployment, and inflame worker discontent. Besides, under socialism there can be no unemployment—an ugly capitalist phenomenon, sign of crisis—so they must maintain the camouflage.*

The average monthly wage of skilled workers is 1,700 forints, the price of an ordinary suit or overcoat. So somehow they must supplement their earnings—at which they are very bold and resourceful. A recent conference of tooling plant managers and engineers produced this tongue-in-cheek proposal: "In our factories we must eliminate the household industries." Laughter greeted this exposure of dual industrial production. The Hungarian worker divides his on-the-job time between factory work output and private projects, using plant equipment, power and his pick of raw materials to make coffee percolators, fishing reels, TV antennas, kitchen stoves, etc. In factory jargon they call this *fusizás* (from the German *fuschen,* bungle). Workers cover up for each other. Carefully they stash away scarce raw materials; but also bail out the chief engineer on rush orders. The factories, too, indulge in a type of "bungling": when missing parts can't be had through state channels, they resort to fantastically expensive "home" tooling. And for ticklish foreign orders they call in the independent small craftsmen —on overtime.

Marx didn't think too much of the peasants, he dubbed them a "bag of potatoes." In his turn, Engels called them the "barbarians of history." Doubtless that is why agriculture scarcely counts (though collectivization is a basic tenet of Marxism-Leninism) in that weird rite of punctiliously assessing the rate of "socialist progress." Once communists seize power, when does a so-called capitalist or feudal-capitalist nation become a "people's democracy"? When does it ripen to "socialism," and

* Some tightening up late in 1965 caused wide-spread unrest, resulting in arrests and stricter police control.

when does the chosen society earn the accolade of having finally "built" communism?

In Poland 12 percent of agriculture has been collectivized, in Yugoslavia 17 percent and in Hungary 97 percent, yet each ranks the same: they are building socialism. (And here we can't resist adding that they buy in America the grain for the bread they eat.) Then why—despite Kádár's repeated promises to the contrary—did they have to force-collectivize Hungarian agriculture?

According to a special report on Hungary by the research branch of Radio Free Europe (München, Germany, 1961), the first phase of the collectivization drive started in mid-January 1959 and was over by March. A second wave came a year later and ended between December 1960 and March 1961. "Although activists were supposed to convert the peasant by words only and, in theory, farmers would join the producers' cooperatives out of their own free will, the first two phases of the campaign (and especially the first) were marked by brutal coercion."

And the third phases of collectivization, though milder, brought the peasant a host of problems with which he was psychologically unprepared to deal. Strong-arm methods were now replaced by sophisticated and less-sophisticated propaganda ranging from mass visits by "patronizing" factory workers to threats, bribes and "promises mixed with appeals to reason and to the peasant's patriotism and self-interest."

Collective agriculture, patterned after the Soviet *kolkhos* system, is the main area where Hungarian communists stubbornly cling to their orthodox, obsolete theories. Marginal reforms have been introduced to improve management and wage systems, but any interference with the concept of collectives is taboo. Up to 96.7 per cent of the land has been collectivized; and the sole privilege Hungarian peasants enjoy is the right to a small garden or strip from the common, which they can cultivate on their own.

The so-called profit system introduced in Hungary's communist agriculture, and interpreted by some Western correspondents as "a means to keep 'em happy down on the collective farms" (*New York Times,* Oct. 25, 1964), is but a modified version of the pre-war feudal form of share-cropping used as an extra stimulus to payments in kind or cash in a grossly underdeveloped economy chronically short of funds. The sole difference between the two approaches is the *ratio*: pre-war Hungarian land-lords took a half to two-thirds of the produce from their sharecroppers, while under the "new system" the Communist State, as super-landlord, grants a twenty per cent bonus per "work unit" to members of certain collectives. Although adjustable, a "work unit" is roughly equal to wages for a ten-hour work day, amounting in the "Nádudvar* experiment" to 16.6 forints ($0.20) by free exchange). So the "profiteering" kolkhos peasants, pooled by brute force into collectives, are now sharecroppers on their own lands.

So-called "profit-sharing," far from being a healthy sign of Hungarian agricultural progress, was rather as an omen of acute crisis. Based on 1938 as 100, at the start of forced collectivization in 1949, the production index (recuperating from war damage) was 85 and at the end of Rákosi's collectivization campaign in 1952 dropped ominously to 70. The next year, during lenient-communist Imre Nagy's "new course," when peasants left the collectives to farm their own lands, the production index jumped to a post-war peak of 97. After the crushed 1956 revolt, it fell again to 88; however, the Kádár regime claims a rise to 115 in 1962 and 121 in 1965. Meanwhile, population grew by 10 per cent between 1938 and 1964.

The troubles of Hungarian agriculture lie in the combination of collective and private operation within the kolkhos system. Each kolkhos member is entitled to an acre of land for private use (expanded to six acres in collectives where the "Nádudvar system" obtains—about half of them) dividing his work between the private and

---

* A turbulent large agrarian community with a long, brave record of fighting for freedom and social justice, Nádudvar became the first "collective town" in the late forties when forced collectivization began under Rákosi in 1950. Now it symbolizes the break with orthodox Communist agricultural methods and management.

collective sectors. According to official data, the private operations, using 24 per cent of the farm labor force, account for 38 per cent of gross agricultural production. In the collectives (as of 1961) out of a total membership of 1,115,000, 410,000 members were over 60, and 260,000 did not participate in the common work. That has left 440,000 active collective members seeking part-time jobs in industry, the building trades or mines, as unskilled hands, or moonlighting as artisans, gardeners, etc. The gross agricultural product in Hungary is valued at 1.5 billion dollars, yielding the farm population of 3.3 million an annual per capita income of $450.00.

Faster development of agriculture is required for steady growth of the whole economy—a view shared by communist leaders, too, but they are loath to admit that collectivization shackles Hungarian agriculture. Instead of a dogmatic approach, the real solution would be de-collectivization and the expansion of private farming; a step they dare not take for fear of disrupting the political monopoly of the party.

FALLING BIRTH RATE

A nation's energy and optimism is measured by its growth. In Hungary natural increase has faltered and slowed to the extent of being the last in Europe, if not in all the world. In 1954, for 223,500 live births there were 106,500 deaths; a net growth of 117,000. In 1962, for 130,000 live births there were 108,000 deaths, the increase being 22,000. With 250,000 abortions yearly the population of Hungary increased by only 1.5 per cent in the last five years. Again it was the writers who sounded the tocsin, just as in the thirties when Endre Bajcsy-Zsilinszky, János Kodolányi, Lajos Fülep, Gyula Illyés, Lajos Zilahy, Géza Féja and others shocked society and the government into the realization of the dire consequences of "only-childism" in the Ormánsag and Sárköz districts. The new alarm at first was viewed as just the "forebodings of aging populist writers." Now even the doubters and cynics admit there is something in their "mad vision" of a nation's death.

The Kádár regime rejects all charges that communism

might have anything to do with the plummetting growth rate. It is a world phenomenon, they argue officially. An easier life, indifference, irresponsibility are the reasons—along the right of women to "bear or not to bear." According to some demographers the Hungarians are in an "underpopulating trough" through war-caused gaps: fewer marry, and there are fewer births.

However, a debate, probing more deeply, encountered complex, many-layered problems.

Collectivization ousted the prolific peasants from the soil and their traditional way of life. The younger age groups switched to industrial jobs in the towns; the wealthier peasants (kulaks) were deported; and within fifteen years (1949–64) a million and a half souls—a third of the agrarian population—dropped out of agriculture. Those who exchanged rural life for the city's found no tranquility or rapport in jammed slum quarters; the last resort of proletarianized couples was surgical intervention.

In Hungary 34 per cent of apartments comprise one room and kitchen, 60 per cent two rooms; 84 per cent have no bathroom, 77.5 per cent have no running water, and 26 per cent no electricity. Birth control has been forced on most couples by extraordinarily unfavorable social conditions; or the assurance of a relatively higher living standard. Still others fell victim to slacker morals, to a sensuous *dolce vita*.

Within a quarter of a century, Hungarian marriage patterns have changed radically. In 1938, 25.8 per cent of the men and 58.7 per cent of the women entering into marriage were 24 years old or younger; in 1962, 47.9 per cent of the men and 70.4 per cent of the women. Hungarians are marrying earlier and divorcing sooner. In 1962, 9.5 per cent of married persons were divorced in less than a year; and of those divorced 44.7 per cent were childless, while 33.7 per cent had just one child.

A young writer, Károly Jobbágyi, who despite his earlier deploring of alarms, now also holds that we need not even necessarily think in terms of nuclear war—a sudden epidemic or natural catastrophe would do and then only the strong peoples would survive, while the weak perished. Dumfounded, he asks, "Can it be that our history, or literature may become just a memory, stuff for scholars?"

YOUNG CYNICS AND OLD HERETICS

The feeling that something has gone wrong with Hungarian communism, widespread among party members, is especially marked in the younger generation. "Politics is a dirty business," said one high school student in a radio discussion, and next day a commentator agreed with him. "Our young friend took these words out of the mouths of adults. They often say that politics is a dangerous trade, a dirty thing. How often a reporter is told, 'Please, I am not interested in politics.'" (Radio Kossuth, January 26, 1965.)

This attitude among the young has made the battle of generations unusually intense, for added to the normal outrage of the young at the follies of their elders is a political disgust over the state of the nation they are to inherit. Three years ago the young poet Ferenc Baranyi published some verses which shook the establishment.

> For seventeen years, we busily filled
> Our heads with the wine of knowledge,
> And yet, from a high shelf, an
> Empty barrel-head arrogantly
> Echoes instructions for us. . . .

The battle continues. In the January 1965 issue of the avant-garde literary monthly *Uj Irás* (New Writing) another young poet, Ferenc Buda, speaks of the attitude of those between 25 and 30: "We were enthusiastic twice and disappointed twice, on both occasions so cruelly that we could hardly survive even with our elastic spirit. It is not easy for us to be enthusiastic; instead of ideas, we try to find strength within ourselves on which we can depend." (The two occasions are obviously the "liberation" of 1945 and the revolt of 1956. The latter is called "the counter-revolution" by the party, but remains a vivid, inspiring memory to people in all walks of life.)

His comments are part of a series entitled "Confessions About Youth." Most of the articles are, in effect, an indictment of the older generation, including the political leaders. A young, idealistic man, argues Buda, cannot hope to make a career because he is always running up against "job security, professional or materialistic jealousy, a kind of bad mood which is impossible to define, and corruption." Buda feels that the younger generation is not understood; that it is underpaid and ignored. Especially hard is the lot of the young professional or intellectual forced to live in the countryside where his ideas and energy beat in vain "against the massive walls of poverty, misery, conservatism, prejudice, resentment, heavy-handed bossism, and hidden hostility."

Peter Veres, an old establishment writer with a slight accent of nonconformity, observed in the December 1964 issue of *Kortárs* (Contemporary) that a prevalent mood in Hungary is indifference, an "apolitical" attitude stemming from "weariness and disappointment." He analyzed its various causes, most of which seemed to lie in the conflict between the "Messianic" promises of Marxism and the uncomfortable facts of reality. This apolitical attitude, he declared, "is the biggest and most difficult problem facing Hungarian Society."

Beneath the calm surface, dark currents are at work. In the late forties and early fifties the regimented writers and artists were made to express the "happiness" of the Hungarians; today, when life is relatively free and the writers and artists are able to create according to their talents and ideas, the new Hungarian literature and art reflect sadness, pessimism, despondency, despair. Their pervasive themes are the unhappiness of man and the emptiness of life; they are obsessed with the horrors of the recent past and the total absence of alternatives. There is no difference here between the older and the younger generations.

THE ADVANCE WESTWARD

While the atmosphere within the country is freer, but not happier, Budapest's foreign policy remains essentially that of the Soviet Union. President Johnson's "bridge-building" approach to Eastern Europe is interpreted Moscow-style as a desire to make Hungary a "bridge-head" against the Soviet Union. Unlike the Rumanians and Poles, Hungarian communists have not exploited the power relations in the communist world to achieve national ends of their own, and until now Kádár has been among Moscow's two or three most reliable sup-porters. This may perhaps be a symptom of the politi-cal vacuum in Hungary. Not one of the top leaders was educated in the West or even visited a free country be-fore he acquired his official post. The technocrats are not interested in foreign affairs, and the better-educated non-communist supporters of the regime have no desire to venture into dangerous fields.

Nevertheless the Kádár regime is trying to improve its international image, and the red carpet is rolled out for every prominent visitor along with 21-gun salutes. In recent years, state guests have included Khrushchev, Gomulka, Novotny of Czechoslovakia, Zhivkov of Bul-garia, Tito, Haile Selassie, the President of the Yemen Republic, Brezhnev, etc. In 1964, Budapest began to ex-plore opportunities for closer contacts with the West. It developed warm relations with Austria, reached an accord with the Vatican, signed a trade agreement with Britain and a cultural agreement with Belgium, and even flirted a little with de Gaulle's formula for a united Europe.

The *rapprochement* with Austria revived memories of the Hapsburg era when Hungary played an important role in Europe. Receiving Hungary's Deputy Premier Jenö Fock in Vienna in 1964, Austrian Vice Chancellor Bruno Pittermann said: "For Austria, Hungary is like the neighbor's flower garden." Austrians and Hungar-ians talked hopefully of some new form of co-operation, and after they had settled their claims it was reported that the two countries were planning joint industrial operations and business deals with the underdeveloped world. At an international Congress of Historians in Budapest, participants openly discussed the lessons to be drawn from the history of the Austro-Hungarian monarchy; some speakers even raised the question whether the Western powers had not been mistaken in pressing for its dissolution in 1918.

The biggest surprise was provided by Foreign Minister János Péter when he visited Paris in January 1965.* On his arrival at the Gare de l'Est this dull, opportunistic bureaucrat announced that he had come "to take a close look at France's idea of an independent, enlarged and 'European' Europe." After he had met with his French counterpart Couve de Murville, he told the press that "Hungary, despite the fact that she is a small country, can in her geographical position help to bring the opposing worlds closer to each other."

His visit to France was called "historic," and the slogan "Europe to the Urals" received great play in the Hungarian press. "Why not?" asked the Budapest radio. "Hungary is a European nation, and it is only natural that she express interest in a Europe whose borders can not be arbitrarily drawn; it stretches from the Atlantic to the Urals. The cultural heritage of Europe is still a force in our culture and traditions."

Kádár was led to discuss the idea in his speech to parliament on February 11, 1965: "Class struggle has not invalidated geography," he said, but he went on—typically—to say that while Hungary is geographically part of Europe it belongs politically to the "socialist world system." On the question of whether the two parts of Europe might be brought closer, he confined himself as usual to the line laid down by Moscow: recognition of the status quo in eastern Europe (including East Germany and a separate West Berlin); the requirement that a withdrawal of Soviet troops can take place only as part of a "give and take" arrangement between East and West; and the levelling of the Common Market tariff wall.

Returning the visit of his Hungarian colleague to Paris, French Foreign Minister Maurice Couve de Murville arrived in Budapest at the end of July, 1966 for a two-day visit which was marked by great cordiality.

* The first state visit of a Hungarian foreign minister to France; others had gone there to sign the peace treaties in 1920 and in 1947 with the Allies.

Immediately a cultural and consular agreement, as well as an agreement on cultural, technical and scientific co-operation, was signed between the countries. During the talks bilateral relations and international problems, primarily the German question and Vietnam, were discussed.

Hungarian Foreign Minister Peter said in his speech at the airport that the visit is a "new stage" in the development of French-Hungarian relations which can be considered a "new step" on the road of détente and the peaceful solution of European problems. Couve de Murville said that his visit is at the same time a beginning and a result. The results of it are shown in the agreements concluded, but at the same time the visit is the beginning of a "certain rapprochement" and the two countries must continue to follow this road: "Europeans must attempt to create a European Europe."

In an article entitled "Promising Results of French-Hungarian Dialogue," central party organ *Népszabadság* stated on August 2, 1966:

> The cordial atmosphere that had prevailed throughout the French Foreign Minister's conversations in Budapest, the goodwill expressed in the same measure by Paris and by ourselves, furnish every reason to be confident in judging the perspectives concerning the relationship between the two countries.

From the end of 1964 until early 1966, Hungarian communist leaders, including Kádár, made occasional public statements about the "common fate" of the Danubian nations and the geopolitical significance of Hungary's location in the center of Europe. These statements were made initially in the context of efforts to improve Hungarian-Austrian relations, but the formulations used by communist Hungarians bore a striking similarity to a concept developed by 19th century Hungarian statesmen such as Kossuth, then at the end of World War I by Oscar Jászi, and later by the communist Imre Nagy. This concept recognized the "community of fate" of Hungary and its Danubian neighbors, and that these smaller nations shared common, indeed vital, interests in counterbalancing the political and economic power of their larger European neighbors.

The "Danubian" statements by Kádár and János Péter raised some hopes that the communist leadership was considering a shift in emphasis toward a more autonomous posture in its relations with the Soviet Union. Since March 1966, however, the statements of Hungarian leaders have taken quite the opposite tack, namely abject subservience to the USSR. *Népszabadság* on March 24, 1966 published a lecture to the political academy of the Hungarian Communist Party by Politbureau member Zoltán Komocsin in which the speaker condemned manifestations of anti-Sovietism in Hungary and in the international communist movement, especially those communist regimes and parties (e.g. Rumanian, Italian) that loosen ties with Moscow in order to improve relations with their own nationals. Since March, Kádár has reiterated this line on several occasions, both in Budapest and in Moscow at the Twenty-third Congress.

It appears that the communist leadership has increasingly stressed its pro-Soviet line in an attempt to stem the tide of history and quash increasing nationalism in the party. However, there is no ready explanation for why they elected to swim against the tide rather than with it. Although it seems highly improbable that Moscow forced this shift by some Stalin-like threat, there may have been Soviet economic pressure (express or implied) and evidently Kádár and his colleagues lacked the skill, fantasy, and political will to parry such Soviet move. Besides, Hungary must still suffer Soviet military occupation.

THE ECONOMY*

Excerpts from the articles of Sándor Kiss: "Hungary's Economic Situation," EAST EUROPE, May 1965, Volume 14, Number 5; "Hungary's Reluctant Workers," EAST EUROPE, August 1965, Volume 14, Number 8. New York, New York.

The general destruction wrought by the 1956 Revolution and the prolonged strike which followed it undermined the Hungarian economy at its most vital points. The country suffered an economic loss of 21 billion forints—one-fifth of the national income. Industrial output dropped heavily, causing a sudden deterioration in the country's balance-of-payment accounts. There was a grave shortage of raw materials, and fuel and electricity were scarce. All this was accompanied by a considerable rise in wages and consumption—more money chasing fewer goods.

The first objective of the Kádár government's reconstruction plan for 1957 was, therefore, to avoid inflation. Investments were reduced, administrative expenses and the defense budget were cut, and production in the heavy industrial sector was curbed. Concurrently, industry began to turn out larger quantities of consumer goods, hoping to meet the population's extra purchasing power.

To help the country back to its feet, Hungary was

---

* The data used in this essay are exclusively from official Hungarian sources. This in certain instances might cast doubt on the conclusions drawn—communist statistics are apt to be sophisticated rather than reliable—but in the case of the Hungarian economy we accept them at face value, because since the 1956 Revolution admissions of failures, shortcomings, and inefficiency have been loud and frequent in all mass media.

granted loans worth 3.5 billion foreign-exchange forints[1] by the socialist bloc—three-quarters of this sum coming from Soviet Russia. Coinciding as they did with the cancellation of Hungary's earlier debts, these loans proved a successful deterrent to inflation.

1957 Loans to Hungary[2]
(In millions of foreign-exchange forints)

	Forints	Per cent
Soviet Union	2,564	72.6
Bulgaria	21	0.6
China	293	8.3
Czechoslovakia	220	6.2
East Germany	176	5.0
Poland	117	3.3
Rumania	117	3.3
Yugoslavia	23	0.7
Total	3,531	100.0

RECOVERY AND AUSTERITY

These factors, plus an exceptionally good harvest, made it possible for the Hungarian economy largely to recover its balance by the second half of 1957. Unemployment was conquered, consumer goods industries were operating at full capacity, heavy industry at 70–75 per cent of capacity—partly by fulfilling Czechoslovak and Soviet orders. Raw materials and consumer goods purchased with foreign loans began to flow again, wage

[1] Calculated by the Hungarian National Bank on export-import results (100 foreign-exchange forints are roughly equal to 4 U.S. dollars).

[2] *Belpolitikai Szemle* (Home Review), Budapest, June 18, 1959. In his speech to the March 1963 session of the Hungarian Parliament, Premier Kádár noted that the "counter-revolution" had caused damages estimated at 22 billion forints. Rebuilding had to be financed partly by short-term, partly by long-term, expensive foreign loans. In 1963 the sum of 7.79 billion forints, or nine per cent of all expenditures, was set aside to pay off both foreign loans and the pre-1956 peace-loan bonds. Kádár said that Hungary had paid back all loans from the "socialist countries" except the Soviet Union, 40 per cent of whose loans had been repaid by 1963. Later, as the economic situation deteriorated, it was widely reported that Hungary requested postponement of repayment of the Soviet loan, but in vain.

demands were checked, and a slow start was made in communist investment programs (housing, school building, etc.).

In 1958, however, sources of foreign credit began to dry up and, apart from a long-term investment loan of 440 million roubles which the Soviet government injected into the economy in addition to its original loan, Hungary had to maintain her freshly attained economic balance by relying almost solely on her own resources. This necessitated a drive for more exports and a cutting back on imports.

A three-year plan (1958, 1959, 1960) drawn up in the spring of 1958 made no allowance for the collectivization of agriculture; nor would such an allowance have been practicable. Repercussions were severe when collectivization did get under way. The government had no funds with which to prop up the newly formed cooperatives. The plan envisaged the stabilization of real wages at their 1957 level, and foresaw reduced investments in heavy industry and the diversion of funds to social and communal programs. Officials were persuaded that it was at this level that some of the winds which had caused the Revolution could best be taken out of popular sails.

By 1958 the reconstructional phase of Hungary's economic plan, with its higher standard of living, had achieved its purpose, and in August 1958 a more austere plan was placed on the statute books. The earlier trend was reversed, and heavy industrial investments were increased by 20 per cent, and the housing program correspondingly reduced.

After the December 1958 resolution which gave the green light to collectivization, there was another raid on the standard of living, and on March 6, 1959 the party decided that, in view of the "encouraging perspectives" in the Hungarian sector of the Soviet seven-year plan, some of the targets of the three-year plan (larger national income, higher rates of investment and productivity) could be brought forward by a whole year. In other words, everyone was going to work harder, and the 1960 targets were to be achieved in 1959. This resolution marked the beginning of an intensive effort throughout the economy, and was accompanied by the usual chorus of propaganda.

To step up production in the favored branches of industry the government had a choice of two alternatives:

(1) It could resort to wage cuts, as was done under Rákosi, plowing back into investment the money thus withheld from the consumer (between 1949 and 1952 real wages dropped by 22 per cent);

(2) It could embark upon a program of rationalization with cuts carried out simultaneously in non-productive investments, such as cultural, social, and building programs.

By and large the second method was preferred, although the drive for a more rational exploitation of the labor force produced wage cuts in some parts of the economy. But these were neither as brutal nor as unfair as they had been in the 1949–1952 period. A start was made in the modernization and the re-tooling of industry, and investments which had no direct relevance to the production effort were gradually turned into local responsibilities. Housing schemes and borough and council projects were shifted onto the shoulders of local authorities. In addition, in the summer of 1960 new and higher norms were introduced, with an attendant cut in real wages.

An industrial survey carried out in the spring of 1960 revealed that industrial production capacity was being only partly exploited. There were delays in the supply of materials, machinery was antiquated, labor inefficiently organized, work norms slack; and there were not enough incentives. Production had risen because more people were employed, but productivity was stagnant. The Minister of Labor complained:

> In many enterprises slack discipline has led to the loss of eight to ten per cent of working time. Owing to the inadequate preparation of labor processes, a further five to ten per cent of time is spent waiting for materials, tools, blueprints, and other things.[3]

If, it was argued, norms could be fulfilled and even

[3] *Népszabadság* (People's Freedom), Budapest, November 4, 1960.

surpassed under such conditions, there was ample reason to set them higher, and on December 4, 1960 the Minister of Labor ordered a general rise in production norms, involving a ten to fifteen per cent increase—a rate higher than the national margin by which the earlier norms had been surpassed (the latter had averaged five to ten per cent).[4]

When news of the reorganization first appeared in the press, government propaganda reassured workers that the higher target figures did not mean automatic cuts in their earnings. Soon, however, the workers learned that their anxiety had been well founded—in the third quarter of 1960 (when the new norms had become effective), the average monthly wage of Hungarian workers fell to 1,580 forints, as compared to 1,660 in the corresponding quarter of 1959.[5] Later it was freely admitted that in certain cases the new norms had produced a drop in earnings.

Nevertheless, the order for a general increase in production norms was executed with great vigor. An essay in the party ideological monthly *Társadalmi Szemle* [Social Review], in November 1961 revealed that the first nine months of 1961 showed an 8 per cent increase in per capita daily production as compared to the preceding year. Two thirds of the net production increase stemmed from the rise in productivity. "The spirit of the workers was better than at any other time when norms were readjusted. . . . Morale was poor only where wages dropped considerably or for a long period of time, where the adjustments were not discussed in advance with the workers, or at places where norms were increased twice."

This second increase was made possible by a decree of June 1961, which provided for a constant tightening of the norms. This decree brought about a worsening of the workers' mood and morale which, in addition to the tense international situation, added to the worries of the government. The Minister of Labor therefore

4 *Munka* (Work), Budapest, November 10, 1960.
5 *Statisztikai Havi Közlemények* (Statistical Bulletin), Budapest, November 1960.

found it necessary, at a radio-press conference, to emphasize that "the regrouping of norms, in general, does not mean a permanent drop in income . . . and only those who have earned more that they deserve will receive less over a long period of time."[6]

The workers disagreed. On a fact-finding tour (October 5, 1961) at one of the largest machine factories in Budapest, GANZ-MAVAG, a *Népszbadság* correspondent was told by the workers that "it is easy to be smart, but while we work we are under constant pressure to meet the norms." Others also complained that the norms were set too high. A one-day strike by construction workers in western Hungary was supported by the local county paper, which blamed management for leading the workers to believe that their rights had been violated by the setting of new production norms. According to the paper the strike was a protest against the effect of the new norms on wages. "Since they were ill-informed, the workers believed that their prospects were bad. They are not to be blamed for taking such a step."[7]

MANAGEMENT AND MERGER

A thorough purge and overhaul of management was one of the original demands of the 1956 Revolution. Reforms were urged—to stop overcentralization, weed out bureaucracy, and remove dogmatism and the slavish imitation of Soviet example. And for some time after the Revolution half-hearted attempts were made to institute such reforms. Hungary was the first among the socialist countries to abolish compulsory delivery quotas in agriculture, and firms and factories were given greater independence and expected to become gradually self-supporting.

As early as in 1957 the government convoked an economic "brain trust" of 200 members. Headed by professor Istvan Varga, former member of the Smallholders Party and a well known economist, the committee embarked upon a painstaking survey of the na-

---

[6] Radio Budapest and *Népszabadság*, October 17, 1961.

[7] *Fejér Megyei Napló* (Fejer County Journal), *Székesfehérvár*, October 23, 1963.

tional economy. The findings of this committee suggested a watering-down of official programs, offering cogent reasons as to why this was necessary: the forced pace of capital investment was retarding a rise in the standard of living; agriculture was being neglected; new and unreasonably large factories had been and were still being erected, while modernizatioin of existing ones hung fire. Insufficient attention had been paid to the generation of electricity, and to many of Hungary's economic and geographic peculiarities. There had been too much centralization, production prices were being calculated on unrealistic bases, and quantity production undermined the skills and standards of industry. Also, there had been excessive imports of raw materials, upsetting the country's balance-of-payment account.

The party's answer to the recommendations was measured but negative. When collectivization got under way and the three-year plan was accelerated, rejection of the comittee's suggestions became dogmatic and final.

Nevertheless, party economists were aware that reforms were needed.

In reorganizing the economy the Kadar regime set out to adapt industrial planning to the country's resources. This meant a complete change from Stalinist policy, which had sought to make Hungary a "land of iron and steel" despite the fact that it had few of the raw materials needed for heavy industrial development. The new policy emphasized industries which had fewer raw material requirements and more labor requirements (particularly in fields such as telecommunications, where Hungary had a pool of skilled labor). The extent to which these industries were pushed can be seen from the following table, comparing their development to that of all state industry (with 1949 as 100.)[8]

	All State Industry	Machinery	Electric Machinery	Tele-communications	Tools	Chemicals
1955	226	237	262	n.a.	816	269
1960	331	461	433	747	1367	594
1963	449	574	586	1406	2195	906

8 *Statisztikai Havi Közlemények*, January, 1965.

This trend continued in 1964, when the telecommunications industry increased its output by 13 per cent, the electrical machine industry by 30 per cent, and the chemical industry by 12.7 per cent, as compared with an average of 9 per cent for all industry.

During the second five-year plan (1961–65) industrial production increased by 47 per cent. Production in heavy industry topped 1960 by 51 per cent. However, certain branches developed more slowly than the average: mining by 30 per cent, metallurgy 30 per cent, machine equipment production 36 per cent, construction industry 36 per cent and metal wares by 47 per cent. Development above the average was:

	Per cent
Electric power production	53
Production of communications facilities	54
Machine industry	58
Machine production of electric industry	60
Precision engineering	84
Chemical and rubber industry	89
Telecommunication and vacuum industry	129

Another aim was to increase the efficiency of industry by merging enterprises. This program was adopted in 1959, and the amalgamation drive continued through 1963. By the middle of that year, 648 enterprises had been merged into 202 large ones.[9] The 10 automobile and tractor enterprises, for example, were merged into 6.[10] Between January 1963 and January 1964 the number of state industrial companies dropped by 416, or one-third. The drop was greatest in the building material industry, where 98 enterprises were merged to form 27. The number of workers employed in the average enterprise rose correspondingly, and some mammoth enterpises employed more than 10,000.[11]

Arguments for merging enterprises were mainly those of greater efficiency. It was contended that mergers would lead to higher productivity, lower overhead, better utilization of equipment and personnel, capital savings,

9 *Népszabadság*, July 21, 1963.
10 *Népszabadság*, October 11, 1963.
11 *Népszabadság*, March 6, 1964.

less administrative labor, etc. The mergers were carried out against rather widespread opposition from managers and plant officials. One of the leading provincial weeklies wrote: "We would be fooling ourselves if we were to pretend that the reorganization and everything involved in it is completely understood by every worker in a leading position. . . . Some people make no secret of their disagreement and predict that the whole business will have to be dropped inside of three years."[12] The party press discussed the problems of the reorganization in detail, particularly the reluctance of management to cooperate in the reshuffling of personnel.

In the outcome, the mergers do not seem to have produced the higher efficiency that was hoped for. Three plants in Diósgyőr that were amalgamated into one reported higher costs and lower profits than before the merger.[13] The United Elevator and Driving Gear Company in Budapest was said to have reaped administrative chaos, and its production sagged. Statements of top managerial personnel were bitter: "Two years ago we tried to tell ourselves that time would solve our problems, but now we have lost all hope and we feel like someone who is totally disillusioned by an unsuccessful marriage," and "They have deprived us of what is basically important: our individuality, initiative, and sense of responsibility."[14] While these two examples may not be typical, the Kádár leadership is apparently not very happy with the over-all results; in a country where every official policy is praised as an example of the leaders' wisdom, this one has received the criticism of silence.

Kádár's decision to let the economy be run by people with proper qualifications even if they were not party members, rather than continue to rely on the old "worker-managers" of the Stalinist era, was dictated by political and economic considerations—implementing the famous slogan "Whoever is not against us is with us." Under it non-party people became eligible for any high-ranking job that was not by its nature restricted to party

12 Dél-Magyarország (South Hungary), Szeged, May 23, 1963.
13 Népszabadság, October 22, 1964.
14 Népszabadság, January 8, 1965.

members; this opened the way for many competent technical and managerial people who were not party members, and it apparently gave the economy an upward impetus at the beginning of the sixties. At the same time these non-party experts had to work with party organs above them and around them—with officials in the ministries, with the party committee in the plant, with the party-run trade union—with the result that even the strongest individual was not free of control.

The apparatus of centralized control was, in fact, so strong that another reform was initiated at the beginning of 1963. This removed the actual direction of most industries from the ministries and gave it to trusts set up by the plants in each industry. Some large enterprises acted as their own trusts. The functions left to the government ministries were mainly those of planning and accounting. The functions having to do with day-to-day operations were given to the trusts, which were free to administer the wages, finances, and production plans of their member enterprises.

The promotion of non-party experts and the re-organization of management apparently did not go very far toward solving Hungary's economic difficulties. For one thing, these measures were strongly opposed—at times even sabotaged—by old party functionaries who had been accustomed to telling the enterprise managers what to do. When they saw their "advice" being ignored or not even asked for, many of them began to agitate against the reforms. Party indoctrinators and the party press marshalled every possible force against them, but often met with passive resistance.

Another factor was that the new task of advising managers how to run things efficiently, rather than compelling them to carry out directives from above, was one for which most factory party leaders have no qualifications. In practice the managers are left to do as they see fit, while the party functionaries tend to complain because they are not consulted in matters that concern them.

Nor has the reorganization of industry been successful in producing the closer relations hoped for between plant

managers and the authorities above them. More authority and responsibility were expected to devolve on the
managers, but the managers have been reluctant to
grasp their new powers. Moreover, the people who staff
the new trusts were taken mainly from the old bureaucracy in the ministries, and their relationship to the
enterprises under them is not essentially different from
what it was previously. While the managers of the enterprises are urged to show independence and to be in-
novators, many of them do not feel strong enough to
oppose the mighty forces above them.[15]

THE PROFILE

Hungary's industrial development has been slowing
down, despite the continued upward movement of production statistics. The meaning of economic statistics
tends to be elusive when they consist mainly of quanti-
tative output series, but it is clear that the Hungarian
consumer is not getting much of a return on his investment of time and energy. The second five-year plan
scheduled a 48–50 per cent increase in total industrial
production; cumulative results were as follows (with
1960 as 100):

1961	111
1962	120
1963	129
1964	140
1965	147

These figures, however, say nothing about the profit-
ability of the whole operation, and it is necessary to look
elsewhere for such information.

Productivity—i.e., output per workers—was expected
to generate 70 per cent of the increase in production.
The actual increase in productivity has been much less
than anticipated, and the difference has been made up
by the employment of more workers and the increase of
overtime. According to Deputy Premier Jenő Fock, barely half of the increased production in the last four years
was due to higher productivity.[16]

15 *Kisalföld* (Little Plans), Györ, January 15, 1965.
16 *Népszabadság*, January 1, 1965.

Production costs have also proved less flexible than planned. They were to have been reduced by 10 per cent over the five years, which would have meant substantial savings in wages and materials, but in the first four years (1961–1964) the actual reduction was reportedly only five per cent.[17]

Foreign trade, which already had a sizable deficit in 1960, has continued in the red (as measured in millions of foreign-exchange forints):[18]

	Imports	Exports
1960	11,455.5	10,259.8
1961	12,039.6	12,079.6
1962	13,485.2	12,905.5
1963	15,326.7	14,155.5
1964	17,471.0	15,853.0
1965	17,848.5	17,721.3

While exports increased, they lagged behind imports except in 1961. A major factor has been the agricultural situation in Hungary. The country's requirements in wheat and rye are between 2.4 and 2.5 million tons a year, while the average crop in this period was only 2.1 million tons. In 1963, only 1.7 million tons of bread grains were produced, and the government had to import 800,000 tons. Of this, 45 per cent came from the United States and 55 per cent from France and Italy, at a total cost of about $64 million. In 1964 the government bought 100,000 tons of wheat from Canada for 7.4 million dollars.

The trends in foreign trade were as follows in 1961-1965 (in billions of foreign-exchange forints):

Countries	Imports from	Exports to
Bloc	52,117	52,078
Capitalist	19,779	16,221
Developing	4,350	4,434
Total	76,246	72,733

Trade balance deficit, 3,513 billion foreign-exchange

[17] *Népszabadság*, January 24, 1965.

[18] *Statistical Pocket Book of Hungary*, 1964 and *Népszabadság*, January 17, 1965.

forints. Thus, for the five-year period the balance of Hungarian foreign trade shows an import surplus. The deficit with the socialist countries was only 39 million forints—*i.e.*, balanced—but there was a deficit of more than 3.5 billion forints in trade with the capitalist countries. There was an 84-million-forint surplus for Hungary in the trade with developing countries.

This picture is quite unfavorable to Hungary, because the deficit in foreign trade is not being balanced by other means (tourism, transit income, etc.). Hungary was in debt even before this period, and the balance of payment has worsened considerably, instead of improving, during the five-year plan.

National income was slated to rise 36 per cent during the five-year plan, but the actual increase was only 25 per cent. There was a gradual reduction in the tempo of increase, which came to a complete standstill during the last two years of the plan period.

GROWTH AND DISTRIBUTION OF NATIONAL INCOME
(In billions of forints)

	1961	1962	1963	1964	1965
Consumption: Population	104	109	115	121	123
Public institutions	5	6	6	6	6
Total	109	115	121	127	129
Investments, stockpiling	38	40	45	48	46
Surplus/deficit			—3	—3	
Total national income	147	155	163	172	175

Sources: Statistical Yearbooks, 1958–64. Estimate for 1965 based on the Plan Fulfillment Report in *Népszabadság*, April 10, 1966.

During the second five-year plan (1961–65) 74.01 per cent of the total national income was spent for consumption was 18.94 per cent for investments; 7.05 per cent was withheld for stockpiles and reserve.

The goal of the original plan was a three-to-four per cent surplus in national income up to the end of 1965, which would have been used primarily abroad, to pay off the earlier debts. But this goal was not reached. On the contrary, the earlier unfavorable ratio between the national income and consumption deteriorated further and as a result the indebtedness of the country increased.

In the last five years Hungary has spent about 850 million dollars for the modernization of her army. The regular military budget is seven per cent of the national income, but it must be noted that only direct defense expenditures are included in this figure. Production in the Hungarian war industry is included in the figures for heavy industry. An additional burden to the population is the expense of the Soviet occupation forces—a well-kept secret.

SOURCES OF NATIONAL INCOME
(Per cent)

Industry (including construction)	67.6	72.8
Agriculture	23.1	21.4
Other	9.3	5.8
	100	100

By the end of the second five-year plan, the share of industry in the production of national income had considerably increased, but at the same time the share of agriculture decreased. There is no doubt that the dynamic development of industrial production played an important role in this, but bad weather in 1961 and 1962 had also unfavorably influenced agricultural production.

Furthermore, in considering the share of agriculture in the creation of national income, it must be noted that agricultural prices are understated, and therefore we do not get a true picture of the share contributed by agriculture. According to data supplied by the Central Statistical Office, in 1963 agriculture paid about 1.5 billion forints extra for industrial goods used for current operations, but on the other hand it received about 12 billion forints less for agricultural products used in industry than it would have received in a price system based on social expenditures.

Wages and salaries were scheduled to rise by 16 or 17 per cent; however, the actual results for the five-year plan period were as follows (with 1960 as 100):

Year	Per cent
1961	100.2
1962	101.7
1963	106.2
1964	109.0
1965	109.0

These are nominal wages, which do not allow for increases in the cost of living. The official price index states that prices for consumers rose by 0.8 per cent in the first three years; if this figure is applied to the wage index for 1963, it indicates that average real wages at the end of 1963 had risen 6.25 per cent above the 1960 level.[19] There is reason to believe that this overstates the actual increase, since it does not allow for the well-known "hidden price increases" by which lower-quality goods are substituted for standard goods at the same price. The Hungarian press is full of examples. Moreover, the wage statistics include amounts earned by working overtime, and since overtime work has increased since 1960 the official wage index must be still further reduced.

RELUCTANT WORKERS

Norm-setting has long been a focus of resentment in the factories. The authorities, on the one hand, argue that tighter norms make for increased productivity, and therefore add to workers' incomes. Managers are blamed for not making these concepts clear to the workers and for not administering the norms properly. In their turn the managers complain about shortages of raw materials and parts due to breakdowns in other sectors of industry. This bureaucratic buck-passing leaves the workers with the impression that they are destined to carry the burden of managerial errors—and that this burden is passed on to them in the norm-setting procedure. To protect themselves the workers have adopted a whole series of hedgehog defenses which the authorities tirelessly condemn as violations of labor discipline.

[19] *Statisztikai Évkönyv 1964* (Statistical Yearbook 1964). The data for 1965 are from the plan fulfillment report of the Central Statistical Office.

So far as norms go, the workers would be happy to have them left where they are. The norm-raisers reply that the existing norms are too low and too easily over-fulfilled. *Népszabadság* reported (September 24, 1964) that "Studies carried out regarding lost time show that this has hardly changed in recent years, and often amounts to 20 to 30 per cent of working time. No doubt some time-losses are due to lack of cooperation and to mismanagement, but they are also due to slack labor discipline."

Whatever the norms happen to be, much ingenuity goes into beating them, and not only the workers are involved. Foremen and managers either cooperate in the process or wink at it, lest workers take even more decisive evasive action. Norms which are set too high are met by falsifying records, or by expanding the assigned task to include fictitious work or nonessential functions. Another way is to cut corners on workmanship, a practice which has led to widespread criticism of poor performance and to consumer complaints about bad quality.

The Kádár regime's view of the Hungarian worker was given in an article in *Magyar Nemzet*[20] which grouped workers in the following three categories: "Those who labor with socialist consciences and with enthusiasm; those who do only as much as is required and not one bit more; and those slackers and parasites who clock in sham work and, when reminded of their obligations, express displeasure and raise the question of their 'rights'." The paper voiced particular concern that "slackers" seemed to be excused by the "decent" workers, and that there was a general feeling of solidarity among workers against the demands for greater discipline.

The litany of complaints against workers also includes charges of moonlighting, using the factory premises and facilities for private work and freelance assignments, illegal overtime beyond the 48-hour work week (a practice in which managers collaborate in their efforts to meet plan targets), stealing (which ranges from petty

[20] *Magyar Nemzet* (Hungarian Nation), Budapest, December 9, 1964.

theft to large-scale embezzlement), job-hopping, and deliberate slowdowns.

To cope with these problems, in 1965 the Presidential Council endorsed a series of amendments to the Labor Code designed to reduce job-switching and to tighten up labor discipline. The penalties for workers who violate the code include loss of vacation and other benefits and loss of seniority. The threat of being laid off without the protection of the trade unions—whose leaders are party apparatchiks concerned first with applying current directives—was probably the most serious provocation to workers, and one which they have met with growing sullenness and resistance.

There is ample evidence that appeals to achieve production goals and to the workers' duty to "build socialism" go unheeded, and that most workers are imbued with a deep sense of cynicism about promises of more jam tomorrow. The experience of 1956, when the Workers' Councils, which were the central sustaining body of the revolution, were crushed by Kádár and the Soviet occupation, has deprived slogans about the leading role of the working class of all credibility. Although pressure on the workers has eased considerably since the revolution, Kádár's most significant peace offer has been made to technicians and engineers, who have been invited to join in building the Hungarian economy without having also to join the party. Nothing of a similar nature has been offered to the workers, not even to letting the trade unions act on behalf of their members' immediate interests.

Under such circumstances, workers tend to believe only in what is tangibly present—their take-home pay and bonuses. The "leading role of the working class," in their eyes, has come to mean special privileges for paid officials of mass organizations such as the trade unions, whose salaries are not based on production according to norm. Moreover, there is a lot of skepticism over official statistics about increases in wage income through the years. Reports of a rise in salaries and wages of 9.6 per cent from 1960 to 1964 are vitiated by the fact that real wages, taking into account *de facto* prices, actually rose only 1.5 to 2 per cent in the period, and lagged considerably behind the average national income increase of five per cent.

The impact of the labor code and the new norms has had a predictable result—more sophisticated methods of evasion, and the application of traditional labor techniques of slowdown. A "conscientious withdrawal of efficiency"—to borrow an old American IWW slogan—has led to a general breakdown of morale in the factories. The charges of poor labor discipline made by the authorities are doubtless true, but from the workers' point of view these acts are simply defensive measures against exploitative policies which demand too much and yield too little. The wide popularity of the derisive *Ten Commandments of Labor*,[21] which emphasize such values as "anything you might want to do today can be done just as well tomorrow," shows a state of mind which sees in directives from above merely edicts that are to be undermined, subverted, or evaded. This attitude runs through the entire working force. The worker looks upon his titular leaders as "they," as strangers to himself and his companions.

It is against this background that the newest squeeze on the workers has been introduced, setting off complaints of bureaucratic oppression and intensifying the workers' disregard of planning targets and of the sanctity of "social property." The class struggle, reappearing in a most primitive form, is now the major industrial problem in a country where it was theoretically obliterated a decade ago.

[21] The popular decalogue of labor contains the following items: (1) Laziness is responsible for one-half of your fitness; (2) Whatever is to be done today can be done just as well tomorrow; (3) Any matter which is not solved automatically in 30 days is not worth taking up; (4) Don't search for zeal lost in looking for work; (5) Failure to do a job means no mistakes, and no mistakes must win a bonus; (6) Don't be misled into working just because someone else is on the job; (7) Don't monopolize all the space at the work bench; (8) Since wages are only minimal, working effort should correspond; (9) The factory is not a café, and it is not necessary to spend all one's time in it; (10) We know the axiom, "Work ennobles," but who needs nobility under socialism?

THE REFORM

In February 1965 Kádár said in a speech to Parliament that "the system of economic direction must be subjected to a thorough review" because it was too centralized, but he declined to engage in "adventurous experiments." Instead he postponed further discussion for a year or so. "Our responsible organs will, after serious research and preparation, deal with the matter . . . and define what measures will be necessary."

The tone of his speech was unusual for a communist, and so was that of other speeches at this session of Parliament: relatively frank and business-like, without the usual political sloganeering. In fact, the three-day session put the nation's real economic situation on the public record with unprecedented thoroughness. Kádár stated that over the past four years industrial production had risen at the rate planned, but that agricultural production had not. Imports had increased faster and exports more slowly than planned. Productivity had risen too slowly, and prime costs had not fallen fast enough.

> Highly centralized economic direction is slow, clumsy, not mobile, and it is partly due to this that at present some of the goods produced from expensive raw materials with considerable labor do not sufficiently meet the requirements of the home and international markets, and remain in stock. The question of our goods being up-to-date is of particular importance nowadays when . . . competition between the two social systems is developing more and more. Modern goods, competitive in price and quality, must be introduced in the international market, because otherwise we shall lag behind. This applies to the Western market, but it must be added that the time is past when within the socialist world anyone, out of feelings of sympathy or charity, should accept shoddy, unsalable goods from us, just as we do not take such goods from others. Material incentives today are designed more to promote overfulfillment of quantitative plans rather than profitable production and improvement in quality. Moreover, unfortunately the system of bonuses and rewards is in effect detrimental to the requirements of quality work.

If Kádár had followed the advice of Hungarian economist István Varga and his colleagues back in 1957, the condition of the country's economy today might be radically different. Then the goverment set up 11 committees of experts, and in a few months they presented their conclusions—which bore strong resemblance to programs adopted eight years later in other communist countries. Like Soviet and Czechoslovak economists today, they favored decentralization and a greater emphasis on profit as a guide to production. "It must be left to the enterprises," ran one of the proposals, "to determine their production themselves within the framework of the long-range plan, and to do this by considering the market situation."[22] These words might have been written by Professor Liberman of the U.S.S.R. five years later, but at the time they were branded by the Hungarian party as "right-wing"; and the economists' proposal for price reform resembled that since adopted in Czechoslovakia and East Germany.

The long-awaited party Central Committee plenum on the proposed economic reform took place on May 25–27, 1966 and was attended not only by Central Committee members, but also by government and trade union leaders, representatives of mass organizations, leaders of county party committees, and economic experts. The session passed "unanimous resolutions" on the outline of the new five-year plan and on directives for reform. *Népszabadság*, May 29, published the text of the latter and the address to the plenum delivered by party economic expert Rezső Nyers. Both documents indicated, as have previous statements on the subject, that one of the main aims of the reform will be to allow the law of demand and supply to play a more important role in the economy, although central direction is to be maintained. Central organs will establish only the long-term tasks, and the enterprises will work out their own short-range plans on the basis of market requirements. Instead of direct control, the state will use indirect economic means —such as credit and interest policies—to influence enter-

[22] *Közgazdasági Szemle* (Economic Review), October and December 1957.

prises, which among other things will also be responsible for establishing their own wage policy. Since income will be tied to profits, the reform is expected to act as an incentive to workers, particularly enterprise managers.

The changes will also involve a price reform, to go into effect at the beginning of 1968. Some prices will be fixed by the state and others will be set by the enterprises on the basis of market demands. The party's plan is for wage increases to surpass price increases, and attempts have been made to allay fears about further hikes in living costs by assurances on this subject. During the next year and a half the new system will be gradually introduced. The entire reform is scheduled to be implemented in 1968.

REPRESSION OF THE CHURCH

I.

BEFORE THE 1964 VATICAN-HUNGARIAN PROTOCOL

Excerpts from the booklet of István Baranko-vics: CATHOLIC CHURCH AND CATHOLIC FAITH IN HUNGARY, *The Hungarian Quarterly*, New York, New York, 1963.

Despite the loyalty of the overwhelming majority of Hungarian Catholics who support the Church with a very commendable financial sacrifice, the situation of the Catholic Church in Hungary is worse today than at any time since 1945. While the pressure of external terror upon the Church decreased during the past few years, the internal undermining of the Church by the Communist Party not only failed to stop, but has continued and was organized even better. The State also intervenes incessantly in the internal affairs of the Church, so that in Hungary today no one can assume the internal administrative autonomy of the Church.

The State has suppressed almost all the cultural functions of the Church, including one of its most important ones, that of teaching.[1] Only its liturgical and ascetic

[1] In the summer of 1948, the State nationalized all schools and boarding houses of the Catholic Church, including its real estate and equipment. Later the State restored to the Church eight secondary schools (six for boys and two for girls); but about 99.7 per cent of the Catholic schools are still nationalized. In the operating Catholic Schools State-published textbooks must be used; though the teachers may explain the position of the Church on the issues taught. The quality of the Church schools is the highest calibre and their reputation is excellent. Every year the number of those applying for admission exceeds the number of free places available.

functions are tolerated, and even these only in a controlled and limited manner. Already in 1950 the State dissolved, with but four exceptions, all religious orders and the present education of clergy is drastically curtailed by it.[2] All the Christian trade unions and vocational organizations were already liquidated by 1945 when the Marxist monopoly was introduced in the field of trade unionism. This was followed by the dissolution of the many thousand Catholic social, cultural and religious associations of peasant, worker and middle-class background, the confiscation of their property without compensation, which in many instances were handed over to the communist and anti-theistic organizations. Today, the Hungarian Catholics have no organized social power.

All the communist governments of Hungary—including the Kádár government—have faithfully followed the Leninist doctrine in their fight against the Church and against religion, although this fight was carried on with varying means and tactics.

Lately, however, there have been indications in Western newspapers and in declarations of Hungarian government officials that changes are impending in the Church-State relations of Hungary. The question is what will these changes amount to and what will they mean to the Church and the State. Will they be in accord with the Leninist doctrine of anti-religious campaign or will they denote *in practice* a departure from it?

On March 21, 1936, János Kádár, President of the Council of Ministers, made the following statement on Church-State relations:

[2] The monasteries and other buildings, together with their installations and furniture, became the property of the State without any indemnity. Only about 500 monk-priests were given permit by the State to continue their ecclesiastic functions within the various dioceses. For the rest, the State forbade to join a diocese and continue their ecclesiastic functions as regular priests. One female and three male religious orders were granted permit to continue their very limited activity with substantially reduced personnel and with the infinitely limited training rights (one order, for example, could admit only two novices annually). Today, the number of monks and nuns is about one per cent of the pre-1950 figure.

The relation between the State and the churches active in Hungary is normal, *regulated by agreements,* and improving from year to year. The scientific and the religious outlooks are, of course, opposed to each other, but the State ensures the freedom of worship, the Church acknowledges the laws of the State, and therefore they do not have to engage in a political fight. There still are, and no doubt there will be in the future, outstanding issues between the Hungarian People's Republic and the churches active in our country. The government believes that all arising issues may be and should be solved in a way which is acceptable to both sides and which *respects* the laws and legal order of the State as well as taking into account the inner laws and order of the Church. Both believers and non-believers are citizens of the Hungarian People's Republic. It is our *common* interest to abolish the last *remnants of the exploiting capitalist society and to build up the free, socialist society of all workers.*[3]

The Hungarian bishops have indeed signed agreements with the state in 1950. Yet it is also, and more importantly, true what Kádár does not say, that the leaders of the Church did not sign these so-called agreements freely, but were compelled to do so under duress. They were confronted with the gravest threats of communist State power and with the irresistible pressures (such as deportations of nuns and monks, threats of mass arrests of bishops and priests) of the same. It seems therefore that Kádár wishes to maintain these so-called agreements and, furthermore, that he desires to gain at least the tacit approval of the Vatican.

Kádár also states that today it is no longer necessary for the State and the Church "to engage in a *political* struggle, since the State ensures the freedom of worship and the churches acknowledge the laws of the state." No one knowing the present situation will deny that millions of the faithful do go to church and participate in the sacraments in Hungary. The State, obviously, does not *explicitly* forbid them to exercise their religion in this sense. Yet this by no means bears out the statement that "the State ensures the freedom of worship." Kádár

[3] *Magyar Nemzet,* Budapest,, March 22, 1963. Italics partly in the text, partly mine.

is silent about the grave limitations upon this same freedom of worship as well as those legal disadvantages which the exercise of religion brings to the faithful. He also neglects to mention that the state denies to the religious citizen his rights as a man and as a citizen (e.g. freedom of speech and press, of assembly, of organization, of forming parties, etc.) which would enable him to defend both his freedom of worship and the rights of the Church. Without these rights, he finds it physically *impossible* to fight politically. Furthermore, the State has deprived the besieged Church even of the right of *spiritual self-defense*. The anti-theists have all the right to wage a campaign against the Church and religion, but the Church and the faithful are forbidden to take up the challenge. Not even to the faithful is the Church allowed to expound its arguments against anti-theism and materialism; it is restricted to the limited exposition of its positive tenets of its creed. The suppression and persecution of the Church, together with the barring of religious citizens from the equal enjoyment of their rights, have forced the Church into a position where it must "acknowledge the laws of the State without public protest, even though these laws embody —besides the infringement of other elementary human rights—the crudest violation of religious liberty and the rights of the Church"[4]

Kádár declares it to be "the common interest" of "both believers and non-believers" to cooperate in "abol-

[4] The Constitution of the Hungarian Communist State, in words, guarantees the freedom of worship, speech and press, etc., but in communist interpretation in reality means the denial of these rights. The communists like to refer to certain Western laws, which are considered harmful by the Church from the points of religious freedom and its own rights, and with reference to these Western laws bring to an equal level the situation of the Church and religious freedom in these free countries and in the communist countries. Disregarding any other difference, there is a decisive difference even in the case of the same concrete discriminations of religious freedom and of the Church. The laws of the democratic countries guarantee the right to the faithful to fight for the changes of the injurious laws freely with legally permitted means, while the Church and the faithful are deprived of this right in the communist countries. The greatest violation of freedom is the denial of the right to fight for freedom.

ishing the last remnants of the exploiting capitalist society," and in "building up the free, socialist society of
the workers." What does Kádár have in mind? What else
can he still wish to abolish as a "remnant of the capitalist society?" Large and medium sized estates have been
abolished in Hungary since 1945. Then the large and
medium industrial plants, the banks and wholesale and
middle-trade firms were nationalized without any indemnification. The almost complete liquidation of small
business followed suit. What, then, does Kádár regard
as "the last remnants of capitalist society," the abolition
of which he declares to be the *common* interest of
Church and State, of believer and nonbeliever? According to communist doctrine, the Church, and religion itself, is a remnant of capitalist society and in order to
promote the "dying out" of religion, the liquidation of
the Church "belongs to the building of socialist society."
Did Kádár actually intend to proclaim in communist
jargon that it is the common interest of believers and
nonbelievers alike that the faithful cooperate in promoting the "dying out" of religion?

Until now the Kádár regime has shown no sign, either
in words or in actions, that it intends to liquidate or,
as far a possible, to remedy the most Stalin-like and most
harmful crimes of Stalinist ecclesiastical policy. Such
crimes include both overt and covert interference of the
rights of the Church in self-government, preaching, and
dispensing the sacraments; they include the denial of
free religious instruction, the withdrawal of the right
of operation from monastic orders, the abrogation of
the Church's cultural rights, and of her right to maintain her own schools; and they include the sentencing
of Cardinal Mindszenty, etc. Even the principles of "socialist legality" and destalinization were discriminately
applied to the Churches and to the ecclesiastical persons
by the Kádár regime and its destalinizing predecessors.
The Kádár regime and some of its predecessors withdrew the charges, one by one, as unfounded, against the
still living or dead communists (and a few non-communist Marxists) who were sentenced during the Stalinist
era. They were in their life or post mortem rehabilitated

and some people even received a certain compensation. Certain Church figures received amnesty and some were released from prison without any formal amnesty. The unfounded charges were, however, not withdrawn against any living or dead ecclesiastical persons who were sentenced during the Stalinist era. No one was rehabilitated either in his life or post mortem, and no one received any compensation. In other words, according to the Kádár regime and its destalinizing predecessors, the charges against the ecclesiastical persons sentenced during the Stalinist era were in accordance with the truth of their sentences justified; the defendants—among them real martyrs of the Christian religion, of national and human freedom—were not innocent but criminals. This distasteful stigmatization and cynical discrimination throws light not only on the principles of "socialist legality" and destalinization, but also on the Leninist doctrine of persecution of Church and religion, and that the changes are in accord with this doctrine.

These changes are twofold. Although the Kádár regime put aside some of the crudest Stalinist methods of Church persecution, it applied the "less vociferous" methods recommended by Lenin more relentlessly and, especially, more effectively than the governments of the Stalin era. This will become clear from the description given below. The Kádár regime has followed Lenin's directions in changing the tactics of the fight against the Church, in accordance with the changing phases of the "class struggle," thus adapting itself to "reality" and to the "concrete situation." Within the limits laid down by Leninist doctrine, the concrete situation of the Church in communist Hungary has undergone some changes even in the past. *Today,* the "interests of the class struggle," the interests of communist rule, and the changed "reality," demand that the ecclesiastical policy of the Kádár government should reckon with the more important elements of the "concrete situation":

1. The spiritual power of the Church in Hungary failed to diminish in proportion to the persecutions and anti-theistic efforts. In spite of a decade and a half of religious and Church persecutions and anti-theistic propaganda, re-

ligion and the Church have remained a part of Hungarian life, a part that must not be underestimated and must be reckoned with as "reality" by the communist regime.

2. József Cardinal Mindszenty, Primate of Hungary, who was liberated from his prison by the Revolution of 1956, was compelled to seek asylum in the American Legation in Budapest because the government threatened him with imprisonment. Cardinal Mindszenty as a prisoner has become, and remains in his asylum, a world-wide symbol of the active ecclesiastical resistance to communism. According to reliable information, the majority of the Hungarian people still regard him as the *highest embodiment of Hungarian national, moral, and religious resistance.* Though he is physically isolated inside the American Legation, he is yet on Hungarian soil. His mere presence on Hungarian soil has a peculiar effect on the Hungarian people. The Revolution of 1956 has undermined the belief in the finality of arrangements among both communists and non-communists. The knowledge that the Cardinal may, in the advent of some unforeseen change, reoccupy his archi-episcopal throne (at least as long as he remains in Hungary and retains his *legal* position as Head of the Hungarian Church) disquiets and restrains the collaborators within the Church, strengthens the waverers and those who resist.

3. The Kádár government has considerable economic, political and prestige interests in the normalizing of diplomatic relations between Washington and Budapest. One obstacle in the way of such a normalization of relations is the asylum given to Cardinal Mindszenty. The government now wishes to eliminate this obstacle by settling the Mindszenty question in a manner favorable to itself and, at the same time, approved equally by the *United States* and the *Vatican.*

Atheism, even militant anti-theism is the doctrine of the present Hungarian State, although it is not included in the Constitution. The State functions as the missionary of atheism by utilizing every available means for its propagation and for the eradication of religious beliefs. Not only State power in the narrower sense, but also economic, cultural and social institutions and organizations (i.e., trade unions) serve this cause, with special emphasis upon institutions of education and those means used in formulating public opinion, such as the press, radio, television, movies, and theaters.

The atheistic State oppresses not only the Church as an organization, but also its individual members-believers. State authorities use legal disadvantages against supporters of the Church or confessors of the faith. Although some relaxation could be observed in recent years in this respect, the possibility of discrimination, however, lingers above the heads of every believer. The legal disadvantages may be different in kind and degree, as the totalitarian State has extended its direct power over almost all areas of human activity.

In spite of the foregoing, the main success of atheistic propaganda consists not so much in the increase in the number of atheists and anti-theists, but in the significant spread of religious indifferentism among certain groups of society. These people adopt, for the most part, *hedonistic materialism* rather than the doctrines of dialectical historical materialism propagated by the State.

The members of the former and new middle class are most apt to refrain from the profession of the religion, from going to church and from sending their children to religious education.

The regime pays special attention to the anti-theistic education of industrial workers and the new intellectuals. In spite of these efforts, however, the majority of the industrial workers, though mostly agnostic, are not atheistic, and another very signifiicant portion not only believes in the Catholic faith but is willing to confess it and unselfishly supports the Church. Among the industrial workers and especially among the young intellectuals there are many so-called seekers. These are people who have been indoctrinated with the philosophy of dialectical historical materialism, which promised to provide answers to the ultimate questions of life. These answers, however, usually fail to satisfy them, and their attention is then turned toward religion, especially toward the Catholic doctrine. Sometimes they do not arrive at the Catholic creed but are, in general, oriented toward *spiritual* values. Among the modern Western Catholic thinkers, Teilhard de Chardin has the greatest influence.

The Church lost most of its followers among the peasantry. The main reasons for this loss follow. One is the former social structure of the village, partly disintegrated and partly changed. Certain Church ceremonies, to which the peasantry were accustomed which they especially loved, ceased to exist, e.g., rogation, benediction of the bread, etc. A significant part of the peasantry—especially the younger generations—became industrial workers and moved into the cities and industrial settlements or commuted there. The new surrounding undermines their traditional customs and morale: the traditional and habitual system of rules. This stratum became isolated from the traditional community of the village but failed to become an integral part of the industrial worker community. These peasants-turned-industrial-workers fell easiest prey to the vulgar atheism and anti-Church propaganda which was especially true of the young people. However, the overwhelming majority of the peasantry who did not sever their relationship with the village's peasant community remained the firm bastions of the Church and the faith.

The number of baptisms, marriage ceremonies and Church burials has slightly decreased (in that order); but almost every Catholic allows his children to be baptized and an overwhelming majority are married and buried by the Church.

In order to provide a substitute for certain Church ceremonies (baptism, marriage, burial), the State has introduced, and by all available means promotes, "social ceremonies," which are festive, memorable and attractive and, moreover, are performed gratis by State officials. The number of these ceremonies, however, is not in proportion to the government efforts.

They are rarely performed in the villages. Their number is largest in industrial areas among factory workers. Yet, it has often happened that industrial workers, after using the "name-giving ceremony" of the State, have clandestinely had their children baptized by a priest. Once the authorities are informed of the subsequent Catholic baptism, the parent must pay a large fee for the name-giving ceremony.

Religious instruction on an optional basis is—at least

theoretically—permitted. In practice, this means that only those pupils whose parents declare before the State authority at the beginning of every school year that they want religious instruction for their children, are allowed to receive it. The instruction is given by the priests. The instructor may only explain the positive doctrines of the Church; the presentation of Catholic arguments against atheism and dialectical materialism is forbidden. It is strictly forbidden to gather children or adults for the purpose of religious instruction in *parish buildings*. Courts have sentenced priests whose "crime" was that they had provided religious instruction outside of the state school buildings. The State often demands the dismissal of the best religious instructions from the Church, and threatens dire retaliatory measures for disobedience. The parents of children receiving religious education, and the children themselves, are subjected to legal disadvantages (non-admission to universities, exclusion from promotion and state employment, etc.). It is the fear of these legal disavantages that explains why only ten per cent of the Catholic children in Hungary receive religious instruction.

Before 1945 Hungarian Catholics maintained several national dailies, weeklies, and periodicals, both in the capital and the countryside, as well as journals of a philosophical, theological, aesthetic, literary or general character. They possessed several large and medium-sized publishing houses and bookstores, and established learned societies. Catholic book publishing occupied an important role. All these firms were nationalized without indemnification. The scientific and cultural societies were either banned, or remain only in nominal existence. Every year only a few Catholic books may be published and these in limited copies. Many excellent Catholic scholars, writers and artists cannot find any way to publish.

At present the Catholic press consists only of these papers:

Magyar Kurir (Hungarian Courier), a lithographed news-sheet which carries only Church news;

Az Uj Ember (The New Man), a weekly; and
Vigilia (The Vigil), a monthly.[5]

Both the *Vigilia* and *Az Uj Ember* are under the secret censorship of the State. This means in effect that
neither *Az Uj Ember* nor *Vigilia* may publish an article, or even a sentence, to which the State privately ob-
jects, and also that the *Az Uj Ember* must occasionally
publish articles secretly requested by the State. Both
publications suffer from economic discrimination by the
government. Since all Catholic printing firms have been
nationalized, both publications have to be printed in
State printing shops, and the State determines the printing costs of Catholic papers quite arbitrarily. Both publications receive permission to buy only the most expensive paper, and even then may not buy enough to satisfy readers' demands. *Az Uj Ember* has a circulation of
64,000 copies, *Vigilia* 10,000 copies and each issue is always sold out. Both publications not only have regular
subscribers but many people buy them at the news-
stands. Many readers prefer to avoid having their names
on the subscription list of a Catholic paper, and therefore buy individual issues. The readers of both the
Vigilia and *Az Uj Ember* are drawn from all classes of
society, priests and lay people, men and women, irrespective of age or occupation. Both publications have a
large number of non-Catholic, even agnostic and atheist
readers, especially among the "seekers."

Deprived of its pre-World War II wealth, the financial resources of the Church are now limited to:
State subsidy; ceremonial fee (*stola*) charged for ecclesiastical functions; and the voluntary contributions of
the faithful in money and natural goods.

The State subsidy consists mainly of the *congrua*, a
supplementary salary of the clergy. This covers, however, only the smaller part of the minimum living ex-

---

[5] The weekly, *Katolikus Szo* (The Catholic Word), should not
be classified among the Catholic press products since it is edited
by "Peace Priests" and remains a mouthpiece of the State rather
than of the Church. The *Katolikus Szo* regularly attacks the hierarchy of the Church, condemns those who remain faithful, and
supports State persecution of the Church.

penses of the priests. The supplementary salary of the clergy is not channeled through the Church or the dioceses as legal persons, but is sent directly to the individual priests. Thus, the *congrua* becomes one of the most effective means of government intervention in the internal affairs of the Church. The State simply withholds the supplementary salary from any priest who does not satisfy governmental demands, or who obeys his own conscience, or obeys the bishop rather than the State. At other times, the State makes the payment of the *congrua* dependent upon the transfer of the priest to another village or function by the bishop. Again, sometimes the bishop or the priest is punished by nonpayment of the *congrua* for refusing to perform a ceremony strictly forbidden by the *Codex Iuris Canonici*. There are innumerable ways of utilizing the *congrua* against the Church. In effect, the State subsidy is intended not to help the Church but is utilized as a powerful instrument of intervention in the teaching, sanctifying and governing rights of the Church. In short, it is used by and large to undermine and subvert the Church. First, the communist State deprived the Church of all sources of material independence; then, it gave State subsidy to put the Church in a materially dependent position; and finally, the subsidy is being used to coerce the Church into the service of State aims and internally corrupt it.

The *stola* is paid voluntarily by the believers. The fees are set low; the really poor people don't pay at all. Thus, it constitutes a very limited source of income for the clergy.

The voluntary contributions of the faithful are paid both in *money* and *in kind*. The importance of contributions paid in kind is manifested by the fact that they are sufficient to feed the members of the seminaries.[6]

6 Before the Second World War, the twelve dioceses and almost all the religious orders in Hungary had their own seminaries. In addition, there was also a Central Seminary in Budapest to educate those seminarists who were studying at the Theological Faculty of the University of Budapest. The seminaries of the orders were liquidated, and today there are only *six* regular seminaries. Between 1945 and 1950 the number of new vocations was higher

Money contributions are twofold: plate collections during the mass; and the so-called ecclesiastical tax which constitutes an incomparably larger source of revenue than plate collections. The ecclesiastical capital tax (paid not by families but per capita) is set annually at 25 forints (one U.S. dollar), which still represents a significant amount for the poorer classes. The ecclesiastical capital tax is not a real tax but a voluntary contribution. The Church may ask the payment by mail or by house-to-house collections. Yet, the overwhelming majority of the faithful spontaneously pay this capital tax, a fact which well demonstrates their fidelity as well as their generosity. In one of the largest archdioceses which is in a poorer section of the country and where the number of children attending religious education is very low, about 80 per cent of the faithful paid this capital tax in 1962.

It is evident from the consistent actions of the communist governments in Hungary that they are determined to systematically infiltrate, polarize and disorganize, but most of all to *behead,* and *internally corrupt* the Church. The main characteristics of this government policy are the following: (a) open and secret intervention in the internal affairs of the Church; (b) ostracism, i.e., the open and secret persecution of the most excellent members of the clergy just because of their excellence; and (c) the use and support of those members of the clergy who suffer from some defect, and, particularly, the coercion of the Church to fill the important Church positions with such priests. The *official* executive organ of this government policy is the so-called State Office for Church Affairs, always headed by a well-known anti-theist. The officials of this government organ are attached to the chanceries of dioceses. The *socio-*

and the quality of applicants more promising than at any time during the last hundred years. Now, new vocations emanate from all classes, but in smaller numbers. In the seminary of one of the archdioceses, there were 90–110 seminarians before 1945, but in 1962 only 29. In the past the number of priests ordained annually in this archdiocese equalled the present number of all seminarists in the five classes. In 1963 the entire student body of the Central Seminary of Budapest numbered only 46 students.

ecclesiastic organ of this government policy is the Peace Priest Movement. This government policy inflicted more harm on the Church than the anti-theistic propaganda and resulted in more open and harsher persecution.

The State Office for Church Affairs continuously intervenes in the internal affairs of the Church. It exercises censorship over the pastoral letters. It forces the bishops and chapters to appoint or elect vicars who are favorites of the regime. Thus, the bishop is impeded in his right to select his own vicar. The State Office for Church Affairs frequently demands the removal, transfer or punishment of parishoners, chaplains and religious teachers. It also forbids certain priests to preach and to celebrate solemn church services (e.g., high mass). Under the threat of reprisals, it frequently demands that priests deliver propaganda speeches from the pulpit in favor of communist institutions or measures (e.g., the kolkhozes, hated by the peasants).

The priest refrains in vain from political and secular affairs and limits his activity to the strict ecclesiastical duties. The more talented a priest may be the more he will be a thorn in the flesh of the government and is subjected to persecution. The State Office of Church Affairs tries to expel the most capable, talented, educated and faithful priests of high character from the important church posts and functions. These priests can avoid persecution and retaliation only if their ordinaries banish (exile) them to insignificant places and posts. The government takes consistent steps for the undermining of ecclesiastic discipline and creating discord and antagonism between the higher and lower members of the hierarchy. No priest can expect any defense of his ordinary against the threats of the government if the priest refuses to obey the illegal demands of the government and obeys the Church laws.

The majority of the Peace Priests consists of honest priests who joined the movement under duress mainly because they wished to stay with their flock. Their co-operation with the Peace Priest Movement is rather formal and is limited to the inevitable. Joining the Peace Priest Movement was for many a great sacrifice.

The majority of the priests resisted the duress and temptation and did not join the Peace Priests.

The bishops created the *Opus Pacis* which was joined by all the clergy. The bishops hoped that they and their loyal clergy would be directing the new organization, but did not achieve their aim. Today, the bishops and the loyal clergy must sit together with the sinful priests in the *Opus Pacis;* the latter are the real powers within the movement, though they themselves are under strong pressure from the government.

Neither Kádár's speech quoted above nor his ecclesiastical policy until now, give any foundation whatsoever in hoping that his government will enter a road which, however gradually, would eventually lead toward a respect of religious freedom. Whatever signs one has seen so far, indicate that the most that can be expected from the Kádár regime is a *limitation* of the Church's servitude, but not a granting of *limited freedom* to the Church.

II.

RECENT DEVELOPMENTS

Reprinted from EAST EUROPE, a Monthly Review of East European Affairs, June 1966, Vol 15, No. 6. New York, New York.

If it is true to say that the war between atheism and religion in communist countries has, on the whole, gone against the communists, one must at the same time observe that the war between Church and state is still going on. True, religious faith is very much alive. As one Hungarian propagandist complained recently, "The invisible empire is still at work." But on the institutional level, where taxes are levied and policies carried out, the churches have had to make concessions.

The direct and heavy-handed repression of the late 40's and early 50's has now been replaced by a policy of pressure, although the police arm is always at hand when needed. Thus in September 1964 the Hungarian government signed a protocol with the Vatican covering relations between the state and the Catholic Church, which ministers to about 65 percent of the population. Three months after this, nine Catholic clergymen were arrested for "conspiracy" because they had been "active in arranging discussions" among young people. In secret trials they were sentenced to long prison terms, and those who had hoped for a new *modus vivendi* between church and state were shown that there had been no basic change in the party's attitude.

The limits within which religious institutions are allowed to function were set in the years after the Communist take-over. By 1954, Catholic elementary and high schools in Hungary had been reduced from 3,148 to only eight; Calvinist schools from 1,057 to four; Lutheran schools from 359 to one; and Jewish and Orthodox schools had been completely eliminated. Religious instruction had been banished from the primary and secondary schools. The State Office for Church Affairs was set up in 1951 with the right to intervene at any point in the conduct of religious organizations and to decide the number of institutions, schools and religious teachers that would be permitted. Today this militantly atheist government bureau maintains fully-staffed offices in 19 Hungarian counties, submits the names of priests for appointment, calls for the punishment or transfer of of those it dislikes, and forces the clergy to support communist policies such as the collectivization of agriculture. Paradoxically, a regime committed to atheism has not been averse to using church groups as propaganda arms of the state; religious leaders, including high prelates, have been pressured into making pronouncements in support of Moscow's foreign policies.

An entering wedge has been the mobilization of so-called "peace priests" who in effect serve the party in the same fashion as the trade unions, the youth groups and the satellite political parties. Though they represent only a small minority of the Catholic clergy they constantly speak in the name of the church. The peace priest movement was abolished during the 1956 revolution by Cardinal Mindszenty, who used his brief period of freedom to break the political shackles of the church.

(Since the regime has a freer hand in nominating pastors to higher positions in the Protestant Churches, a closer relationship has developed between them.)

In furtherance of its political aims where the churches are concerned, the state employs the power of the purse. Under the agreements signed in 1948 with the Protestant churches and in 1950 with the Catholic Church, the government undertook to subsidize the religious denominations for a period of 20 years, the amount of the subsidy decreasing by 25 percent every five years. Between 1956 and 1961, however, the subsidies were increased. The subsidy represents only a small percentage of the church income from the assets which were expropriated when the communists came to power in 1947. The state payments include the so-called "congrua" designed to cover the minimum expense of carrying out the priests' clerical duties. The congrua is paid directly to the individual clergymen, thus making them dependent for a vital source of income on the state; and the authorities have not hesitated to use this as a means of keeping stubborn individuals in line. Against this, the churches have only the resources left through fees paid for specific religious ministrations, and voluntary contributions from the faithful.

The limitations thus imposed on the functioning of the church have been generally effective. Because of the reduced influence of the church in daily affairs, the state has been able to adopt a more pragmatic approach. Thus Hungarian delegations were permitted to attend the sessions of Ecumenical Council in Rome in 1963, 1964 and 1965. They included bishops, episcopal vicars, canons, a number of Catholic laymen, and a contingent of peace priests. At home, however, the church is held on a much shorter leash. The Central Seminary in Budapest in 1963 had 43 theologians as opposed to 120 during the 1958-1959 school year. Some 700 priests were forbidden to practice their calling in 1951 and were told to take jobs in industry where, because of their background, they have not been permitted to rise to advanced positions open to other workers. Moreover, they are closely watched to see that they do not promote religion on the job. The two Calvinist and one Lutheran seminaries still permitted to function have few applicants. There is one Rabbinical Institute, which is expected to provide spiritual leaders for Hungary's remaining 100,000 Jews.

In the eight Catholic high schools (six for boys, two for girls), nuns and priests are free to teach the doctrines of their church, but they are permitted to use only textbooks published by the state, and similar restrictions apply to the one Calvinist and one Lutheran high schools. Nevertheless, the schools have established reputations as the best in the country, and there is a waiting list for entrance. Since 1963 the state has abolished automatic restrictions on entrance to college for graduates of religious schools. Such entrance, however, is limited to graduates of exceptional talent. While parents may enroll their children for a limited amount of religious instruction in the schools, this is hedged about with so much open hostility and delay that only the more fervent believers take the trouble. Paradoxically, party members with religious inclinations are forbidden to enroll their children for religious instruction, and efforts in this direction are reported to the higher party authorities. Classes cannot be held for children or adults in church buildings, and several priests have been jailed for conducting such "anti-state" activities. Particularly stringent penalties are applied to priests who give private religious instruction.

What has been the effect on religious belief? Church attendance has certainly fallen off, but this seems partly a result of demographic changes. Since 1948 there has been a heavy migration from the farm to the city. The churches remain strong in the rural areas, but many youngsters who drifted off to the cities have lost their religious roots. In dropping their traditional faith, they have not, of course, made the leap into total scientific materialism as required by communist dogma. Instead, childhood beliefs have been replaced by disillusionment, cynicism and the quest for material possessions.

Even if there has been a drift away from religious belief under the combined pressure of urbanization and state-inspired opposition, there is still a wide acceptance of traditional rituals, particularly christenings, marriages and funerals. The state has accordingly recognized this by setting up its own non-religious ceremonies. Old mansions have been converted to marriage halls where, under the sponsorship of the youth organizations, women's leagues, and trade unions, non-religious ceremonies are performed free of charge. Christenings have been re-titled "name-giving feasts," and confirmations are called "promotion to adult status." Funerals are very elaborate, even to choirs and bands.

The press claims that these secular rituals are growing in popularity, but at the same time one can find articles complaining that people fail to take advantage of the state's generosity. Villagers generally shun the state-subsidized ceremonies, while in the cities many use them and then repair to church for an additional ceremony. When this is discovered, the culprits must repay the state for its services and return its gifts.

While the rank-and-file priests and worshippers can to some extent defy the constraints imposed on their religion by the state, church spokesmen are under constant pressure. They have at their command only one weekly, *Uj Ember* (New Man), with a circulation limited to 50,000 and subject to close censorship. It accepts "socialism," but maintains that believers have equal obligations to God and fatherland. An editorial stated on August 7, 1960, "Catholics must partake of the nation's work notwithstanding the new mold of our relationship with the state. . . . To make new life rise on the ruins, to break down social barriers, to raise the status of the working man, to stop man's exploitation by man, to raise the people's welfare and culture, to secure peace within and outside our country, to reject war and all nuclear weapons—such are our common duties."

A smaller and less representative group of clergymen, however, offer more resistance to the state goals. They view political persecution as having a positive value, as a return to Christian martyrdom in a modern setting. This existentialist approach sees life under a communist dictatorship as posing an ultimate problem for the truly religious person. The communist challenge to Christianity must be met by an assertion of the superior spiritual quality of religion. This will appear in the way a Christian believer acts in a hostile environment, proving by his readiness to be a witness for his faith that his service to man is equal to that proclaimed by the communists. Further, there is the implication that even communists can be brought to a more sympathetic acceptance of religion by such an example.

The debate, in view of the unequal resources of the participants, has an unreal quality. On the communist side there is little inclination to enter a dialogue on the spiritual significance of religion, most of whose practices are dismissed as belonging to another, backward era. Official church leaders, on their part, are ready to sanction most of the social aims of the communists in return for being allowed to practice their religion. The communists are ready to cooperate only to the extent that the church joins in expressing support for their programs, particularly their international policies.

TRANSYLVANIA AND THE HUNGARIAN MINORITY

Reprinted article of Ferenc A. Váli: "Transylvania and the Hungarian Minority," JOURNAL OF INTERNATIONAL AFFAIRS (Volume XX, No. 1, 1966). School of International Affairs, Columbia University, New York, New York.

Transylvania is a high plateau surrounded by the semi-circle of Carpathian and Transylvanian Alps, and separated from the Hungarian Plains by other ranges of lower mountains and hills. Most of its rivers flow toward the Hungarian fluvial basin, but some, such as the Olt, join the Danube or its tributaries in the Walachian or Moldavian Plains.

The word Transylvania is frequently used in a wider sense (though incorrectly, both from the geographical and historical point of view) to denote all the regions which, following World War I, were ceded by Hungary to Rumania: that is, in addition to Transylvania proper, the areas of Crisana and Maramures, and the eastern portion of the Banat. In this wider sense, Transylvania lies between Hungary and the *Regat,* a kingdom created in 1881 out of the original Rumanian principalities of Walachia and Moldavia, which had been united in 1859–60. Transylvania, in either the narrower or the wider sense, is inhabited by a mixed population of Rumanians and Hungarians, in an approximate ratio of three to one in favor of the former, and also by a smaller number of Germans (known in Transylvania proper as Saxons, and in the Banat as Swabians).

Among the factors dividing Hungarians and Rumanians in Transylvania, religious differences played an outstanding role. Hungarians (and Germans) are either

Catholics or belong to one of the Protestant denominations. Rumanians are adherents of Eastern Orthodoxy; they belong to the national Rumanian Orthodox Church or, as many did before 1948, to the Uniat Rumanian Church which concluded a union with Rome while still preserving its orthodox rite and liturgy.[1] The religious cleavage added significantly to the ethnic and linguistic differences.

The politico-ethnic strife over Transylvania between Hungarians and Rumanians is accentuated by the historical controversy over whether Rumanians are the autochthonous inhabitants of Transylvania. It is incontrovertibly established that with the Magyar occupation of the Carpathian basin in the last decade of the ninth century the Transylvanian region also came under the control of the Hungarians. Furthermore, until the creation of the autonomous Principality of Transylvania, this region was always considered an integral part of the Kingdom of Hungary.

Whether Transylvania was largely uninhabited when the Magyars occupied it or whether a people descended from Latinized Dacians already living there, as claimed by the adherents of the Daco-Roman theory, is a question of more than academic significance. The intellectual source of Rumanian national consciousness and pride has been and still remains based on the claim that Rumanian culture is a direct offspring of the classical Roman civilization.[2] The theory of the Daco-Roman origin of the Rumanians, formulated first in the eighteenth century, contributed greatly to the creation of

[1] In 1948 the Uniats were forcibly reincorporated into the national Rumanian Orthodox Church after their five bishops had been arrested by the communist authorities.

[2] The Latin origin of the Rumanians and of the Rumanian language was tempered during the Stalinist and post-Stalinist periods when an allegedly Slav kinship was emphasized. At present, Daco-Romanism has again become the *leitmotiv* of Rumanian historiography and linguistics. Besides being used to prove the Western-Latin origin of Rumanians, it is also exploited for irredentist motives: for example, an article recently wished to prove that the (now Soviet-held) Northern Bukovina was also part of Roman Dacia. See Dan Zamfirescu, 'Rumania—Land of Civilization and Synthesis," *Gazeta Literara*, July 22, 1965.

Rumanian national awareness. According to this theory, Transylvania, which had come under Rumanian control only in 1918, and not the Danubian Principalities, should be regarded as the real cradle of Rumanian *ethnicum*.

Hungarian as well as many Western historians rely, however, on the clearly established historical fact of the Magyar occupation and colonization in the tenth and eleventh centuries.[3] The Székelys, a Hungarian-speaking people of controversial origin, were settled in the far eastern part of Transylvania to serve as guardians of the border against the onslaught of nomads from the East. These same historians also argue that Rumanians (originally known as Vlachs) began their infiltration into Transylvania from the twelfth century onward. On the other hand, the neo-Latin character of the Rumanian language and, accordingly, the ethnic-linguistic tie between Rome and the Rumanians cannot be questioned, irrespective of the fact whether Rumanians were in the area prior to the Magyar occupation.

The Rumanians in Transylvania, although their number constantly increased in proportion to the Hungarian-speaking element, politically played an insignificant role for many centuries. More important, from this point of view, were the German colonists, settled by Hungarian kings during the twelfth and thirteenth centuries, who created flourishing urban communities.

After the fateful Battle of Mohács (1526), as a consequence of the Turkish invasion of Hungary and the establishment of Hapsburg rule over the remaining "royal" Hungary, an autonomous Principality of Transylvania was formed by the three "nations" of that region: the Hungarians, the Székelys and the Saxons. Al-

[3] It is also pointed out that the Roman legions were withdrawn from Dacia in 272 A.D. (Dacia became a Roman province under Trajan around 106 A.D.), and until the 12th century no convincing trace of Daco-Romans was found in Transylvania. Dominic G. Kosary, *A History of Hungary*, Cleveland-New York, 1941, pp. 13-14. Among the chief advocates of the Daco-Roman theory are to be mentioned: A. D. Xenopol, *Histoire des Roumains*, Paris, 1896; N. Jorga, *Geschichte des rumänischen Volkes*, Bucharest, 1905; R. W. Seton-Watson, *History of the Roumanians from Roman Times to the Completion of Unity*, New York-London, 1934.

though nominally a vassal of the Sultan, independent Transylvania rested on a balance of power between the Hapsburgs and the Ottoman Empires. As soon as the balance tilted in favor of the former and the Turks were forced to abandon their Hungarian possessions at the end of the seventeenth century, Transylvania came under the rule of the House of Hapsburg.

The demand for constitutional and administrative fusion between Hungary and Transylvania was an important part of the program of the Hungarian reform-party during the first half of the nineteenth century. The union was proclaimed by one of the momentous Acts of 1848. Before the implementation of the fusion, the revolutionary war of 1848–49 erupted, a war marked by Rumanian insurgency serving the cause of Vienna against Hungarian nationalism. After the suppression of Hungarian independence in 1849, Transylvania was governed as an Austrian province. Only following the *Ausgleich* of 1867 between Austria and Hungary, was the union of Hungary and Transylvania fully implemented.

Between 1867 and 1918, Rumanians in Hungary expressed frequent and often vehement discontent with discrimination and attempts at their Magyarization. They resisted this latter pressure most successfully. In fact, despite Magyar constraints and lack of schooling facilities in the Rumanian language, the Rumanians retained their identity and increased faster in population than the Hungarians. Rumanian members in the Hungarian Parliament upheld the cause of their co-nationals, and from across the border of Transylvania the authorities of the Kingdom of Rumania supported morally and financially their Trans-Carpathian brethren. The aim was no longer their emancipation but the union of all Rumanians in a *România Mare* (Great Rumania).

During World War I, the Allies, in order to induce Rumania to join their cause against the Central Powers, promised to cede Transylvania and other parts of Eastern Hungary to Rumania.[4] But the Rumanian entry

---

[4] Agreement of August 17, 1916. For details see C. A. Macartney, *Hungary and Her Successors,* Oxford, 1937, p. 275.

into the war in 1916 ended in disaster, and Bucharest was compelled to sue for peace. Only after the defeat of Germany and Austria-Hungary in the fall of 1918 did Rumania again consider herself at war. Her forces, under an elastic Armistice Agreement, entered Transylvania, and drove deeper and deeper into Hungary proper. An Allied ultimatum, demanding from Hungary the surrender of further areas west of Transylvania, caused the resignation of the republican Károlyi regime in March 1919 and prompted the establishment of the first Hungarian Communist regime under Béla Kun. Three months later, the Rumanian advance toward Budapest contributed to the collapse of Béla Kun's proletarian dictatorship. Only in November 1919 did the Rumanian forces withdraw behind the demarcation line that was to become the Hungarian-Rumanian frontier under the Peace Treaty of Trianon. This demarcation line is today still the boundary between these two states.

The transfer of Transylvania and other territories placed about 1,700,000 Hungarians under Rumanian control. A Minority Treaty, concluded between the Principal Allied and Associated Powers, and Rumania, was to safeguard the Hungarian and other minorities under the guarantee of the League of Nations. From 1921 until the collapse of the League's authority, the Hungarian Government championed the interest of the Hungarian minority in the committees and councils of the League, before international courts, and in the chancelleries of diplomacy. The transformation of the Hungarians from a dominant into a minority element presented inevitable hardships. These were augmented by some discriminatory measures introduced by the Rumanian Government. One of these was a drastic agrarian reform which resulted in the confiscation of Hungarian properties and gave rise to a prolonged and heated dispute between the two countries.[5]

One must bear in mind, in any comparison between

[5] This conflict was incorrectly known as the "optants" dispute; see Francis Deak *The Hungarian-Rumanian Land Dispute*, New York, 1928. For Hungarian grievances in general see Zsombor de Szasz, *The Minorities in Roumanian Transylvania*, London, 1927.

the post-World War I and post-World War II situation, that in the previous period Rumania was an "open" country, ruled by a relatively liberal-constitutional regime. Even if often unsuccessfully, Hungary could and did avail herself of the diplomatic and other procedures open to it which, together with Western pressures, prevented a gross abuse of power and more flagrant violations of treaty rights. Neither Hungary nor the West is at present able or willing to exert such pressures; nor are they likely to find reactions in Rumania similar to those in the interwar period.

The main concern of Hungarian foreign policy in the era following World War I was to bring about a revision of the territorial clauses of the Trianon treaty, a policy which forged Czechoslovakia, Yugoslavia and Rumania together into the alliance known as the Little Entente. The distribution of the Hungarian-speaking element in Rumania was, however, of a nature that excluded any practical and sound compromise solution. Along the Rumanian side of the international border lay a strip populated by about half a million Hungarians. Although economically disadvantageous, the return of this area would have rendered some justice to the ethnic principle. It would, however, still have left the majority of Hungarians under Rumanian rule. These other Hungarians were dispersed in various parts of Transylvania, while the solid mass of the Hungarian-Székely element (about 700,000) lived in the east and southeast corner of Transylvania, separated from compact Hungarian districts by regions populated mainly by ethnic Rumanians.

In the summer of 1940 the Soviet Union forced on Rumania the return of Bessarabia (together with Northern Bukovina). Hungary then threatened her eastern neighbor with war if the Transylvanian question was not solved. Germany and Italy intervened and under the (second) Vienna Award (August 30, 1940) Northern Transylvania and the four Székely counties were given back to Hungary. For the first time in history, Transylvania had become politically divided. With the division of the Vienna Award almost as many Rumanians were returned to Hungarian rule as were Hungarians, while hundreds of thousands of the latter continued to live in the Rumanian part of Transylvania. In 1944, after the Rumanian surrender, Soviet forces entered Transylvania and advanced into Hungary proper. The administration of Hungarian Transylvania was first left by the Soviet occupation forces to local elements but later, as the Sovietization of Rumania progressed, it was handed over to the Rumanian Government.

At the Paris Peace Conference of 1946–47, the Hungarian delegation attempted to preserve for Hungary the Hungarian-inhabited frontier belt of Rumania. While the United States favored such a solution, the Soviet Union, wishing to please Rumania rather than Hungary, prevented its acceptance.[6] Thus the Trianon border was integrally restored. However, the Peace Treaty concluded between the Allied Powers and Rumania on February 10, 1947, contained in Part II, Section I Article 3, the following protective provisions:

> (1) Rumania shall take the steps necessary to secure to all persons under Rumanian jurisdiction, without distinction as to race, sex, language or religion, the enjoyment of human rights and fundamental freedoms, including freedom of expression, of press and publication, of religious worship, of political opinion and of public meeting.

> (2) Rumania further undertakes that the laws in force in Rumania shall not, either in their content or in their application, discriminate or entail any discrimination between persons of Rumanian nationality on the ground of their race, sex, language or religion, whether in reference to their persons, property, business, professional or financial interests, status, political or civil rights or any other matter.

As could have been foreseen by the Western signatories of the treaty, an implementation of these exemplary provisions was from the beginning incompatible with the existence or survival of a Communist dictatorial regime which, in practice, denies freedom to the entire

[6] Stephen D. Kertesz, *Diplomacy in a Whirlpool,* Notre Dame, Ind., 1953, *passim;* John C. Campbell, "The European Territorial Settlement," *Foreign Affairs,* October, 1947, pp. 211-213.

population and not only to particular groups.[7] Nevertheless, as experience shows, certain generally conceived measures may inflict greater harm on certain groups or segments of the people than on the rest of them. Thus, for instance, the nationalization of industries and business, and the restrictions imposed on the artisan class, affected the Hungarians in Transylvania more severely than the Rumanians because the former composed a larger proportion of the urban population than the latter. Hungarian schools in Transylvania were to a large extent run by Catholic or Protestant religious organizations; but under the Communist regime, religious communities were generally barred from maintaining educational institutions. Catholics and Uniats (the former almost exclusively Hungarians), because they maintained contacts with Rome, were subject to more violent persecution than members and priests of the Rumanian Orthodox Church.

However, within the general context of Communist dictatorial rule, the Hungarian minority fared relatively well in the first decade of the Rumanian People's Republic. Within the extremely weak Rumanian Communist Party, as it was in the immediate postwar period, the Transylvanian organizations, having many members of Hungarian stock, were proportionately stronger than those of other parts of the country. It was perhaps due to the influence of the Transylvanian organizations but certainly to Soviet pressures that the second Communist Constitution of 1952 contained a number of provisions in favor of ethnic minorities, including special arrangements for the Hungarians in Transylvania.[8]

The Constitution of 1952 guaranteed to all national minorities the use of their mother tongue, and provided that instruction be given on all levels of public education in their respective languages. In minority areas,

[7] See Henry L. Roberts, *Rumania—Political Problems of an Agrarian State,* New Haven, 1951, p. 307. Attempts by the Western Powers at inducing Rumania (and also Hungary and Bulgaria) to comply with the human rights clause failed after proceedings before the U.N. and the International Court of Justice.

[8] See R. V. Burks, *The Dynamics of Communism in Eastern Europe,* Princeton, 1961, pp. 155-158.

officials were to use the language which prevailed in their district. Discrimination against members of the national minorities was to be considered a criminal offense. In other words, the so-called Leninist principle of nationalities was to be put into effect.

Article 19 and 20 of the Constitution of 1952 created for the Hungarian minority in Transylvania the Hungarian Autonomous Province consisting of the entire Székely region. The population of this area, according to the 1956 census, was made up of Hungarians (77.3 per cent), Rumanians (20.1 per cent), and some splinter minorities. The autonomy of this province was to serve the cultural and educational needs of the Hungarian majority. In addition to institutions of higher learning in Targu-Mures (Marosvásárhely), the capital of the Hungarian Autonomous Province, a Hungarian University continued to function, alongside a Rumanian one, in Cluj (Kolozsvár, in Hungarian; Klausenburg, in German), the historic capital of Transylvania.[9]

This preferential status of the Hungarian minority came to an end in 1958, the year of the withdrawal of Soviet forces from Rumania. It was no accident that this occurred two years after the abortive Hungarian Revolution and its final denouement in the execution of revolutionary Prime Minister Imre Nagy. The uprising in Hungary of October-November 1956 made an electrifying impression on the citizens of Rumania and especially on the population of Transylvania, where students (not only Hungarian ones) demonstrated in a number of towns. Had the revolution in Hungary not been quickly suppressed, the position of the Rumanian Communist regime would have been seriously jeopardized. Russian army units were strategically positioned to crush the demonstrators if they got out of hand. The Bucharest government collaborated in every possible manner with the Soviet Union: some Soviet units passed through Ru-

[9] The original Hungarian University in Cluj was converted after 1920 into a Rumanian University. In 1940, it was reconverted into a Hungarian institution. After 1947, the Rumanian Government divided it into a Rumanian (University of Babes) and a Hungarian (Bolyai University) institution.

mania on their way to Hungary. The leaders of the Hungarian Revolution, captured by the Russians, were interned on Rumanian soil, while Hungarian-speaking Rumanian security officers assisted the Soviet Security organs in their task to hunt down freedom-fighters in Hungary. The reward for the loyalty and collaboration of the Rumanian Party and Government was the withdrawal of Soviet forces, an expression of trust which was denied to the Hungarians. The demonstrations in Rumania gave the pretext for arresting the regime's known or suspected opponents, most of them members of the Hungarian minority. According to unconfirmed reports, many thousands were arrested and hundreds among them executed.[10]

The Hungarian Revolution manifested the weakness of the Hungarian Communist regime and compromised its leaders in the eyes of world communism. But the Polish and Hungarian events also compromised the Soviet claim to be the leader of the communist camp. The beginnings of the Sino-Soviet split, the official recognition of legitimate "independent roads toward communism," and the evolution of a global climate favoring a more pronounced nationalism encouraged the Rumanian leaders gradually to implement a program which had probably been conceived earlier. The objectives of this program were liberation from the fetters of Soviet governmental and Party control, internal emphasis on the "national" character of the regime, and independence in foreign policy. Such a program corresponded to the conceptions of the Party leadership—now consisting of "home" communists, after the elimination from leadership of earlier, Moscow-trained, "internationalists." It also served to make the regime more popular in the eyes of the ardently nationalist and essentially anti-Russian population, and to strengthen it in every respect.

National minorities, in the philosophy of "integral" nationalists, were an obstacle to the desired "national unity," in other words, a source of debility and of perils.

[10] The story is told by George Bailey, "Trouble Over Transylvania," *The Reporter*, November 19, 1964, pp. 25-30.

The national society, according to this view, should be made more cohesive, more uniform and monolithic by the assimilation and absorption of the national minorities. In the eyes of the Rumanian leadership the compact mass of Hungarians (Székelys) in the very center of the country, as well as other Hungarian settlements in various parts of Transylvania constituted a potential danger. This reasoning was reinforced by some historical precedents. A highly nationalistic Rumanian regime—whatever its political color—was bound to turn against the Hungarian minority and to seek to end its alleged privileged status.

The anti-Hungarian campaign was carried out in successive stages. The most vehement onslaught was against the flourishing Hungarian educational institutions. Its prime victim was the Hungarian Bolyai University at Cluj, which was compelled to join the Rumanian Babes University.[11] In Hungarian schools not immediately closed down, parallel sections in which the teaching was done in Rumanian, were set up. During the following years the Rumanian sections grew while the Hungarian ones dwindled.[12] According to prevailing practice, only the eldest of the children in a family was allowed to attend Hungarian classes where they still existed. At the end of 1962, no independent Hungarian schools, not even a primary school, functioned in Rumania.

The official dismantling of the Hungarian Autonomous Province was carried out in 1962. A Presidential Decree arbitrarily changed the boundaries of this province by cutting away Székely-inhabited districts and by merging these areas with an overwhelming Rumanian population. At the same time, the name of the province was changed to "Mureş-Hungarian Autonomous Province," because the territory was increased largely with sections along the Mureş (Maros) River. In the capital of the province the Hungarian Medical and Pharma-

[11] *Bulletin of the International Committee of Jurists,* No. 17, Geneva, December 1963, p. 40.

[12] Stephen Fischer-Galati, "Rumania," in Stephen D. Kertesz, *East Central Europe and the World: Developments in the Post-Stalin Era,* Notre Dame, Ind., 1962, p. 165.

ceutical College was simply closed. Use of the Hungarian language by officials (including the employees of the state-owned industrial and commercial firms) was first discouraged, then forbidden, both within the Autonomous Province and outside. The Hungarian influence in this province has been weakened to the extent that members of the local councils and cultural institutions are mostly Rumanians.[13]

All the available sources appear to indicate that the Rumanian Government is practicing severe discrimination against the Hungarian minority and that the clear intention once again is to Rumanize them, to reduce their numbers by absorbing them into the Rumanian ethnic community. The Rumanian regime may believe that it has a much better chance now to proceed with such an attempt. As it has been noted, in the interwar period Hungary and the Western Powers possessed legal, political and moral weapons for intervening against the de-nationalization process, and in the immediate postwar situation the Soviet Union was able to impose the application of the Leninist principle of nationalities. At the present juncture, no such interposition seems likely or possible.

The Hungarian Government and Party were caught in their own trap: since 1945 they have constantly condemned the chauvinist and irredentist attitudes of the Horthy regime. Expressions of disapproval with the ethnically unjust Trianon frontier were branded as reactionary and fascist attitudes. Should the Hungarian Government now launch protests, it could be accused of violating the friendship between Socialist fraternal countries, and of intervening in the internal affairs of a sister nation and Party. The West does not now possess any means of exerting pressure on the Rumanian Government and, in fact, the Western Powers approve of the independent foreign policy of Rumania even if they disapprove of the persecution of a national minority. The Rumanian leading circles may also have counted on Soviet complacency in this matter. Moscow would be

13 George Bailey, op. et loc. cit.

unwilling to see its relations with Bucharest further deteriorate for the sake of the Hungarian minority.

The facts concerning the fate of Hungarians in Rumania are generally well-known in Hungary, where they are often discussed *in camera*, even on higher party levels, in a way which almost amounts to a whispering campaign.[14] But, thus far, none of the Rumanian actions have been mentioned, let alone condemned, in the Hungarian press, nor has any official protest been lodged by Budapest. From June 15 to 19, 1965, a Hungarian Party delegation led by Politburo member Gyula Kállai (who shortly thereafter became Prime Minister) visited Bucharest, in order "to develop further the co-operation between the two Parties," and was received in a "comradely spirit." It is not known whether the question of the Hungarian minority in Transylvania was even discussed. Thus, while Kállai preaches "socialist patriotism" which should be "free of nationalism,"[15] the brotherly Rumanian Party undertakes to eliminate their Hungarian minority in the name of Rumanian nationalism.

It is, however, hardly to be expected that, in the long run, the discontent over the Rumanian developments, keenly felt by Hungarian popular, intellectual and even Party elements, will fail to erupt into the open. The feeling of the present writer is that dissatisfaction has so far been silenced by the promise that the most effective assistance to Transylvanian Hungarians could be administered via discreet and confidential Party-to-Party channels. Intercession by the Soviet Government or Party may also have been sought.

In the meantime, the Rumanian authorities have undertaken to isolate Transylvanian Hungarians from outside Hungarian influences, a policy which, with the help of communist methods of control and restriction, has not been too difficult to put into effect. Hungarian

[14] See Ghita Ionescu, "Communist Rumania and Nonalignment," *Slavic Review*, June 1965, p. 252.

[15] From Gyula Kállai's address before the Political Academy of the Hungarian Party's Central Committee on the subject "From Bourgeois to Socialist Nation," on June 14, 1965; *Nepszabadsag*, June 16, 1965.

visitors are not permitted to move freely in Transylvania as a whole; they can only stay at the place indicated in their visas. Importation of Hungarian publications, including the daily press, is severely curtailed, and few books printed in Hungary reach Transylvania. The implementation of the Hungarian-Rumanian cultural agreement depends on Rumanian authorities, and it is not being used to foster relations between Transylvanian intellectuals and their colleagues in Hungary. Rumania is, however, unable to prevent people from listening to the Hungarian radio.

The official Rumanian Party line has since 1958 been ardently nationalistic. Ideologically, this is a strange matrimony between Marxist-Leninist pragmatism and conservative-nationalist thinking.[16] Even the history of Rumania has, under the direction of the Party, been rewritten to demonstrate that Communist Rumania embodies the continued development of earlier features of her national tradition.[17] It is perhaps remarkable that the present die-hard Communist Party policy is associated with the traditional nationalist school of thought, essentially alien to Marxist-Leninist internationalism, whereas the liberal trend in the Party, as represented by young writers, while approving the Government's policy for independence, is more indifferent to nationalist concepts and wishes to rely more on "human values."[18]

Flexibility, so characteristic of the Rumanian position,

[16] Nicolae Ceausescu, the Party leader, in his speech before the Ninth Congress of the Rumanian Communist Party pointed out that Socialism depended on the existence of a strong national state.

[17] The four volumes of the new *History of Rumania*, published so far, present the development of the various parts of the country within a unitary framework, from the time of Roman conquest of Dacia, as if this development were shared by Moldavia, Walachia, and also Transylvania. At the conference of historians held in Budapest in May 1964 on the fall of Austria-Hungary, Rumanian historians maintained that the formation of national states on the territory of the Monarchy was a historic necessity, while Hungarian and Soviet historians contended that the dissolution of Austria-Hungary was not inevitable and that a federation of democratic states could have been set up in its place; *Contemporanul*, May 29, 1964.

[18] See *New York Times*, August 31, 1965.

is however manifested by the fact that *within*, and under the discipline of, the Communist Party, Hungarian elements, as such, are still permitted to function. It was officially reported during the Ninth Party Congress that among Party members 87 per cent are ethnic Rumanians, 9 per cent Hungarians and more than 3 per cent Germans and other nationalities.[19] The new Party Statutes, adopted by the Congress, again emphasized that members of the Party consist of different categories of workers, "irrespective of their nationality."[20] Among the leading members of the Party are still some of evidently Hungarian origin, though often their names have been Rumanized.[21] At the time of this writing it is not known whether the new Constitution which is now being prepared will continue to pay lip-service to the protection of national minorities.

The question of the Hungarian minority in Rumania is linked with the future evolution of Soviet-Rumanian relations. Should these relations deteriorate, should the presently existing differences between the two countries and Parties be openly aired, as the Sino-Soviet conflict was after a number of years, the dispute arising from the treatment of Transylvanian Hungarians is likely to develop into an overt conflict. As things are now, Hungary could openly support the rights of her fellow-nationals only if permitted by Moscow to do so. On the other hand, Moscow might prefer to exert pressure on its former satellite "by proxy." Of course, such developments might demonstrate even further the disunity of the socialist camp, which is not in the interest of the Soviet Union.

Resurgent nationalism in the East Central European

[19] *Scinteia*, July 21, 1965.

[20] *Scinteia*, June 3, 1965; the draft text, published in this issue was subsequently adopted by the Congress.

[21] Most prominent are: Alexander Moghioros (Magyaros), member of the Executive Committee of the Party; Leontin Salajan (Szalagyan), Executive Committee member and Minister of Armed Forces; Ion Fazekas, Alternate member of the Executive Committee and newly-appointed Deputy Premier; Iosif Bank, another newly-appointed Deputy Premier; Ghisela Vass, Central Committee member in charge of relations with other Parties. Prime Minister Ion Gheorghe Maurer is of Transylvanian-German origin.

arena may, as the impact of communist internationalist ideology recedes, become even more vehement and harmful than in the interwar period when it deprived the small nations, squeezed between the German and Russian giants, of means of joint diplomatic and military defense. Because communism has weakened humanism and individualism in this area, the new "socialist" nationalism might prove more devastating than the prewar traditional one, just as the national sentiment of the *ancien régime*, as advocated by Burke, was a gentlemanly game compared with the popular ultra-nationalism of the French Revolution.

With the notable difference of the potential intensity of this new nationalism, it appears that not much has changed: Hungarians in Transylvania are again oppressed; now another Great Power, this time the Soviet Union and not Germany, may use the Transylvanian Question as a lever for its own expansionist ambitions, and may even promise the return of Transylvania to Hungary. *Plus ça change, plus c'est la même chose.*

HUNGARIAN MINORITIES UNDER COMMUNIST RULE

Original study by István Révay.

Emerging vanquished from World War I, Hungary lost ethnically Hungarian areas and thus over three million Hungarians were shifted to a minority status. Today they, too, live under Communist rule.

In Rumania, according to a 1956 census, there were 1,652,-000 persons whose mother tongue was Hungarian; in 1930 1,554,500. In Yugoslavia, according to the 1953 census there were 506,000 Hungarians as against 468,200 in 1931. In Czechoslovakia the 1961 census listed 534,000 Hungarians, while in 1930—within today's frontiers, not counting the Carpatho-Ukraine—there were 603,800. Through post-World War II population exchanges and expulsions 15 per cent of the Hungarian minority in Czechoslovakia had been expatriated. In the Carpatho-Ukraine—annexed by the Soviet Union in 1945—a 1959 Soviet census listed 149,000 Hungarians; in 1930 there were 115,800.

In 1930 74.5 per cent of all Hungarians lived in Hungary proper, and 25.5 percent in three neighboring countries, not counting Austria. The percentage today stands at 76.2 per cent for Hungarians in Hungary and 23.8 per cent for Hungarians in the three neighboring Communist states and the Ukraine.

According to official data on demographic trends, in the respective countries—with the exception of Yugoslavia—Hungarian minorities are increasing at a surprising rate. The rate of natural increase for Hungarians in Czechoslovakia in 1955 was 15.5 per thousand, in 1956 15.4 per thousand as against

6.6 per thousand for the year 1936. The population growth rate among Hungarians in Rumania between 1948 and 1956 averaged 14.5 per thousand yearly, while population growth for the same group averaged 5.7 per thousand between 1934 and 1937. The rate of increase for these two Hungarian minority groups at present exceeds that for the population of Hungary which—in 1955, the year before the Revolution —showed an 11.5 per thousand growth rate. The average annual rate of population growth for Hungarians in Yugoslavia between 1948 and 1953 was only 3.8 per thousand, which cannot be compared with the situation between the two World Wars, as Yugoslav statistics for those years did not deal separately with the development of minority populations. In the Carpatho-Ukraine, the Hungarian minority showed a yearly 9.9 per thousand increase between 1930 and 1959. In 1936 the increase was 9.0.

Hungarian ethnic groups in Slovakia and Carpatho-Ukraine have preserved their linguistic frontiers. Although Slovak population exchanges and settlements have considerably inflated Slovak and Ruthenian-Ukrainian minority groups, the national character of Hungarian linguistic areas has remained unchanged. The situation is similar in Transylvania: no changes have taken place in the territorial distribution of Hungarians.

Hungarian-inhabited towns where Rumanians have been settled comprise an exception. In Transylvania in 1930 the population of the twenty-five most important towns was 46.6% Hungarian and 32% Rumanian; in 1956 51.9% Rumanian and 36% Hungarian. The name of the Hungarian autonomous Region established in 1952 was changed in 1960 to Maros-Hungarian Autonomous Region and its territory was gerrymandered at the expense of the Hungarians. In 1952 34.8% of all Rumanian Hungarians lived in the autonomous region; after 1960 29.8%. Through gerrymandering the percentage of Hungarians in the region fell from 77.6% to 61.7% while the number of Rumanians rose from 19.9% to 34.8%

Eighty-eight per cent of the Hungarians in Yugoslavia inhabit the Vojvodina [Vajdaság], making up 25 per cent of the population; 10 per cent are located in the Croatian, 2 per cent in the Slovenian Republic

EDUCATION AND CULTURAL LIFE

Today in Czechoslovakia there are 611 Hungarian-language schools on the primary and secondary levels, in Yugoslavia 283, in Carpatho-Ukraine 110. According to the last statistics, in Rumania there were 1660 Hungarian-language schools, but between 1958 and 1962 these were merged with the state-language schools. In the merged schools there are so-called "Hungarian" classes, but they only teach certain subjects in Hungarian. Hungarian kindergartens also exist (307 in Czechoslovakia, for example). As for university level there is, in Czechoslovakia the Hungarian language and literature chair at Komensky University in Bratislava and the Pedagogical College, at Nyitra; in Yugoslavia the Hungarian language and literature chair at the university of Novisad; in Carpatho-Ukraine the Hungarian pedagogical faculty at the university in Uzgorod. In Rumania there is a Hungarian language and literary chair at the Babes-Bólyai University in Cluj; Hungarian is an auxiliary language. In Tirgu Mures the College of Medicine and Pharmacology is a Rumanian-language institution, with Hungarian only an auxiliary language.

Literary groups: Hungarian section of the Slovak Writers Association, the Literary Society of the Vojvodina (Vajdaság). In Rumania there was a Hungarian section of the Rumanian Writers Federation, but that was merged with the main body. In Carpatho-Ukraine the Trans-Carpathian Division of the Ukrainian Writers Federation has a Hungarian branch.

Publication of Hungarian books: 437 in Rumania for 1956, 60 in Yugoslavia for 1957, and 40 in Czechoslovakia for 1957. The average number of books published is roughly the same every year. As for content, the books are works of Communist and Russian authors, Hungarian classics, a rather high percentage of translations of world literature and works by Hungarian minority authors. Each year one or two Hungarian anthologies are published in Carpatho-Ukraine. Hungarian minority groups publish through a Hungarian editorial office in the Slovak Publishing House for Creative Writing which has replaced the recently abolished Hungarian Publishers in Czechoslovakia, the Hungarian Department of the Forum Publishing House in Novisad (Ujvidék), and the Hungarian Division of the Trans-Carpathian Publishers. In Rumania there was a Hungarian branch of the Rumanian Literature and Arts Publishing House, but it was disbanded. Now various Rumanian publishing firms print the Hungarian-language books.

Hungarian minorities have nine legitimate theatres: the Hungarian Regional Theatre in Komarnó (Komárom), the Hungarian Opera House and Theatre in Cluj (Kolozsvár), the Theatre in Tirgu Mures (Marosvásárhely), at first Hungarian, now Rumanian-Hungarian, the National Hungarian Theatres of Satu Mare (Szatmár), Oradea (Nagyvárad), Timisoara (Temesvár) and Sfintu Gheorghe (Sepsiszentgyörgy), The Hungarian Ensemble of the Subotica (Szabadka) People's Theatre. There are also three professional, or semi-professional, people's ensembles of national importance: the Young Hearts Hungarian People's Ensemble of Czechoslovakia, the People's Ensemble at Tirgu Mures, and the Hungarian People's Ensemble of Carpatho-Ukraine.

The total number of Hungarian-language newspapers and periodicals in the four countries comes to nearly 100; important dailies are *Előre* of Bucharest with a circulation of 110,000 *Uj Szó* of Bratislava (Pozsony), circulation 100,000, and *Magyar Szó* of Novisad (Ujvidék) with a circulation of 50,000.

The Hungarian minorities do not have any important radio station; however, the radio stations of Bratislava (Pozsony), Kosice (Kassa), Uzgorod (Ungvár), Cluj (Kolozsvár), and Novisad (Ujvidék) all have Hungarian desks and Hungarian-language broadcasts.

The Hungarian minorities engage in cultural movements within which they preserve their national existence and foster their culture. The Communists urge activities "socialist in content and national in form" but our minorities have learned how to stress the latter. The cultural activities of Hungarian minorities have such verve, that the Communists willy-nilly, are swept along, too.

Cultural festivals held by the Hungarians are the highlights of today's minority life. Whether these festivals be of national or only regional importance, thousands of performers and spectators gather each time to enjoy the spirited performances of their traditional folk-groups, actors, singers and dancers.

In Czechoslovakia cultural activities are carried on within

the framework of the organization called *Csemadok* (Cultural Association for Hungarian Workers of Czechoslovakia). *Csemadok* has 500 local (that is, village and municipal) and 12 district organizations and national centers in Bratislava.

In Rumania, Hungarians have no nationwide cultural organization; regime organs manage Hungarian cultural life. In Yugoslavia the Hungarian Cultural Association, founded in 1948, was abolished in May 1956. Minority cultural organizations have been replaced by an integrated Cultural Community. *Magyar Szó* (May 8, 1957) reports on experiments with new types of organizations in order to fight more effectively against retrogressive nationalist and petit-bourgeois phenomena.

EFFECT OF THE HUNGARIAN REVOLT

During the 1956 Hungarian Revolution, the world press carried news day by day on the unrest among Hungarian minorities. It was reported, for instance, that, due to demonstrations, Hungarian-inhabited regions of Slovakia had been occupied by Czech troops. The same was reported from Transylvania where Rumanian troops were concentrated and foreigners banner from areas bordering on Hungary. *Newsweek* of New York (November 11, 1956) carried news of a widespread rising among Hungarians in Carpatho-Ruthenia. *The New York Times* of July 26, 1957 reported that Romanian Communists finally had admitted to internal troubles at the time of the Hungarian Revolt. A staff writer of the *Neue Zuricher Zeitung* wrote on August 14, 1957, that he hardly met anyone in Southern Slovakia who did not at once start talking about the Hungarian Revolt. There was general sympathy with the Hungarian cause, disturbances occurred in several places.

A few quotations from the local press will help to make this picture even clearer:

Edgar Balogh, Hungarian university professor in Romania, a minority Communist intellectual, declared on November 6, 1957: "Let us not fool ourselves. The counter-revolution of last October in Hungary, and its waves reaching us, have given ample proof that Hungarian nationalism is still rampant." Laszlo Batky, a Hungarian columnist of Slovakia, writes on June 27, 1957: "We have no right to claim that we are living in an atmosphere free of the after-effects of the Hungarian events of last fall. It is evidently the confused echo of last year's events that finds expression in the views and behavior of certain persons, in the evaluation of events. And since these people do not live in an isolation booth . . . there is a danger of contagion against which we have to protect ourselves." *The New York Times* of December 10, 1956, reported that Hungarian events strongly affected 500,000 Hungarians of the Vojvodina (Vajdaság); they became aroused and awaited with feverish excitement the outcome of happenings in Hungary.

Eight Hungarians of Rumania are reported to have been executed and forty-four others sent to prison for terms ranging from five years to life for "separatist plotting" in Rumania at the time of the Hungarian uprising (*The New York Times*, September 6, 1958).

According to records, 50,000 Hungarians were going to be deported from Transylvania to Soviet Russia. The reason: a big and active anti-Red underground. Soviet security boss, General Ivan Serov, arrived in Rumania to look into the matter. He recommended the deportation of these Hungarians as a lesson to all (*Newsweek*, New York, October 6, 1958).

Minority youth has fully adopted the views and atttitudes of the older generation. *Magyar Szó* of Novisad complains that, at a meeting of university students in Zenta, demands were voiced for the establishment of an Association of Hungarian University Students of Yugoslavia (April 17, 1954). The same paper reports that Hungarian young people of Yugoslavia are "of a destructive, corrupt mentality" and cannot get along with their Serbian counterparts (May 10, 1957). After fourteen years of Russian rule, a Hungarian-language youth paper published by the local Komsomol appeared in February of this year in Carpatho-Ukraine. In Bratislava Laszlo Batky complains that nationalist and revisionist manifestations of the Hungarian Revolution had a tremendous effect, above all on the Hungarian intelligentsia. One must add—he writes—that the overwhelming majority of this intelligentsia are young people of twenty or younger, who could hardly have any personal contact with Hungarian revisionist efforts. (July 23, 1957.)

The Communists have kept the question of the revived na-

tional self-consciousness of Hungarian minorities in the fore-
ground since the Revolution. Khrushchev himself mentioned
the Hungarian minorities in his *Leipzig* speech of March 7,
1959. He alluded to the fact that antagonism between the
Hungarian and Rumanian populations still exists. *(Pravda,*
Moscow, March 27, 1959.) At the 1958 Congress of the Slovak
Communist Party, Karol Bacilek, First Secretary of the Party
declared that the nationalism of the Hungarian minority must
be suppressed.

Moscow evidently deemed it necessary to counter this phenomenon. János Kádár was sent to Bucharest and Prime
Minister Munnich to Prague, with the intent of suppressing
the nationalistic sentiments of the Hungarian minorities.
Both Kádár and Munnich (the former in Rumania, on February 27, 1958, the latter in Czechoslovakia, on December 10,
1958) declared that Hungary had no territorial demands on
her neighbors, and that anyone who suggested this was an
enemy of the unity of peoples building socialism.

However, this action was apparently restricted to preventing strife between the satellite countries on account of their
Hungarian minorities because, in the above-mentioned Leipzig speech, Khrushchev also discussed the Hungarian minority
of Yugoslavia. He said that the Hungarian territories annexed
to Yugoslavia contained a Hungarian population of 1 million. *Kommunist,* the official weekly of the Yugoslav Communist League, took Khrushchev to task for this, on April 2,
1959, for accusing Yugoslavia of possessing Hungarian territories.

Changing Policy

Unlike the situation between the two World Wars, today's
Hungarian minorities are not covered by any internationally
valid agreements guarding the rights of minorities. Communist countries ostensibly treat their minorities on the basis
of the so-called Leninist policy of nationalities, involving a
tolerant attitude toward the use of the mother tongue, a
preservation of national "peculiarities," concessions regarding
the cultivation of national traditions which are augmented
or restricted according to the momentary stance by which the
respective regime attempts to win the sympathy of minorities

for cooperation in the "building of socialism." Like all other matters, the nationalities policy is handled inconsistently, on the basis of expediency. In Rumania and Czechoslovakia the minority remnants of the *Little Entente states*, based on proportional nationality figures, are still recognizable, while in Yugoslavia the nationalities are made to accept a supranational concept of the Communist Yugoslav nation.

A lengthy article in *Magyar Szó* (Ujvidék) of April 17, 1954, dealing with the problem of minorities summarizes the nationality policies of the three Communist neighbor-states: "The process of democratization has created the possibility of a true rapprochement of peoples, and their amalgamation into one community. The social economic management has swept away the administrative solution of the minority problem on the basis of nationality figures, making possible the realization of a true equality of rights."

What insecurity this vague conception of equal rights meant to the minorities is evident from a comment by Gyula Duba, Hungarian writer of Czechoslovakia (June 9, 1956): "Unfortunately we have not been told yet where the limits of our obligations toward our mother tongue and Hungarian nationality are, and where the area of chauvinism and bourgeois nationalism begins."

The respective Communist regimes, so as to win over their Hungarian minorities and manufacture a tradition of evolution for minority consolidation as advocated by them, identify themselves with the pre-World War II nationalities' struggle to maintain their existence, and speak as if those efforts had been precursors of today's actions.

This standpoint is complemented by a policy condemning the "bourgeois" methods of the three states with regard to their minorities. László Bànyai, Rumanian Deputy Minister of Education, who is a Hungarian, writes thus on Rumania between the two World Wars (September 1, 1957): "In the past, the exploiter classes of our Fatherland, in order to assure their oppressive rule and to split up the worker class, engaged in a policy of chauvinistic hate-mongering, oppression and the forcible assimilation of national minorities."

After seizing power, the communist regimes sought to crush the Hungarian minorities' so-called "bourgeois nationalism," meaning the national sentiments guiding their whole outlook and character. In that period the strategy of survival for minorities was nationalist separatism.

The effects of the 1956 Hungarian Revolution, plus the realization that the Hungarian minorities were too strong to be simply liquidated or integrated, led the Yugoslav and Czech communist regimes to make concessions. Rumania chose another path: stepped-up oppression. In the quite altered social structure of Yugoslavia and Czechoslovakia, nationalist separatism had scant prospects; the Hungarian minorities saw they would prosper by making the best of the new possibilities. Meanwhile the Rumanian regime began eliminating the already attained minority institutions and prerogatives.

Because of chaotic conditions in the Hungarian-inhabited regions, in March 1959 the Central Committee of the Yugoslav Communist Federation passed a series of resolutions more exactly regulating minority rights as to language, schools, culture, etc. The same occurred in March 1960 in Czechoslovakia where, at a national conference of the Czechoslovak Communist Party, President Novotny affirmed recognition of their Hungarian minority as a separate nationality group. The 1960 constitution of Czechoslovakia specifically mentions the rights of the Hungarian minority; the 1963 Yugoslav constitution details in several sections the special rights of the "nationalities." Vice President Kardelj noted that the new Yugoslav constitution had replaced the term "minority" with "nationality" so that with this, too, it might stress their complete equality of rights in language, education and culture. The so-called system of self-administration (local autonomy) advances the use of the minority language.

In December 1964, at the Eighth Congress of the Yugoslav Communist Federation, President Tito dealt at length with the legal rights of minorities. Those on the frontier can be the means of rapprochement between their country and the motherland, he said. In 1965 a book by Juraj Zvara, a noted minorities specialist affiliated with the Chair of Marxism at the university in Bratislava, appeared under the title, "The Solution of the Hungarian Minority Question in Slovakia." The work roundly condemns the cruel persecution of Hungarians from 1945 to 1948, blaming the Communist Party, too, for its participation. Zvara depicts the political, economic, educational and cultural situation of the Hungarian minority, at the same time calling attention to deficiencies still present.

In Yugoslavia and Czechoslovakia, as regards the most vital question of the Hungarian minorities—schooling, the equal use of Hungarian in official administration—grave inadequacies continue. Professor Zvara's book, as well as the Czechoslovak and Yugoslav press, repeatedly ascertain that the "dual language concept" is being sabotaged by local officials and exponents of the state language. In vain has an extensive network of Hungarian schools been built. About thirty per cent of the Hungarian children still attend the state-language schools both in Yugoslavia and Czechoslovakia. Evidently local officialdom has managed to maintain an atmosphere of intimidation, and a third of the Hungarian parents dare not enroll their children in Hungarian schools.

The condition of Hungarians in Rumania is far worse. Instead of improving, the state of their rights and circumstances shows a downward trend. This is all the more striking since, after the war, the Groza government of those days got back all Transylvania from the Soviet Union on condition that it would respect the rights of the Hungarian minority—which actually is not so much a minority as the second nationality in a dual-nation province. This is also reflected in the fact that the Soviet military government introduced a dual-language, Rumanian-Hungarian administration.

The Groza government established for the Hungarians a national cultural and social organization called Hungarian People's Federation, which co-ordinated the work of local and district groupings. Had it continued to exist, it would have assured cultural and social autonomy for the Hungarians in Rumania through the numerous independent Hungarian local cultural societies it set up. The Hungarian-language university at Cluj (named after the Transylvanian Hungarian scholar, Bólyai) was retained. A Hungarian university-level Medical and Pharmacological Institute was founded at Tirgu Mures. A complete network of schools for Hungarians was formed in regions they inhabited. Hungarian-language newspapers, publishing firms and theaters were organized.

In 1951 they dissolved the Hungarian People's Federation, integrating its cultural groups with the Rumanian network of cultural associations.

In 1952 they set up the Hungarian Autonomous Region,

which comprised the whole territory of the Székely-Hungarians. This improved the lot of a third of the Hungarian minority, but worsened that of the other two-thirds outside the autonomous province.

In 1958 they began dissolving the minority institutions. Within four years, by 1962, they completely fused independent Hungarian schools into the Rumanian school network. Bólyai University at Cluj was absorbed by the Rumanian Babes University; the Tirgu Mures Institute also became primarily Rumanian; and in 1960, by altering the boundaries of the Hungarian Autonomous Province, they changed its Hungarian character to Hungarian-Rumanian. Into Hungarian-inhabited towns they systematically settled Rumanian elements and began resettling Hungarian craftsmen and intellectuals in Rumanian-inhabited sectors. Henceforth the Hungarian-language press was forbidden to write the word "Magyar" or to write on Hungarian themes or about Hungarian cultural events. All this was aimed at crushing Hungarian consciousness and influence, with the final goal of having the Hungarian minority regard itself as an organic part of the Rumanian nation.

All this also conflicts with the Leninist concept of nationalities, and as justification for their minority-treatment methods they came up with a unique interpretation. In July 1965 the Ninth Rumanian Party Congress re-evaluated its stand on proletarian internationalism, giving precedence to socialist patriotism. Today in Rumania a school with one purely Rumanian branch plus a second branch teaching in Rumanian and Hungarian, is rated a minority school. In vain does the new Rumanian constitution of 1965 ensure instruction in the mother tongue at every level of schooling, if schools do not actually teach in that tongue. These and like measures result from the denial of Hungarian ethnic entity. They represent grave minority oppression even from a Marxist standpoint.

Representation: The 61 member Central Committee of the Rumanian Workers' Party has 6 Hungarian members, the 70 member Central Committee of the Slovak Communist Party, 5 Hungarian members. The Rumanian Parliament has 44 Hungarian Communist deputies, the Czechoslovak Parliament 8, the Yugoslav Federal Chamber of Deputies 6. In the Slovak

National Council, (a Regional Parliament of Slovakia), there are 13 Hungarian Communist deputies, in the Federal Assembly of the Vojvodina 29. The rights stipulated in the Constitutions and representation in high legislative bodies is practically meaningless for the inner life of the Hungarian minorities, the fact that they give evidence to the outside world of their continued existence.

Transylvanian Local Councils and lower-grade administrative councils have more than 13,000 Hungarian members (1956), in Czechoslovakia there are 7,000 (1960). According to an official announcement, 22.6 per cent of Local Council members in the Vojvodina (Vajdaság) are of Hungarian nationality.

As regards Local Councils, Iván Galy, a spokesman for the young Hungarian Communist intelligentsia in Slovakia, voices complaints (June 11, 1955): "Bourgeois nationalism is responsible for the mistrust of state organs felt by some of our Hungarian workers. Despite the fact that . . . in all organs of state administration a great number of Hungarian workers participate in the management of public affairs, the view is rather widespread that the Local Councils are 'agencies alien to us,' what is more, there are some who regard [the councils] with more scepticism than the parish hall of older times." The Hungarian minorities instinctively avoid participation in the work of Local Councils directed from above. Participation, they feel, would amount to surrendering their right to self-determination."

THE REACTION IN HUNGARY

The Kádár-Kállai regime of Hungary is passive in the face of the Rumanian minority oppression policy. Though it has taken care not to transgress ideological precepts relating to minorities, for years it has blinked at such transgressions by their Rumanian comrades. On behalf of Hungarians in Rumania it thus far has failed to get that government to act in line with either proletarian internationalism or the concept of equal rights for minorities. The world press reported repeatedly that influential party circles have publicly urged the regime to intervene more energetically. They also have moral grounds for this, since every concession has been given to the Rumanian minority in Hungary, despite its small size.

As regards Czechoslovakia and Yugoslavia the regime informed the people of concessions made to the Hungarians there. On October 3, 1964, during the Budapest reception for President Novotny of Czechoslovakia, Kádár himself evaluated favorably the Czech treatment of the Hungarian minority. And in December of that year Deputy Premier Lajos Fehér reported in the main party paper, *Népszabadság,* on the favorable outlook for the Hungarian minority in Yugoslavia. Examples show that along with the "solidarity of socialist lands" the life of minorities in adjacent countries is a permissible public theme. The exception is Rumania. Due to its subservient role, the Budapest regime keeps silent, and won't let others speak up either.

Hungarian minorities are more insistent in their claims for a national existence today than ever before, and they are an important factor in the question of consolidating the Danube states. Their attitude of insistence is not due to submission to the communists' cause. On the contrary, it results from their consistent and resolute exploitation of current possibilities and a conscientious effort to increase their influence and importance.

HUNGARIAN POLITICIANS IN EXILE

On orders from the Soviet Union, with the help of the Russian occupation forces, in the summer of 1947 the Hungarian Communist Party took over the country. The democratic leaders either landed in jail or were forced into exile.

Premier Ferenc Nagy was vacationing in Switzerland when General Sviridov, the Russian Chairman of the Allied Control Commission, on May 28 sent an ulti-matum-style note to Acting Premier Mátyás Rákosi, head of the Hungarian Communist Party, containing the confessions extorted in a Soviet military prison from Béla Kovács, then Secretary General of the Smallholders Party and former Minister of Agriculture, whom the Red Army had seized in February. One of the "documents" in his own hand stated: "The leaders of the Smallholders Party, including Ferenc Nagy, Béla Varga, and myself, are at fault and responsible that the instigators of the conspiracy against the Republic came from our ranks."

This sounded like a death knell.

Next day Mátyás Rákosi summoned a cabinet meeting and called on Ferenc Nagy to return home at once or resign his post. On the same day (May 29) from Bern, Switzerland, Mr. Nagy personally informed President Zoltán Tildy by phone that he was resigning his premiership and all other offices. The discourse was taped and sent as an official document to Msgr. Béla Varga, President of Parliament, who, in accordance with the Constitution, summoned its Political Committee to accept the resignation and designate a new premier.

Despite the protest of the democratic parties, General Sviridov forced the Political Committee to name as premier his agent, the former landowner Lajos Dinnyés. With this brutal Russian intervention began the cruelest of dictatorships in Hungary.

Facing arrest on charges of active participation in the "conspiracy," Béla Varga at the eleventh hour fled at the risk of his life through the Russian zone of Austria to Switzerland.

Within a short time most of the other democratic leaders also fled to free soil: Dezső Sulyok of the Freedom Party, Zoltán Pfeiffer of the Independence Party, Károly Peyer of the Social Democratic Party, István Barankovics of the Christian Democratic People's Party, and Imre Kovács of the Peasant Party.

Right after his resignation Ferenc Nagy left Switzerland for the United States, where he was joined by Msgr. Varga. They at once launched into consultations with the competent Hungarian and American factors. On November 15, 1947, at the instance of Msgr. Béla Varga, the Hungarian National Council was formed to represent the oppressed Hungarian people in the free world. The Council established a headquarters in New York City and its first diplomatic representation at Washington. In the interest of national unity, all democratic politicians (save for extremists) joined, aware that the most important mission of exile politics was to free the Hungarian people from communist rule. The Hungarian National Council, established on a coalition basis, rejected partisan standpoints on the logical ground that a return to party politics would be possible only in a free Hungary, when the Hungarian people could again elect their parliamentary representatives.

The legality of the Hungarian National Council derived from the Hungarian Constitution. Law—I—1946 prescribes that if the Hungarian chief of state becomes permanently unable to carry out his duties, then these devolve upon the President of Parliament. Since the Hungarian lawmakers on free soil ascertained that the takeover had made the President of the Hungarian People's Republic a captive of the communists—unable to act of his own free will, and *permanently* prevented from carrying out his high official duties—on the basis of legal continuity through rights assured by the Hungarian Constitution, they recognized Msgr. Béla Varga as competent to exercise the presidential functions. The Hungarian lawmakers on free soil, elected in 1945 and 1947, also declared that they continued to regard themselves the lawful representatives of the Hungarian people; thus the Hungarian National Council could exercise parliamentary jurisdiction and supplement membership. They also chose an Executive Committee which filled the role of a government-in-exile.

THE HUNGARIAN NATIONAL COUNCIL
(1950)

PRESIDENT:

Msgr. Béla Varga

VICE PRESIDENTS:

János Dombay   Vincze Nagy

EXECUTIVE COMMITTEE

Paul Auer   Joseph Közi Horváth
George Bakách Bessenyey   Ferenc Nagy
István Barankovics   Károly Peyer
Tibor Eckhardt   Zoltán Pfeiffer
Béla Fábian   Dezső Sulyok

MEMBERS

László Acsay   Sándor Borsos
Dezső Albrecht   Antal Braunecker
Béla Andaházy Kasnya   Ferenc Chorin
Mihály Andrássy   István Csorba
Ödön Antl   Antal Czermann
György Apponyi   László Czipó
Paul Auer   Bálint Czupy
Ferenc Babóthy   Ferenc Dajkovich
István Barankovics   Gyula Dessewffy
Lipót Baranyai   János Dombay
Ferenc Barkányi   Tibor Eckhardt
Albert Bartha   Gyula Erőss
Gyula Belső   György Eszterhás

János Eszterházy
Pál Fabry
Árpád Falcione
Valér Fricke
Ferenc Gordon
László Gunde
Béla Hadik
Lajos Hadju-Németh
Béla Halter
Károly Hokky
János Holota
Tibor Hám
Tibor Horányi
Imre Hunyadi
Miklos Horthy, Jr.
Jozsef Jankovich-Besán
László Jékely
Miklós Kállay
Kelemen Krizosztom
Tamás Keresztes
János Korányi
Móric Kornfeld
Imre Kovács
Zoltán K. Kovács
Gusztáv Kövér
József Közi Horváth
Iván Lénárt
Gyula Maár
István Medey
Miklós Mézes
Zsigmond Mihalovics
Ferenc Nagy

Vincze Nagy
Sándor Nyirjesy
Jenő Padányi-Gulyás
Ferenc Palinay
György Papp
István Papp
József Pálffy
Ferenc Pete
Károly Peyer
Zoltán Pfeiffer
Lajos Pócza
István Révay
Kálmán Saláta
Tibor Scitovszky
István Séra
Dezső Sulyok
Gyula Szabó
Pál Sz. Szabó
Károly Széchényi
Sándor Szent-Iványi
Mrs. Marton Szily
Béla Teleki
Béla Varga
László Varga
László Vatai
Ferenc Vándor
Imre Veér
Károly Vértessy
Mátyás Vészy
Miklós Villányi
Pál Zoltán
Dezső Zserci Molnár

OFFICIAL PERIODICALS:
Bizottmányi Közlöny
Hungarian Observer

In accordance with its government-status the Hungarian National Council established the following diplomatic representations:

Argentina	Arnó Bobrik
Australia	George Barcza
Austria	Lászlo Bartók
Belgium	György Apponyi
Brazil	Miklós Horthy, Jr.

Canada	Imre E. Vladár I
Chile	Ferenc Rosthy Forgách
Colombia	Mrs. Lola Riegler-Rosenberg
Egypt	Lászlo Páthy
France	Paul Auer
Germany	Gusztáv Hennyey
Great Britain	Antal Ullein Reviczky
Greece	Iván Bogdán
Italy, Vatican	Gábor Apor
Morocco	Iván Éliassy
Mexico	Sándor Hollán
Portugal	Tibor Bartheldy
Spain	Ferenc Marosy
Switzerland	Alfréd Nickl
Turkey	George Perényi Lukács
Uruguay	Imre E. Vladár II

Refugee Offices: Brussels, Munich, Paris, Salzburg, Rome

Most Western governments semi-officially recognized the Hungarian National Council, received its representatives at the foreign ministries, accept its memoranda, and informed it of their stand on international developments and questions relating to Hungary. The president and members of the Executive Committee maintained regular contact with the governments of the free world, conducted consultative discussions with them. They unmasked and countered Communist machinations in the free world.

Two factors greatly helped the activities of the Hungarian National Council. One was the increasing resistance of the Hungarian people to rampant communist terror; clear proof that the Rákosi regime could not create a popular base for communism in Hungary, for inalterably the Hungarians yearned for freedom and independence. The other was the West's firm stance as regards the Soviet Union and the communist drive for world dominion. Recognizing the perils of Moscow's policies that had forced communism on the Eastern European countries. the Western great powers regarded it as their political and moral duty to free the oppressed peoples from communist rule and Soviet domination.

The *liberation* policy—stressed at international con-

ferences, in declarations and special messages—filled the
iron-curtain peoples with hope and satisfaction. It also
played an essential role in the outbreak of the 1956
Hungarian Revolution.

So long as the Western liberation policy and the interests of Hungary coincided, the Hungarian National
Council could carry on its work smoothly and effectively.
However, the representatives of the Hungarian people
on free soil were put in a very difficult situation when
the illusion of the so-called "thaw" after Stalin's death
weakened Western policy towards the Soviet Union and
East Europe. A new concept was born, *liberalization*,
which, along with the basic principle of self-determination, has been a leitmotif ever since.

They no longer aim to *free* the East European nations but just liberalize the communist regimes, so they
may be milder, more acceptable. But a "milder" or
"more acceptable" form of communism means one thing
in a Western interpretation and quite another to those
whom the new policy actually condemns to live forever
under communism, only under slightly better conditions.

The concept of self-determination also changed. Right
from the Geneva summit conference, in the summer of
1955, U.S. Secretary of State John Foster Dulles went to
see Marshal Tito on the Isle of Brioni. After their consultations Secretary Dulles informed the press that they
recognized the right of the East European peoples "to
freely choose the economic and social system under
which they want to live." This was the first indication
that the West was ready to accept even the communist
system if it were the choice of the people. But evidently
it did not occur to them that communism bars free elections. At the same time the Brioni statement formally
ended the era of the "crusade against communism."

The Hungarian Revolution of 1956 demonstrated that
the Hungarian people want no form of communism. Unfortunately its changed viewpoint and policy so mud-
dled the West that it proved incapable of energetic intervention. It was not only because of Suez that the free
nations could not hurry to the aid of the Hungarian
freedom fighters, but rather because Western chancel-

leries did not size up the situation clearly—unaware of communism's relentless march,—while over-rating liberalization, they under-rated and disregarded the people's yearning for freedom.

They did not recognize that the mainspring of history is the wish for liberty!

Before and during the Hungarian Revolution of '56, memoranda of the Hungarian National Council called the attention of the Western governments to the gravity of the situation and the neglect of their responsibilities and obligations.

Alarmed by the intensity of the Russian armed intervention in the first days of the Revolution, the following letter was sent to the U.S. Secretary of State:

October 26, 1956

The Honorable
John Foster Dulles
Secretary of State
Department of State
Washington, D.C.

Dear Mr. Secretary

It is the fourth day of the waging of regular warfare by the Soviet Red Army against the Hungarian nation. By now it has transformed the entire country into a battlefield. This tragic act of violence is endangering international peace and the lives of the Hungarian people. It is being perpetrated in flagrant violation of the Peace Treaty concluded with Hungary. Whereas minor acts of violence have been repeatedly dealt with by the United Nations and the continuation of violent acts has been successfully stopped—no action has yet been taken in this major violation of the peace. It is the right and primary duty of the United Nations to give its urgent attention to the dangerous situation which has developed in Hungary through Soviet aggression. Paragraph 4 of Article 2 and Article 34 of the United Nations' Charter demand that the United Nations take action in this conflict. The high moral prestige of the United Nations would suffer a deadly blow should the present situation created by the Soviets in Hungary continue to be overlooked.

In view of these facts, the Executive Committee of the Hungarian National Council respectfully submits to you, Mr. Secretary, the following urgent requests:

1.) To take action with the United Nations Security Council in order to prevent further bloodshed in Hungary by immediately sending truce commissions to Hungary with full authority to intervene in the armed struggle and compel the Soviet Red Army to stop its acts of war against the Hungarian people;

2.) To insist with the United Nations that the Hungarian civilians and armed forces that are fighting for the restoration of national independence and human freedom be declared to be a regular national force and not individual criminals to be convicted on the basis of the Hungarian Penal Code. Effective measures should also be taken by the United Nations to prevent these patriots from being deported to Soviet Russia. A broad amnesty is needed to save Hungarian patriots from further persecution.

I beg you, Mr. Secretary, to accept the expression of my highest consideration.

Respectfully yours,

Msgr. Bela Varga
Former President of the
Hungarian Parliament

After the crushing of the Revolution some two hundred thousand Hungarians arrived in the free world. The leaders of the revolutionary councils held a Congress in Strasbourg, France, authorizing the formation of a political organization: The National Representation of a Free Hungary. Its chairman was Madame Anna Kéthly, minister of state in the revolutionary Nagy Government; vice-chairmen were Major General Béla Király and Mayor József Kővágó, (of Budapest), the general secretary was Sándor Kiss, former director of the Hungarian Peasant Alliance. The National Representation of a Free Hungary had offices in New York and Paris. However the New York office was dissolved after a time.* In order that the representatives of the revolutionary forces and freedom fighters might be included

*Madame Kéthly settled down in Brussels, Belgium. Since then she has been very active in Europe as head of the Hungarian Social Democratic Party in Exile. The party's general secretary, Imre Szélig, former regional secretary of Greater Budapest, now resides in London. Another member of the '56 revolutionary Nagy cabinet, József Fischer, since his arrival in 1965, lives in New York.

in a supreme political body, now the newly organized Hungarian Committee replaced the Hungarian National Council in March 1958. On the basis of legal continutiy, Msgr. Béla Varga remained its head; but its composition reflected a fuller cross-section of the nation.

THE HUNGARIAN COMMITTEE
(1960)

CHAIRMAN:
Magr. Béla Varga

VICE-CHAIRMAN:
József Kővágó

MEMBERS:

József Adorján	Imre Kovács
Paul Auer	Ferenc Nagy
István Barankovics	Zoltán Pfeiffer
Lajos Hajdu-Németh	Pál Sz. Szabó
Pál Jónás	László Varga
Béla Király	Ferenc Váli
Sándor Kiss	Ferenc Vidovics

OFFICIAL PERIODICALS:
Szabad Magyar Tudósitó
Free Hungarian Information Service
The Hungarian Quatrerly

The Hungarian Committee concentrated its activities on the illegality of the Kádár regime, demanding in memoranda and at press conferences that the freedom of the Hungarian people be restored. The Hungarian Committee also challenged Soviet leaders visiting Western countries to carry out the U.N. resolutions: the withdrawal of Russian troops from Hungary and the granting of self-determination to the Hungarian nation. During the 1959 visit to the United States of Nikita S. Khrushchev, then leader of the USSR, the Hungarian Committee sent the following letter to President Eisenhower:

New York, August 19, 1959

The Honorable
Dwight D. Eisenhower
President of the United States of America
White House
Washington, D.C.

Mr. President,

In the name of the Hungarian Committee, the free spokesmen of the silenced Hungarian people, we respectfully submit to your kind consideration the following plea:

After World War II, the Hungarian people did their utmost to organize their public life on the principles of democracy. The unparalleled result of the national elections of November, 1945, were an auspicious augury for success, since the Communists were not able to muster more than 17 per cent of the votes, despite Soviet occupation and Communist terror.

However, unfortunately, the Hungarian people were not duly sustained by the Western Allies in their efforts at developing and preserving the democratic institutions of the Hungarian Republic. The fact that there was no rotation in the Chairmanship of the Allied Control Commission in Hungary had enabled the permanent Soviet chairman to gradually intensify direct Soviet influence in all domestic matters of the country. This situation was decisively instrumental in the preparation of Communist usurpation of power in Hungary.

However, even after the elimination of the leading personalities of the Hungarian Republic, the Hungarian people made a new demonstration of their unshakeable will to maintain the democratic system, when the Communist Party attained only 20 per cent of the votes in the August 1947 elections ordered by the Communist Party Chief Rakosi in order to erase the non-Communist majority by fraud and terror, exploiting the psychological effect of the presence of Soviet troops.

Thansformed in 1949 into a so-called People's Republic whose institutions were set up on the Soviet pattern, Hungary's entire public life, economy and territory were placed under the Kremlin's control in defiance of the agreement on a liberated Europe and the Hungarian Peace Treaty, both signed by the Allied Powers and the Soviet Union.

The nation-wide Hungarian Revolution of October 23, 1956, left no doubt that the Hungarian people, even youth and the working class, in spite of ten years of indoctrination, were fed up with the Communist system and foreign domination. However, while they stood ready to sacrifice their lives for freedom and democracy, they very realistically stressed in their political manifestations the necessity of good neighborly relations with the powerful Soviet Union. The authentic spokesmen of the Revolution many times declared that they were not intent on converting Hungary into a country hostile to the Soviet Union. On the contrary, they have strongly advocated the idea of an internationally controlled neutrality.

All these facts were impeccably established by the UN Special Committee on the Problem of Hungary, and accepted by the UN General Assembly as trustworthy evidence of the bad faith of the Soviet Union, which did not shrink from the assertion that the spontaneous Hungarian Revolution was the result of a plot of Hungarian fascists and foreign secret services.

The UN General Assembly successively adopted ten political resolutions on Hungary demanding the withdrawal of Soviet troops and free elections under international control, and condemning the Soviet Union for the brutal crushing of the victorious Hungarian Revolution. The Soviet defiance of these resolutions has gravely affected the prestige of the world organization, thus creating a dangerous precedent for the impunity of members who do not comply with the General Assembly resolutions.

For all these reasons we believe, Mr. President, that your forthcoming meeting with the Soviet dictator will provide for you the first and unique opportunity [since the tragic events in Hungary,] to use your high authority in order to induce the Soviet Union to comply with the UN resolutions on Hungary.

You will certainly share our opinion that the sojourn in the United States of the Soviet leader most responsible for the massacre of the Hungarian people, again will subject this people's morale to a very severe test. We believe, Mr. President, that it is in your power to help them stand up successfully to this test, and we are convinced that in so doing, you would act according to the noble principles which guide the conduct of international affairs of your great country and serve the vital interests of the world. The United States has consistently followed a policy of non-recognition of illegal conquests.

We, therefore, solemnly appeal to you, Mr. President, to

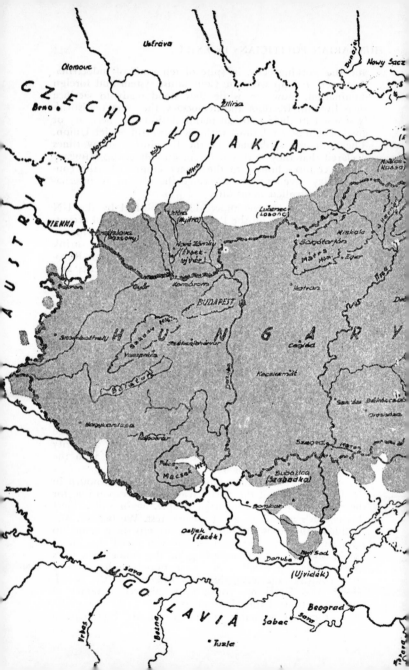

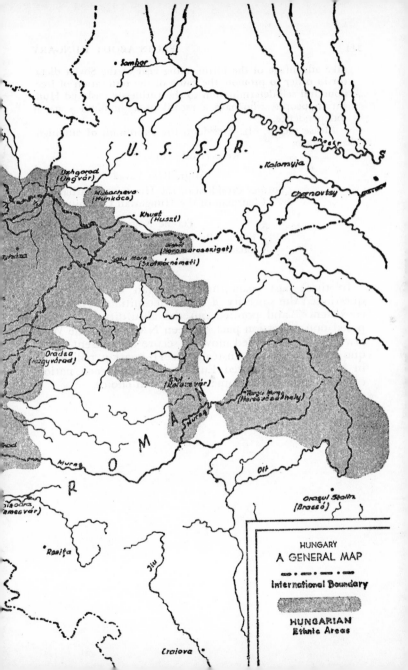

U. S. S. R.

Sombor

Dnsst

Kolomyja

Uzhgorod
(Ungvár)

Chernovtsy

Mukachevo
(Munkács)

Khust
(Huszt)

Sighet
(Máramarossziget)

Satu Mare
(Szatmárnémeti)

Nyíregyháza

Oradea
(Nagyvárad)

Cluj
(Kolozsvár)

A

Târgu Mureş
(Marosvásárhely)

Turda

R   O   M   A   N   I   A

Mureş

Oradea

Timişoara
(Temesvár)

Oraşul Stalin
(Brassó)

Reşiţa

Jiu

Oft

Craiova

HUNGARY
A GENERAL MAP

━━ • ━━ • ━━ • ━━
International Boundary

HUNGARIAN
Ethnic Areas

take advantage of the forthcoming visit of the Soviet dictator in order to promote the cause of the restoration of freedom and self-determination to the ruthlessly enslaved Hungarian people, who have a record of a thousand years of
independence.

Please accept, Mr. President, the expression of our highest esteem.

Respectfully yours,

Msgr. Béla Varga
Former President of the Hungarian Parliament,
Chairman of the Hungarian Committee.

Ferenc Nagy
Former Prime Minister of Hungary,
Chaiman of the Foreign Relations
Committee.

In these past years the Hungarian Committee has
questioned the sincerity of the Soviet-initiated "peaceful-
coexistence" and pointed out the absurdity of its proposed non-aggression pact between NATO and the Warsaw Powers as a veiled move to secure the present status
quo in East Europe. Instead, the Hungarian politicians
in exile favor a united Europe in which each nation
can live under a government of its own choice.

MODERN HUNGARIAN HISTORIOGRAPHY

By István Borsody

Excerpts from the article of István Borsody, "Modern Hungarian Historiography," THE JOURNAL OF MODERN HISTORY, Volume XXIV, No. 4, December 1952. University of Chicago Press, Chicago, Illinois. Brought up to date.

Hungarian historiography during the period of the *Ausgleich* (1867-1918) presents a very heterogeneous picture. The two great historians of the nineteenth century, László Szalay (1813-64) and Bishop Mihály Horváth (1809-78), both of whom were active politicians in the 1848-49 revolution against Austria, are typical of the *national-liberal school*. To them the dominant element in Hungarian history was the struggle for national freedom and independence. They were influenced to a considerable extent by the French liberal historians—François Guizot, for example, had a marked effect on Horváth. They were also pioneers in the use of primary sources. Szalay was especially successful in reaching objective conclusions from his studies of sources, but his *History of Hungary* (in Hungarian) (1851-62, 2d ed., 4 vols.; Budapest, 1871), on the other hand, was regarded as the standard historical work in liberal Hungary, achieving eight editions in the period between 1852 and 1882.

The national-liberal school was soon out-numbered by the adherents of *scientific positivism*, but the establishment of the modern historical sciences was the joint achievement of both groups. At the Hungarian Academy (founded in 1825) and the National Museum (1802) new historical sections were created after the *Ausgleich* of 1867, when the cultural and economic life of the country developed in rapid strides.

In 1874 the Historical Society was founded, and in the next year *Századok* (Centuries), the review of the society and the first in a long line of scientific periodicals, was established. Of especial importance was the *Monumenta Hungariae historica,"* a series of source editions started by the academy in 1880. The study of sources was accompanied by a rapid development of the auxiliary historical sciences and related fields.[1]

The historians of the scientific school were excellent in detailed research and analysis; they made lasting contributions to the study of various segments of the past, but in synthesis they did not achieve anything similar to the works of the earlier national-liberal authors. The great collective work of this generation, the ten-volume *History of the Hungarian Nation* (in Hungarian) (Budapest, 1895–98)—edited under the direction of Sándor Szilágyi, the dean of the historians—was more or less a chronological record of events.[2]

The general concept of history during the period of Austro-Hungarian dualism was saturated with the spirit of independence and hostility toward Austria. It emphasized the "liberal" and "national" aspects of the past; in a sense it identified the nation with liberty—a practice followed everywhere in Central Europe.

This concept was called the "lay" interpretation of history, the word "lay" expressing not only a contrast to earlier theological concepts but to an even greater extent the contempt later critics felt for its unscientific nature. By the turn of the century this concept overshadowed all the other contemporary trends in historiography. Institutions and university chairs passed into the hands of politician-historians, devotees of the

---

[1] The historians who initiated Hungarian historiography into the systematic study of sources were: Gyula Pauler (1841-1903), Ferenc Salamon (1825-92), Árpád Károlyi (1853-1940), Sándor Szilágyi (1827-99), Dávid Angyal (1857-1943), Sándor Márki (1853-1925), and Bishop Vilmos Fraknói (1843-1924), a belated exponent of the theological interpretation of history but also a modern promoter of the study of sources, since he was the founder of the "Monumenta Vaticana Hungariae."

[2] This was called the "Millennium History" because it was published at a time when the country was celebrating the thousand-year anniversary of the conquest of Hungary by the Magyars, set at A.D. 896. The best parts of it were written by Henrik Marczali and Ignác Acsády (see below).

lay concept, who did not continue the scientific work of the positivists. They busied themselves in adjusting history to current political needs and failed to maintain contact with the development of Western scholarship.[3]

During this period of so-called "decadence" (*ca.* 1890–1920), among the historians enjoying position and influence only Henrik Marczali (1856–1940) fought against national isolation. Calling himself the pupil of Georg Waitz, Wilhelm Wattenbach, and Gabriel Monod, he stood for continued co-operation with the foreign schools; furthermore, his seminar at Budapest University was the center of the study of sources. Marczali was the most prolific Hungarian historian, the finest exponent of scientific historical writing.[4]

The period of decadence, however, was not altogether decadent. Under the noisy surface dominated by the lay concept, the silent work of the scholars continued.

Historical criticism was one of the cherished tendencies among the serious scholars. German positivism was rejected for being bogged down in sheer recording of facts. The more "spiritual" positivism of Herbert Spencer and Auguste Comte was followed instead. Among the exponents of historical criticism, Károly Tagányi (1858-1924) had a decisive influence. Although Tagányi never held a professional chair, the younger generation regarded him as their teacher and master. He specialized in the social and economic problems of medieval Hungary, depicting also the analogous developments and relationships among the Hungarian, Germanic, and Slavic peoples. Among other things, Tagányi established the fact that Hungary did not experience feudalism proper but adapted many feudal social forms, as did other nations living outside the truly feudal area of Europe.[5]

3 Typical representatives of the politician-historian were Kálmán Thaly (1839-1909), an able organizer and founder of the Historical Society; Aladár Ballagi (1853-1928); and Gusztáv Beksics (1847-1906).

4 Marczali's *History of Hungary* (in Hungarian) (Budapest, 1911) was a basic work on the political history of the country. Outstanding among his many monographs were *Hungary in the Eighteenth Century* (Cambridge, 1910) and *Ungarische Verfassungsgeschichte* (Tübingen, 1910). He also edited the twelve-volume *Illustrated World History*, the great collective work of the universal historians in pre-war Hungary.

5 Tagányi's chief works are available also in German; see K.

Tagányi, together with Ignác Acsády (1854–1906), founded Hungarian economic history. Acsády specialized in the period of the sixteenth, seventeenth, and eighteenth centuries, and his *History of the Hungarian System of Serfdom* (in Hungarian) (Budapest, 1908) was the first of its kind. Though written with some of the democratic bias of the twentieth century, it is a remarkable synthesis, and so is his *History of the Hungarian Empire* (in Hungarian) (Budapest, 1903–4). Sándor Takáts (1860–1932) also made a valuable contribution with his studies concerning economic and social conditions during the Turkish occupation (1526–1686).

Also active in the field of historical criticism was Lajos Thallóczy (1854–1916), who extended the scope of Hungarian historiography to include the Balkans. He founded the oriental or Balkan commission at the Academy and continued the pioneer work of the statesman-historian Béni Kállay (1839–1903), a Hungarian expert on the Eastern question and Serbian history.[6]

Another, rather isolated, group consisted of the radicals, who followed to varying extents the theories of historical materialism; their interest was focused on the social and minority problems, the two neglected aspects of both the past and the present. Grouped around the review *Huszadik Század* (Twentieth Century) (1901–'9), they were the extreme antithesis of everything that contemporary Hungary stood for. Well trained in Western sociology, they applied Western standards of measurement to Hungary. Their conclusions, pointing out as they did the backwardness of the country, made them unpopular. Their bitterness, as well as the bitterness against them, was aggravated after the failure of the democratic experiment in 1918–19; sooner or later they were all forced to emigrate.

Oszkár Jászi (1875–1955), who became a professor at Oberlin College in 1925, was the leading spirit of this group. The wide range of his scholarly works covered the nationality problem, the abortive revolution, and the fall of the Haps-

Tagányi, *Lebende Rechtsgewohnheiten und ihre Sammlungen in Ungarn* ("Ungarische Bibliothek," Ser. 1, No. 3 [Berlin, 1922]).

[6] Rumanian history was studied by Benedek Jancsó (1854-1930). Endre Veress edited the "Fontes rerum Transylvanicarum." The Slovak problem found its first student in Lajos Steier (1885-1942).

burg empire. Bitter political experiences did not undermine Jászi's striving for objectivity. His recent analyses offer not only a clear historical presentation of the Danubian problems, concerning which much has been written from a propaganda viewpoint, but also a lucid sociological evaluation of the present confused situation.[7] Ervin Szabó (1877-1918), another illustrious representative of the radical group, wrote with mature historical sense.[8] József Diner-Dénes (1857-1937) applied to the fullest measure historical materialism.[9] An outstanding member of this group was Rusztem Vámbéry (1872–1948), a sociologist of international fame, whose last historical work, however, was a rather unfortunate exhibition of personal grudge.[10]

Among the historians working in silence after the turn of the century, some followed the German currents known under the name of *Geistesgeschichte*. Wilhelm Dilthey, Gustav Schmoller, Georg von Below, Karl Lamprecht, Max Weber, Ernst Troeltsch, and Werner Sombart were their models. However, the excesses of the German school were checked in its Hungarian version. The Hungarian name, *Szellemtörténet*, meaning *"intellectual history,"* or *"history of ideas"* was a rather happy mixture of French- and English-inspired historical criticism and German *Geistesgeschichte*. In other words, the new school, though German in name, was essentially a Hungarian phenomenon. It became all-powerful in the period between the two World Wars (1919–1939).

According to the new school, the task of the historian is not just to establish the facts but to penetrate into the spiritual background of the facts. Human history, said Gyula Szekfü, who first applied *Geistesgeschichte*, is the history of

[7] Jászi's chief works are: *The Formation of the National States and the Nationality Problem* (in Hungarian) (Budapest, 1912); *Revolution and Counter-revolution in Hungary* (London, 1924); *The Dissolution of the Habsburg Monarchy* (Chicago, 1929). Among his recent works, outstanding is *Danubia: Old and New* (reprinted from *Proceedings of the American Philosophical Society*, Vol. XCIII, No. 1 [1948]).

[8] Ervin Szabó, *Social and Party Struggles during the Hungarian Revolution, 1848–1849* (in Hungarian) (Vienna, 1921).

[9] Joseph Diner-Dénes, *La Hongrie: Oligarchie—nation—peuple* (Paris, 1927).

[10] Rustem Vábéry, *Hungary: to Be or Not to Be* (New York, 1946).

the human soul. The spiritual approach encouraged the historians to reconstruct the ideas of the past and evaluate the facts in the spirit of the times when they occurred. As Elemér Mályusz, the best social historian of the post-war period, expressed it: It is the *Weltanschauung* which is to be properly understood. He even proposed that the new school be called "history of the *Weltanschauung*."[11]

The favorite slogan of the new historians was "synthesis." They wanted to re-create the past in its fullness. They rejected the romanticism of the national-liberals, held insufficient the rigid fact-finding methods of the scientific-positivists, detested the narrow-mindedness of the lay conception, and condemned the radicals, both for their ahistorism and their disregard of Hungarian peculiarities. Their work began in times of stress; the last war and its consequences had left Hungary in a desolate situation. Nevertheless, thanks to the sympathetic understanding of an able minister of education, Count Kluno Klebelsberg (1873–1932), and the enthusiasm of the scholars, the disrupted organizations of the historians were rapidly rebuilt.

The Historical Society assumed the responsibility for the edition of sources, with the publication, beginning in 1923, of the *"Fontes historiae Hungaricae aevi recentioris, 1686-1918."* The huge volumes of the "Fontes," with exact reproduction of the sources and scientific commentaries, were justly regarded as the pride of Hungarian historiography. Another important venture of the society, the *Manual of Hungarian Historical Sciences* (in Hungarian) (Budapest, 1923), standadized the methods of research. A new society and review, called *Minerva*, were founded by the new school (1922). Foreign contact was established in the research institutions at Vienna, Rome, Berlin, Paris, Warsaw, and also by means of the following foreign-language periodicals: *Corvina* (1920), *Ungarische Jahrbücher* (1920), *Revue des études hongroises* (1923), *Archivum Europae centro-orientalis* (1935), *Revue d'histoire comparée, nouvelle série* (1943).

[11] For the credo of the new school see Bálint Hóman, "The Road of History," and Gyula Szekfü, "Political Historiography," both in Hóman (ed.), *New Ways of Hungarian Historiography* (in Hungarian) (Budapest, 1932), pp. 7-53, and 397-445, respectively. Cf. J. Bartha, "Spirit, Spiritual Science, Spiritual History" (in Hungarian), *Athenaeum*, Vol. XVII (1931), considered one of the most important studies on *Geistesgeschichte* in Hungary.

With an organization relatively better developed than that of many greater nations, Hungarian historiography after the First World War was pursuing a double objective: specialization and synthesis. That specialization in the cultural-intellectual field was especially detailed and successful would seem obvious for a trend which stressed the importance of ideas. But in the neglected areas of economic and social relations the work of the specialists was also significant.

The representative work of the new school was the *Hungarian History*,[12] the ancient and medieval part written by Bálint Hóman (Vols. I–II), the modern by Gyula Szekfü (Vols. III–V).[13] Written in a brilliant style, it was a tremendous success; approximately nine thousand copies of it were sold in a country with a population of 9,000,000. It was a synthesis of the labor of more than one generation, the first work which integrated the political, cultural, social, and economic aspects of the past into one great picture.[14] Hóman and Szekfü portrayed—by scientific and not ideological argument—the history of the multi-national Hungarian state as showing distinctive marks of the Magyar nation and possessing organic ties with the Christian-Germanic, i.e., central European, brand of Western civilization. Szekfü's narrative ends with 1914; the ensuing chapters were written but kept in manuscript. An English translation was in preparation when the Second World War halted its publication.

Gyula Szekfü (1883–1957) was the dominant figure of Hungarian historiography in the period between the two World Wars. His first synthesis of Hungarian history, written during

12 In Hungarian (1st ed. in 8 vols.; Budapest, 1928-34; 2d and 3d eds. in 5 vols.; 1935-36).

13 The bibliographical notes of *Hungarian History* offer the most complete list as well as a critical evaluation of practically every work of importance written on Hungarian history.

14 Shorter syntheses of Hungarian history were given by Ferenc Eckhart (see below), *A Short History of the Hungarian People* (London, 1931); Sándor Domanovszky (see below), *Die Geschichte Ungarns* (Munich, 1923); Miklós Asztalos and Sándor Pethö (1885-1939), *History of the Hungarian Nation* (in Hungarian) (Budapest, 1933); George Balanyi, *The History of Hungary* (Budapest, 1930); Count Paul Teleki (1879–1941), *The Evolution of Hungary and Its Place in European History* (New York, 1923); Dominic G. Kosáry (see below), *A History of Hungary* (Cleveland and New York, 1941).

the First World War,[15] already clearly set forth his national-Christian concept, which, often linked with the so-called "Christian-national" trend of the postwar reactionary regime of Admiral Horthy, was branded as Catholic, pro-Hapsburg, and antiliberal.

Szekfü's much criticized "antiliberalism" consisted mainly in the exposure of liberalism's failure to live up to its own ideals. Liberalism's drifting away from its spiritual sources and devoting itself to egotistical materialism was, in Szekfü's view, a world-wide phenomenon and one of the principal causes of the crisis of democracy. His severe but constructive criticism of Hungarian social conditions made him popular with both the enlightened conservatives and the progressive democrats. He supported the conservative policies of Count Stephen Bethlen (1874–1948) and was editor of *Magyar Szemle* [Hungarian Review], a prominent politico-sociological monthly sponsored by Bethlen. During the Second World War Szekfü became the rallying point of spiritual resistance. He edited *What Is Magyar?* (in Hungarian) (Budapest, 1939), a collective work of Hungarian scholarship presenting a challenge to totalitarianism on the eve of Hungary's entrance into the war on the side of Germany (1941). Until the German occupation of Hungary (1944) he was editorial writer for the anti-Nazi daily, *Magyar Nemzet* [Hungarian Nation]. After spending a year of the German occupation in hiding, Szekfü became in 1946, democratic Hungary's first envoy to Moscow. In his last book, *After the Revolution* (1947), written partly in Moscow, he is at his best in describing the inglorious end of the old regime; but his analysis of Russian Communism, corroborating

15 Julius Szekfü, *Der Staat Ungarn* (Stuttgart and Berlin, 1928); in Hungarian: Gyula Szekfü, *The Biography of the Hungarian State* (Budapest, 1920). In addition to the volumes of the *Hungarian History*, discussed above, Szekfü dealt with the recent period, with a quasi-sociological approach, both in his *Three Generations*, a popular work which strongly influenced the new generation (in Hungarian) (Budapest, 1920; enlarged under the title *Three Generations and After* [1935]), and *After the Revolution* (in Hungarian) (Budapest, 1947). His other chief works are: *Rákóczi in Exile*, 1715–35, branded as antinational when published (in Hungarian) (Budapest, 1913); *Gabriel Bethlen* (in Hungarian) (1929). Szekfü greatly encouraged the study of minority nationality problems; his own studies in this field were collected in *State and Nations* (in Hungarian) (Budapest, 1942); in French: *Etat et nation* (Paris, 1945).

the views of the "red dean," Hewlett Johnson, whom he cites with approval, was a grave disappointment to his old friends and adherents. In 1948 Szekfü resigned his post in Moscow and returned to his professorial chair at Budapest University.

The career of the co-author of *Hungarian History* was very different. Bálint Hóman (1885–1951) died while serving a life sentence, convicted as a criminal for his wartime collaboration as minister of education and leader of pro-Nazi political movements. Hóman's political views were by no means characteristic of a group or faction among the Hungarian historians. They were solidly anti-Nazi. Hóman's case was rather an isolated one.[16] The circumstance, however, that Hóman was a convicted war criminal cannot alter the fact that he was the great medieval historian of the new school. He started—like most of the members of the new school—as an advocate of historical criticism. He wrote many important monographs besides the great synthesis presented in *Hungarian History*, and was an efficient organizer and editor.[17]

Specialization brought substantial results in the study of the different periods. Ancient history was explored by the exemplary teamwork of historians, archeologists, anthropologists, ethnographers, and linguists.[18] A valuable contribution was made to the exploration of the middle ages by Sándor Domanovszky; many results of his profound studies were incorporated into *Hungarian History)* by Hóman.[19] Other

[16] Another isolated victim of Nazi influence was Ödön Màlnàsi, author of *A sincere history of the Hungarian nation* (in Hungarian) (Budapest, 1937), who was sentenced to forced labor.

[17] Hóman's chief works were: *Towns in Hungary under the Árpáds* (in Hungarian) (Budapest, 1908); *History of Hungarian Money, 1000–1325* (in Hungarian) (Budapest, 1916); *Financial and Economic Policy of Hungary under Charles Robert, 1308–42* (in Hungarian) (Budapest, 1921); *Settlement of the Hungarians* (in Hungarian) (Budapest, 1923); *King Stephen the Saint* (in Hungarian) (Budapest, 1939); "Hungary, 1301-1490" in the *Cambridge Medieval History, Vol. VIII* (1932), chap. xix.

[18] Gyula Németh, *The Formation of the Hungarian People* (in Hungarian) (Budapest, 1930); *Attila and His Huns* (in Hungarian) (Budapest, 1941); see also the works of Count István Zichy, János Melich, Zoltán Gombocz, Károly Visky, Lajos Bartucz, and István Kniezsa.

[19] Domanovszky edited two volumes, on the *History of Hungarian Culture, Vol. I, The Middle Ages*, and Vol. II, *Hungarian Renaissance* (in Hungarian) (Budapest, n.d.).

important medieval researchers were István Miskolczy and, among the young historians, J. Deér and P. Váczy.[20] Elemér Mályusz did outstanding work with his studies of both medieval and modern times. He clarified many problems of the medieval minorities, though his main interest was in the bourgeoisie.[21] He maintained that the bourgeoisie was the prisoner of the nobility until the end of the nineteenth century. Mályusz, a Protestant, was often out of step with the new school, and his criticism of Catholicism, Hapsburgs, and nobles was decried by Szekfü as "a historical antipathy."

Among the students of modern times, Ferenc Eckhart explored economic problems.[22] Imre Lukinich widened the horizon of Hungarian historiography with important studies concerning relations with Hungary's neighbors, especially Rumania.[23] Jenö Horváth excelled with studies on foreign relations.[24] Gusztáv Gratz, in his monograph, *The Age of Dualism,* 1867–1918 (in Hungarian) (Budapest, 1934), produced the long-awaited pragmatic work on the period of *Ausgleich.* Gratz, a liberal statesman-historian, had ready in manuscript the history of Hungary between the two World Wars, but after his return from a German concentration camp in 1945 he looked in vain for a publisher.

[20] Their chief works are: István Miskolczy, *Hungary in the Age of the Anjous,* 1308-1386 (in Hungarian) (Budapest, 1923); Joseph Deér, *Heidnisches und Christliches in der altungarischen Monarchie* (Szeged, 1934); Peter Váczy, *Die erste Epoche des ungarischen Königtums* (Pécs, 1935).

[21] Elemér Mályusz, "Geschichte des Bürgertums in Ungarn," *Vierteljahrschrift für Sozial- und Wirtschaftsgeschicte,* Vol. XX (1928). He has also written a biography, *Matthias Corvinus* (in the series "Menschen die Geschichte machten," ed. Peter Richard Rohden and Georg Ostrogorsky, Vol. II); outstanding is his *Development of the County Turócz* (in Hungarian) (Budapest, 1922).

[22] Ferenc Eckhart, *Economic Policy of the Vienna Court in Hungary under Maria Theresa* (in Hungarian) (Budapest, 1922).

[23] Imre Lukinich, *Territorial Changes of Transylvania* (in Hungarian) (Budapest, 1918); he published in the "Fontes" series, *History of the Peace of Szatmár 1711* (in Hungarian) (Budapest, 1928); edited the *Mohács Memorial* (in Hungarian) (Budapest, 1926); and the *Matthias Corvinus Memorial* (in Hungarian) (Budapest, 1940).

[24] Jenö Horváth, *Hungarian Diplomacy,* 1815–1918 (in Hungarian) (Budapest, 1928); *The Diplomacy of the Arpads,* 1101–1250 (in Hungarian) (Budapest, 1931).

István Szabó specialized in the study of the peasantry;[25] with firm historical sense he maintained a scientific point of view in treating the sorry plight of the peasants.

Among the younger historians, outstanding were the scholarly works of Domokos Kosáry, whose latest studies deal with Kossuth.[26] Gyula Mérei made valuable contributions to the understanding of the social and political background of the nineteenth century.[27] Kálmán Benda covered both medieval and modern periods; and many other historians, trained in the "new school," undertook with great skill the detailed examination of the past—sometimes so detailed that, as Szekfü once put it, the more general explorer of the past had "to pull himself together" to follow them.[28]

The art and literary historians contributed much to the synthesis of the new school. Tibor Gerevich was one of the real builders of Hungarian *Geistesgeschichte*; his major contribution was the reappraisal of medieval Hungarian art.[29] Antal Hekler (1882–1939), the other leading art historian, was an authority on Hungarian baroque. Among the listerary historians the most important figures were: János Horváth, Tivadar Thienemann, Sándor Eckhardt, József Huszti, Gyula Farkas, Béla Pukánszky, and Jénö Pintér (1881–1940), author of the scholarly, precise, ten-volume *Hungarian Literary History*. The American student will find extremely valuable the illuminating essays on Hungarian literature by Joseph Reményi, professor of comparative literature at Western Reserve University, USA.

There were some first-class historians who specialized in universal history, ancient, medieval, or modern, such as Károly Kerényi, András Alföldi, Gyula Moravcsik, István Hajnal, and Antal Balla. A four-volume *Universal History*, edited by Bálint Hóman, Gyula Szekfü, and Károly Kerényi (in Hun-

---

[25] István Szabó, *History of the Hungarian Peasantry* (in Hungarian) (Budapest, 1940).

[26] Domokos Kosáry, *Kossuth in the Age of Reform* (in Hungarian) (Budapest, 1946).

[27] Gyula Mérei, *Political Party Programs, 1867-1914* (in Hungarian) (Budapest, 1934); *The Agricultural and Agrarian Society, 1790-1848* (in Hungarian) (Budapest, 1948).

[28] Gyula Szekfü, "Mathias Memorial" (in Hungarian), *Magyar szemle*, XXXVIII (1940), 612.

[29] Tibor Gerevich, *L'arte antica ungherese* (Rome, 1929).

garian) (Budapest, n.d.), was the representative work of the
world historians.

The aftermath of the Second World War threw Hungary
into the Russian sphere of influence. In 1947 Hungarian historiography was described by an American expert on central
European affairs as "iconoclastic, partisan, and dialectical,"
by which he meant that it was rebelling against the trend
between the two World Wars and emphasizing the importance
of historic Russia and the Soviet Union. He cited as a prime
example of Marxist revaluation of Hungarian history the
work of the Communist Erik Molnár, *History of Hungarian
Society from Antiquity to the Age of the Árpáds* (in Hungarian) (rev. ed.; Budapest, 1945; first published in 1942–43).
Molnár, who achieved prominence after 1945, maintained that
"knowledge of the law of social mechanism and evolution . . .
makes it possible to arrive at unknown historical facts from
known ones." Thus, for instance, he came to the conclusion
that "Géza and his son St. Stephen are the first great revolutionaries in Hungarian history."[30]

Supplemental references follow: Louis J. Lekai, "Historiography in Hungary," 1790–1848," *Journal of Central European Affairs*, XIV (1954), an outline of the author's detailed
study on the subject in manuscript. Tibor Baráth, "L'histoire
en Hongrie 1867–1935," *Revue historique*, CLXXVII (1936),
84–144, 595–644; CLXXVIII (1936), 25–74, a detailed history
of Hungarian historiography. No study of similar scope is
available in English. Dominic Kosáry, "Gabriel Bethlen, Transylvania in the XVIIth century," *Slavonic Review*, XVII
(1938), 162–73. In this study of seventeenth century Transylvania the author summarizes the treatment of the problem
by Hungarian historiography. Imre Lukinich, *Les éditions
des sources de l'histoire hongroise 1854–1930* (Budapest, 1930).
List of source editions with short commentaries, Zoltán Ma-
gyary (ed.), *Die Entstehung einer internationalen Wissenschaftspolitik: Die Lage der ungarischen Wissenschaftspolitik*
(Leipzig, 1932), a collective work on the state of Hungarian
sciences, including historiography. James Westfall Thompson,

---

[30]Leslie C. Tihany, "Post-Armistice Hungarian Historiography"
(in manuscript); the bibliographical part of the study was published in *American Slavic and East European Review*, VI (1947),
158-78.

History of Historical Writing (New York, 1942), II, 639–41, a sketch of Hungarian historiography brought up to Marczali.

After the Communist take-over, the "five-year plan of the historians" pledged the exploration of the neglected fields and the revision of distortions. No doubt there were neglected fields—especially in the economic, social, minority, and international domains; and there were distortions, favoring the former ruling classes, which called for corrections.

While the new historiography of the second half of the twentieth century has produced new distortions favoring the new rulers, it has also scored great successes. Since the revolution of 1956, the trend has been particularly encouraging. *Acta Historica*, a journal of the Hungarian Academy of Sciences, written in English, French, German, and Russian, offers a wide range of information on the current state of Hungarian historiography. For general information, the following articles are of particular interest: Unsigned, "Institutions de science historique en Hongrie," *Acta Historica*, VII (1960), 175–187; L. Katus, "Rapport sur les travaux de la Bibliographie Hongroise d'Histoire," *Acta Historica*, VII (1960), 183–189; A. Urbán, "La recherche historique dans les Universités de Hongrie (1957–1962)," *Acta Historica*, X (1963), 115–154.

The achievements of the new historiography are particularly noteworthy in the field of bibliography. In this field, by its very nature, the political interference of the Marxist exponents of the Communist regime is least noticeable. Domokos Kosáry covered the period up to 1825 in his three-volume work, *Introduction to the Sources and Literature of Hungarian History* (in Hungarian) (Budapest, 1951–57). The period from 1825 to 1867 is the subject of a five-volume work, *Hungarian Historical Bibliography 1825–1678* (in Hungarian); the first three volumes (Budapest, 1950–52), edited by Zoltán I. Tóth, contain material relating to the history of the Hungarians (Magyars) in historic Hungary, while the fourth volume, edited by Gábor G. Kemény and László Katus (Budapest, 1959), deals with the development of modern nationality problems in general as well as with the South Slav and Slovak nationalities in particular; the fifth volume, in preparation, will cover the literature concerning the other nationalities. An even more ambitious undertaking is the six-volume bibliography dealing with the period between 1867 and 1918. The first three volumes have been completed and publication will shortly begin. Also, the Institute for Historical Science of the Hungarian Academy of Sciences, organizer of all these activities, is now compiling a select bibliography for the history of the Hapsburg monarchy between 1526 and 1918. For further information, see the following bibliographical articles: Emil Niederhauser, "A forthcoming bibliography of Hungarian history, 1867–1918," *Slavic Review*, XXIV (1965), 291–296. Péter Hanák, "Recent Hungarian literature on the history of the Austro-Hungarian monarchy, 1849–1918. A historiographical survey," *Austrian History Yearbook*, I (Rice University, 1965), 151–163.

SELECTED BIBLIOGRAPHY
ON HUNGARY

Compiled by Zoltán Sztaray

GENERAL WORKS

Baranyai, Zoltán. *Ungarn, das Antlitz einer Nation.* Budapest, Königl, ungarische Universitäts-Druckerei, 1940. 869 p. Illust.

Boldizsár, Iván. *Hungary, A Guide-Book.* Budapest, Corvina, 1959. 391 p. Illust. Maps.

Companion to Hungarian Studies. Budapest, Society of the Hungarian Quarterly, 1943. 532 p.

Dami, Aldo. *La Hongrie de demain.* Paris, Les Œuvres représentatives, 1933. 317 p.

Grunwald, Constantin de. *Portrait de la Hongrie.* Paris, Plon, 1939. 243 p.

Halász, Zoltán. *Hungary.* Budapest, Corvina, 1956. 391 p.

Hanzely, Victor E. *The Hungarians.* New Haven, 1955. 267 p. Illust. Maps.

Hegedüs, Ádám. *Hungarian Background.* London, H. Hamilton, 1937. 302 p. Illust.

Hongrie (La) et la civilisation. Histoire, ethnographie, constitution, rapports internationaux, lettres, arts, sciences, vie sociale et économique. Paris, La Renaissance du livre, 1927. 3 vols. 430, 413 and 232 p.

Humphrey, Grace. *Hungary, Land of Contrasts.* New York, Scott & More, 1936. 296 p.

Hungary Today. By the Editors of Survey, New York, Praeger, Inc., 1962. 104 p.

Hungary, Yesterday and Today. London, Grant Richards, 1936. 237 p.

Kubiatovicz, Lucjan. *Wegierska Republika Ludowa.* Odczyt. Warsawa, Czytelnik, 1950. 71 p. Map.

Mende, Tibor. *Hungary.* Cross Roads Series. London, Macdonald, 1944. 175 p.

Paget, John. *Hungary and Transylvania; with Remarks on Their Condition Social, Political and Economical.* 2 vols. London, 1855. Illust.

Reismann, J.—Illyés, Gy. *Lake Balaton.* Budapest, Corvina, 1962. 40—162 p. Illust.

Sauvageot, A. *Découverte de la Hongrie.* Paris, F. Alcan, 1937. 244 p.

Schreiber, Thomas. *Hongrie.* Paris, Nagel, 1957. 174 p.

Szabó, Stefan. *Ungarisches Volk, Geschichte und Wandlungen.* Budapest-Leipzig, Ungarisches Institut für Geschichtsforschung—Danubia, 1946. 328 p.

Takács, László. *Der Ungar in der Welt.* Budapest, Dr. G. Vajna and Co., 1934. 364 p. Illust.

Ungarn, ein Reisebuch. Budapest, Corvina, 1956. 391 p.

Ungheria (L'). Roma, Instituto per l'Europa orientale. 1930. 454 p. Illust.

Visages de la Hongrie. Paris, Plon, 1938. 622 p. Bibliography.

Vredenburg, W. S. A. van. *Hongarije en de Hongaren.* Leiden, A. W. Sijthoff—N. W. Uitgeverij, 1936.

GEOGRAPHY, GEOLOGY

Chardonnet, Jean. *Géographie économique de l'Europe Danubienne et de la Pologne.* Paris, 1959.

Fillitz, Franz. *Die Donau—Vermittlerin zwischen West und Ost.* Wien, Donaueurop. Inst., 1959. 8 p.

Holland, Clive. *Hungary: The Land and Its People.* London, J. Miles, 1935. 356 p.

Hungary. Central Statistical Office. *Administrative Directory of Hungary.* Budapest, Közgazdasági és Jogi Könyvkiadó, 1956. 755 p.

Lóczy, Louis and Papp, Charles. *Geological Map of Hungary.* Budapest, 1922.

Lóczy, Lajos. *A Geographical, Economic and Social Survey of Hungary*. Budapest, Pátria Press, 1919. 121 p. Illust.

Kakas, J. *Climatic Atlas of Hungary*. Budapest, Publishing House of the Hungarian Academy of Sciences, 1960. In Hungarian and German. 20 p. text, 130 colour maps.

Pécsi, M.–Sárfalvi, B. *The Geography of Hungary*. Budapest, Corvina, 1962. 360 p.

Petri, Edith. *Geographie de la Hongrie*. Budapest, Bulletin Hongrois, 1950. 96 p. Maps.

Road-Atlas of Hungary. Budapest, Cartographic Enterprise. 1963. 23 maps.

Rónai, A. *Atlas of Central Europe*. Budapest, 1945.

Sárfalvi, B. ed. *Problems of Applied Geography in Hungary*. Budapest, Publishing House of the Hungarian Academy of Sciences, 1964. 230 p. Illust.

Treitz, Péter. *Geographical Unity of Hungary*. Budapest, F. Pfeifer, 1920. 19 p.

Winkler, A. *Ungarns landwirtschaftsgeografische Gestaltung*. Berlin, 1938.

Witthauer, Kut. *Die Bevölkerung der Erde. Verteilung und Dynamik*. Gotha, Haak, 1958. 336 p. Maps, illust.

ECONOMICS, STATISTICS

Balassa, Béla A. *The Hungarian Experience in Economic Planning*. New Haven, Yale University Press, 1959.

Basch, Antonin. *The Danube Basin and the German Economic Sphere*. London, Kegan Paul, Trench-Trubner, 1944. 288 p.

Dewar, Margaret. *Soviet Trade with Eastern Europe 1945–1949*. London, Royal Institute of International Affairs, 1951.

Eckstein, Alexander. *National Income and Capital Formation in Hungary, 1900–1950*. Cambridge, International Ass'n for Res. in Income and Wealth, 1956.

Hungarian National Bank. *Annual Reports*. Budapest, National Bank of Hungary. Annually.

Kemény, George. *Economic Planning in Hungary 1947–49*. London, Royal Institute of International Affairs, 1952. 146 p. Tables.

Marczewski, Jan. *Planification et croissance économique des démocraties populaires*. Paris, Presses universitaires, 1956. 2 vols. 572 p.

Matolcsy, Mathias and Varga, Stephen. *The National Income of Hungary, 1924–1925, 1936–1937*. London, King and Son, 1938. 116 p.

Nyárády, Nicholas. *My Ringside Seat in Moscow*. New York, Crowell, 1952. 320 p.

Soviet Reply to U.S. Note on Hungarian Economic Situation, July 27, 1946. Washington, D.C., Department of State Bulletin, Vol. XV.

Spulber, Nicolas. *The Economics of Communist Eastern Europe*. New York-London, The Technology Press of MIT and John Wiley and Sons, Inc., — Chapman and Hall, Ltd., 1957. 525 p. Bibliography.

Statistical Pocket Book of Hungary. Budapest, Central Statistical Office, Tables, maps. Annually.

Statistical Yearbook of Hungary. Budapest, Central Statistical Office. Annually.

Statistical Yearbook. New York, United Nations. Annually.

Sztaray, Zoltan. *Hungary. A Survey*. New York, The Kossuth Foundation, Inc., Part I. 1959. 61 p.; Part II. 1960. 75 p.

U.N.R.R.A. European Regional Office. *Agriculture and Food in Hungary*. London, 1947. 41 p.

—— *Economic Rehabilitation in Hungary*. London, 1947. 93 p.

U.S. Joint Publications Research Service. *Monthly Digest of Hungarian Statistical Periodicals*. Washington, D.C.

HISTORY

Borsody, Stephen. *The Triumph of Tyranny*. London, Jonathan Cape, New York, Macmillan Co., 1960. 285 p.

Contre-révolution (La) et les évènements d'octobre en Hongrie. Livre blanc publié par le Bureau d'Information du Conseil des ministres de la République populaire de Hongrie. Budapest, 1956–1957. 4 vols. 62, 1957, 140 et 136 p.

Eckhart, Ferenc. *Histoire de la Hongrie*. Paris, Œuvres Représentatives, 1932. 209 p. Illust.

Hóman, Bálint. *Geschichte des ungarischen Mittelalters*. Berlin, W. de Gruyter, 1940.

Jászi, Oscar. *Revolution and Counter-Revolution in Hungary*. London, King, 1924. 268 p.

Kecskeméti, Paul. *The Unexpected Revolution. Social Forces in the Hungarian Uprising.* Stanford University Press, 1961. 178 p.

Kosáry, Dominic G. *A History of Hungary.* Cleveland, Ohio, Benjamin Franklin Bibliophile Society, 1941. 482 p. Illust.

Lasky, Melvin J. *The Hungarian Revolution.* The Story of the October Uprising as Recorded in Documents, Dispatches, Eyewitnesses' Accounts and Worldwide Reactions. New York, Praeger, 1957. 318 p. Illust.

Macartney, C. A. *Hungary, A Short History.* Chicago, Aldine Publishing Company, 1962. 262 p.

—— *October Fifteenth. A History of Modern Hungary 1929–1945.* Edinburgh, Edinburgh University Press. 1956–57. 2 vols. 493 and 519 p.

Pethö, Tibor and Czebe, Jenö. *Hungary in World War II. A Military History of the Years of War.* Budapest. Atheneaum, 1947. 509 p.

Sinor, Denis. *History of Hungary.* London, George Allen & Unwin Ltd., 1959. 310 p.

Seton-Watson, Hugh. *Eastern Europe between the Wars 1918–1941.* New York-Cambridge, Macmillan-Cambridge University Press, 1946. 442 p.

Szekfü, Gyula. *Der Staat Ungarn. Eine Geschichts-Studie.* Stuttgart, Deutsche Verlags-Anstalt, 1918. 224 p.

Teleki, Count Paul. *The Evolution of Hungary and Its Place in European History.* New York, Macmillan Co., 1923. 312 p.

Vérité (La) sur l'affaire Nagy; les faits, les documents, les témoignages internationaux. Préface de Albert Camus. Paris, Plon, 1958. 256 p. Illust.

Zinner, Paul E. *Revolution in Hungary.* New York-London, Columbia University Press, 1962. 380 p.

FOREIGN AFFAIRS

Aide mémoire économique du gouvernement hongrois présenté aux 21 puissances réunies en conférence à Paris en vue de l'élaboration des traités de paix. Budapest, Ministère Hongrois des Affaires Etrangères, 1946. 59 p.

Conference (The) at Malta and Yalta, 1945. Washington, D.C., Department of State, 1955. 1032 p.

Deák, Francis and Újváry, Dezsö. *Papers and Documents Relating to the Foreign Relations of Hungary.* Budapest-New York, Royan Hungarian University Press, 1939. 1125 p.

Edgecumbe, O. P. *The British Military Mission in Hungary.* In Journal of Royal Unit. Service Inst., No. 95, 1950; pp. 207–220.

Hungarian Ministry of Foreign Affairs. *Hungary and the Conference of Paris.* Budapest, University Press, 1947. Vol. 1. 190 p.; Vol. 2. 172 p.; Vol. 4. 202 p.

Hungarian Society for Foreign Affairs. *The Deportation of the Hungarians of Slovakia.* Budapest, 1947. 24 p.

Kertesz, Stephen D. *Diplomacy in a Whirlpool. Hungary Between Nazi Germany and Soviet Russia.* Notre Dame, Ind., University of Notre Dame Press, 1953. 273 p.

— — *The Fate of East Central Europe. Hopes and Failures of the American Foreign Policy.* Notre Dame, Ind., University of Notre Dame Press, 1956. 463 p.

Lukacs, J. A., *The Great Powers and Eastern Europe.* New York, American Book, 1953. 878 p.

Report of the Special Committee on the Problem of Hungary. New York, United Nations, 1957. 148 p.

Treaty of Peace with Hungary of February 10, 1947, Entered into Force September 15, 1947. Washington, D.C., Government Printing Office, 1947. 165 p.

U.S. Congress. Committee on Foreign Affairs. *Report of the Special Study Mission to Europe on Policy toward the Satellite Nations.* June 4, 1957. House Report No. 531, 25 p.

LANGUAGE, DICTIONARIES

András-Murvai. *How to Say It in Hungarian. An English-Hungarian Phrase Book with Lists of Words.* Budapest, Publishing House of the Hungarian Academy of Sciences, 1966. 238 p.

Bánhidi, Z.-Jókay, Z.-Szabó, D. *Lehrbuch der ungarischen Sprache.* Budapest, Publishing House of the Hungarian Academy of Sciences, Budapest, 1966. 495 p.

Bánhidi, Z.-Jókay, Z. *Text-Book of the Hungarian Language.* Budapest, Publishing House of the Hungarian Academy of Sciences, 1966, 460 p.

Décsy, Gyula. *Einführung in die finnische-ugrische Sprachwissenschaft.* Wiesbaden, Otto Harrassovitz, 1965. 261 p.

Eckhardt, Sándor. *French-Hungarian Dictionary.* Budapest, Akadémiai Kiodó, 1953. 1643 p.

— *Hungarian-French Dictionary.* Budapest, Akadémia Kiadó, 1958. 2376 p.

Gáldi. *Hungarian-Spanish Dictionary.* Budapest, Akadémiai Kiadó, 1958. 736 p.

— *Spanish-Hungarian Dictionary.* Budapest, Akadémiai Kiadó, 1958. 800 p.

Halász-Elöd. *German-Hungarian Dictionary.* Budapest, Akadémiai Kiadó, 2 vols. 696 and 827 p.

— *Hungarian-German Dictionary.* Budapest, Akadémiai Kiadó, 1957. 1232 p.

Herczegh. *Italian-Hungarian Dictionary.* Budapest, Akadémiai Kiadó, 1952. 2 vols. 747 and 712 p.

— *Hungarian-Italian Dictionary.* Budapest, Akadémiai Kiadó, 1958. 766 p.

Lotz, János. *Das ungarische Sprachsystem.* Stockholm, 1939.

Országh, Laszló. *Hungarian-English Dictionary.* Budapest, Akadémiai Kiadó, 1953. 1448 p.

— *English-Hungarian Dictionary.* Budapest, Akadémiai Kiadó, 1960. 2333 p.

Ortutay, Gyula. ed. *Congressus Internationalis Fenno-Ugristarium Budapestini Habitus 20–24.IX.1960.* Budapest, Publishing House of the Hungarian Academy of Sciences, 1963. 490 p.

Seböck, Tamas. *Spoken Hungarian.* Bloomington, Ind., The Author, 1948. 482 p.

Sivirski, A. L. I. *Leergang voor de Hongaarse taal.* Amsterdam, Becht, 1957. 148 p.

Statistical Dictionary in Seven Languages. Budapest, Central Bureau of Statistics, 1961. 171 p.

Várady, Emerico. *Grammatica della lingua ungherese.* Roma, 1931.

Whitney, Arthur H. *Colloquial Hungarian.* London, Routledge and Paul, 1950. 264 p.

CULTURE, CIVILIZATION AND EDUCATION

Allen, Walter Jr. *The Four Corvinus Manuscripts in the United States.* New York, The New York Public Library, 1938.

Fraknói, Vilmos-Fogel, József-Gulyás, Pál-Hoffmann, Edith.

Bibliotheca Corvina. La bibliotheca di Mattia Corvino re d'Ungheria. Budapest, Addademia di Santo Stefano, 1927.

Hajnal, István. *L'Enseignement de l'écriture aux universités Médiévales.* Budapest, Maison d'Edition de l'Académie des Sciences de Hongrie, 1959. 302 p. Illust.

Juhasz, William. *Blueprint for a Red Generation.* New York, Mid-European Studies Center, 1952. 101 p.

Kornis, Julius. *Education in Hungary.* New York, Teachers College, Columbia University, 1932. 289 p.

—— *Hungary and the European Civilization.* Budapest, Royal Hungarian University Press, 1938. 37 p.

Kurucz, Jenö. *Die Opposition der Jugend als philosophische Strömung in der deutschen Philosophie des 19. Jahrhunderts und als politische Aktion in der Ungarnrevolution.* St. Gallen, Magyar Diák, 1958. 97 p.

Nékám, Louis. *The Cultural Aspirations of Hungary from 896 to 1935.* Budapest, Central Committee of the Thermal Baths Health Resorts, 1935. 319 p.

Radisics, Elemér. *Hungary; Pictorial Record of a Thousand Years.* Budapest, Athanaeum, 1944. 190 p.

—— *La Hongrie d'hier et d'aujourd'hui.* Paris, Les oeuvres représentatives, 1932. 232 p.

Ráth, Sándor, *Juden in Ungarn. Kulturleben in der 2. Hälfte des 19. Jahrhunderts.* Berlin, 1934.

Szentkirályi, Joseph. *Modern Trends in Hungarian Education.* New York, Hungarian Reference Library, 1939. Pamphlet No. 1.

CHURCHES

Barth, Karl, *Christliche Gemeinde im Wechsel der Staatsordnungen. Dokumente einer Ungarnreise.* Zollikon-Zürich, Evang. Verlag, 1948, 76 p.

Bereczky, Albert. *Die Entscheidung der Kirche und Ihre Mission.* Budapest, The General Synod of the Reformed Church. 1963. 146 p.

—— *Die ungarische Christenheit im neuen ungarischen Staat.* Zollikon-Zürich, Evang. Verlag, 1948.

Bucsay, *Mihály. Die Geschichte des Protestantismus in Ungarn.* Stuttgart, Evangelisches Verlagswerk, 1959. 228 p.

Documents sur l'affaire Mindszenty. Livre jaune hongrois. Budapest, Athenaeum, 1949. 104 p.

Four-Year Struggle of the Church in Hungary. Facts and Evidence Published by Order of Cardinal Mindszenty. London, New York and Toronto, Longmans, Green & Co., 1949. 206 p.

Gombos, Gyula. *The Lean Years. A Study of Hungarian Calvinism in Crisis.* New York, The Kossuth Foundation, Inc., 1960, 131 p.

Juhász, William. *Church and Society in Hungary. A Study in the Church and Society.* New York, Arts Int., 1952. 100 p.

Kádár, Imre. *The Church in the Storm of Time.* Budapest, Bibliotheca, 1958.

Lévai, J. *Black Book. L'histoire de l'antisémitisme.* Budapest, Editions d'Etat, 1951. 386 p.

Meyer, Peter. *The Jews in the Soviet Satellites.* Syracuse, University Press, 1953. 637 p.

Mindszenty, Joseph Cardinal. . . . *The World's Most Orphaned Nation.* New York, The Book Mailer, Inc., 1962. 111 p.

Procès de József Grösz et ses complices. Budapest, Editions d'Etat, 1951. 411 p.

Révész, Imre. *History of the Hungarian Reformed Church,* Hungarica Americana. Washington, D.C., The Hungarian Reformed Federation of America, 1956. 163 p.

Sharpe, E. *Faustus Socinus and the Unitarians in Hungary.* London, 1901.

Shuster, G. N. *Religion Behind the Iron Curtain.* New York, Macmillan, 1954. 281 p.

Soós, Géza. *Quelques pages de l'histoire de l'Eglise Réformée Hongroise entre deux guerres mondiales, 1919–1945.* Genève, 1950. 174 p.

Szlavik, M. *Zur Geschichte des Anabaptismus in Ungarn.* Leipzig, 1897.

LITERATURE AND HISTORY OF LITERATURE

Cushing, George F. *Hungarian Prose and Verse. A Selection with an Introductory Essay.* London, University of London; Athlone Press, 1956. 197 p.

Duczynska, Ilona and Polanyi, Karl. *The Plough and the Pen. An Anthology of the Hungarian Literature.* London, Peter Owen, 1963.

Farkas, Gyula. *Der Freiheitskampf des ungarischen Geistes, 1867–1914* Berlin, W. de Gruyter & Co., 1940. 280 p. Illust.

Farkas, Julius von. *Der ungarische Vormärz; Petöfis Zeitalter.*
Berlin, W. de Gruyter & Co., 1943. 186 p.

— *Die Entwickklung der ungarischen Literatur.* Berlin, W,
de Gruyter & Co., 1934, 306 p.

Gara, László, ed. *Anthologie de la poésie hongroise du XII*
siècle à nos jours. Paris, Editions du Seuil, 1962. 502 p.

Hankiss, János – Juhász, Géza. *Panorama de la littérature*
hongroise contemporaine. Paris, Editions Kra, 1930. 348 p.

Hankiss, János – Mohos-Müller, L. *Anthologie de la poésie*
hongroise. Paris, 1936.

Hungaria. An Anthology of Short Stories by Contemporary
Hungarian Authors. London, Nicholson & Watson, 1936.
302 p.

Hungarian Short Stories—19th and 20th Centuries. Hungarian
Library, Budapest, Corvina, 1962. 391 p.

Juhász, William and Rothberg, Abraham. *Flashes in the Night.*
New York, Random House, 1958. 87 p.

Kirkconnell, Watson. *The Magyar Muse: An Anthology of*
Hungarian Poetry. Winnipeg, Canada, Canadian-Hungarian
News Co., 1933. 349 p.

Klaniczay, Tibor – Szabolcsi, M. – Szauder, J. *History of Hun-*
garian Literature. Budapest, Corvina, 1964. 361 p.

*Panorama de la littérature hongroise du XX*ᵉ *siècle, I.–II.*
Edited by György Bodnár, Budapest, Corvina, 1965. 416–
356 p.

Remenyi, Joseph. *Hungarian Literature.* Washington, D.C.,
American-Hungarian Federation, 1946. 48 p.

— *Hungarian Writers and Literature: Modern Novelists,*
Critics, and Poets. New Brunswick, N.J., Rutgers University
Press, 1964. 512 p.

— *Sándor Petöfi, Hungarian Poet (1823–1849).* Hungarian
Americana 1. Washington, D.C., The Hungarian Reformed
Federation of America, 1953. 46 p.

Riedl, Frigyes. *A History of Hungarian Literature. Short*
Histories of the Literatures of the World. Vol. XIII. London, Heinemann, 1906.

— *A History of Hungarian Literature.* New York, D. Apple-
ton and Co., 1906. 293 p. Illust.

Sötér, I. – Süpek, O. ed. *Littérature hongroise—littérature*
européenne. Budapest, Publishing House of the Hungarian
Academy of Sciences, 1964. 480 p.

Tabori, Paul, ed. *Hungarian Anthology*. London, Bale and Staples, 1943. 147 p.

FINE ARTS

Balás-Piry, László von. *Die ungarische Malerei des XIX. und XX. Jahrhunderts*. Berlin, 1940. 104 p.

Csányi, Karl. *Gesichte der ungarischen Keramik des Porzellans und ihre Marken*. Budapest, Verlag des Fonds fur Bildende Künste, 1954. 159 p. Illust.

Czobor-Szalay. *Die historichen Denkmäler Ungarns*. Budapest, 2 vols. 465 p. Illust.

Divald, Kornél. *Old Hungarian Art*. London, Oxford University Press, 1931. 228 p.

Gál, Ladislaus. *L'Architecture réligieuse en Hongrie du XI. au XIII. siècles*. Paris, 1930. 300 p. Illust.

Genthon, Etienne. *La Peinture médiévale hongroise*. Paris. A la croisée des chemins—Budapest, Officina, 1948. 16–32 p.

Héjj Détári, A. *Old Hungarian Jewellery*. Budapest, Corvina, 1964. 36–19 p.

Huszár, Lajos. *The Art of Coinage in Hungary*. Budapest, Corvina, 1963. 96–48 p.

Kampis, Antal. *Holzildhauerei in Ungarn*. Budapest. Officina, 1940. 150 p.

Koczogh, Á.*Modern Hungarian Metalwork*. Budapest, Corvina, 1964. 36–49 p.

Pataky, D. –Brestyánszky, I. *Modern Hungarian Ceramics*. Budapest, Corvina, 1961. 46–40 p.

Pataky, D. *Zeichnungen und Aquarellen in Ungarn*. Budapest, Corvina, 1961. 240–192 p.

Pogány, Gábor Ö. *Hundert Jahre ungarische bildende Kunst*. Budapest, Corvina, 1948. 56 p. Illust.

—— *19th Century Hungarian Painting*. Budapest, Corvina, 1959. 88 p. Illust.

Pogány, Gabriel Ö. *Les révolutionnaires de la peinture hongroise*. Budapest. Officina, 1946. 79 p. Illust.

Radocsay, D. *Gotische Tafelmalerei in Ungarn*. Budapest, Corvina, 1963. 68–48 p. Illust.

The Treasures of the Hungarian Museum of Fine Arts. Budapest, Corvina, 1954. 28 p. Illust.

FOLK ARTS, FOLKLORE

Domanovszky, Georges. *L'Art pastoral hongrois*. Budapest, Officina, 1948. 40 p., 14 tables.

Fél, Edit-Hofer, Tamás-Csilléry, Klára. *Hungarian Peasant Art*, Cambridge, Steffer and Sons, 1959. 280 p. Illust.

—— *Ungarische Bauernkunst*. Budapest, Corvina, 1958. 85 + 242 p. Illust.

Hölbrigl, Joseph. *Historic Hungarian Costumes*. Officina, 1948. 27 + 16 p.

Hungarian Ethnographical Museum. *Hungarian Decorative Folk Art*. Budapest, Corvina, 1954. 36 + 208 p. Illust.

Illyés, Gyula. *Once Upon a Time—Forty Hugarian Folk Tales*. Budapest, Corvina, 1964. 286 p.

Károlyn, Alexander F. *Hungarian Pageant. Life, Customs and Art of the Hungarian Peasantry*. Budapest, G. Vajna, 1939. 113 p.

Ortutay, Gyula. *Kleine ungarische Volkskunde*. Budapest, Corvina, 1963. 230 p. Illust.

—— *Hungarian Folk Tales*. Budapest, Corvina, 1962. 543 p.

Tarr, László. *Hungarian Rhapsody. The Hungarian State Folk Ensemble*. Budapest, Corvina, 1956.

Undi, Mária. *Hungarian Fancy Needlework and Weaving. The History of Hungarian Decorative Embroideries and Weavings*. Budapest, 1934. 87 p.

Viski, Charles. *L'Art des pasteurs hongrois*. Paris, Duchartre, 1928. 2 vols.

Viski, Károly. *Hungarian Dances*. London, Simpkin Marshall-Budapest, G. Vajna, 1937. 192 p.

—— *Hungarian Peasant Customs*. Budapest, G. Vajna, 1937. 187 p.

—— *Volksbrauch der Ungarn*. Budapest, G. Vajna, 196 p.

MUSIC

Bartók, Béla. *Das ungarische Volkslied*. Walter de Guyter, Berlin, 1925.

—— *Die Volksmusik der Magyaren und der benachbarten Völker*. Berlin, Walter de Guyter, 1935

—— *Hungarian Folk Music*. London, Oxford University Press, 1931.

SELECTED BIBLIOGRAPHY ON HUNGARY 341

—— *La musique populaire des Hongrois et des peuples voisins.*
Budapest, 1937.
—— *Scritti sulla musica popolare.* Torino, Edizioni Scientifiche
Einaudi, 1955.
Bartók, Béla and Kodály, Zoltán. *Transylvanian Hungarian
Folksongs.* Budapest, Rózsavölgyi, 1921. 212 p.
Bonis, F. *Béla Bartók—Sein Leben in Bildern.* Budapest, Cor-
vina-Bonn, Boosey und Hawkes, 1964. 27 + 224 p.
Eösze, L. *Zoltán Kodály—Sein Leben und sein Werk.* Buda-
pest, Corvina-Bonn, Boosey und Hawkes, 225 + 18 p.
Juhász, William. *Bartók's American Years.* Washington, D.C.
Occidental Press, 1959. 125 p.
Kodály, Zoltán–Bartha, Dénes. *Die ungarische Musik.* Buda-
pest, 1943. 118 p. Illust.
Moreux, Serge. *Béla Bartók, sa vie, ses oeuvres, son language.*
Paris, Richard Masse, 1949.
—— *Béla Bartók.* London, Harvill Press, 1953. 156 p.
Stevens, Halsey. *The Life and Music of Béla Bartók.* New
York, Oxford University Press, 1953. 366 p.
Szabolcsi, Bence. *Béla Bartók. Weg und Werk. Schriften und
Briefe.* Bonn, Boosey und Hawkes, 1957. 371 p.
Szabolcsi, Bence. *Geschichte der ungarischen Musik.* Budapest,
Corvina-Leipzig, VEB Breitkopf und Härtel, 2nd ed. 1965.
248 p. Illust.
—— *The Twilight of Franz Liszt.* Budapest, Publishing House
of the Hungarian Academy of Sciences, 1959. 136 p. Illust.
Vigné, Jean et Gergely, Jean. *La musique hongroise.* Paris,
Presses universitaires de France, 1959. 127 p. Illust.

POLITICAL AND SOCIAL LIFE

Andrássy, Count Julius. *The Development of Hungarian Con-
stitutional Liberty.* London, Kegan and Co., 1908. 456 p.
Bibó, István. *La Révolution hongroise et la troisième voie.*
Paris, Esprit, November, 1957. 605–613 pp.
Delaney, Robert Finley. *This Is Communist Hungary.* Chi-
cago, Henry Regnery Company, 1958. 260 p.
Gunther, John. *Derrière le rideau de fer.* Paris, Gallimard,
1951. 375 p.
Healthy, Denis, ed. *The Story of Social Democracy in Eastern
Europe.* London, Lincoln-Prager, 1951. 353 p.

Horthy de Nagybánya, Nicolaus, de, régent de Hongrie. *Mémoires.* Paris, Hachette, 1954. 288 p.

Jaszi, Oscar. *Die Kriese der ungarischen Verfassung; eine Denkschrift.* Budapest, Politzer, 1912.

Kállay, Miklós. *Hungarian Premier. A Personal Account of a Nation's Struggle in the Second World War.* New York, Columbia University Press, 1954. 518 p.

Károlyi, Michael. *Faith without Illusion.* London, Jonathan Cape, 1956. 392 p.

Kecskeméti, Károly. *Notes et rapports français sur la Hongrie au XVIIIème siècle.* Bruxelles, Institut Imre Nagy de Sciences Politiques, 1963. 179 p.

Király, Ernö. *Die Arbeiterselbstverwaltung in Ungarn. Aufstieg und Niedergang 1956-1958. Ein Dokumentarbericht.* München, Verlag R. Oldenbourg, 1961. 111 p.

Kovács, Imre. *D'une occupation à l'autre.* Paris, Calman-Lévy, 1949. 301 p.

—— *Im Schatten der Sowjets.* Zürich, Thomas Verlag, 1948. 298 p.

Kövágó, József. *You Are All Alone.* New York, Frederic A. Praeger Publishers, 1959. 295 p.

Kracauer, Siegfried and Berkman, Paul L. *Satellite Mentality: Political Attitudes and Propaganda Susceptibilities of Non-Communists in Hungary, Poland and Czechoslovakia.* New York, Praeger, 1956. 194 p.

Nagy, Balázs. *Formation (La) du Conseil Central Ouvrier de Budapest en 1956.* Bruxelles, Institut Imre Nagy de Sciences Politiques, 1961. 78 p.

Nagy, Ferenc. *Struggle behind the Iron Curtain.* New York, MacMillan Co., 1948. 471 p.

Nagy, Imre. *On Communism, in Defense of the New Course.* New York, F. A. Praeger, 1957. 306 p.

Sulyok, Dezsö. *Zwei Nächte ohne Tag.* Zürich, 1949, 297 p.

Tildy, Zoltán. *Discours choisis.* Budapest, Parti de petits propriétaires, 1946. 29 p.

United States. Department of State. *America's Interests in the Hungarian Struggle for Independence.* Documents and State Papers, Vol. I. No. 5. Washington, D.C.

—— House of Representatives. *Select Committee on Communist Aggression. Communist Takeover and Occupation of Hungary.* Special Report No. 10. 83rd Congress, 1954.

—— Department of State. *Soviet Activities in Hungary: Soviet-American Exchanges of Notes*. Vol. XVI. 1947.

Varga, Béla. *Genocide by Deportation*. New York, Hungarian National Council, 1951. 131 p.

LAW, HUMAN RIGHTS

Bedö, A.K.-Kálnoky, H.-LeNard, L.-Torzsay-Biber, G. *Laws on Nationalization in Hungary*. Washington, D.C., Library of Congress, 1956.

Carlton, Richard K. ed. *The Economic Role of Forced Labor in Eastern Europe*. New York, Mid-European Studies Center, 1954.

Criminal Code of the Hungarian People's Republic. Budapest, Corvina, 1962. 133 p.

Forced Labor and Confinement without Trial in Bulgaria, in Czechoslovakia, in Hungary, etc. Washington, D.C., National Committee for a Free Europe, Inc., 1952. 146 p.

Gsovski, Vladimir and Grzybowski. *Government, Law and Courts in the Soviet Union and Eastern Europe*. London, Stevens and Sons Ltd., The Hague, Monton and Co., 1959. Vol. I. 917 p., Vol. II. 2067 p. Bibliography.

Hungarian Civil Code. Budapest, Corvina Press, 1960. 208 p.

Hungarian (The) Situation and the Rule of Law. The Hague, International Commission of Jurists, 1957. 144 p. Bibliography.

Justice (La) dans la Hongrie d'aujourd'hui. Le rapport de la Commission internationale de juristes sur la situation en Hongrie et la règle de droit. La Haye, 1958. 74 p.

Kertész, Stephen D. *Human Rights in the Peace Treaties*. In "Law and Contemporary Problems," Durham, N.C., 1949.

Library of Congress. Law Library. *Hungary: Confinement without Trial. (Forced Labor.)* Digest Index of East European Law, Washington, D.C., 1951. 9 p.

—— *Hungary: Labor Law. (Prior to Labor Code.) Historical and Legal Background*. Digest Index of East European Law, Washington, D.C., 1951. 13 p.

Rappart, Daniel *Ilegalna madarizácia, 1790–1840*. Turč-Sv. Martin, Vydala Matica Slovenská, 1947. 246 p.

Rumania Ten Years After. Deputation from the American Committee on the Rights of Religious Minorities. Boston, Mass., The Beacon Press, 1928. 143 p.

Strafgesetzbuch der Ungarischen Volksrepublik. Budapest, Corvina, 1963. 144 p.
Zivilgesetzbuch der Ungarischen Volksrepublik. Budapest, Corvina, 1960. 147 p.

BIBLIOGRAPHIES

Banner, János. *Bibliographia archeologica hungarica 1793–
1943.* Szeged, Institutum Archeologicum Universitatis de
Nicoalo Horthy nominatae szegendiensis, 1944. 558 p.

Bobula, Ida. *The Hungarian Material of the Library of Congress.* Washington, Mid European Studies Center, 1951. 38 p.

Bogyay, Thomas v. und Krallert-Sattler, Gertrud. *Ungarische
Bibliographie 1945-1950.* München, n.d. 118-182 p.

Braham, Randolph L. *The Hungarian Jewish Catastrophe. A
Selected and Annotated Bibliography.* New York, Yivo Institute for Jewish Research, 1962. 86 p.

Byrnes, Robert F. *Bibliography of American Publications on
East Central Europe 1945–1957.* Bloomington, Ind., Indiana
University Publications, Slavic and East European Series,
Vol. 11. 1959. 213 p.

Csicsery-Rónay, István, ed. *Bibliográfia.* Supplement of the
Hungarian Periodical "Hirünk a Világban," Washington,
D.C., 1957–to present.

East European Accessions Index. Vol. 7–15. Washington, D.C.,
The Library of Congress, 1958–to present.

East European Accessions List. Vol. 1–6. Washington, D.C.,
The Library of Congress, 1951–1957.

Gragger, R. *Bibliographia Hungarica.* Berlin, 1920.

Halasz de Beky, I. L. *Bibliography of the Hungarian Revolution 1956.* Toronto, University of Toronto Press. 1964.
179 p.

*Index Translationum. International Bibliography of Transla-
tions.* Paris, UNESCO, Published yearly. 1948–to present.

*Index Translationum. International Bibliography of Transla-
tions.* Paris, League of Nations. International Institute of
Intellectual Co-operation, Published quarterly. 1932–1940.

Kálnoki, Bedö, Alexander and Torzsay, George; Gsovski, Vladimir, Gen. ed. *Legal Sources and Bibliography of Hungary.* New York, F. A. Praeger, 1956. 157 p.

Kont, Ignace. *Bibliographie française de la Hongrie (1521–*

1910), avec un inventaire sommaire des documents manuscrits. Paris, E. Leroux, 1913. 323 p.

Leval, André. *Supplement à la Bibliographie française de la Hongrie de I. Kont.* In Revue de Hongrie, Vol. 13. pp. 52–66. Budapest, 1914.

Lynn, Meda. comp. *Reconstruction in Hungary, 1924–1935. Bibliography of Magazine Articles.* New York, Th. H. W. Wilson Co., 1935. 27 p.

Markovitz, Augusta. comp. *Recent Additions to the Hungarian Collections. A Selected List.* New York, The New York Public Library, 1930. 21 p.

—— *Recent Additions to the Hungarian Collections. A Selected List.* New York, The New York Public Library, 1931. 112 p.

Pálinkás, Ladislas. *Bibliografia italiana della lingua e letteratura ungherese.* Roma, 1943. 160 p.

Petrik, Géza. *Bibliographia Hungarica, 1712–1910.* Budapest, 1885-1928. 10 vols.

Roberts, H. L. ed. *Foreign Affairs Bibliography 1942–1952.* New York, Harper and Brothers, 1955. 727 p.

Schreiber, Thomas. *La Hongrie de 1918 à 1958.* Etat des Traveaux et Annexe Documentaire. Paris, Fondation Nationale des Sciences Politiques, 1958. 42 p.

Shaw, J. T. ed. *The American Bibliography of Slavic and East European Studies for 1957.* Vol. 10. Bloomington, Ind., Indiana University Publications, 1958. 103 p.

—— *The American Bibliography of Slavic and East European Studies for 1958.* Vol. 18. Bloomington, Ind., Indiana University Publications, 1959. 112 p.

—— *The 1956 American Bibliography of Slavic and East European Studies in Language, Literature, Folklore, and Pedagogy.* Vol. 9. Bloomington, Ind., Indiana University Publications, 1957. 89 p.

Szabó, George. *Corvinus Manuscripts in the United States. A Bibliography.* New York, The Kossuth Foundation, Inc., 1960. 20 p.

Szebenyi-Sigmond, Judith. *Libraries and Information Services Behind the Iron Curtain.* In American Documentation, Vol. 10. No. 2. April, 1959. pp. 108–115.

Sztaray, Zoltan. *Bibliography on Hungary.* Hungarian Bib-

liography Series, No. 1. New York, The Kossuth Foundation, 1960. 101 p.
—— *Books on The Hungarian Revolution. A Bibliography.*
Brussels, The Imre Nagy Institute for Political Research,
1960. 14 p.
Ungarisches Institut, Universität, Berlin. ed. *Bibliographia
Hungariae . . . zusammengestellt vom Ungarischen Institut
an der Universität Berlin.* Vols. 3. Berlin, W. de Gruyter
and Co., 1923–1928.

ETHNIC, CULTURAL
AND SOCIAL DATA

GEOGRAPHY

The 93,030-square-kilometer (35,855-square-mile) territory of Hungary lies largely in the main basin of Central Europe, the Middle Danube depression, also called the Hungarian Carpathian, or Pannonian Basin. Hungary occupies a compact area, approximately 122 miles wide and 280 miles long. It falls between 45° 48′ and 48° 31′ north latitude and between 16° 01′ and 22° 58′ east longitude. Hungary has only two stretches of natural frontier, the Danube and Ipoly rivers along the western half of the northern border, and the Drava and Mura rivers in the southwest. The total length of the present boundaries is approximately 1,400 miles, of which 228 miles border on Austria in the west, 446 miles on Czechoslovakia in the north, 66 miles on the Soviet Union in the northeast, 268 miles on Rumania in the east, and 397 miles on Yugoslavia in the south.

The almost perfectly flat plain covers nearly two-thirds of the central and eastern part of Hungary. On the basis of geological setting, relief, and climate, Hungary may be divided into three major geographical regions: Transdanubia, the Great Plain, and the Northern Upland. Lake Balaton, covering 160 square miles, the largest lake of East Central Europe, lies in Transdanubia.

Hungary's mean annual temperature ranges from 48° in the north to 52° in the south. Precipitation varies from 30 to 35 inches in the Bakony Forest to less than 15 inches in the east; most of the rain falls in May and June. High summer temperatures and a long autumn are favorable to agriculture.

Before 1950, Hungary consisted of twenty-five counties, traditional administrative units of various sizes. In that year their number was reduced to nineteen by merging the smaller ones, and their sizes became more proportionate. The counties (megye) are in turn subdivided into districts (járás). Communities numbered 3,291 in 1941, and 3,288 in 1947. This number declined to 3,222 in 1950, as a result of administrative mergers. The absorption of 24 suburbs and towns created greater Budapest. Besides these, there are 65 towns.

All ethnic, cultural and social data are taken from the official STATISTICAL POCKET BOOK OF HUNGARY, 1965 (Publishing House for Economics and Laws, Budapest, 1965).

CHANGING TERRITORY AND POPULATION OF HUNGARY

YEAR	TERRITORY (*square miles*)	POPULATION (*thousands*)
1914 (including Croatia)	125.641	20.886
1920 The Treaty of Trianon ceded to:		
Austria	1.552	292
Czechoslovakia	23.797	3.518
Italy	8	50
Poland	227	24
Rumania	39.804	5.257
Total	89.748	13.272
1921 (after Trianon)	35.893	7.914
1938 (January)	35.893	9.129
1938 (On Nov. 2nd, by the 1st Vienna Award, part of South Czechoslovakia was returned)	40.498	10.187
1939 (Carpatho-Ukraine was retaken)	45.154	10.857
1940 (On Aug. 30th, by the 2nd Vienna Award, North Transylvania was returned)	61.796	13.490
1945 (June)	35.893	8.740
1947 (The Paris Peace Treaty Allotted 38 square miles and 3.379 Hungarians to Czechoslovakia)	35.855	9.048
1965	35.855	10.135

ETHNIC COMPOSITION

(percent)

Mother Tongue	1910	1930	1941	1956
Hungarian	88.4	92.1	92.8	97.0
German	7.3	5.5	5.1	2.2
Slovak	2.2	1.2	0.8	0.1
Romanian	0.4	0.2	0.2	0.1
Serb and Croat	0.8	0.4	0.3	0.3
Other	0.9	0.6	0.8	0.3

The Germans are settled mainly west of the Danube, with a small group in the southeast. The Slovaks are scattered, except for a small group in the southeast. The Romanians are near the Romanian frontier and the Yugoslavs near the Yugoslav, but there is dispersal here too.

POPULATION BY RELIGION

(percent)

Religion	1910	1930	1941	1956
Roman Catholic	62.8	64.9	65.7	67.0
Greek Catholic	2.2	2.3	2.5	2.5
Protestant	27.8	27.0	26.8	27.3
Jewish	6.2	5.1	4.3	1.5
Others	1.0	0.7	0.7	0.7

POPULATION OF MAJOR CITIES
(January 1, 1965)

Budapest	1.935.531
Miskolc	166,927
Debrecen	145.692
Pécs	133.993
Szeged	113.594

POPULATION INCREASE

Year	Live births	Deaths	Natural increase	Deaths under 1 year of age
1938	182 206	130 628	51 578	23 933
1949	190 398	105 718	84 680	17 933
1950	195 567	106 902	88 665	16 759
1951	190 645	109 998	80 647	15 993
1952	185 820	107 443	78 377	12 987
1953	206 926	112 039	94 887	14 647
1954	223 347	106 670	116 677	13 556
1955	210 430	97 848	112 582	12 622
1956	192 810	104 236	88 574	11 332
1957	167 202	103 645	63 557	10 543
1958	158 428	97 866	60 562	9 204
1959	151 194	103 880	47 314	7 926
1960	146 461	101 525	44 936	6 976
1961	140 365	95 410	43 955	6 185
1962	130 053	108 273	21 780	6 232
1963	132 335	99 871	32 464	5 676
1964	131 899	100 594	31 305	5 253

	Per 1000 of population			Per 1000 live births
1921—1930	27,7	18,4	9,3	180,0
1931—1940	21,1	14,9	6,2	144,4
1941—1950	19,9	14,4	5,5	111,8
1951—1960	18,8	10,7	8,1	63,2
1960	14,7	10,2	4,5	47,6
1961	14,0	9,6	4,4	44,1
1962	12,9	10,8	2,1	47,9
1963	13,1	9,9	3,2	42,9
1964	13,0	9,9	3,1	39,8

POPULATION BY AGE AND SEX
(percent)

Year	Under 15	15—39 years	40—59	60 years and over	Total
1920	30,6	41,3	19,1	9,0	100,0
1930	27,5	42,6	20,1	9,8	100,0
1941	26,0	40,6	22,7	10,7	100,0
1949	24,9	38,8	24,7	11,6	100,0
1960	25,4	36,8	24,0	13,8	100,0
1963	24,6	36,1	24,5	14,8	100,0
1964	24,1	36,1	24,6	15,2	100,0
Males	25,5	36,9	24,0	13,6	100,0
Females	22,7	35,4	25,2	16,7	100,0
Females per 1000 males	954	1 027	1 125	1 311	1 070

MARRYING PERSONS BY AGE
(percent)

	Males			Females		
	1938	1949	1963	1938	1949	1963
Under 20 years	3,2	3,2	6,0	30,0	26,3	33,2
20—24 years	22,6	33,2	43,8	28,7	39,0	38,8
25—29 years	39,7	35,1	24,4	21,2	18,7	10,2
30—34 years	16,6	10,1	8,9	9,0	5,3	5,3
35—39 years	7,7	7,8	5,0	4,7	4,7	3,7
40—49 years	5,9	6,5	5,1	4,5	4,1	4,7
50 years & over	4,3	4,1	6,8	1,9	1,9	4,1
Total	100,0	100,0	100,0	100,0	100,0	100,0

MARRIAGES – DIVORCES

	Marriages			Divorces		
Year	Number	Per 1000 of population	Number	Per 1000 of population	Per 1000 marriages concluded in the year	Per 1000 prevailing marriages
1938	70 276	8,1	5 754	0,6	77,5	2,8
1949	107 820	11,7	12 556	1,4	116,5	5,8
1960	88 566	8,9	16 590	1,7	187,3	6,5
1961	83 072	8,3	17 480	1,7	210,4	6,8
1962	81 354	8,1	17 410	1,7	214,0	6,8
1963	84 387	8,4	18 364	1,8	217,6	7,1
1964	87 511	8,6	..	..	..	..

EDUCATIONAL STANDARDS*

Year	College, University degree	Secondary school qualification	Primary school qualification	Illiterates at 10 years and over
	Thousands			
1941	85	266	1 039	454
1949	91	356	1 425	347
1960	163	615	2 439	244
1963d)	178	714	2 901	211
	Percentages			
1941	1,6	4,2	15,1	5,9
1949	1,7	5,5	20,6	4,5
1960	2,7	8,8	32,8	3,0
1963d)	2,9	10,0	38,2	..

* The number of persons with lower qualifications also includes those with higher qualifications.

** As percentage of the population of 25 years and over in respect of graduates of universities and other institutions of higher (post-secondary) education, 18 years ola and over for persons with secondary and 15 years old and over for those with primary school qualification.

NATIONAL INCOME 1964
MILLION FORINTS

SOURCES

		%
Industry (incl. mining)	107 812	62,8
Construction industry	17 110	10,0
Agriculture	36 813	21,4
Transport, communication	7 820	4,6
Home trade	11 447	6,7
Foreign trade	− 10 942	− 6,4
Other	1 610	0,9
Total	*171 670*	*100,0*

SOCIAL SECTORS

State	123 417	71,9
Collective and cooperative	37 991	22,1
Other socialist	4 820	2,8
Socialist sector, total	*166 228*	*96,8*
Private	5 442	3,2
Total	*171 670*	*100,0*

EXPENDITURES

Consumption	128 050	74,6
Accumulation		
Increase of fixed assets	31 240	18,2
Increase of circulating funds	17 215	10,0
Net import	− 4 835	− 2,8
Total	*171 670*	*100,0*

LABOR FORCE
(thousands)

	1960	1961	1962	1963	1964
Industry (incl. mining)	1 323,6	1 361,3	1 393,7	1 443,8	1 503,9
Construction industry	269,2	264,7	266,3	281,3	284,6
Agriculture	1 929,1	1 782,7	1 701,1	1 634,4	1 559,6
Transport and communication	282,0	287,9	293,9	298,7	306,7
Trade	314,1	331,4	328,9	344,2	
Services	133,9	140,2	146,7	149,5	151,3
Welfare, cultural and health institutions	237,4	245,2	262,1	278,8	297,9
State administration	101,5	103,0	103,1	103,9	106,2
Other	235,7	259,7	269,7	270,5	281,0
Total	4 022,7	4 826,5	4 776,1	4 746,9	4 805,1	4 857,9

AGRICULTURE 1964
CULTIVATE AREA
(1000 hectares

Arable land	5.086,2
Gardens	156,1
Orchards	153,4
Vineyards	242,6
Meadows	430,1
Pastures	911,4
Forests	1.400,9
Reeds	28,1
Cultivated land	8.408,8
Uncultivated land	894,6
Land area, total	9.303,4

SECTORS

Farms	Units	1.000 hectars	%	Employment
State	245	2.997**	32.2	235.500
Collectives	3.417	5.779	62.1	760.400*
Auxiliary**		292	3.2	
Private		235	2.5	

* Members, without those in pension (313 500 persons).
** Land allotments and farms of 0,5754 hectare or smaller.
NOTE: Households plots of members of agricultural co-operatives amounted to 492 000 hectares of arable land on 31 May 1964.

PRODUCTION (1962)

Coal	28.648.000	Ton
Crude Oil	1.641.000	
Iron ore	682.000	
Bauxite	1.473.000	
Steel	2.330.000	
Pig iron	1.382.000	
Aluminium	233.000	
Wheat	1.959.000	
Corn	3.240.000	
Potatoes	1.882.000	
Sugar	357.000	
Electricity	9.118.000	Kw
Shoes	22.804.000	pairs
Textiles	369.000.000	sq. m.
Washing Machines	132.000	units
TV Sets	210.000	
Diesel Motors	1.470	
Tractors	2.550	
Motorcycles	49.405	

LIVESTOCK (1963)

Cattle	1.906.000
Pigs	5.428.000
Horses	339.000
Sheep	3.043.000
Poultry	30.000.000

PER CAPITA CONSUMPTION

Commodity	Unit	1950	1962	1963
Flour (incl. bread)	kg	141,2	131,6	131,6
Rice	kg	0,9	3,6	3,7
Potatoes	kg	108,7	94,1	88,9
Sugar	kg	16,3	28,0	28,7
Meat	kg	25,9	40,1	39,9
Poultry	kg	8,4	9,8	10,4
Eggs	piece	85	159	163
Milk	kg	96,4g)	103,5	97,3
Pig fat	kg	14,4	18,8	19,5
Butter	kg	1,0	1,6	1,6
Edible oil, margarine	kg	1,9	1,6	1,9
Wine	litre	33,0	28,8	29,3
Beer	litre	8,3	39,4	41,1
Spirits	litre	1,5	3,1	3,3

FOREIGN TRADE 1962

	Export	Import
TOTAL IN MILLION DOLLARS		
	550	573

BY COUNTRIES (%)

	Export	Import
Soviet Union	35.6	36.3
Communist bloc	37.2	34.5
Free World	27.2	29.2

MAIN ITEMS (%)

	Export	Import
Machinery and instruments	36.2	30.0
Industrial consumer goods	21.8	4.7
Raw materials and semi finished goods	22.3	55.7
Food	19.7	9.6

PRIVATE CRAFTSMEN, 1964

Tool-and locksmiths	2 795
Mechanics (incl. radio mechanics)	1 242
Joiners	3 909
Cartwrights and wheelwrights	486
Upholsterers and decorators	747
Tailors	5 001
Dressmakers	6 035
Shoe- and bootmakers	8 029
Butchers	56
Barbers and Hairdressers	4 985
Photographers and enlargers	758
Carpenters	1 130
Bricklayers	3 894
Plumbers	787
Painters	1 610
Glaziers	355
Electricians	1 162
Total	*66 008*

AVERAGE MONTHLY EARNINGS*
(Forints)

Economic branch (state sector)	*1949*	*1963*	*1964*
Industry and mining	638	1 723	1 761
Construction industry	656	1 803	1 816
Agriculture	405	1 446	1 509
Transport and communications	606	1 604	1 739**
Trade	619	1 489	1 557
State administration, health and institutions	606	1 644	1 684

* *Average earnings include sums subtracted from wages (income tax, old age contribution, and state loans), but exclude items over and above wages such as sick-pay, family allowances, and aids, etc. (In official exchange rate, 100 Forints = $8.3; in tourist exchange = $4.15; free exchange = $2.00.)*

** *Including the redemption-money of working-clothes.*

MEDICARE 1963

	Total	Per 10.000 inhabitants
Doctors	17.865	17.9
Pharmacists	3.777	3.8
Nurses	20,945	20.9
Midwives	2.283	2.3
Hospital beds	75.179	75.2

DWELLINGS 1960

Units	2.757.625

Inhabitants per 100 dwellings	343
Inhabitants per 100 dwelling rooms	140
Dwellings with one room (%)	62.2
two rooms	32.6
three or more rooms	4.7
electricity	74.0
running water	22.5
bathroom	1.2

TOURISM

Year	Foreigners visiting	Foreigners on transit	Hungarians travelling abroad
1937	383 113	... ...	220 000
1958	153 575	163 491	205 003
1959	189 732	221 103	222 066
1960	244 351	280 261	299 282
1961	336 696	328 757	373 009
1962	463 395	310 325	453 943
1963	584 688	336 333	569 775
1964	1 302 361	497 581	1 485 712

DESTINATION OF HUNGARIANS TRAVELLING ABROAD
(percent)

Country	1961	1962	1963	1964
Austria	5,0	5,3	7,6	4,1
Bulgaria	1,0	0.7	0,6	0,4
Czechoslovakia	50,8	48,1	46,6	71.9
France	0,7	0,7	1,1	0,6
German Democratic Republic	11,4	9,7	7,8	3,6
German Federal Republic	2,3	2,4	3,7	2,1
Italy	0,6	0,7	1,4	1,1
Poland	5,5	5,6	4,5	3,6
Romania	12,4	15,7	13,2	5,3
Scandinavian states	0,3	0,6	0,6	0,5
Soviet Union	6,6	5,0	4,4	2,1
United Kingdom	0,4	0,5	0,7	0,4
Yugoslavia	1,3	2,9	3,9	2,6
Canada	0,0	0,1	0,2	0,1
United States of America	0,0	0,2	0,5	0,3
Total	*100*	*100*	*100*	*100*

FEATURE FILMS SHOWN

1950	59
1963	150
1964	167
Of which:	
Soviet	34
Hungarian	24
Italian	20
Czech	16
Polish	14
English	11
American (USA)	9
Yugoslav	7
French	7
German (GDR)	5
Romanian	4
Bulgarian	4
German (GFR)	3

BELLES LETTRES BY GENRE AND NATIONALITY OF THE AUTHORS, 1964

BOOKS PUBLISHED

Nationality of the author	Poetry	Novels, short stories	Dramas	Other	Total
Total:	106	471	54	106	737
Written in Hungarian	65	228	31	67	391
Translated from foreign languages	41	243	23	39	346
American (USA)	1	14	1	2	18
Bulgarian		2			2
Czech	2	22		1	25
English	3	10	7	1	22
French	5	53	2	6	66
German	1	22	4	9	36
Italian		10		2	12
Polish		12	1		13
Romanian	9	17		2	28
Russian a)	4	53	1	9	67
Yugoslav		1			1

COPIES OF BOOKS, THOUSANDS

Nationality of the author	Poetry	Novels, short stories	Dramas	Other	Total
Total:	737,3	9 695,8	330,3	1 346,9	12 110,3
Written in Hungarian	461,9	4 549,0	156,6	804,5	5 972,0
Translated from foreign languages	275,4	5 146,8	173,7	542,4	6 138,3
American (USA)	6,1	482,9	12,5	20,7	522,2
Bulgarian		20,0			20,0
Czech	1,8	102,9		0.8	105,2
English	18,3	303,8	77,3	18,4	417,8
French	29,6	1 681,5	20,2	104,1	1 835,4
German	5,9	469,2	35,3	153,6	664,0
Italian		257,5		33,3	290,8
Polish		229,5	0,5		230,0
Romanian	6,8	42,5		2,5	51,8
Russian	34,8	1 102,9	19,1	55,3	1 212,1
Yugoslav		4,6			4,6

a) Including literature in the non-Russian languages of the Soviet Union.

INDEX

APPENDIX

APPENDIX

CAPTIVE NATIONS WEEK

BY THE PRESIDENT OF THE UNITED STATES OF AMERICA

A PROCLAMATION

WHEREAS many nations throughout the world have been made captive by the imperialistic and aggressive policies of Soviet communism; and

WHEREAS the peoples of the Soviet-dominated nations have been deprived of their national independence and their individual liberties; and

WHEREAS the citizens of the United States are linked by bonds of family and principle to those who love freedom and justice on every continent; and

WHEREAS it is appropriate and proper to manifest to the peoples of the captive nations the support of the Government and the people of the United States of America for their just aspirations for freedom and national independence; and

WHEREAS by a joint resolution approved July 17, 1959, the Congress has authorized and requested the President of the United States of America to issue a proclamation designating the third week in July 1959 as "Captive Nations Week," and to issue a similar proclamation each year until such time as freedom and independence shall have been achieved for all the captive nations of the world:

NOW, THEREFORE, I, DWIGHT D. EISENHOWER, President of the United States of America, do hereby designate the week beginning July 19, 1959, as Captive Nations Week.

I invite the people of the United States of America to observe such week with appropriate ceremonies and activities, and I urge them to study the plight of the Soviet-dominated nations and to recommit themselves to the support of the just aspirations of the peoples of those captive nations.

IN WITNESS WHEREOF, I have hereunto set my hand and caused the Seal of the United States of America to be affixed.

DONE at the City of Washington this seventeenth day of July in the year of our Lord nineteen hundred and fifty-nine, and of the Independence of the United States of America the one hundred and eighty-fourth.

By the President: *DWIGHT D. EISENHOWER*

DOUGLAS DILLON
Acting Secretary of State

COMMUNISTS AND FREE ELECTIONS

The methods of military occupation in the war-affected countries were regulated by the provisions of the 1945 Yalta agreement. The Yalta agreement not only insured rights for the armies of occupation, but also contained certain provisions to benefit the occupied areas. Thus, the Yalta agreement stated that the armies of occupation should aid the occupied countries to hold free elections as soon as possible and to create democratic governments and institutions. The Soviet Union, naturally disregarded these provisions of the Yalta agreement. No free elections were held in the countries of Eastern Europe under Soviet occupation. Hungary was an exception. A few weeks after the Yalta agreement was signed, in the spring of 1945, the leaders of the democratic political parties initiated discussions with the present Soviet authorities, asking for an opportunity to hold free elections. Today, we must believe that the Soviet Union agreed to hold elections in Hungary during the fall of 1945 because at the time of the spring discussions, it was not yet clear whether the great U.N. powers, the United States and Great Britain, would demand compliance with the provisions of the Yalta agreement. It is possible that it was for this reason that the Soviets did not reject the request of the democratic Hungarian parties to hold an election.

It is well known that in the countries of Eastern Europe occupied by the Soviet Army, Allied control commissions had been established comprised of an American and a British representative. But in every case and in every country, the presiding officer was a Soviet general. Therefore, in Hungary, as well as in the other Eastern European countries, Soviet authority had three bases of operation: the commander of the occupation army, the head of the Soviet Legation and the president of the Allied Control Commission. During the discussions concerning the elections, Soviet authorities clearly indicated they expected that even after the elections a coalition government should govern the country—regardless of the outcome of the elections. Under the given circumstances, the leaders of the non-Communist parties reluctantly accepted this idea of a coalition. Recognizing the complete cooperation between the Communist Party and the Red army, they felt that it was better to share in the responsibility for the government than to force the Communist Party into opposition and allow it to carry on subversive work with the support of the Soviet Army.

(Statement by Ferenc Nagy for the Committee on the Judiciary United States Senate: A Study of the Anatomy of Communist Takeovers. Washington, D.C., July 25, 1966).

AMNESTY FOR POLITICAL PRISONERS IN HUNGARY

Declarations of American Citizens

We, the undersigned, fully recognizing the great responsibility incumbent upon us in this age when man has the means of total destruction, solemnly declare our intention to serve the most important cause, the preservation of peace.

We agree that all efforts must be directed to that end and every possibility must be employed to ameliorate those problems which result in the present dangerous world tensions. To attain the desired goal all nations must show evidence of their good faith.

We firmly believe that one of the disturbing elements in the effort toward mutual understanding is the fate of those Hungarians who participated in the revolt of 1956. If there is a spirit which radiates understanding and forgiveness, we think that those Hungarian political prisoners, regardless of their age and sentences, must be forgiven, too.

Therefore, we are appealing to the understanding and consideration of the Communist leaders to grant an amnesty to Hungarian political prisoners, gratifying those throughout the world who are yearning for peace and justice. We hope that the Communist leaders will recognize their own responsibilities in connection with our demand and they will act according to their conscience, and with humanity.

Done in the month of March, 1960, in the United States of America.

Conrad Aiken	**P. W. Bridgman**
Andreas Altoldi	*Clifford P. Case*
Eugene Barnothy	*Leo Charne*
Magdolna Barnothy	*Richard Cardinal Cushing*
Charles E. Bennett	**Richard J. Daley**
Alvin M. Bentley	*Thomas J. Dodd*

Mark van Doren
Christopher Dowson
Ralph Ellison
Paul Fejos
Harry Emerson Fosdick
Israel Goldstein
Oscar Halecki
Dietrich von Hildebrand
Henry W. Hobson, Right Rev.
William E. Hocking
Sidney Hook
Theodor de Karman
Kenneth B. Keating
Frank Lausche
Ashley Montagu
Marianne Moore
Thomas Merton, Rev.
R. J. McCracken

John W. McCormack
Lewis Mumford
Charles Munch
Ernest Nagel
Katherine Anne Porter
Eleanor Roosevelt
Budd Schulberg
George N. Shuster
Upton Sinclair
Albert Szentgyergi
Joseph Szigeti
Norman Thomas
Charles de Tolnay
Eugene P. Wigner
Thornton Wilder
G. Mennen Williams
Alexander Wolsky
Lajos Zilahy

"ACTION COMMITTEE"
AMNESTY FOR POLITICAL PRISONERS IN HUNGARY, 125 EAST 72nd STREET, NEW YORK, N. Y. 10021

Reprinted from *The New York Times*, March 31, 1960.

THE HUNGARIAN FREEDOM CROWN

**Issued in Commemoration of the 1956 Revolution
in Hungary**

Renewing the medieval custom of marking great
events through special coins, the minting of two
thousand serially numbered silver-clad Hungarian
Freedom Crowns has been authorized by the Hungarian Committee to commemorate the tenth anniversary of the 1956 Revolution in Hungary. The
obverse features the Hungarian Freedom Fighter as
visualized by the famous painting of Boris Chaliapin.
The reverse shows the torn Freedom Flag, symbol
of the Revolution. Each coin is struck in proof condition and is housed in a special presentation case.

The proceeds will aid the cause of liberty.

The Hungarian Freedom Crown
may be ordered at $9.75 from

**HUNGARIAN COINS FOR FREEDOM
10 East 49th St., New York, N.Y. 10017**